DISCARD

AIR POWER

AIR POWER

A Global History

Jeremy Black

ROWMAN & LITTLEFIELD
Lanham • Boulder • New York • London

Published by Rowman & Littlefield
A wholly owned subsidiary of
The Rowman & Littlefield Publishing Group, Inc.
4501 Forbes Boulevard, Suite 200, Lanham, Maryland 20706
www.rowman.com

Unit A, Whitacre Mews, 26-34 Stannary Street, London SE11 4AB,
United Kingdom

British Library Cataloguing in Publication Information Available

Library of Congress Cataloging-in-Publication Data
Black, Jeremy, 1955– author.
Air power : a global history / Jeremy Black.
pages cm
Includes bibliographical references and index.
ISBN 978-1-4422-5096-3 (cloth : alk. paper) — ISBN 978-1-4422-5097-0
(electronic)
1. Air power—History. 2. Cold War. I. Title.
UG630.B48 2016
358.4'03—dc23
2015031855

Printed in the United States of America

For Augusta Kyte

CONTENTS

ABBREVIATIONS

Add.	additional manuscripts
ADIZ	air defense identification zone
AFC	Australian Flying Corps
ALCM	air-launched cruise missile
AWACS	airborne warning and control system
AWM	Canberra, Australian War Memorial, archive
BBC	British Broadcasting Corporation
BL	London, British Library, Department of Manuscripts
BSA	Bosnian Serb Army
CAB	Cabinet Office papers, British
CENTO	Central Treaty Organization
CMTC	Combined Maneuver Training Center
COIN	counterinsurgency
DARPA	Defense Advanced Research Projects Agency
DEW	Distant Early Warning
DRO	Exeter, Devon Record Office
EAF	Egyptian Air Force
ECM	electronic countermeasures

FIS	Islamic Salvation Front
FLN	Front de Libération Nationale
FMLN	Farabundo Marti National Liberation Front
GAM	Gerakan Aceh Merdeka
GLCM	ground-launched cruise missile
GPS	Global Positioning System
HARM	high-speed antiradiation missile
IAF	Indian Air Force
ICBM	intercontinental ballistic missile
IFOR	NATO-led Implementation Force
IPKF	Indian Peace-Keeping Force
IRBM	intermediate-range ballistic missile
ISAF	International Security Assistance Force
ISR	intelligence, surveillance, and reconnaissance
JDAMs	joint direct attack munitions
JRTC	Joint Readiness Training Center
JSTARS	Joint Surveillance and Target Attack Radar System
KV	records of the security service
LH	London, King's College, Liddell Hart Library
LMA	London Metropolitan Archives
MANPAD	Man-Portable Air Defense Systems
MDAP	Mutual Defense Assistance Program
MM	Montgomery-Massingberd papers
MVAF	Malayan Volunteer Air Force
NA	London, National Archives
NATO	North Atlantic Treaty Organization
NTC	National Training Center
OPFOR	opposing force
PAF	Pakistan Air Force

PLA	People's Liberation Army
PLAAF	People's Liberation Army Air Force
RAAF	Royal Australian Air Force
RAF	Royal Air Force (British)
RCAF	Royal Canadian Air Force
RFC	Royal Flying Corps
RFMAF	Royal Federation of Malaya Air Force
RMA	Revolution in Military Affairs
RNAS	Royal Naval Air Service
RNLEIA	Royal Netherlands East Indies Army
RPV	remotely piloted vehicle
RUSI	Royal United Services Institute/*RUSI Royal United Services Institute Journal*
Rutgers, Fuller	Rutgers University Library, New Brunswick, New Jersey, Fuller papers
SAC	Strategic Air Command
SAGE	Semi-automatic Ground Environment
SAM	surface-to-air missile
SFOR	NATO-led Stabilization Force
SSM	surface-to-surface missile
TAC	Tactical Air command
Thomson papers	papers of Alan Thomson, private collection
TRADOC	Training and Doctrine Command
UAV	unmanned aerial vehicle
UN	United Nations
UNEF	United Nations Emergency Force
UNITA	National Union for the Complete Independence of Angola
USAAF	United States Army Air Forces

VLR   very long range
WO   War Office papers, British

PREFACE

I have benefited greatly from the opportunity to teach military history for more than three decades, at the universities of Durham and Exeter, and more generally. For this book, I particularly profited from opportunities to speak at the United States Air Force Academy, the United States Naval War College, and Waseda University, and to visit Cuba, Denmark, France, Germany, Hungary, Japan, and Serbia. The papers of Alan Thomson are used by permission of his great-granddaughter.

Writing about a means of delivering lethal force, and of killing, can appear bloodless, if not worse. I am well aware that my subject deals with death and loss. On a personal level, a young uncle died as a fire spotter during the German "blitz" on London. I can recall one of my grandmothers telling me about seeing a zeppelin (German airship) over London during the First World War and my father explaining why German V-2 rockets, which gave no warning, were more terrifying than their noisier V-1 counterparts, a point also made by others. We owe to those who suffered a response that makes sense of their experience; one at once more and less than an emotional reaction.

The two anonymous reviewers who commented on the proposal greatly improved it. So did the comments of Floribert Baudet, Richard Connell, Christ Klep, Andrew Lambert, John Olsen, John Peaty, Anthony Saunders, Mark Stevens, and Jason Warren on earlier drafts, and of Rodney Atwood, Jonathan Fennell, John Ferris, Robert Foley, Holger Herwig, Peter Hugill, Peter Lee, Jean-Baptiste Manchon, and Gary Sheffield on parts of the book. I much appreciate their efforts, but I alone am responsible for any errors that remain. To be a colleague for many years of Richard Overy has been a great inspiration. His works are fundamental guides to the subject. I have benefited from advice on specific points or the loan of books from Charles Ashcroft, Gabor Agoston, Alejandro Amendolara, David Anderson, Michael Axworthy, Simon Barton, Harry Bennett, Ahron Bregman, Michael Bregnsbo, Pete Brown, Andrew Buchanan, Ong Wei Chong, Paul Cornish, Michael Epkenhans, Xu Erbin, Norman Friedman, Jack Gill, Blake Goldring, John R. Grodzinski, Selim Güngörürier, Peter Hanley, Jan Hoffenaar, Charles Ingrao, Brian Linn, John Maurer, Kenneth Maxwell, Richard Muller, Tim Niblock, James Onley, Russell Parkin, Ryan Patterson, Maarten Prak, Ralph Porch, Roger Reese, John Reeve, Matt Rendle, Nicholas Rodger, Kaushik Roy, Nick Sarantakes, José Sardica, Gary Schaub, Stephen Schuker, Georges-Henri Soutou, Daniel Steed, Dave Stone, Harold Tanner, Martin Thomas, William Thompson, Richard Toye, Tim Travers, Ashley Truluck, Katsuya Tsukamoto, Maurice Vaisse, Arthur Waldron, Peter Waldron, and Geoffrey Wawro.

The collaborative nature of the project is further exemplified by the important role of my editor, Susan McEachern. She has provided the necessary mix of enthusiasm, skill, and wisdom that makes for a great editor. This book is dedicated to Augusta Kyte, a good friend and an amusing companion.

I

INTRODUCTION

On January 25, 1904, at a meeting at the Royal Geographical Society in London, Halford Mackinder (1861–1947), then the most influential British academic geographer as well as the director of the London School of Economics, presented a paper titled "The Geographical Pivot of History."[1] In this paper, he focused on Eurasia, the largest landmass on Earth, and advanced a notion of a Eurasian "Pivot." This was the basis for Mackinder's view of the importance of what he termed the "Heartland," which he defined as "that vast area of Euro-Asia which is inaccessible to ships, but in antiquity lay open to the horse-riding nomads." Taking conflict as normal, Mackinder claimed that, thanks in part to the invention and spread of railways, and the resulting reconfiguration of distance and space, the nature of the military challenge in Eurasia had fundamentally altered, while, he argued, control over the "Heartland" would be the basis of global power.

At the meeting, however, Mackinder's interpretation was challenged by the young Leo Amery, then a *Times* journalist, later a Conservative cabinet minister and prominent exponent of British imperialism. Moving on from Mackinder's stress on new rail links, notably the Trans-Siberian Railway linking European Russia to the distant Russian Far East, Amery emphasized the continuing onward rush of technology and the role of industrial capacity. He told the gathering that sea and rail links and power would be supplemented by air.

This was a prescient remark, given that the Wright brothers had only had their first powered flight on December 17, 1903. Meanwhile, although greatly facilitating the development of indirect artillery fire, balloons, without any power plant, had earlier failed to fulfill the more ambitious hopes of their potential, being capable of flying from but not to a position.[2] However, the Wright brothers' success was the culmination of efforts by a number of individuals, for example Clément Ader, who achieved a short hop. Hopes about balloons were to be revived later in the 1900s with the arrival of the internal combustion engine and the resulting use of airships.

Amery added that, once air power played a role, then

> a great deal of this geographical distribution must lose its importance, and the successful powers will be those who have the greatest industrial basis. It will not matter whether they are in the centre of a continent or on an island; those people who have the industrial power and the power of invention and of science will be able to defeat all others.

In contrast, Mackinder, both in 1904 and in 1919, failed to rise to the geopolitical challenge of comprehending air power.[3] The United States, where manned powered flight—flight that was both controlled and sustained—had begun thirty-nine days earlier, was an obvious candidate for the role envisaged by Amery, and this was indeed to be the case. It was to be *the* air power, and notably so, from the 1940s, after major earlier air-power roles for France and Britain, just as Britain had been *the* sea power.

The history of air power is that of the period since 1903, the situation today, and suggestions about the future. Indeed history, the record of what happened in the past and the accounts subsequently presented of these events, very much bridges to current concerns when considering air power. Its capabilities, potential, use, limitations, and ethics are all strongly debated, across a range of subjects from military planning and international relations to ethics. This interest is sharpened by the awareness that, despite the difficulties of responding to challenges, not least when under the pressure of multiple commitments, air power, nevertheless, is a dynamic, rapidly changing, force.

Furthermore, with the changes brought about by the introduction of precision weaponry, the capacity of air power to tackle military and political problems has been much to the fore in literature about international relations over the last quarter century. For the West, air power has become largely the politician's weapon of choice, replacing gunboat diplomacy and providing maximum destructive and other effects with the minimum of commitment. Thus, air power played a central role in discussions about the supposed Revolution in Military Affairs (RMA) in the 1990s and early 2000s, and in the related, but also subsequent, debate about a military "transformation." The range and accuracy of weapons were readily demonstrated, but questions arose over impact and effectiveness, notably the role of lethal force in geopolitics and, in particular, the physical effects of destruction combined with the psychological effects of its potential use in coercion.

There is an extensive literature on air power, particularly, but not only, by American scholars, and most of it is excellent. The history, capability, future, and ethics of air power have all been ably tackled. However, this literature also has limitations. Often, because of the differing roles of navies and air forces, the literature fails to integrate, or to integrate adequately, the important naval dimension, that of air power both at sea (whether sea or land based) and from the sea. This is because many of the writers have been airmen. The American air force, essentially for historical reasons related to its origins in the army, focuses on operations overland. For the American navy, air power is seen primarily as sea power. However, far from being an appendix, air power at sea, and from the sea, has been a highly significant form of air power since the 1910s and was (and is) very important to American and British air power. Increasingly, moreover, it is the air weapon itself that counts; precisely where it is launched from is largely immaterial to the receiver.

Second, the literature on air power generally focuses on the leading air powers and is commonly national in tone, emphasis, and perspective. Much of it, indeed, is written from an American or a British perspective. There is also a degree of coverage of other leading air powers, notably the rivals of the United States and Britain, particularly Germany in the two world wars. A global approach, however, is far less common, and especially from the perspective of states that were neither leading powers nor competitors for this role. Third, much of the writing is for specialists rather than for students or a general audience.

Fourth, there is a tendency among air force historians to overrate air power, one that is more pronounced than that of army and navy historians to underrate it. This overrating may take the form of an emphasis on the real or alleged strategic potency of air power or, currently more frequently, a stress on its value as a tool of integrated warfare. Air force commanders rise to the fore based on which component of air power is in favor. In America, bomber pilots long dominated the chain of command, only to be replaced more recently by fighter pilots. It is likely that rocket and space commanders in the American air force will soon come to the fore: the air force certainly dominates the American rocket and space commands.

The common theme is that of a crucial role for air power. This situation is linked to the extent to which, despite much lip service about cooperation, and some success in providing it, for example in the German blitzkrieg in 1939–41 and with the British Eighth Army and Desert Air Force in North Africa in 1941–43, historically individual branches of the military have tended to fight separate wars at the same time. As a result, interservice frictions color not only military affairs, but also their history. Particular tensions arise over the utility of strategic air power, over control of armed helicopters, over close air support, and over naval air power. These elements can be readily seen in the history of American and British air power, but not only there.

Thus, there is a need for a study of air power that gives due weight not only to its use in bombing and in aerial conflict, and by the major powers (which are the established issues in the literature, issues that are well covered), but also that considers a broader range of topics and perspectives. In particular, there is the importance of air power as a political weapon and its employment by the minor powers, each of which is a key and necessary topic in capturing the variety of air power, but also the roles of maritime, air power, and logistic support for ground operations, of transport by air, and of the use of air assault to deliver troops to the battlefield. As a reminder of the differences between the uses of air power, there were not only contrasts in doctrine, practice, and historical accounts about its proactive and aggressive role, but also varying emphases on the counters to air power, on defensive weaponry, tactics, strategy, and doctrine directed against air's offensive role. These contrasts and emphases had consequences for the nature of air combat, and therefore for all the combatants involved. Thus, a stress on interceptor fighters for the defending power had different consequences to one on antiaircraft guns and control systems.

Moving beyond this action-reaction dialectic, there are questions about the fundamental nature of war. More particularly, is an enemy a network of systems that can be bombed, or is war primarily a matter of imposing will on the enemy through very human elements of combat that can only be brought to bear on the ground? In short, is it about pure physical destruction or, psychologically, about subjugating the enemy's will? These questions will recur throughout the book.

Moreover, as another instance of the room for difference in scholarly emphasis, the significance of events and developments in the years since the Cold War between the communist and anticommunist blocs which ended in 1989 is such that they need to be given due weight in any account. The perceptions of overwhelming asymmetry that arose following the end of the Cold War and from the First Gulf War have colored international and substate relations ever since. Air power, in the sense of powered flight, began only in 1903, and was not employed in conflict until 1911. As a result, despite the vast air armies by the end of the First World War and, even more, during the Second World War, most of the history of air power and of its political utility has in fact occurred since the Second World War ended in 1945. Such an emphasis needs to be apparent in any study, and notably so for a book that is to be published and read from the second decade of the twenty-first century.

With the exception of this introduction, and of a lengthier conclusion, this book will adopt a chronological approach. This approach reflects the degree to which the technology of aircraft and of air warfare has changed over time, creating new parameters for effectiveness and related assumptions about use. The chronological approach also captures the role of particular conjunctures, notably of conflict, international relations, and air-power capability, in providing resources and in framing governmental and public views about the use of air power, including the ethical, legal, and political views about civilian casualties. Under the pressure of events, these views change very rapidly. Given the crucial impact of technology and such conjunctures, a thematic approach linked to particular spheres for the use of air power, for example a chapter on airlift and another on ground support, important as these topics are, would not work well.

A key dimension throughout will be to assess governmental and social dimensions of the response to air power, and how these changed. Since the Second World War, air power has been seen as a quintessentially American strength, which is correct as far as that period was concerned. In practice, however, Britain made a major attempt to engage with air power far earlier. It offered a range appropriate for an empire that was spread across the globe. In addition, air power for Britain was an apparent substitute for conscription, which was judged undesirable, as well as a crucial means of home defense. Thus, air power formed an acceptable form of "standing" or permanent military force, one that also appeared both modern and as no threat to political stability. Nevertheless, the political and cultural commitment to the navy remained strong in Britain, and, in the wake of the ethical issues surrounding the strategic bombing campaign against Germany during the Second World War, there was not the central commitment to air power seen with the United States, particularly after the Second World War.

The American commitment was cultural and psychological, as well as grounded in power, whether economic, political, or military. Indeed, as a continental power with no neighboring enemies but with worldwide interests, aviation provided a way for Americans to conceptualize and exploit a claim to represent a progressive form of global power, as the navy had earlier done for the United States in the 1890s and 1900s. International competition in air transport and power was helped by the fact that the technologies were new, they diffused easily, and there was little attachment to traditional ways of doing things. A means to extend American influence, and to demonstrate, affirm, and confirm strength and dominance, aviation and air power lacked the colonial connotations associated with other empires,[4] notably that of Britain. As a consequence, the very discussion of air power was, and is, significant for the understanding of views, both American and non-American, of the American century. A belief that air power could bring victory at least cost, and thus overcome attrition, was a major strand from the 1920s to the present. In 1943, *Victory through Air Power*, a book by the Russian-born but American-based former aircraft designer and entrepreneur Alexander de Seversky, sold hundreds of thousands of copies in the United States, led to a Disney cartoon of the same name, and helped color American geopolitics.[5]

Air power played a key role in the Second World War, not only in reducing German and Japanese industrial capacity, but also in providing the Allied air superiority without which land success would have faltered, as well as in the war at sea and in bringing Japan to surrender through the air delivery of atomic bombs. Chapter 6 discusses this conflict. Moreover, thereafter, as assessed in chapter 7, air power had a major part in the early stage of the Cold War. Air power, crucially with the nuclear capability it offered, was probably the one factor that prevented a possible Western rout in the late 1940s and 1950s; it was the one trump card that the West had. Underlining the challenge, the Korean War (1950–53), despite Allied air superiority, became a stalemate; demonstrated how Western, mostly American, ground forces could be blocked; and showed vividly that an effective classic Eurasian heartland dynamic was in force, but not to the West's advantage. Despite their serious tensions,[6] the Soviet Union and China together formed an imposing ad hoc alliance whose populations and ground forces were overwhelmingly greater than those of the West. In response, American and British bombers with atomic bombs, U-2 overflights, and, later, missiles kept the Soviet Union and China in perpetual anxiety. From the early 1960s, the Sino-Soviet split was the West's next greatest ally. By the time the Soviet Union had appreciably strengthened its bomber and missile forces in the mid-1960s, the Sino-Soviet split was beyond remedy. Specialized air technology and sheer luck had enabled the West to keep the communist bloc at bay.

A more critical response to air power developed from the 1960s. While part of a general antiwar culture in the West, the criticism of air power was particularly pointed. It owed much of its energy to opposition to the Vietnam War, in the United States and elsewhere. Unequivocally, the North Vietnamese won the propaganda war, and air operations were portrayed as both immoral and ineffective. This propaganda entered the American conscience and is a theme that has continued to the present. Thus, Peter Brooks, the popular cartoonist of the *Times* (of London), in its issue of October 3, 2014, depicted a British jet carrying nine missiles, each with a price tag from £30,000 to £790,000, with the pilot saying, "If we don't hit schools and hospitals in Iraq, we certainly will back home," a reference to the high cost of air operations and the extent to which defense and social welfare are competing forms of expenditure. This is ironic as defense costs far less than health, education, or social welfare. In the United States, the elimination of the entire Department of Defense would still leave trillions of dollars of unfunded liabilities in the form of social programs. In Britain, defense expenditure is a quarter of that spent on health, half of that spent on education, and a seventh of that spent on social programs.

The same cartoonist, in the issue of September 12, 2014, captured another aspect of contemporary ambivalence, with President Obama painting "Sorry" on an American jet, the pilot saying, "I guess he's still a bit reluctant." The perception of the president is of particular interest, as, because it can be controlled so centrally and immediately, air power is a visible statement of presidential resolve. Air power is also in part a narrative about American strength, about the American century, and concerning aspirations into the future. This narrative, and the related analysis, is linked to debates about the causes, consequences, and prospects of American power, whether political, economic, or military. The cultural and psychological aspects of the situation are of great significance. Air power is part and parcel of American identity. It reflects the frontier cowboy mentality of Americans in always seeking to be on the cutting edge and conquering new frontiers, as well as the post-Vietnam preference for a military intervention that produces few body bags and hence has low political costs.

The conceptual framework of the book will be one in which public and governmental senses of opportunity and fear are regarded as key drivers in the understanding of air power. In the more specific military dimension, there will also be an assessment of the value of air power as opposed to that of armies and navies. Moreover, an action-reaction dialectic of air power, and of responses designed to mitigate its impact, will be considered. How this dialectic varied through time, and in specific military, political, and social environments, will be assessed, alongside the press of technological development. By its nature, air power is an exclusive capability. The very costs associated with the highest-tech air systems exclude all but the few. In contrast, the book will also consider how air power might be the weapon of the underdog, where the imposition of costs might deter, if not actually coerce, a stronger power. Last, alongside air power as the new military means of the twentieth century will come consideration of its capacity to capture the imagination, both with politicians and the public, which indeed has been the case from the outset.

2

THE START OF A NEW ARM

If they can conduct the balloons in the same way as they do ships, how could an army subsist when the enemy can throw force and destruction upon their stores and magazines at any time? How can an armed fleet attack any sea-coast town, when the people of the country can swarm in the clouds and then fire upon it in the middle of the night? Do you not think that this discovery will put an end to all wars and thus force monarchs to perpetual peace or to fight their own quarrels among themselves in a duel? —Jan Ingenhousz[1]

In 1784, Jan Ingenhousz, a Dutch-born scientist who lived in Britain, suggested that the new use of balloons for manned flight might lead to perpetual peace. Man indeed does not naturally fly, and the possibilities offered by manned flight appeared genuinely revolutionary, as for many they have always done. This helps account for the capacity of air power to capture the imagination, a capacity, seen in the drawings of Leonardo da Vinci, that has encouraged bold views about what flight can lead to.

The possibilities of air power excited interest well before the Wright brothers officially achieved manned heavier-than-air powered flight in 1903. Much of this interest focused on fantasies of flight that were impossible in light of the technology of the time, including fantasies about flying to the moon, the subject of *Il Mondo della Lune* (The World on the Moon), a satirical libretto by Carlo Goldoni, written in 1750 and set by six composers before Haydn used it for an opera buffa performed in 1777. In military terms, the use and effectiveness of plunging fire, whether of arrows, stones and javelins, or, later, exploding

shells, encouraged speculation about the possibilities of launching projectiles from aerial vehicles.

This interest was taken forward with the development of manned
balloon flight. Kites and rockets had long been used in China, but their
use was advanced as a result of scientific work in the West in the
eighteenth century. In 1766, Henry Cavendish, a master of quantitative
analysis, was the first to define hydrogen as a distinct substance. A
decade later, he ascertained that it was lighter than air and thus would
rise. In 1778, another British scientist, Joseph Black, suggested that
hydrogen should be released into a bladder, and in 1783 hydrogen was
utilized as a lifting agent in a balloon commissioned by the French
Académie des Sciences and manufactured by the physicist Jacques
Charles, who flew in it. Earlier that year, employing the expansive power of heat, the Montgolfier brothers had used hot air to send up two
balloons, one with animals, the second with men, a feat that attracted
much attention.

Experiments and designs rapidly followed, notably Jean Baptiste
Meusnier de la Place's designs for cigar-shaped steerable balloons. A
French mathematician and engineer, Meusnier presented an idea for a
balloon airship to the Académie des Sciences in Paris in 1784. He
proposed an elliptical balloon eighty-four meters long, with a capacity
of 1,700 cubic meters, powered by three propellers driven by manual
labor. The basket, in the form of a boat, was suspended from the canopy
on a system of three ropes. In 1783, Charles and the Robert brothers
built an elongated steerable craft that followed Meusnier's proposals.
On July 15 that year, the brothers flew for forty-five minutes in their
elongated balloon. It was fitted with oars for propulsion and direction,
but these proved useless, while the absence of a gas release valve
obliged them to slash the envelope to prevent it from rupturing when
they reached an altitude of about 4,500 meters. On September 19,
1784, in the first flight over one hundred kilometers, the brothers and
M. Collin-Hullin drifted in the wind for 186 kilometers, a journey that
took them six hours and forty minutes.

The outbreak of the French Revolutionary Wars in 1792 saw a military application of the new technology, rather as the First World War,
breaking out in 1914, was to encourage the manned flight that had
begun in 1903. The French used hot-air balloons to carry messages in
1793, and in 1794 a tethered hydrogen-filled silk balloon played a valu-

able reconnaissance role for the French at the Battle of Fleurus in Belgium. Thereafter, about twenty more balloons were sent to French armies. However, Napoleon, who took power in France in 1799, decided to disband the balloon force. This decision can be seen as conservative,[2] but the difficulties of transporting the gas-generating apparatus, and the time required to inflate the balloons, gravely limited their tactical value.[3] Moreover, the amount of smoke on contemporary battlefields obscured the view. Indeed, tethered observation balloons only really became a practical instrument when smokeless gunpowder was invented and adopted at the close of the nineteenth century, an invention that was also crucial for reconnaissance by aircraft during the First World War. Tethered balloons, furthermore, were affected by the weather, notably with their vulnerability to high winds, and, due to the reliance on flags, pigeons, or landing, there were delays in the transmission of messages to the ground.

More success, in a different manner, was achieved with the use of rockets, which were of the form of giant fireworks.[4] Rockets were fired from land and from ships. The British drew on the Indian use of rockets for their inspiration. Congreve's rockets had a range of two thousand yards by 1805, but they were expensive to produce and highly inaccurate. Their use serves as a reminder that what air power was to mean was quite varied, but also that its potential was not to be reached until the electronic improvements of the twentieth century. It was only in the second half of that century that accurate guidance systems ensured that the potential of rockets could be realized. However, a weapon that is launched from the ground is different from aircraft, which are secondary systems because they are not in themselves weapons, but rather are weapons platforms with flexibility in deployment and range of operation.

In the nineteenth century, there was continuing interest in the potential of aerial vehicles. Balloons were first used in Europe to bomb a town in 1849, when Austria bombed the rebellious city of Venice with grenades. The need for observation and reconnaissance was more significant, not least due to the increase in the range of artillery: for fire at long ranges to be effective, enhanced observation was required. The use of balloons to get up as high as possible provided a way for artillery observers to increase their range and field of vision and helped further the accuracy of indirect fire. Balloons gave a perspective limited by weather, not topography.

During the American Civil War (1861–65), balloons were deployed by both sides for artillery observation and reconnaissance. For example, George McClellan's Army of the Potomac used gas-filled observer balloons in 1862, although they proved of little value. During the German siege of Paris in 1870–71, balloons were employed to carry letters and people out of the city, notably enabling Léon Gambetta to leave in order to organize French resistance elsewhere.

Having been impressed with military ballooning in the American Civil War, Captain Beaumont of the British Royal Engineers tried unsuccessfully from 1862, when balloon trials took place at Aldershot, to 1873 to persuade the army of its value. Moreover, the American balloon producer Henry Coxwell had offered to provide two silk balloons to Garnett Wolseley's expedition of 1873–74 against the Asante (Ashanti) of West Africa, at a total cost of £2,000, only for the offer to be declined as too costly.[5] In 1874, the first official British experiment was conducted by the Balloon Equipment Store at the Woolwich Arsenal. Although cumbersome to deploy, observation balloons were employed by the British in Africa from 1884 to 1885, with the Bechuanaland expedition, followed in 1885 by the second of two expeditions to Suakin in Sudan. In neighboring Eritrea, the Italians successfully used three balloons in 1887–88: the Italian Engineers had formed a company-sized aeronautical section in 1884 with two balloons bought from France. In 1889, a balloon detachment took part in the annual British Army Manoeuvres at Aldershot. It was so successful that a Balloon Section of the Royal Engineers was established in 1890, with its work and personnel supported by a balloon factory and school.

During the Second Boer War (1899–1902), the British sent eleven balloons to South Africa and overcame the problem of providing a constant supply of gas for them. Compressed gas was stored in robust portable retorts that were transported to the front in oxcarts. Balloons were employed for artillery observation to note the fall of shot during the Battle of Magersfontein (December 11, 1899), the siege of Ladysmith (November 2, 1899–February 28, 1900), and the Battle of Tugela Heights (February 14–27, 1900). Balloons were sent back to Britain in 1900, however, after the Boer switch to guerrilla tactics made balloon observation less effective and less worth the trouble and expense: balloons took ten hours to inflate.

Balloons had serious deficiencies in terms of navigable free flight. Nevertheless, as with submarines, the application of engine technology was significant, and in the 1870s engines and balloons were joined to create "airships." "Gondolas" for the crew were slung underneath. This was followed by the transformation of the balloon aspect by enclosing it within a metal frame. The resulting rigid airship was more navigable.

Air power, however, was anticipated by futurologists rather than general staffs. On October 27, 1883, the French writer Albert Robida published in *La Caricature* an anticipation of warfare in the twentieth century. This included cannon-firing streamlined balloons, as well as electric-powered, armored trains firing cannon and machine guns. Indeed, imaginative literature, such as that of the British novelist H. G. Wells, prepared readers for the impact of powered, controlled flight. He warned also of the dangers of air attack on cities. In Wells's 1897 serial *The War of the Worlds*, Martian missiles convoy war machines that overrun England.

The focus was in part on the design of the gas-filled airship developed by the German Graf (Count) Ferdinand von Zeppelin who, in 1899, began experimenting with a cylindrical, rather than a globular, container for the gas, along with a rigid metal frame. In 1908, Zeppelin's LZ-4 airship flew over 240 miles in twelve hours, leading to a marked revival of interest in airships, with enthusiastic support by the German government, which had ten in service by the start of the First World War in 1914. In Britain, there were scares about a possible attack by German airships, as in 1913. Science fiction offered some speculation as to how airships might be used, as in Wells's *War in the Air* (1908) and in Edgar Rice Burroughs's *John Carter of Mars*, which was first serialized in 1912. In the former, a disastrous air war, waged with airships and aircraft that focus on the destruction of cities, causes the collapse of worldwide civilization.[6]

The successes of Sir George Cayley (1773–1857) with airfoils and manned flight with full-sized gliders were only thwarted by the lack of a suitable small power plant. The arrival of the internal combustion engine, via steam power, enabled both heavier-than-air and lighter-than-air progress. The achievement of the Wright brothers in 1903 was anticipated by experiments and advances with aircraft in the late nineteenth century, for example by Clément Ader who, on October 9, 1890, was able to fly a brief distance with powered flight. In 1911, Ader published *L'Aviation Militaire*, a book that discussed the use of air power in war. It was the success of the Wright brothers, bicycle manufacturers who recognized the need to bank in order to turn, that made controlled flight possible. Moreover, the Wright brothers had anticipated a market for military reconnaissance and in February 1908 obtained a contract for a military aircraft, one able to fly 125 miles at forty miles per hour. The first, however, crashed that September, and by the time its replacement was delivered in 1909, Louis Blériot had flown across the English Channel from France on July 25. Lord Northcliffe, the influential British press baron, remarked, "England is no longer an island."

Nevertheless, not all were concerned. That year, when Field Marshal Sir William Nicholson, the chief of the (British) General Staff and then the Imperial General Staff from 1908 to 1912, sought views on the likely effectiveness of air attack, he met with a skeptical response from General Ian Hamilton, who was unimpressed with the possibilities of bombing. Hamilton wrote, "The difficulty of carrying sufficient explosive, and of making a good shot, will probably result in a greater moral than material effect."[7] Similarly, General Ferdinand Foch, director of the French École Supérieure de Guerre, argued in 1910 that air power would only be a peripheral adjunct to the conduct of war. Admiral Tirpitz, the key figure in the German navy, was doubtful of another "museum of experiments."

However, there was a rapid pace of change from 1908, when the Wrights marketed their aircraft in Europe, and, even more, from 1910. On January 13, 1908, Henry Farman, in a Voisin-Farman 1, a French aircraft, was the first officially to succeed in flying one kilometer on a circuit. A British report on foreign forces in 1910 noted,

> Great activity has been displayed in the development of aircraft during the year, particularly in France and Germany. The main feature in the movement has been the increased importance of the aeroplane, which in 1909 was considered to be of minor military value. This importance was due partly to the surprising success of the aeroplane reconnaissances at the French manoeuvres, and partly to the successive disaster of the Zeppelin dirigibles. . . . Aviation schools have been started in almost every country.[8]

THE START OF A NEW ARM

The Balloon Factory at Farnborough was enlarged and switched to become the Royal Aircraft Factory. The following year, the distinguished British veteran Lord Roberts wrote to Nicholson telling him that the army ought to acquire more aircraft. Roberts had read R. P. Hearne's *Aerial Warfare* (1908), the introduction of which was written by Hiram Maxim, a key figure in the development of machine guns.[9] The following year, Maxim predicted raids on cities launched by one thousand bombers. General Douglas Haig was also in favor of air power. In Britain, which rapidly integrated air power into army maneuvers, an Air Battalion was established in 1911, followed by the Royal Flying Corps in 1912. It was to incorporate a central flying school.[10]

Institutional differentiation was a key development. Thus, in France in 1910, a military aviation service was created, as was a permanent inspectorate of military aviation. In 1912, the first law of the French army concerning aviation was issued, while in November 1913 a directory of the army responsible for military aviation was established.[11] In Austria, the Luftschifferabteilung, for airships, but not yet aircraft, was formed in October 1909. The following year, a few aircraft arrived as gifts from private individuals, and in 1911 orders for aircraft were made. The city of Wiener Neustadt went ahead and built an airport to attract the air force.[12] Across Europe and the United States, aircraft captured the public's imagination. At a series of air meets, successive height, speed, and endurance records were continuously exceeded, and the potential of the aircraft appeared unbounded.

There were also new capabilities as part of the fast pace of development. Instruments for mechanically plotting from aerial photography were developed in 1908, while a flight over part of Italy by Wilbur Wright in 1909 appears to have been the first on which photographs were taken. Invited to Italy by the head of the Aeronautics Section in order to train Italian officers to fly and to bring improved aircraft, the Wright brothers introduced more reliable types. In a significant display of interest and favor at the highest level of government, the king attended their demonstrations.

In the United States, the Jamestown Exposition of 1907 saw attempts by pilots and engineers to demonstrate the usefulness of aircraft to the American navy. The first aircraft takeoff from a ship occurred there in November 1910, and the first landing on a ship the following January.[13] The first night flight took place in 1910. The potential for armament was rapidly pursued. In America, with Glenn Curtiss playing the key role, dummy bombs used on target ships in June 1910 were soon followed by live ones, and the trials, moreover, saw the employment of primitive bomb-aiming sights. He also developed seaplanes. Separately, an aircraft-mounted low-recoil machine gun was tested by the Army Ordnance Department. Strategic uses for air power were rapidly suggested. In 1910, an American admiral, Bradley Fiske, felt able to propose that the defense of the distant and recently conquered Philippines should be left to air power. He sought to develop torpedo-carrying aircraft. Russia, with its vast land empire, designed and tested gigantic four-engine, long-range aircraft in 1913, although relatively few were built, and their safety record was questionable.

More generally, the military attempted to work out what air power could do. The schemes they put money into (always a good indication of actual thinking) were mostly realistic and viable or, if not, were explicitly experimental. German advances with airships were so rapid that they left a strong impression, though there was an awareness of airship vulnerabilities and disasters.

Aircraft were first employed in conflict during the Italian-Turkish War of 1911 and the Balkan Wars of 1912–13. In the former, a conflict that also saw the earliest use of armored cars, the Italians initially deployed twelve aircraft as well as airships in Libya. The pace of action was rapid. On October 22, 1911, the first combat reconnaissance flight occurred; the next day an Italian Bleriot XI monoplane took a photograph of the Turkish lines; the first aircraft was hit by ground fire on the 25th; and, on November 1, a two-kilogram grenade was dropped from an Austrian-designed and -built Taube aircraft on Turkish troops. This was followed by a further bombing attack on the main Turkish camp at Ain Zara, one where more heavy grenades were dropped. Fabric ribbons were used to produce a parachute effect, but the Italians developed purpose-built bombs and devices for launching them, including finned cylindrical bombs. The Italian airships were used extensively for reconnaissance and for artillery spotting. However, there were no means to communicate in real time. Weighted notes in small metal containers were dropped. Infrastructure was developed, including an artificial airstrip that was built at Benghazi in Libya in 1911 because of the soft nature of the ground: it proved necessary to lay down a wooden platform for aircraft to take off and land. The Turks sought to make propaganda from the Italians allegedly bombing a hospital.

The Italian use of air power impressed observers and led a number of states to establish air forces, including Bulgaria, Greece, and Turkey. Turkish-held Edirne (Adrianople), besieged by the Bulgarians in 1913, was the first town on which bombs were dropped from an aircraft. "The New Arm's Fearful Strength: Death from the Air," an illustration published in the widely circulated *Illustrated London News* of January 13, 1912, of the impact of a bomb on Turkish forces, was misleading, as the real effect was less deadly, not least as Ottoman forces learned to scatter upon the approach of an aircraft. Indeed, the use of aircraft had little impact on operations in any of these wars, although the Italians benefited from the development of aerial photography, using it to correct their maps, a process that on the ground was vulnerable to attack.[14]

By the outbreak of the First World War, the European powers had a total of over one thousand aircraft in their armed forces. Statistics vary greatly, in part due to issues of flyability, but estimates included 244 aircraft and 300 pilots in the armed forces of Russia (as well as twelve airships), 232 aircraft for Germany, 138 (as well as six airships and two hundred pilots) for France, 154 for Britain, and 56 for Austria-Hungary. In Hungary, a military training school for pilots was established in 1911, while a military aviation section was established in Russia in 1912.[15] There were also smaller air forces, which, individually and in combination, led to a sense that air power was desirable and should be normal. For example, the Danish army and navy had air-defense sections attached to them from 1912 and 1911, respectively, although a Danish air force did not become a service of its own until 1950. The Dutch air force started in 1913 as part of the Royal Netherlands Army. It did not become a separate branch of the armed forces until 1953. Belgium had 24 aircraft in 1914. In Portugal, the first civilian air club was established in 1909. However, it was only the new republican regime that seized power in 1910 that started to think about adding aviation to the armed forces. In 1914, in parallel with the debate over whether Portugal should enter the First World War (or not), the government established what was called the Military Aeronautic Service and bought from France the first military aircraft in Portugal. These efforts were made in the army, with the navy not following until 1917, by which time Portugal had joined the war.

Air power was also spreading on a global scale, both within imperial systems and beyond them. Thus, military aviation in Australia can be dated to 1914, just before the war, when the Australian Flying Corps (part of the army) was set up.[16] Turkey first had military aircraft and trained officer pilots in 1912. There were two of the latter, with eight more under training in France. By mid-1912, an "aviation school" was inaugurated in Constantinople (Istanbul), followed by a "naval air force school" in 1914. Turkish aircraft played a relatively more important role in the Second Balkan War (1913) than they had done in the First (1912–13). In Siam (Thailand), the origins of air power can be traced to February 1911 when a *"semaine de l'aviation"* (week of flying) staged by Charles Van Den Born, a visiting Frenchman, was followed by the designation of the first Siamese pilot officers. China received its first twelve aircraft (Caudrons from France) in the summer of 1913, and France sent an instructor. In Japan, the first locally manufactured aircraft flew on October 25, 1911, and Japan then organized an air service. On September 1, 1914, four Japanese seaplanes attacked the German base of Qingdao in China.

The global spread of air power was in part a matter of the use of aircraft within far-flung imperial systems. Thus, in the French Empire, the world's second most extensive empire after the British, the governor general of Madagascar sought to establish a local air capability, an attempt prevented by accidents in 1911. In Indochina (Vietnam, Cambodia, and Laos), tentative attempts to do the same failed, but in Senegal an airport was created in 1911, and military maneuvers involving aircraft were staged in 1912. The use of military aircraft in Algeria began in 1912. These cases did not involve conflict, but, in the French zone in Morocco, aircraft were deployed as part of a campaign of "pacification": on October 14, 1911, a French aircraft made the first reconnaissance as part of a campaign. There was no air-ground communication, so aircraft had to land to report what they had seen. And they often could not land near the "front lines." On September 23, 1913, Roland Garros was the first pilot to fly across the Mediterranean.

The French soon moved from aircraft only as reconnaissance vehicles to aircraft as fighting platforms. In the spring of 1913, by which time the use of aircraft by the French in Morocco was more frequent, they were the first to drop incendiary bombs.[17] The Spanish army first employed aircraft in offensive operations in "their" sphere of Morocco in 1913. The use of French aircraft in Morocco, however, was affected by their technical limitations, and this led in 1914, prior to the outbreak of the First World War, to the return of most aircraft to France. In 1914, the British planned to use three airships to attack opponents in British Somaliland, only to have to abandon the plan because they needed parts from Germany.[18]

At the same time, naval requirements were to the fore for Britain. In Bernard Partridge's cartoon "Neptune's Ally," published in the British magazine *Punch* on May 25, 1914, Winston Churchill, the ever-active First Lord of the Admiralty, was depicted as blowing aircraft and airships forward to aid Neptune and the Royal Navy in protecting Britain from invasion. The first British airship in 1911 was followed in 1912 by the first launch of a British seaplane. Churchill had played a central role in the formation of the Royal Naval Air Service, devoting considerable attention to the details and displaying a personal interest that was shown in his flying over the fleet in 1914. In 1913, Churchill pressed for the fitting of radios in seaplanes.[19] On a pattern that was to be all too typical of air power, his interest was competitive, with a clear argument that naval air power was more significant than the land equivalent. On February 10, 1914, Churchill wrote,

> The objectives of land aeroplanes can never be so definite or important as the objectives of seaplanes, which, when they carry torpedoes, may prove capable of playing a decisive part in operations against capital ships. The facilities of reconnaissance at sea, where hostile vessels can be sighted at enormous distances while the seaplane remains out of possible range, offer a far wider prospect even in the domain of information to seaplanes than to land aeroplanes, which would be continually brought under rifle and artillery fire.[20]

In 1912, the navy carried out trials to discover if submarines could be detected and attacked from the air. Integration with other services and goals was a significant theme. By 1914, with the active support of Churchill, the Eastchurch naval air station had created a defensive system in which British aircraft fitted with radios cooperated with ground observers. At the start of the war, the Royal Naval Air Service contained thirty-nine aircraft, fifty-two seaplanes, seven airships, and about 120 pilots. The French had the first warship able to transport seaplanes: the

Foudre, modified in December 1911, entered active service in August 1912 and transported four seaplanes in 1914.

Plans were bold. The *Daily Mail* prize offered in 1913 for the first transatlantic flight encouraged new ideas, including Zeppelin's commitment to a four-engine aircraft, which was to be significant for the development of German bombers in the First World War. In 1913, the German flier Hellmuth Hirth proposed a six-engine seaplane that would be able to cross the Atlantic by 1915. However, most of the aircraft in 1914 were little more than flying boxes, as they were slow, underpowered, and unarmed. Indeed, the issue of armament did not really arise until after the outbreak of the war. Despite bold hopes, the general emphasis was on using aircraft for reconnaissance, a readily grasped role already seen in prewar maneuvers. Thus, aircraft were already seen as being part of armies' combined-arms operations. Assumptions about the likely effectiveness of air power had moved from fiction, journalism, and advocacy to the institutions, procurement, and training of the military, but what this would mean in practice was unclear. It was not clear that airships were to become a cul-de-sac vis-à-vis aircraft. There was a poor understanding of the reliability of aircraft, and, more generally, of the reality, as opposed to the perception of the capability, of the system.

3

THE FIRST WORLD WAR

"Flying Men: The Chivalry of the Air" was the title of a piece in the *Times* of London on March 20, 1917. This article suggested that air battles represented the "last chivalries," whereas the "desolation" of conflict on the ground threatened to destroy traditional values. Pilots were presented as "a race apart" and as "air warriors" taking part in one-to-one fighting, "wing to wing."[1] The advent of flight indeed led young men to do something "different and exciting," but the reality was much bleaker. Conflict in the air was brutal as well as dangerous, and death there was as unpleasant as that among the "desolation" on the ground. Pilots lacked parachutes.

The scale of change in air power really escalated from 1914, in part because, in the existing situation, change was bound to be radical and impressive. In part a matter of new types of aircraft and new weapon technologies, change also involved the rapid and significant development of doctrine and production. Most important was a sense of air power as an integral aspect of other branches of conflict, including its use for reconnaissance, artillery spotting, bombing, and action against submarines. The flexibility of air power, its use for land and sea conflict, and its potential for tactical, operational, and strategic ends all emerged clearly. These factors were important in their own right and looked to the future. They encouraged an interest in such concepts as air superiority, command of the air, and strategic warfare.

Air power played a role from the opening campaigns in 1914, developing the potential already glimpsed prior to the war. Reconnaissance was a key capability, with aircraft more flexible and less vulnerable than tethered balloons, and far better and more responsive than the cavalry widely used by all armies. Despite the serious operating constraints posed by the weather, aircraft came to supplement and then replace the reconnaissance functions of cavalry, although the pace of change varied. Over land, French aircraft reported the significant change of direction of the German advance near Paris, creating the opportunity for the successful Allied counterattack in the Battle of the Marne. Aircraft reconnaissance also helped the Germans in the Tannenberg campaign as they responded victoriously to the Russian invasion of East Prussia. In contrast, German aircraft saw and reported the crucial French redeployment of forces from Lorraine to Paris but were not believed. Over water, Admiral Sir John Jellicoe, the commander of the British Grand Fleet, warned that "the German airships will be of the greatest possible advantage to their fleet as scouts."[2]

From the outset, bombing was one of the most modern and terrifying aspects of the war. In 1910, Colonel Frederick Trench, the British military attaché in Berlin, reported that Germany was aiming to build "large airships of great speed, endurance and gas-retaining capacity."[3] Supporting the German invasion of Belgium, a zeppelin raid bombed Liège on August 6 where the garrisons in the fortresses surrounding the city held up the German advance. German airship raids on Antwerp, Paris, and Warsaw soon followed. In response, and indicating what was to be a key element in the employment of air power, its use against other air forces, the aircraft of the British Royal Naval Air Service (RNAS) conducted effective raids from Antwerp in September and October 1914. Twenty-pound bombs were dropped on zeppelin sheds at Düsseldorf on October 8, destroying one airship. The zeppelin base at Friedrichshafen on Lake Constance was attacked on November 21. As a result of this success, the British Admiralty developed an interest in strategic bombing.

As yet, the scale of activity was still modest. Austria, for example, only had five aircraft on the Eastern Front, and only two worked. Cavalry, not aircraft, was used by the Austrians to locate the Russian armies in the vast space of western Ukraine in August. The Austrians were relatively late in appreciating and deploying aircraft. At the start of the war, the British Royal Aircraft Factory at Farnborough could produce only two air frames per month, but its artisanal methods (which encouraged the dependence on French aircraft) were swiftly swept aside by mass production. The first important aircraft built at Farnborough was the BE (British Experimental) aircraft, which was designed for reconnaissance and observation. Entering service in 1912, it was a very stable aircraft, making it ideal for reconnaissance. About 3,500 were built between 1912 and 1918. Existing factories were rapidly converted to war uses. The Birmingham and Midland Carriage Company built Handley Page bombers, while Sunbeam, Wolverhampton's carmakers, manufactured aero-engines.[4] Drawing on the experimentation of Igor Sikorsky, who had built and flown the first four-engine aircraft in 1913, the Russians developed four-engine bombers capable of a considerable range and bombed East Prussia, but Russian air power suffered from the limitations of its industrial base.

A report in the *Times* on December 27, 1914, noted of the Western Front,

> The chief use of aeroplanes is to direct the fire of the artillery. Sometimes they "circle and dive" just over the position of the place which they want shelled. The observers with the artillery then inform the battery commanders—and a few seconds later shells come hurtling on to, or jolly near to, the spot indicated. They also observe for the gunners and signal back to them to tell whether their shots are going to, whether over or short, or to right or left.

As far as the British were concerned, the Aisne fighting on the Western Front in September and October 1914 was the first time aircraft and artillery were used in this fashion. The French had done so slightly before.

1915

Air warfare became bolder in conception as the war continued, with the strategic impasse, and the mounting casualties and attritional character of the war on the ground, providing a search for added capability and alternative means, as well as the time necessary in order to develop innovations. From January 19, 1915, zeppelins attacked Britain, while they continued to bomb French cities, being joined by aircraft. The material damage was relatively modest. A total of 51 zeppelin attacks on

Britain (involving 208 sorties) during the war dropped 196 tons of bombs that killed 556 people and caused £1.5 million worth of property damage. These attacks, which continued on Britain until August 1918, had considerable impact in terrorizing civilian populations, with up to a million people decamping into the countryside, and inflamed British and French opinion.[5] These attacks also affected troops at the front, collapsing the distance between it and the home front. Lieutenant Colonel Alan Thomson, a gunner, was worried about his wife in London and referred to the zeppelins as "those infernal devils."[6]

Bombing raids on civilians were both an application of new technology for the established goal of targeting civilians and a preparation for a new type of total war, in which the centers of opposing states could be attacked with increasing speed and scale. While the sense of what air power might achieve expanded rapidly, many ideas were not feasible, as when the British Committee of Imperial Defence considered using long-range aircraft based in Russia to drop incendiary bombs that would destroy German wheat and rye crops.[7] Although overrating the vulnerability of agriculture, this idea, impracticable as it was, indicated how quickly military planners began to envisage that this form of conflict should be war virtually without limits. This was not the same as air power itself being novel as a new form of war without limits because antisocietal goals and means were long established, a point that some discussion underplays. Instead, air power represented a new delivery system. Other ideas were considered unacceptable, as when Major Lord Tiverton recommended the use of potato blight, which would also have provided a more pointed instance of the food shortages that naval blockade was intended to produce. This would also have been the first use of biological warfare.

While there were only limited changes in airships, the capabilities of aircraft swiftly improved, and tactics for the effective use of aircraft were worked out. The ability of aircraft to destroy balloons and airships with explosive and incendiary bullets spelled doom for the latter. The British spent much effort developing antizeppelin rounds. The main ones were the Brock, the Pomeroy, and the Buckingham, the first two explosive and the last incendiary. Incendiary rounds had a problem with range: the pilot had to get very close because otherwise the phosphorus burned up too early as it was ignited when the round was fired. The zeppelin had impressed contemporaries as a bomber, but it was expensive compared to aircraft and its vulnerability to aircraft firing explosive and incendiary bullets became apparent. That zeppelins tended to attack at night, could fly at a great height, and could climb rapidly created challenging requirements for the intercepting fighters, one of which was flown by Arthur Harris, later a key figure in the Second World War. Explosive and incendiary bullets were also used against artillery observation balloons and, again, helped account for the value of aircraft.

Meanwhile, the ability of aircraft to act in aerial combat with other aircraft was enhanced thanks to increases in aircraft speed, maneuverability, and ceiling. Engine power increased and size fell, while the rate of an aircraft's climb rose. The air-combat capability of an aircraft was helped by improved structural designs.

The need to shoot down reconnaissance aircraft, the first shot down on October 5, 1914,[8] resulted in the development of the fighter as well as an emphasis on antiaircraft guns fired from the ground. Initially reliant on small arms, generally revolvers and carbines fired by the observer, rather than on fixed arms, the fighter soon carried machine guns. In trials, the British fired Lewis guns through the propeller, merely binding the blades with tape to prevent splintering. Adding deflector plates or wedges to propeller blades permitted the firing of machine guns ahead and thus on the axis of attack. Because of the ballistic complexities of firing off axis, it soon became clear that firing along the aircraft's flight path was far more accurate. Adopting this device enabled the French to establish Escadrilles de Chasse (hunting squadrons). Roland Garros was the first French pilot to use deflector plates or wedges on propeller blades. He shot down three German aircraft with the system in April 1915.[9]

In turn, the interrupter gear ensured that the machine gun would not fire when the gun muzzle and the propeller were aligned. Interrupter and synchronizing mechanisms work by allowing a pulse to be sent from the engine to the firing mechanism to fire the gun, which effectively fires on semiautomatic. The impulse was often generated by a cam while a rod linkage fired the gun. In essence, each pulse fired one round, hence the gun firing on semiautomatic, but this was at a sufficient rate to produce a stream of bullets, albeit much reduced compared to a conventional full automatic. Had the guns tried to fire on full automatic, the system would have stopped the gun from firing altogether. These mechanisms did not interrupt the guns or the engines.

Effective synchronizing gear, which enabled bullets to pass through the arc of a propeller without hitting the propeller, was developed by a Dutchman, Anthony Fokker, although Fokker was sued for patent infringement by Franz Schneider, a Swiss engineer, and the case continued until 1933 despite the courts finding in favor of Schneider every time. Schneider, who worked for Luftverkehrs Gesellschaft, had patented a synchronizing gear in 1913. Neither Schneider's nor Raymond Saulnier's French 1914 gear were really reliable enough for employment in combat, partly because of inconsistencies with the propellants used in the machine-gun ammunition, which led to misfires.

Fokker's synchronizing gear, utilized by the Germans from April 1915, enabled aircraft to fire forward without damaging their propellers, and thus to fire repeatedly in the direction of flight. The Fokker Eindecker aircraft, a speedy and nimble monoplane that the Germans deployed from mid-1915, gave them a distinct advantage for the rest of the year, which was appropriately known as the "Fokker Scourge." The BE-2 was to be referred to as "Fokker fodder" in Britain's Parliament. The first British gear, invented by George Challenger, an engineer at Vickers, went into production in December 1915. The first French synchronizing gear was used operationally from mid-1916.[10] Whereas on the eve of the war there had been no armed aircraft designed to attack other armed aircraft, now the situation was different, although emerging air power did not as yet affect the planning of campaigns and the pursuit of strategy.

The continuous nature of the front line as campaigning ceased for the winter in late 1914 led to a very different requirement for aerial reconnaissance including aerial photography. Instead of the emphasis being on the location and movement of opposing armies, as in 1914, the stress now was on information that would enable accurate artillery targeting of opposing trench positions. In 1915, aircraft took a greater role in reconnaissance and artillery spotting (which improved the accuracy of shot), to both tactical and operational effect. For the Battle of Neuve Chapelle on March 15, 1915, the first British trench-warfare attack, the plan was based on maps created through aerial photographs. General Callwell remarked of the plans for the Gallipoli operation, the Allied attempt to break through to Constantinople (Istanbul), "As a land gunner I have no belief in that long range firing except when there are aeroplanes to mark the effect."[11] At an operational level, the Turkish columns advancing on the Suez Canal were spotted by British aircraft, which helped prepare the repulse of the attack in February 1915. Russian aircraft were mainly used for reconnaissance.

The value of reconnaissance and the vulnerability of the reconnaissance aircraft as they maintained straight and level courses to take their photographs made them vital, yet ideal, targets, and considerable effort was spent in chasing, if not destroying, these aircraft and, in turn, in preventing this from happening. Thomson recorded at Gallipoli a British aircraft chasing off a German one and another German one flying low and machine-gunning a sailor on a destroyer.[12] Another officer at Gallipoli noted, "The Germans have been dropping bombs and proclamations," although the former did little damage.[13]

That year, an exchange program began, with some German pilots serving in the Turkish army and some Turkish pilots under advanced training in Germany. The Turks used aircraft more than they had done in the Balkan Wars of 1912–13. More aircraft were purchased by Turkey, and they were organized as air companies. In 1915, because of the increasing number of aircraft, they were organized as the Ninth Department of the Armed Forces, which was followed by the formation of specialized units such as the Aviation School, Air Stations, Air Companies, Fixed Balloon Companies, Anti-Aircraft Artillery Units, and a meteorology department. The aircraft were to participate in most of the fronts on which the Turks operated, including Gallipoli, the Hijaz (Arabia), the Caucasus, and Palestine, spreading an impression of aircraft and touching off reports and rumors.

In Iraq, the Turks faced the first Australian Flying Corps (AFC) unit to see active service. In 1915, Australia was asked for air assistance by the British government of India, which had sent forces to invade Turkish-ruled Iraq. The Australians provided aircrews and ground staff, while the Indian government contributed three aircraft, which, however, were not suited to desert conditions. The aircraft were used for reconnaissance, and two more aircraft were added. The Australians were then added to a British squadron, which had four aircraft and had another seven added. The aircraft made no appreciable difference to operations, which culminated in Allied forces being besieged in Kut in 1915.

Meanwhile, that same year, specialized bombing developed using adapted aircraft. Both Britain and France made significant advances, with Britain using bombers against German rail links in the Battle of Neuve Chapelle in March. Accuracy, however, was a major problem, as was the vulnerability of fighters. Hugh Trenchard, who became the head of the Royal Flying Corps (RFC) in France in August 1915, keenly fostered a sense of aggression and persistent attack for his aircraft, but this attitude led to high casualties. The following month, the French offensive launched in Champagne was accompanied by a large-scale air assault, leading to an aero-terrestrial battle. The bombing of Germany was relegated to the second rank, in part because of the losses suffered by the French in bombing the Rhineland that November. The Champagne offensive led, on November 21, 1915, to the adoption by France of a program of large-scale expansion. An air force of 1,310 aircraft was planned.

1916

The distinct benefit the Germans had gained from their use of Fokker Eindecker aircraft enabled them to seek the aerial advantage over Verdun in the key battle on the Western Front in early 1916. French vulnerability to German fighters was swiftly demonstrated. In addition, troops on the ground increasingly had to be mindful of the risk of air attack. The order of October 26, 1916, for the British 169th Infantry Brigade noted, "When hostile aeroplanes are in sight, troops will halt and clear the road as far as possible."[14] The effectiveness of aircraft machine guns, and their psychological impact, was underscored by the use of the German verb for such an attack, *strafen*, "to punish." In just one pass, an aircraft could kill or wound twenty to thirty soldiers.

Nevertheless, in an abrupt demonstration of the action-reaction cycle that was so significant, the French, who sought what they termed air superiority, were eventually able to drive off German reconnaissance aircraft from Verdun because they succeeded in contesting the German Fokker fighters through their employment of large groups of aircraft and because they now had the agile "Bébé" Nieuport fighter. The first French fighter with a synchronized forward-firing machine gun, the Spad VII, became effective at the end of the year. Thus, war accelerated technological development, but, with equal speed, this resulted in another stalemate of sorts.

Over Verdun, each side complained about the other's aircraft and pursued a battle for air superiority with large-scale air-to-air conflict, but neither side had control of the air. In contrast, in the Battle of the Somme in the second half of the year, air power came to the fore. The German infantry and artillery complained bitterly about the way the British used aircraft for spotting and ground attack, and about the lack of a German response. Although the British were limited by bad weather, the Germans were impressed during the Somme offensive by the skill the British brought to coordinating the action of artillery, aircraft, and infantry. Because the long arm of the British artillery and aircraft reached well into the German rear, units out of the front line lacked restorative time. This was a key aspect of Trenchard's insistence on taking the war to the enemy, a stance the Germans were to copy in 1917 to good effect. In their zone, the French also gained air superiority and launched effective air attacks on the German artillery. Aircraft proved a particular problem for the Germans due to the exposed nature of the terrain.[15] This situation caused a real change in how the Germans thought about air power and control of the air, and they poured resources into developing their own air power, while also bringing aircraft and antiaircraft guns under the same corps. Now a key goal, air superiority required technological proficiency as well as the mass expressed in large formations.

1917

In turn, the Germans gained the advantage in the air in the winter of 1916–17, thanks in part to their Albatross D-1 with its top ceiling of eighteen thousand feet. Aerodynamically efficient, faster than the Nieuport, maneuverable, and armed with two synchronized machine guns, the Albatross entered service in September 1916. Indeed, the British, many of whose pilots had received insufficient training, referred to April as "Bloody April." The advantage was apparent on the ground, the report on the operations of the British 56th Division noting for January 21, 1917, "The hostile bombardment was very accurate, evidently as a result of aerial reconnaissance carried out the previous day."[16] However, artillery frequently could not hit anything even with good spotting. Aircraft were also useful for aerial mapping: aerial photographs were employed to create the maps, but the correct method of reading maps taken from the air was still in its infancy in this period.

The Germans lost their aerial advantage from mid-1917 as more and better Allied aircraft entered service, especially the French Spad VII and Spad XIII and the British Bristol Fighter, with its forward- and rearward-bearing armament, and the extremely nimble Sopwith Camel. These aircraft, in turn, offered the Allies a qualitative superiority. At the same time, this process was one of experimentation, including with people's lives. For example, the Sopwith Camel proved highly dangerous to its pilots, while the RE-8, a descendant of the BE-2, was substantially and successfully redesigned to remove its deadly operating flaws, flaws that led to considerable public criticism.

The British abandoned mechanical synchronizing gears and, in 1917, adopted the superior synchronizing gear (the CC gear) invented by a Romanian engineer, George Constantinesco. This gear employed no mechanical linkages, but a column of fluid in which wave pulses were generated and transmitted. This was not a hydraulic system because of the use of the pulse, but the process produced the hydraulic equivalent of an alternating current in electricity. It was more reliable than mechanical systems and allowed for a faster rate of fire. The CC gear was fitted to British fighters from March 1917 (Bristol Fighters, DH-4s and SE-5s), until the Gloster Gladiator of 1934 (it entered squadron service in 1937). Because Constantinesco's theory of sonics was kept secret, the Germans failed to copy the gear from shot-down aircraft (a regular source of technical intelligence) because they wrongly assumed the device to be purely hydraulic and could not make it work. They still used synchronizing gears in the Me-109 and FW-190 of the Second World War.

On the Western Front, the use of air power increased in 1917, both in scale and in type, not least with an increase in ground attack. This could be seen in the Allied Third Ypres Offensive, although the weather did not permit much flying in August, while in September dust often prevented accurate spotting. Nevertheless, in late September and early October, when the weather improved, the spotters helped the successful "bite and hold" limited offensives of the Second Army under Herbert Plumer. In the Battle of Cambrai, from November 20 to December 5, the British made a large-scale use of tanks for the first time, and both they and the Germans first used ground attacks extensively. Already, on May 23, the Italians had used 109 aircraft in an attack on Austrian positions in advance of an offensive, a mass use of aircraft for ground support. Aircraft use was therefore part of a more general embrace of the new. In contrast, during the April Chemin des Dames offensive, the French air force concentrated on trying to win a separate victory in the air.

In 1917, paralleling the turn to unrestricted submarine warfare, the Germans launched an air assault on Britain, because they believed, possibly due to reports from Dutch intelligence, that the British were on the edge of rebellion, which was very much not the case. As a result of this belief, the attacks were intended not so much to serve attritional goals, but rather to be a decisive, war-winning, strategic tool. This, the first attempt to use air power as a truly strategic weapon, rather than simply as a renewal of the zeppelin offensive, was a form of war that was novel. The targets were not fortresses. The use of bombers—the twin-engine Gotha—from May 25 reflected the rapid improvement of capability during the war. The Germans imitated the design of the Russian Ilya Mourometz four-engine bomber, a development of the prewar Sikorsky model, which made over four hundred raids on Germany. The Gotha MK IV could fly for six hours, had an effective range of 520 miles, could carry 1,100 pounds (or 500 kg) of bombs, and could fly at an altitude of twenty-one thousand feet (6,400 meters, or four miles), which made interception difficult. The need for bombers to be able to outperform fighters was crucial. A rear machine gun that could depress to fire below was designed to thwart fighters firing up from below where aircraft were vulnerable to a surprise attack. Furthermore, the crews were supplied with oxygen and with electric power to heat their flying suits. The first (and deadliest) raid on London, a surprise daylight one on June 13, 1917, led to a public outcry in Britain. Fourteen aircraft (six had dropped out), approaching at 16,500 feet, each carrying six 110-pound bombs, killed 162 people and injured 432, not least as a result of a direct hit on the North Street School in Poplar that killed sixteen children.

In the characteristic action-reaction cycle, the raids resulted in the speedy development of a defensive system involving high-altitude fighters based on airfields linked by telephone to observers. This led to heavy losses among the Gothas and to the abandonment of daylight raids. Britain's early detection and response system, which was effective, provided the model for that used in 1940 when the Germans launched a deadlier air assault.

Moreover, the rationale of the 1917 German air campaign was misplaced because, as with the air attacks on France, those on Britain, far from hurting British morale, led to a hostile political, media, and public response. This remained the case in the winter of 1917–18, when the Germans unleashed large, four-engine Riesenflugzeug, or R-series, bombers, difficult to control but able to fly for eight hours and drop 4,400 pounds (2,000 kg) of bombs. These aircraft, which themselves required a major logistical support system and thus a significant opportunity cost, failed to inflict serious and sustained damage, which did not set an encouraging example for strategic bombing.[17] As earlier with the zeppelins, British troops at the front were concerned about the fate of loved ones at home.

1918

New weapon systems rapidly developed during the war. However, in 1918, aircraft remained particularly significant for reconnaissance, notably in spotting for artillery, the key weapon on the Western Front. This spotting was fundamental to the effectiveness of the earlier aerial reconnaissance work, which had produced the photography necessary for the accurate mapping of opposing positions, as well as for identifying targets. Thanks to spotting, by aircraft such as the French Breguet XIV A-2, the German Albatross C-3, and the British RE-8, the accuracy of artillery fire could be assessed and fresh targets of opportunity found. Radio permitted air-ground communication. The British ground stations were operated by RFC personnel attached to artillery batteries. The radio communication, however, was one way: the operators had to take down and interpret the signals from the aircraft but could only reply by laying out cloth strips. By the end of the war, about six hundred reconnaissance aircraft were fitted with the Tuner Mark III, and there were one thousand ground stations and eighteen thousand wireless operators.

Air spotting aided counterbattery work and deep shelling: targeted fire on opposing positions behind the front that were within range. Douglas Haig, the commander of the British forces on the Western

Front, and Trenchard both saw artillery-aircraft cooperation as crucial. Enhanced accuracy, which transformed the nature of range, was central to a modernization of artillery effectiveness, one that, paradoxically, while dependent on air power, nevertheless ensured that ground-based fire remained far more significant as the essential form of firepower. Although limited by the range of the guns, artillery could deliver far heavier weights of firepower than the aircraft alone. This modernization has been seen as akin to a revolution in military affairs.[18]

The capability and range of ground-support operations expanded. There was also a development in low-level ground attack, including trench strafing by machine gun, while there was also ground support in the form of interdiction: isolating the battlefield through attacking targets, notably supply links such as bridges, to the rear of the front line. In 1918, the Germans used specially organized ground-attack squadrons, coordinated in what became known in the Second World War as blitzkrieg attacks, to saturate and overrun Allied defenses on the Western Front. This forced the Allies to focus on repelling the German air assault, while, in turn, frequent Allied air attacks on their supply links inhibited German advances. The Fokker D-7 fighter, which entered German service in April 1918, suffered problems at first, such as rib failure, shedding fabric on the upper wing, fuel tanks splitting at the seams, and engine heat igniting phosphorus in the ammunition. However, the D-7 provided the Germans with a highly maneuverable and effective aircraft able to outclimb its British opponents, and British ground attacks on the Western Front that August were affected by German air power: "During the whole of these operations, enemy low flying aircraft were extraordinarily active, bombing and machine gunning our troops."[19] The Allies also had some good aircraft, notably the British SE-5, a fast, durable fighter that played a major role in the closing stages of the war. The French Spad XII was well armed, agile, and robust, and was used by the British and Americans as well. The French Breguet XIV, which entered service in June 1917, proved very successful in both reconnaissance and tactical bombing versions.

The impact of Allied fighters on the Western Front, not least in challenging the advantages on the ground that the Germans won with their Spring Offensive, led the Germans to call off their Gotha attacks on London and, instead, to use these aircraft to take part in the air war over France. This involved both interdiction in the shape of attacking railway stations and the pursuit of air supremacy by means of raiding Allied airfields. The bombing of Paris, however, continued.

The range and scale of air activity increased in 1918, notably with the Allies carrying the fight to the enemy. The diaries of German corps and army commanders, such as Oskar von Hutier of the Eighteenth Army, reported that strafing had replaced artillery as the greatest threat to German troops, who, as a result, could only move by night.[20] The casualty rate among aircrew was high, not least due to the deployment of more fighters, and, moreover, in larger groupings. Despite serious problems with recognition and accuracy (which led to "friendly fire" losses), as well as the limited time aircraft could stay in the air, aircraft, tanks, artillery, and infantry were combined by the British and French to provide mobile firepower. German aircraft destroyed moving French tanks in Champagne, while the British used air strikes in their advances on the Western Front and in Palestine and Macedonia.

Numerical superiority was a key element in Allied success. By the end of the war, Germany had a frontline strength of 2,500, but France had 3,700 and Britain 2,600. Moreover, the combined Franco-American-British force of 1,481 aircraft employed to support the American attack on the St. Mihiel salient on September 12 was not only the largest deployment so far but also gained air control, which was not usually possible during the war. The French had done so with six hundred aircraft, the "Division Aérienne," in support of a counteroffensive launched south of Montdidier on June 11. The French bombers participated in the ground battle, attacking German artillery positions and lines of communication and helping to stop the German forces. Prefiguring the situation in the Second World War, there was a major problem providing French fighters with a range able to escort the bombers. This was not settled until the Caudron R-XI entered service and was integrated with the bomber units. The French had played a major role in providing the US Army Air Service with 3,300 aircraft and with training.

Massed offensive tactics were also employed by the Americans, under Colonel Billy Mitchell, in support of the Meuse-Argonne offensive at the end of September. This was an instance of the so-called American Way of War, namely the use of massed force at the decisive point for victory. In 1918, these tactics were also employed by the French and the British.

The big dogfight philosophy gave fighters an apparently enhanced role comparable to that of bombing to victory. This role was detached from the need to protect bombers and from the realities of the difficulties of managing large-scale clashes. Nevertheless, scale on a level inconceivable before the war was now on offer. On October 7, 1918, Haig recorded being impressed by the promise from the Royal Air Force that it could provide three hundred aircraft practically at once to attack the Germans if their position collapsed around Busigny. He had good relations with Trenchard.

The aircraft and techniques used by the British on the Western Front were also employed successfully in Palestine. There, the British defeated their German and Turkish opponents in the air and then used this advantage to great effect in the Battle of Megiddo that September. Australian and British aircraft inflicted great damage by strafing on retreating Turkish forces, notably at Wadi el Fara, and made it difficult for them to rally.

The British established the Royal Air Force (RAF) as a separate force on April 1, 1918. It had about twenty-two thousand aircraft, although most were not frontline. This independence from the army, which anticipated service rivalries and tensions in other states, was not only a testimony to the argument that such an organization would make it easier to pursue control of the air, both for offense and defense, but also a reaction to the demand for retribution for the German raids on Britain. Envisaging a strategic potential and outcome, air power was designed to surmount the deadlock of the trenches by permitting the destruction of the enemy where vulnerable.[21] The German cities of Cologne, Frankfurt, and Mannheim were all attacked in 1918, but the purpose of degrading industrial and logistical capability proved difficult in practice. Moreover, there were civilian casualties, which underlined popular bitterness. At any rate, in a pattern later familiar with the RAF and other air forces, notably the American, the British exaggerated what their bombers had achieved. This greatly affected interwar (1919–38) discussion of strategic bombing, leading to a misrepresentation of its potential.[22] The Italians launched a bomber offensive against Austria in 1918, just as Britain directed one against Germany. Austrian aircraft had bombed Italian targets including Venice, although the wife of Emperor Charles expressed concern about the damage to the city. The French preferred to focus on ground attack and not on distant bombing, but they produced nine hundred Voisin Renault type X, capable of dropping three hundred kilograms of bombs, and had 245 of them in service in August; they specialized in night attacks.

Although they had already used the Handley Page 0/100 and 0/400 with success, the war ended before the British could use the large Handley Page V/1500 bombers they had built to bomb Berlin, but, had the war continued, bombing would have become more important. These aircraft could carry 7,500 pounds of bombs and fly for over twelve hours, but large bombers faced many problems in performance and handling, not least unreliable engines. Moreover, the Germans had deployed fighters, including the Fokker D-8, a high-wing parasol mono-plane with excellent visibility and a tubular steel fuselage structure, which could have posed a major problem for any bomber offensive. Entering service in July, the D-8 initially suffered a few fatal accidents when the wing collapsed due to poor manufacture. The French had similar aircraft from March 1915.

The British idea of a separate air force was influential in the British dominions, notably in Australia. A two-squadron Canadian air force was established, only to be ended in 1918. It never went overseas. However, an estimated twenty thousand Canadian aircrew were in British service during the war. In France, the army opposed an independent air force and wanted air power to focus on the Western Front, not on long-range bombing.

At the same time, antiaircraft capability increased considerably. It was particularly dangerous for low-flying ground-attack aircraft. In 1918, the antiaircraft guns of the German Air Service shot down 748 Allied aircraft. Aside from such guns, which had to be rapid firing and able to elevate to a high angle, there were specialized spotting and communication troops, as well as relevant training, manuals, and firing tables. In September 1918, Arthur Child-Villiers, a British officer on the Western Front, noted greater British success "in bringing down the night-flying [German] aeroplanes."[23]

NAVAL AIR POWER

Air power also developed at sea. Airships were much used for recon-naissance. Although their range was shorter, aircraft proved less exposed to the weather. Prior to the conflict, Britain and France had converted ships to provide seaplane tenders. Seaplanes, generally operated from naval bases but also able to perform sea takeoffs and landings and to be catapulted from ships, and aircraft operated from coastal air stations were most important at sea during the war. Britain took a lead in the use of aircraft for reconnaissance, spotting naval gunfire (in order to improve accuracy), patrols against submarines, and attacks on shipping, although the French also played a role. On December 5, 1914, a French squadron of seaplanes was deployed at Port Said, with French pilots and British observers, in order to protect the Suez Canal and observe Turkish naval and land moves. In April 1916, the squadron was moved to Greece.[24] In 1915, British seaplanes used torpedoes against Turkish supply ships. In 1916, both the British and German fleets failed at Jutland in the North Sea, in poor visibility, to use their air reconnaissance adequately when they clashed in the largest naval battle of the war.

Airships and aircraft offered an advantage in dealing with submarines, as viewing submerged objects is far easier from above than from sea level. With the limited submerged endurance of the submarine, aircraft were most effective in searching large areas for surfaced submarines, and then in possibly attacking them as they dived. However, aircraft were not yet able to make a fundamental contribution to antisubmarine operations because key specifications they had by the Second World War were lacking during the First, while the antisubmarine weapons dropped by aircraft were fairly unsophisticated compared to those of the Second World War. The French aircraft operating from North Africa from January 1916 to November 1918 against German submarines in the Mediterranean only sank one.[25]

In July 1918, Britain conducted the first raid by aircraft flown off an improvised aircraft carrier, a technique not used by any other power. In the following month, British seaplanes eliminated an entire naval force: six German coastal motorboats. In September 1918, *Argus*, an aircraft carrier capable of carrying 20 aircraft, with a flush deck unobstructed by superstructure and funnels—in short the first clear-deck carrier—was commissioned by the British, although she did not undergo sea trials until October 1918. At the end of the war, the Royal Naval Air Service had 2,949 aircraft and was planning an attack on the German High Seas

Fleet in harbor at Wilhelmshaven on the North Sea, an attack that had been postponed to 1919.

Naval air power was also introduced elsewhere. For example, the antecedents of Australian naval air power began during the war, with seaplanes used off the major ships of the Royal Australian Navy and Australian personnel in the Royal Naval Air Service. There was also a short-lived Royal Canadian Naval Air Service, which served from Nova Scotia hunting for German submarines.[26]

CONCLUSIONS

The extension of air power to the sea made scant impact on the course of the war. Moreover, on land, many of the hopes of air power were based on a misleading sense of operational and technological possibilities. In practice, the prime value of air power remained aerial reconnaissance throughout the war. This was not the lesson taken by those in command. Indeed, leading air-power advocates of the interwar years took command positions in the war. These included Giulio Douhet, author of *Il Dominio dell'Aria* (The Command of the Air, 1921), who, despite insubordination, had been appointed head of the Italian Central Aeronautical Bureau in 1917; Billy Mitchell, the senior American air commander in the war; and Hugh Trenchard, who commanded the British Royal Flying Corps in France during the war and was the first chief of the Air Staff in 1918 and from 1919 to 1929. Hermann Göring, Hitler's head of the Luftwaffe, served in the German air force throughout the First World War, eventually as a squadron leader. Ernst Udet, who served under Göring in the war, was put in charge of the Luftwaffe's technical office in 1936.

Artisanal methods in aircraft production had been swept aside by mass production so that France was able to manufacture over fifty-two thousand aircraft during the war, Germany forty-eight thousand, and Britain forty-three thousand. This mass production was a response to the high rate at which aircraft (as well as pilots) were lost, as well as to the need to invest in new generations of aircraft. Wear and tear was also a major problem, and the life expectancy of aircraft remained below a year in 1925. Air power also exemplified the growing role of scientific research in military capability: wind tunnels were constructed for the purpose of research. Strutless wings and aircraft made entirely from metal were developed. Huge improvements in design, construction, engines, and armaments, as well as effective systems of procurement,[27] had turned the unsophisticated machine of 1914, such as the German Taube and the French Blériot 9, into a more potent weapon. There was a marked specialization in aircraft type, with bombers, such as the British Handley Page 0/400 and the Italian Caproni Ca-34, very different from reconnaissance aircraft and fighters. There were separate units for the particular functions. Parachutists on operational missions were first used, by the Italians, in 1918.

However, as yet, air superiority did not have the same effect that was to be seen in the Second World War and certainly did not lead to air supremacy in the sense of an ability to command the air. For example, on November 8 and 9, 1918, on the Western Front, Alan Thomson benefited from information from an aircraft about the situation ahead, and, on November 9, he watched British aircraft dropping ration boxes by parachute as the cratered roads had made it impossible to bring up supplies. Yet he was bombed that night, and on the last night of the war, a German aircraft flew over.[28] Moreover, the tactical and operational effectiveness of air power remained heavily dependent on the weather. There were also serious technological issues, notably with engine development.

The limitations of air power did not prevent a marked spread in familiarity with it, not least because of the articulation of powers into alliance systems. For example, within the Portuguese Expeditionary Corps deployed to northern France in 1917, an air-combat unit was planned. It was not sent, but single officers with flying expertise were posted to British and French units and thus became the first Portuguese fighting pilots. Also in 1917, the Portuguese navy established its Aviation Service and School, while, in the Portuguese colony of Mozambique in 1917–18, there were Portuguese air operations against German forces invading from neighboring German East Africa (now Tanzania).

The extension of the use of air power in Africa had particularly unpleasant aspects, notably in September 1916, when, in reprisal for Senussi tribal attacks on a French border position in southern Tunisia, the French on one occasion bombed the Libyan town of Nalut with gas bombs.[29] The more general French use of air power in North Africa from 1916, and notably in southern Tunisia, southern Algeria, and Morocco, in part prefigured the policy of "Air Control" that was to be associated with the RAF. However, the British were to prove willing to give the air force a degree of independence that the French did not pursue. Moreover, the British also had an example from the First World War with the use of aircraft in Egypt in 1916 against Senussi tribesmen raiding from Libya.

It was the potential for the future that was most striking, not the amount of damage air attack had inflicted, nor its integration with war on land or at sea, nor the range and scale of operations. However, the image of a different world was chilling. Blackouts to make targeting by bombers harder demonstrated both the consequences of the war for civilian life and the range of government. In July 1916, John Monash, an Australian divisional commander, wrote to his wife from London, "You can hardly imagine what the place is like. The Zeppelin scare is just like as if the whole place was in imminent fear of an earthquake. At night, the whole of London is in *absolute darkness*."[30]

A year later, the fear reached Australia. There were claims that a seaplane from a German merchant raider had flown over Sydney harbor. The German Spring Offensive on the Western Front began the following year, and people in Australia became nervous and began to see mystery aircraft everywhere. The navy and the army fruitlessly searched for hidden German bases or raiders from which these aircraft could be flying. This was an impetus for the creation of the Royal Australian Air Force (RAAF), as there were only two or three aircraft available in Australia for this search, and the first memorandum from the army chief of staff calling for an independent air arm dates from then.[31] There was a similar scare in New Zealand at the same time, although air power there did not effectively start until 1923.[32]

In a reaction to the misery in the trenches, the image of the war in the air that was widely propagated was that of individual heroism personified by fighter aces, such as Manfred von Richthofen (German), Charles Guynemer (French), René Fonck (French), and Eddie Rickenbacker (American), and their duels with each other. This image, which reflected the novelty of aerial combat and served as a contrast to the intractable nature of land warfare, did not, however, capture the reality of this warfare. Instead, this reality was of aircraft that could be difficult to fly, exposure to the elements, deadly combat, very high casualties,

and extraordinary mental strain.[33] The latter two elements were captured in *Winged Victory* (1934), a semiautobiographical novel by Victor
Maslin Yeates. Joining the Royal Flying Corps in 1917, he crashed four
times and was shot down twice during his 248 hours of combat flying. In
the novel, the pilots loathe war, seeing it as boredom interspersed with
horror; they drink heavily; and all the pilot friends of the protagonist
die, while he is left a broken man. This was the reality of air warfare, as
was the plight of bombed civilians.

4

THE 1920s

In the aftermath of the First World War, air power was considered, at least in part, as a way to learn lessons from the conflict, notably for waging another major war of this type more successfully. At the same time, national variations played a key role, as each state interpreted air power in a different fashion, particularly in light of its specific wartime track record, its institutional organization of air power, and its unique requirements of the moment.[1] Looking to the future, and fearing another major conflict, commentators sought to make sense of the experience of the First World War and to present that experience as a war-winning formula. They were influenced by a belief in the fragile nature of morale, both military and civilian, and the problems and opportunities this would provide for future conflict.

PLANNING FOR THE FUTURE

This belief provided the basis for the theory of the knockout blow that could be delivered only by air and that would lead to a rapid victory. As a result, it was argued, for example by Giulio Douhet of Italy, that air power would be able to overcome the stasis and high casualties of intractable conflict at the front, which was how the First World War was recalled. The idea of the Lost Generation tied into this interpretation. Air power also might lessen social ills by avoiding high casualties among the troops. In addition, the major impact on public morale of

German raids on London in the "Gotha Summer" of 1917 appeared a menacing augury of what could happen as a result of the deployment of more powerful aircraft. There was an idea, prevalent in Britain in particular, but not only there, that aerial bombardment in any future war was going to be more devastating in practice and decisive in consequence, more strategic in impact, than in fact it proved to be until supplemented by atomic bombs in 1945. The Air Ministry in Britain was more moderate in its claims about the potential of air power than independent air enthusiasts.[2]

However, the latter made the running in public and had an impact. Concerns were vented in the press, in novels, and in supposedly analytical works, such as Basil Liddel Hart's *Paris, or the Future of War* (1925). There were particular air scares in Britain in 1922 and 1935. In John Galsworthy's novel *A Modern Comedy* (1929), Sir Lawrence Mont wondered how the English nation could exist with "all its ships and docks in danger of destruction by aeroplanes." The prospect of civilian losses in the millions arising from attacks with gas and high explosives on major cities was frequently held out.[3] Widespread international concerns about air attack indeed encouraged the idea of "qualitative disarmament": banning aggressive weapons such as aircraft, submarines, and gas. Much speculation and some diplomatic and legal activity were devoted to the subject in the 1920s and early 1930s.

In practice, there was no genuine danger in the 1920s, as Britain's principal opponent then, the Soviet Union, a threat to the Middle East, Persia (Iran), Afghanistan, and India, was in no position to mount an attack on Britain. In the mid-1920s, British bombers with a full load of fuel were designed to take off from Kent, bomb Paris, and return home. However, despite serious concerns, France, as was widely appreciated, was not the principal threat to Britain.[4] Moreover, the French were using virtually the same aircraft as in the First World War into the early 1930s, while the Soviet Union did not develop a modern long-range bomber capability until the 1930s. Even then, aimed against Japan, this capability was not suited for any attack on more distant Britain.

However, concern about the Soviet Union was a reason for the British deployment of air power in Iraq, formerly part of the Ottoman (Turkish) Empire, where Britain, with League of Nations mandates, had become the imperial power as a result of the First World War. There was therefore a strategic purpose alongside the counterinsurrectionary use of aircraft based in Iraq that tends to attract attention. The Soviet-Turkish Treaty of Friendship in 1925 brought the threat that the Soviets would support Turkey in its claims on the oil-rich region of Mosul, which Britain occupied under the League of Nations mandate granting it control over Iraq.

RUSSIAN CIVIL WAR

The use of air power in the 1920s was part of a more fluid practice and style of war than that employed in the First World War. This practice involved civil conflict over big areas, notably in Russia and China, and this conflict did not provide the opportunities for air attack seen in 1918. There were not the relatively fixed front lines that needed to be reconnoitered for purposes of planning and directing artillery fire. In addition, the rapidly changing position of ground forces meant that it was not practical to build up an infrastructure of developed bases to support air operations; airfields frequently had to be abandoned. More-over, the large areas in dispute ensured that aircraft, when used, were operating in a very different operational density to the situation on the Western Front in the First World War.

In theory, the Bolsheviks (the successful communists, as opposed to the Mensheviks and others) in Russia inherited the capability of the Tsarist state, including its air force. In reality, however, the civil war destroyed much of Russia's infrastructure, while the military, already much weakened, was decimated after the October 1917 revolution, and there were huge shortages of fuel, as well as problems with the availability, reliability, and maintenance of equipment. In January 1918, a decree called for the preservation of all existing aviation units and schools for the new regime. The air force, officially the "Workers and Peasants Red Air Force," contained about 350 aircraft. During the civil war, the air force was involved in defending Moscow, Petrograd, Tula, Kronstadt, and Saratov against advances by White and foreign forces, notably the British. Aircraft were also used to communicate between different forces within the Red Army, as well as for intelligence missions and to drop propaganda, in the shape of pamphlets and flyers.[5] In 1924, the air force became subordinate to the Red Army.

The Russian Civil War also led to the expansion of air power elsewhere. For example, Finnish air power began in March 1918 with aircraft used against Finnish communists. The first pilots and the first commander were Swedish volunteers. During the short-lived Hungarian Soviet Republic in 1919, a Hungarian Red Air Force was established.

IMPERIAL AIR POWER

The foreign powers, notably Britain, that intervened against the communists in the civil war used aircraft, although not on the scale of 1918 on the Western Front and with only limited effect. However, there was a large-scale use of air power by imperial states against insurrections in the 1920s. This was seen, for example, with Britain in Somaliland and Iraq, with France in Syria, and with the United States in Nicaragua, which was not a colony but a state where American power was dominant. This use of air power, in an asymmetrical fashion and in small-scale conflicts, looked ahead to more modern patterns, notably with the role of air power in COIN (counterinsurgency) operations. Anticipating arguments made by American advocates of air power in the 1990s and 2000s, air attack was seen as a rapid response combining firepower and mobility; it did not entail the deployment of large forces and was therefore presented both as cost efficient and as appropriate for the much-reduced military establishments arising from postwar demobilization and expenditure slashing.

Reflecting the institutional independence of the RAF from 1918; the size and problems of the British Empire, the largest in the world; and Britain's role in protecting the postwar order, the British proved particularly active in their use of aircraft and discovered great potential in their use. In May 1919, in response to Afghan attacks on neighboring British India (which included Pakistan) in the Third Anglo-Afghan War, the RAF bombed the town of Jalalabad and the Afghan capital, Kabul. British aircraft operated successfully from the modern Pakistani part of then British India, across higher mountains than they had faced in Europe. The bombing, which demoralized the Afghans, acted as a demonstration of power, one of considerable symbolic interest. The war swiftly ended as both sides wished to contain it.[6]

In British Somaliland (the northern part of modern Somalia), in a struggle that was not so contained, the British were opposed by the charismatic Sayyid Mohammed Abdille Hassan (to them the "Mad Mullah"). Sir Hugh Trenchard, the chief of the Air Staff from 1919, saw this conflict as an opportunity to demonstrate that the independent RAF could end a colonial war successfully and at lower cost than the army. The Army Council had envisaged an expedition there of "considerable magnitude," but, instead, Winston Churchill, from his base in the Air Ministry, persuaded Viscount Milner, the secretary of state for the colonies, that, with the assistance of the RAF, the task would be more rapidly and cheaply accomplished. Milner's deputy, Leo Amery, had pointed out the potential of air power to Mackinder in 1904. The chief of the Imperial General Staff, Sir Henry Wilson, an army man, was opposed to reliance on the RAF, but the scheme prevailed with government backing. Trenchard was able to bring together Colonial Office and Air Ministry officials.

Aircraft played a key role in seeing the Mullah totally defeated. The operation also highlighted the need to regard air power as part of a larger package, a package that multiplies the impact of aircraft but also provides other elements. The RAF's Unit Z of twelve DH-9s was the strike force. On January 21, 1920, only one of the six aircraft sent to find Medishe, where the Mullah was based, found the target, but it dropped a bomb that killed his key advisor (who had not seen the danger), following this with machine-gun fire. Four of the aircraft bombed the nearby fortress of Jid Ali and attacked the livestock (sheep and camels) that were the key source of food and mobility for the Mullah's force. Bombing on the succeeding days hit the targets and the livestock, although engine trouble repeatedly affected the aircraft. The Somaliland Camel Corps, a British unit, followed up by advancing and taking the positions. In subsequent operations, aerial reconnaissance played a key part, as did air-dropped messages, while the stronghold at Tale was bombed on February 4. The Mullah fled from there into the Ogaden region of neighboring Ethiopia where he was to die of influenza.

The RAF emphasized its role, not least the demoralizing impact of air attack, in destroying the enemy's willingness to fight, an argument made at the time, as well as frequently in the 1920s and again in the 2000s when the history of the use of air power in COIN operations was advanced. The impact of the aircraft was indeed impressive. Nevertheless, the operation also benefited from the Somaliland Camel Corps; from tribal levies and "friendlies," especially from the Ogaden; and from naval support, not least in transporting the aircraft from the colony of Egypt on the carrier *Ark Royal*. Together, these elements provided the necessary combination of force and mobility.

This pattern of multiple actors, and of the combination of air power and tribal factions, was one also to be seen in the overthrow of the Taliban regime in Afghanistan in 2001. Correspondingly, this pattern highlighted the problem if the package was too weak and, as a result, excessive reliance was based on air power (and air-mobile troops), as in South Vietnam in the 1960s and Afghanistan in the late 2000s and early 2010s. Thus, one of the most effective ways to weaken air power was to strike at "friendlies," a strategy that was difficult to resist with aircraft, whatever their tactical potency.

Also in 1920, the British faced a major revolt in the mid-Euphrates valley in Iraq. To crush it, they deployed a substantial force from Britain's Indian Army as well as the RAF, which was keen to demonstrate what it could do and how this capability also entailed reducing the need for troops. However, the impact of the RAF in Iraq was initially restricted by the limited number of aircraft available. The civil commissioner in Baghdad reported in May 1920 that only eleven aircraft were in working order, of which eight were obsolete BE-8s. The following month, the General Staff in London claimed, "Whatever the possibilities of replacing troops by aircraft in the future may be, at the present moment the impotence of the Royal Air Force in Mesopotamia to carry out even their present tasks becomes clearer every day." Nevertheless, the British air presence in Iraq rapidly increased.[7]

Indeed, the British use of new technology was exemplified by the employment of air power. This was a policy very much encouraged by Churchill, successively as secretary for war and air (1918–21), and then as secretary of state for the colonies (1921–22). Already very interested in aircraft prior to the First World War, he was keen on H. G. Wells, who had written *The War in the Air*. Churchill recalled Trenchard, the first chief of the Air Staff, to office in 1919. Trenchard used the success in British Somaliland in 1920 in order to support his policy of "air control," which was applied in Iraq and elsewhere. It was argued that this policy was particularly effective and required relatively few personnel and little expenditure. The emphasis was on substituting firepower for mass, and this provided a key element in the view of warfare by early air-power theorists as well as in the measure of actual operations.

The variety of this firepower was rapidly enhanced. Gasoline, incendiary, and delayed-action bombs were all employed by the RAF in COIN operations in the 1920s. Arthur Harris, later, as commander-in-chief of Bomber Command, the leading figure in the British bombing campaign against Germany, but then commander of a squadron in Iraq, rigged up improvised bomb racks and bomb-aimer sights in slow-flying Vickers Vernon transport airplanes, as their slowness was conducive to accuracy. More generally, aircraft were developed or adapted for imperial policing duties, for example the Westland Wapiti, a day bomber in service from 1928 to 1939 that was used for army coordination, especially on the North-West Frontier of British India, now of Pakistan. In 1925, an independent air campaign in which there was night bombing as well as daytime bombing and strafing resulted in the Mahsud tribesmen of South Waziristan seeking an honorable peace on British terms.[8] No ground troops were used, and the RAF proved a less expensive and quicker means to ensure consent, thus demonstrating Trenchard's arguments, and in a region that had long been one of great concern to the British.

The RAF spent the 1920s protecting distant British imperial interests, notably (but not only) in the Middle East, where a reliance on its use developed rapidly, in part because, due to factors of cost and prioritization, there was not the availability of British troops on the scale of that enjoyed by the British in India. Despite interservice rivalries, air control worked. In November 1921, a raid on Jordan of Ikhwan (Brethren), fundamentalists from Arabia, was caught in the open and suffered heavy casualties. The RAF served against the Nuer in Sudan in 1927–29, was successfully used against Yemeni incursions into the Aden Protectorate in 1928–29, and in 1928 bombed the Wahhabi tribesmen of Arabia who threatened Iraq and Kuwait. "Aeroplane action" helped stabilize the situation in Kurdistan in 1923 and 1931,[9] while its use against the Yemenis served as a background to the 1934 treaty of friendship. The modest cost of the last, and its result in a treaty, was much praised by air-power commentators. The RAF benefited in such operations from their opponents' lack of effective antiaircraft fire. The presence of British land forces was frequently an element, but air power was provided and presented as crucial to success.

Drawing on its experience in Iraq, the RAF was convinced that air power could suppress opposition, not least by crippling the morale of opponents. The mock bombing attack on an "enemy village" at the Hendon Air Display of 1921, the second year of RAF pageants there, and conveniently close to London, suggested great effectiveness. The effect of bombing on the native economy was also noted, not least the damage to infrastructure and food supplies. Moreover, the capabilities of British air power increased. For example, in 1922, the Vickers Vernon entered service, the first of the RAF's troop carriers. It was based in Iraq. In 1928, Vickers Victorias based there evacuated over five hundred civilians from Kabul, which was threatened by insurgents. However, air assault was not developed.

The cause of air control was pushed hard. In 1921, the Gold Medal Prize essay of Britain's prominent Royal United Services Institute (RUSI) went to Flight Lieutenant C. J. Mackay for "The Influence in the Future of Aircraft upon Problems of Imperial Defence." Published in the *RUSI Journal* the following year, this contribution was followed by numerous articles, notably in that leading periodical, on the potential of aircraft, including their ability to bring about rapid victory by the use of gas.[10]

However, the claims of air-power enthusiasts were exaggerated. As a 1922 report by the General Staff of the British Forces in Iraq noted, "Aeroplanes by themselves are unable to compel the surrender or defeat of hostile tribes."[11] This is a point that was pertinent then and one that remains relevant to the modern use of air power. Aside from this key strategic point, the tactical, and thus operational, effectiveness of aircraft was probably overestimated once their novelty wore off and tribesmen learned how to evade their attacks, not least by employing cover and moving by night.[12] The same was to be the case with the use of American air power in Afghanistan in 2001–2, and there are other modern counterparts.

The debate over the value of air power reflected the RAF's attempt, at a time of stringent public expenditure cuts, to avoid being abolished as a separate body and subsumed into the army. If the RAF could promise that an independent air force could act effectively (and more cheaply) to police the empire than could the army, then it had a rationale for its continuing existence and budget. This argument was important at the time, and examples from the 1920s are still frequently deployed in supporting the case for the RAF and its use.[13]

Air power was also employed by other imperial powers. In the colonies, France organized separate *"régiments de l'air"* as part of the Army Air Force from 1925 onward, first in Morocco, then in Syria, and then in Indochina (Vietnam, Laos, and Cambodia). The Breguet XIV, which had entered service in June 1917 in Europe, was used in the empire until 1929–32. These aircraft and air operations were largely geared to low-intensity bombing and casualty evacuation, which remained the pattern until the use of napalm in Vietnam in the early 1950s and the advent of helicopters. In Morocco, however, French aircraft could not save the isolated posts in the early stages of the Riff War against local insurgents. Instead, aircraft dropped messages and bottles of water on their garrisons, albeit very inefficiently. The aircraft did not have much range, required airfields and logistical support, and were far less effective in the mountainous areas that were plentiful in Morocco and were where the opposition was concentrated. In 1925–26, the French used naval and land-based aircraft when they joined the Spaniards in successfully overcoming Moroccan opposition to the latter, but typhus and lack of food did more to end the Riff rebellion than air power. The French dropped surplus First World War mustard gas on their opponents in Morocco, where Spain also used large quantities of mustard gas, dropped by air on civilians and fighters alike: heavy casualties resulted.

Facing a Druze rebellion in their new colony of Syria in 1925–27, the French had an aircraft shot down in 1925, but they employed bombing as one of the means to thwart a Druze advance into the capital, Damascus, in 1926. In Vietnam, the French used air attacks in 1924 and 1929 in an attempt to deal with highland opposition, although they found they had to rely on the devastation wrought on the ground by advancing columns of troops and on the control these troops represented. Air policing in the French colonies was effective, probably to the same degree as in the British case. However, as with the latter, the psychological impact of air bombardment generally proved temporary.[14] Nevertheless, in both cases, there was a conviction on the part of the colonial powers that air power was effective. This reflected not only the wishes of its advocates, but also, in the face of the large and difficult areas that had to be controlled, a wish to believe that success had been

achieved, as well as the important point that these areas were frequently marginal to the centers of imperial presence. This conviction represented a variant of the argument that air power had a clear strategic
dimension.

In the East Indies (now Indonesia), the Dutch had a separate army,
the Royal Netherlands East Indies Army (RNLEIA). In 1914, a Test
Flight Service was founded. In 1921, this became the Aviation Service
of the RNLEIA, and in 1939 the Military Aviation of the RNLEIA.
Initially, there was some resistance on the part of the RNLEIA leadership, which felt that the climate was unsuitable for wooden aircraft and
that the air was too thin. New leadership, however, led to the introduction of aircraft in 1914. Although convinced of the importance of military aviation, the army leadership faced financial constraints that led to
relatively modest activity, with a focus on training rather than actual
operations. However, in the face of Japan's military buildup, the Dutch
increased their colonial air force from the mid-1930s.[15]

The Americans used air power to support their quasi-imperial position in the Caribbean. Interventions to protect American interests, in
Haiti in 1915 and the Dominican Republic in 1916, essentially by marines backed by the navy, had led to persistent nationalist resistance. In
the 1920s, popular guerrilla movements proved able to limit the degree
of control enjoyed by occupying American forces who found that rebel
ambushes restricted their freedom of maneuver. American bombing
was no substitute for control of the ground, especially in the face of
guerrilla dominance of rural areas at night, but such control was not
feasible. However, the Americans were not defeated in pitched battles,
and in 1922 the guerrillas in the Dominican Republic conditionally
surrendered.[16]

Nicaragua proved a harder task. Ambushes on American marines in
the forested countryside were countered with air power, although the
guerrillas responded to aircraft with machine-gun fire.[17] This was an
aspect of the degree to which, across the world, aircraft were increasingly opposed by ground fire. The latter frequently lacked precision,
but the slowness of aircraft greatly enhanced their vulnerability at the
low level at which they operated. American aircraft and pilots were also
used to bomb Mexican rebels in 1923. In 1927, two American "free-
lance airmen" working for the Nicaraguan Conservatives bombed positions held by the rival Liberals.[18]

The use of air power for imperial or quasi-imperial control and power projection did not look toward its employment during the Second World War. Nevertheless, this use was highly significant, both in terms of the 1920s and with reference to the situation since 1945. The capacity for mobility and tactical advantage offered by air power ensured that it was increasingly seen as a major strategic asset and one that offered a new approach to geopolitics.[19] Indeed, geopolitical considerations encouraged the development of air services to link imperial possessions, notably by the British to Hong Kong, Australia, and South Africa, a process encouraged by Trenchard. These services enjoyed government support and were regarded as an important counterpart to the development of an imperial military air presence. This prefigured the American case after the Second World War. Imperial Airways, a company founded with government support in 1924, pioneered new routes and services. The Britain-to-Australia airmail service began in 1932. Weekly flights began to Cape Town (1932), Brisbane (1934), and Hong Kong (1936). Air travel was very important to the development of individual British colonies and offered a way to administer a global empire.[20] The same was true of the Dutch Empire: from 1930, there was a weekly service between Amsterdam and Batavia (modern Jakarta). French airlines crossed the Sahara en route to French West Africa. The Soviet Union also saw the possibilities of air travel for political integration in the 1920s.

Western public opinion readily accepted the use of air power for imperial and quasi-imperial control. Indeed, air power appeared to marry what was presented as inherently desirable Western control to modernization, which was very much a theme of imperial ideology and governance in this period. The logic of air power was empire, while empire's logic was enhanced by air power. The interwar use of air power, however, had already suggested that it might be less effective in conflict and deterrence in the future than its proponents claimed.

AIR POWER AROUND THE WORLD

Another indication of the future, a future of variety as well as use, limitations as well as capabilities, was provided by the relatively slow spread of air power outside the Western sphere. Nevertheless, air power brought advantages, and the use of aircraft in conflict became common. In the 1920s, the largest conflict, in terms of geographical range and international involvement, was the Russian Civil War. After this came the Chinese civil wars of the 1920s. Air power was used then, but with only scant effect. In 1921, the Guomindang (Nationalist) air force, supporting the defense against an invasion from Guangxi, consisted of only a few biplanes that, in the absence of bombs, had to drop logs. A report in the *Times* (of London) on September 26, 1924, noted,

> The few bombs dropped hitherto on the front [at Shanhaiguan] have done practically no damage and have killed only a few civilians, because ill-directed from a great height and weighing only about 15lb. The earlier explosions made holes in the ground only 3 ft across, but when trying to damage the railway bridge larger bombs were used, making a crater 10 ft across. The prospect of bombing has caused some flutterings in Beijing, where foreigners are resident all over the city, but none so far have thought it worth while to remove outside.

Aircraft were more important for reconnaissance.[21] As elsewhere, the potential of air power in China improved as more sophisticated aircraft were supplied. Seeking to expand their influence, the Soviets shipped aircraft to Guangzhou (Canton) in the mid-1920s. These aircraft were used by Chiang Kai-shek, the Guomindang leader, in the Northern Expedition of 1926–28 that brought control over much of China.

The value of Soviet aircraft was also demonstrated in 1929 when Soviet forces invaded Manchuria, which was not under Guomindang control. They defeated Zhang Zueliang, the powerful regional warlord, thanks in part to using modern artillery, tanks, and, in particular, aircraft. This was one of a number of campaigns involving air power that have received insufficient attention.

In fact, aircraft were used around the world in the 1920s and in very varied contexts. As instances of this variety, the Yugoslav invasion of northern Albania in 1920 was accompanied by the bombing of towns. Very differently, the following year, the outbreak of violence linked to labor problems in the coalfields of West Virginia led the governor to ask for troops and aircraft. The government response included the dispatch of three DH-4B bombers, personally led by Brigadier General William (Billy) Mitchell as commander of the First Provisional Air Brigade. Mitchell, a key and vocal figure in the early propagation of American air power, told newspaper reporters that the Army Air Service could end the unrest by dropping tear gas on the miners. In the event, the immediate crisis passed and Mitchell left. However, fighting in early September saw the local opponents of the miners use civilian aircraft to drop homemade bombs filled with nails and metal fragments. In response to the escalating crisis, twenty-five military aircraft were ordered to West Virginia, although mechanical and other problems ensured that only fourteen arrived. They were used for reconnaissance missions rather than for the bombing for which they were prepared. The concurrent deployment of troops led to the end of the crisis, although Mitchell, of course, claimed much of the credit.[22]

In neighboring Canada, an Air Board formed in 1920 led to the Royal Canadian Air Force that was formally established in 1923. This worked for the federal government, mapping, taking photographs, and firefighting. The ability of air power to provide strength and capability to the state was demonstrated there in a very different fashion in 1919 when Wilfrid Reid May, a prominent aviator, flew a detective in pursuit of a fugitive from Edmonton to Edson. In Mexico, in 1926–27, the army, with air support, suppressed the Yaqui Indians in the troublesome province of Sonora. In such cases, air power brought an impression of greater strength to long-established practices of asserting control over recalcitrant people and regions. Moreover, this impression had substance as far as mobility, range, and firepower were concerned.

Meanwhile, independent non-Western states developed air power, encouraged by seeing its use by Western states. In Turkey in March 1922, ten aircraft were sent by the Atatürk government to the Anatolian front for reconnaissance activity against the Greeks who had invaded. In addition, the French handed over fourteen scout aircraft to the Turks as part of their peace agreement: in 1919–21, five French squadrons had supported the French army in operations against Turkish forces in Cilicia. The Atatürk government also bought twenty aircraft from Italy, equipping them with machine guns from old German fighters. A delegation sent to Germany bought twenty aircraft, which were sent to the Black Sea via Russia, but only two arrived fit for service. The Turks were able to use their aircraft to support their surprise attack on the Greek positions on August 30, 1922, and in the end were successful in preventing the Greek aircraft from attacking and conducting reconnaissance. The key fighting in Anatolia was on land, but air support was of more than symbolic value.

There was also rapid development of air power in Persia (Iran). By 1924, when an independent air force was established there, sixteen French, German, and Russian aircraft had arrived. Persian air cadets were trained in France and Russia. There were occasional bombing missions in campaigns against rebel tribesmen. However, as elsewhere in the spread of air use, both military and civilian, there were serious problems in Persia in providing supplies and sufficient pilots, and many aircraft were lost to wear and to accidents. These problems underlined the extent to which sustaining an air force required a considerable level of organizational sophistication and the provision of plentiful resources. Many states could not provide these. In the Hijaz (western Arabia), in 1925, Ali bin Hussain, the opponent of Ibn Saud, had an air force of two drunk pilots and two aircraft. Although they bombed Mecca, they achieved little.[23]

Aircraft became a major currency of international influence, one that reflected their role as symbols of modernization and as new forms of power, as well as the fact that they were only manufactured in a few states. In addition, however, there were surplus aircraft available after the First World War. This prefigured the situation after the Second World War. Britain supplied aircraft to Ibn Saud of Arabia. The Italians provided the Iman of Yemen and King Amanullah of Afghanistan with aircraft, in each case as a way of challenging British influence, while the latter also received them from Britain and the Soviet Union as the two states competed for influence in this buffer zone. The Afghans, however, were handicapped by a shortage of mechanics. Amanullah used aircraft against tribal opponents, but the latter prevailed in 1929, and he was overthrown.[24] In 1929, in contrast, the future Haile Selassie of Ethiopia owed success over his rival, Ras Gugsa Wolie, in part thanks to his use of a triplane, flown by a French pilot who made bombing runs that caused panic among the Ras's supporters.

Reconnaissance was an important capability of air power. In Persia, observation aircraft helped in operations against the hostile tribesmen, notably Baluchis in 1930, while, in 1920, aerial reconnaissance and intelligence reports warned the British of the likelihood of further raids on Palestine from Bedouin tribes coming from east of the River Jordan.[25] In 1927, the British Chiefs of Staff recommended the use of

British Shanghai-based aircraft to gather military information in China.[26]

NAVAL AIR POWER

There was no experience, from the First World War or subsequently, with conflict between carriers, but there was considerable confidence in the potential of carriers. In 1919, the year in which an American Coast Guard NC-4 flying boat became the first aircraft to cross the Atlantic (a feat the British claimed for a bomber),[27] Admiral Jellicoe, who was very concerned about the strategic relationship with Australia and New Zealand, pressed for a British Far East Fleet, to include four carriers as well as eight battleships, in order to deter Japan,[28] while, in 1920, Rear Admiral Sir Reginald Hall MP argued in the *Times* that, thanks to aircraft and submarines, the days of the battleship were over. The British Admiralty remained convinced of the value of battleships but was not opposed to carriers. Interwar planning called for one carrier to every two or three capital ships. The key to British attitudes was that aircraft had to be integral to the fleet, whereas, in the American and Japanese navies, carriers operated separately and were variously regarded as auxiliaries and rivals to battleships. In America, the National Defense Act had placed air power under the Army Air Service (rather than creating an equivalent to the RAF), but naval aviation was kept separate.[29]

A determination to employ the new capability offered by naval aviation was rapidly apparent. Carriers were used when Britain intervened against the communists in the Russian Civil War. In addition, the carrier *Argus* was stationed near the Dardanelles during the Chanak crisis between Britain and Turkey in 1922, when Britain sought to deter the Turks from attacking British forces in the region. There was also a carrier on the China Station in the late 1920s, first *Hermes* and then *Argus*. *Argus* landed six aircraft at Shanghai in 1927,[30] strengthening the Western position in the International Settlement in the face of the conflict between Chinese forces. Another carrier, *Furious*, took part in the major naval exercises of the late 1920s.[31] The *Eagle*, commissioned in 1923, was the first British flush-deck carrier, while the Fleet Air Arm of the RAF was formed the following year. The number of aircraft in the Fleet Air Arm rose, but, due to the RAF's clear focus on land-based power, only to 144 by the end of the 1920s.

The *Eagle* was a converted dreadnought battleship, while *Argus* was built on a hull intended for a passenger liner, and *Furious*, *Glorious*, and *Courageous* were converted from the battle cruisers of those names. Prior to the *Illustrious* class, only *Hermes* (commissioned in 1924) of Britain's original six carriers was built from the keel up as a carrier. *Furious*, when first converted, had separate fore and aft decks, separated by the ship's original centerline battle-cruiser superstructure, and therefore did not become a flush-deck carrier until a subsequent more radical reconstruction.

The Americans and Japanese made major advances with naval aviation and aircraft carriers, in part because they would be key powers in any struggle for control of the Pacific. They also built carriers on hulls made for battle cruisers and battleships that were canceled as a result of the 1921–22 Washington Naval Conference.[32] The *Langley*, a converted collier, was, in 1922, the first American carrier to be commissioned, followed, in 1927, by two converted battle cruisers, the *Lexington* and the *Saratoga*. This basis helped ensure that American carriers were very fast: thirty-three knots against a twenty-one-knot battle fleet, which forced the carriers to operate separately and made it difficult for the American navy to develop an integrated naval system. The *Lexington* and *Saratoga* were each designed to carry sixty-three aircraft.

The Japanese commissioned six carriers between 1922 and 1939, some converted and others purpose-built as carriers. The *Akagi*, a converted battle cruiser commissioned in 1927, was designed to carry ninety-one aircraft, with the *Kaga*, with ninety aircraft, following in 1928. There were many similarities between the American and British navies. Indeed, a British civilian mission under William Forbes-Sempill, a RAF veteran, which was in Japan in 1920–23, trained Japanese aviators, including in torpedo bombing. Sempill brought plans of British carriers and passed on sensitive information, and in 1925 a prosecution of him under the Official Secrets Act was seriously considered.[33] In 1927, as part of his graduation exercises at the Japanese Naval War College, Lieutenant Commander Tagaki Sokichi planned an attack by two Japanese carriers on the American Pacific base at Pearl Harbor, although, in the evaluation, he was held to have suffered heavy losses.

At sea, however, whatever their apparent potential, air power was restricted in the 1910s and 1920s by the difficulty of operating aircraft in bad weather and in the dark, by their limited load capacity and range, and by mechanical unreliability.

CONCLUSIONS

In his *Il Dominio dell'Aria* (The Command of the Air) of 1921, which was soon translated into English, Giulio Douhet claimed that aircraft would become the most successful offensive weapon and that there was no viable defense against them. Stressing the value of wrecking enemy morale and thus creating a demand for peace, a theme he had advanced from 1915, Douhet advocated the use of gas and incendiary bombs against leading population centers. Thus, bombing would accelerate the potential earlier seen to rest in blockade. He came to argue that air defense was impossible. [34]

Brigadier General Billy Mitchell, the top American combat air commander and assistant chief of the American Air Service in 1919–25, emphasized strategic bombing as well as coastal defense, arguing that aircraft could sink any ship afloat. The latter assertion, which resulted in the test sinking of a seized German battleship, the *Ostfriesland*, in twenty-one and a half minutes of bombing in 1921, led Mitchell to furious rows with the American navy. The value of the test sinking was compromised because the battleship was stationary. Mitchell was eventually court-martialed. The success of his tests led to prominent calls, especially in the *New York Herald*, to convert incomplete capital ships into carriers and resulted in the navy creating a Bureau of Aeronautics and improving the air defenses of its warships. Mitchell, however, was critical of carriers, as he feared they would make it harder to wage a unified air war under a single air command. [35]

More generally, the political struggle entailed in creating separate air forces caused air-power advocates to make grandiose claims for the ability of strategic bombing alone to win wars. This political-institutional context encouraged an emphasis on long-range strategic bombing at the expense of tactical air power, and of procurement accordingly. In 1925, Mitchell told the presidential inquiry on air power that the United States could use Alaska to launch effective air attacks on Japan, which was already seen as a major and growing threat to American interests in the Pacific and the Far East.[36] Visiting India in 1926 on behalf of the British War Office, J. F. C. Fuller, who, in *The Reformation of War* (1923), had argued that the bombing of cities would be important in future war, emphasized the need for the Indian army to modernize, contrasting it with the British navy and air force, which he depicted as "mechanized forces, materially highly progressive."[37]

However, critics argued that these commentators exaggerated the capability of air power. Thus, in Italy, Armedeo Mecozzi, a former pilot, criticized Douhet, not least by emphasizing the capacity of antiaircraft guns. Indeed, the transition from First World War biplanes, used mostly for reconnaissance, with very light bombing, to more modern aircraft had to take place before major strategic bombing could develop.[38] This transition only really happened in the 1930s, although, from the First World War, water-cooled aircraft engines were replaced by the lighter and more reliable air-cooled engine. Similarly, it was important that aircraft came to be made of Dural or Duraluminum (and a number of other variations, all of them trade names), an alloy of aluminum, which was stronger and more durable than aluminum. Dural was first used in the Junkers J1 monoplane of the First World War. In the 1920s, foreign offices and war ministries anticipated the development of strategic bombing, but it had only just begun to happen in reality.

In part, this was a matter of capability in the shape of the implementation of technological possibilities, but tasking was also a key issue. In the late 1920s, Russia seemed contained, Japan was not pursuing expansionism, and Germany was engaging actively and positively with the Western international community, notably in the Locarno treaty negotiations. The United States, the world's leading industrial economy, and Britain, its most far-flung empire, each followed policies of maintaining the status quo and cutting expenditures. The interaction in the 1930s of paranoia and justified fear that began with the Japanese invasion of Manchuria in 1931 was to drive forward investment in symmetrical warfare capability and cutting-edge technology. Despite anxieties, this was not the case in the 1920s.

5

THE 1930s

[T]he Nationalist air forces that smashed the iron ring of defences round Bilbao were almost entirely made up of German machines piloted by Germans. The final attack was launched by eighty of these bombers in the air at one time, and they created havoc. The German aviation groups have continued to play a leading part in the present Asturian campaign, both in bombing attacks on cities and in cooperation with ground troops. —G. H. Thompson[1]

In January 1931, an Italian squadron of eleven double-hulled flying boats reached Brazil after a journey of 10,400 kilometers. This first for a squadron of such a size exemplified the drama of flight, which was very much to the fore in the 1930s, but also its politics. The planes were sent by Benito Mussolini, Italy's Fascist dictator, and were under the command of Italo Balbo (1896–1940), the young commander of his air force. The Italian-made Savoia-Marchetti S-55s stayed in Brazil, where they served the interests of Getúlio Vargas, the president, who had seized power in 1930. He looked to Mussolini for inspiration and support. A prominent Fascist, Balbo, one of the leaders of the March on Rome that took Mussolini to power in 1922, became secretary of state for air in 1926, general of the air force in 1928, and finally minister of the air force in 1929, serving until 1933. In that year, Balbo led a mass flight of twenty-four S-55s to the United States, and he also became governor of Libya. Mussolini had held the air minister title until 1929.

Alliance building and political display were not the sole issues in air power. This decade saw a shift toward a clearer focus on the potential of air power in symmetrical conflict: war between similarly armed states. In particular, there was an emphasis on the apparent war-winning capacity of the bomber in such conflict, conflict that increasingly appeared a prospect. Centering on bombing, there was a growing social and governmental concern about what air power would bring in a new large-scale war; and the apparent possibility of social breakdown as a result, notably in the cities, underlined military concern about the need to be able to respond adequately. Deterrence through inflicting serious damage by means of bombing appeared the best response.[2]

More generally, there was a greater sophistication of aircraft in the 1930s, notably the development both of improved fighters and of more effective bombers. These were seen as bringing the potential of air power to fruition, similar to how the development and diffusion of new aircraft and munitions toward, and after, the close of the Cold War were, in turn, to be presented. In each case, there was the press of the modern. In the 1920s and 1930s, major advances in aircraft technology, including improved engines and fuels and variable-pitch propellers, provided opportunities to enhance military aircraft. They came to the fore with metal aircraft in the 1930s. The massive adoption in the 1930s of German aerodynamic developments was important to a general process of change. Major advances included all-metal monocoque construction, which gave aircraft strength and lightness: loads were borne by the skin as well as by the framework. Retractable (as opposed to fixed) landing gear was significant. The importance of wind resistance led to an emphasis on these undercarriages. The range of advances in the 1930s was impressive and included flaps, variable-pitch propellers, stressed skin construction, night-flying instrumentation, radio-equipped cockpits, and high-octane fuels.[3]

The range, payload, and armament of bombers all increased, notably with the introduction of the American B-17 Flying Fortress bomber, an aircraft that reflected the sophistication of the Boeing company. In the 1930s, the range and armament of fighters also improved. Wooden-based biplanes were replaced by all-metal cantilever-wing monoplanes with high-performance engines capable of far greater speeds. Examples included the American P-36 Hawk, the German Me-109,[4] and, less successfully, the Soviet I-16 Rata. The British developed two effective and nimble monoplane fighters, the Hawker Hurricane and the Supermarine Spitfire.

As ever, the placing of priorities in discussing both developments and usage is problematic, not least because these priorities can suggest a clarity to patterns of causation that, in fact, was absent. In the 1930s, there was no abrupt demonstration of a new capability comparable to the use of atomic bombs in 1945, and therefore no obvious new start. Instead, it was the combination of a more menacing international environment, the extent of change in aircraft technology, and the greater apparent capability of air power that provided the key element in encouraging a renewed and more urgent move from ideas about air warfare to detailed planning and procurement for it. In this, and notably in the contextualization of these ideas, an ideology of modernity, movement, and power, focused on what aircraft could apparently do, played a highly significant role. The ideology was so potent that Colonel Emilio Canevari, the most prominent Italian commentator, covering the successful Italian invasion of Albania in 1939, reported the attack of nonexistent motorized formations in cooperation with the air force.[5] The Italians, however, did transport part of the invasion force by air.

Alongside the implication so far of a clear developmental pattern in air power, it is important to note the impact of particular economic and political contingencies. The economic and fiscal crisis known as the Great Depression led, across the world, to a marked fall in government expenditures in the early 1930s, and this fall greatly affected aircraft procurement. So did the pressure to order aircraft from national companies, a pressure that influenced the response to technological possibilities.[6] Similarly, domestic political demands pressed on military spending, as did the perception of the international situation.

INNOVATION IN THE 1930S

There was a marked improvement in the flying standards and combat characteristics of aircraft in the interwar period. The potential of air power was also investigated in other ways. Airships still appeared to have a potential, and there was interest in their cooperation with aircraft. In 1926, two Gloster Grebes, British fighters, were launched from an airship as an experiment. However, accidents, notably the crash of the British R-101 on October 5, 1930, and of the *Hindenburg* on May 6, 1937, ended British and, later, German interest in airships. More centrally, they were too vulnerable to airplanes, lacked the maneuverability of the latter, and required the availability of helium.

The British Ministerial Committee on Disarmament dealing with Air Defence noted in July 1934 that "development in aircraft design and construction is rapid in these days," with consequent risks of obsolescence.[7] The range and armament of fighters, and the range, payload, and armament of bombers all increased.[8] The Handley Page Heyford, which served from 1933 to 1937, was the last of the RAF heavy bomber biplanes. In contrast, introduced from 1937, the American B-17 Flying Fortress was the first effective all-metal, four-engine monoplane bomber. It was seen as a key expression of American power. Thirty-five were deployed by 1941 at Clark Field, America's leading air base in the Philippines. This bomber was not simply a weapon, but it also embodied the dreams of glory of American air-power enthusiasts.[9] Both Boeing, with the XB-15, and Douglas, with the XBLR-2, renumbered as the Douglas B-19, had developed gigantic long-range bombers, the latter named the "Hemisphere Defender," as part of the air force's XBLR-Experimental Bomber, Long Range program; but success came with the B-17. It was conceived of as extending America's coastal perimeter by attacking an incoming fleet well out to sea, in short as a form of a mobile coastal fortress and not as a strategic bomber, but, despite its relatively small bomb load, it was pressed into that role in the Second World War.

Both Britain and the United States procured bombers that were designed or redesigned as strategic bombers at a considerable rate in the 1920s and 1930s, whereas Germany and the Soviet Union preferred tactical attack aircraft. Britain and the United States were also more concerned than Germany and the Soviet Union with defensive fighters or pursuit aircraft and procured many more aircraft designs. Quite a few of the British and American designs did not work out, but excellent fighter bombers (the Typhoon and P-47) resulted, able to fight their way home in hostile airspace in a way that attack aircraft such as the German Stuka and the Soviet Il-2 could not: against fighter opposition, the last two were very vulnerable.

As an example of the pace of change, the Blenheim I, a fast monoplane bomber, first entered British service in 1937, in which year the Miles Magister entered the RAF as its first monoplane trainer. The British Air Ministry issued specifications for a four-engine bomber in

July 1936, followed, in September, by specifications for a twin-engine all-metal medium/heavy bomber. A series of new planes entered British service in the late 1930s. These included the Wellington, the first model of which flew in December 1937. Until the arrival of the four-engine bombers, the Wellington played a key role for Britain's Bomber Command. Its airframe offered more resistance to opposing fire than earlier models, as it was made with a geodetic metal "basket weave" or lattice construction. The Hampden I, which entered service in September 1938, was a twin-engine monoplane, although it was an example of an aircraft designed without an understanding of how the bomber would fare against fast single-seat fighters. It proved ineffectual and poorly protected, and it also carried a small payload. The Hampden was last used on bombing operations in September 1942, with almost half of those built having been lost. Another example of an ill-conceived multi-role aircraft, the Fairey Battle, proved ineffective in France in May 1940 and was withdrawn that year after heavy losses. Also in 1938, the Short Sunderland I was the first RAF monoplane flying boat, replacing earlier biplanes. It was to be important to Coastal Command in the Second World War.

Innovations spread. Although they largely turned out 1932-design aircraft until 1938, the French development of power-operated turrets for bombers strengthened hopes that they would be able to beat off fighter attacks. The Boulton Paul Overstrand, a biplane that began service in 1935, was the first RAF bomber with a power-operated turret.

Improvements ensured the obsolescence of existing planes, such as the He-51 and He-60 biplanes flown by the Germans in 1935, and the need for fresh investment. In Britain, the Hawker Fury I, a biplane fighter with a maximum speed of over two hundred miles per hour that entered service in 1931, was made obsolete by the introduction of the Hawker Hurricane I in 1937. Alexander de Seversky, a veteran of the Russian naval air arm who had become a protégé of Billy Mitchell, inventing an air-refueling system and a gyroscopically stabilized bombsight, developed, in the early 1930s, an all-metal aircraft with an enclosed cockpit, the BT-8, which was a forerunner of a sort of the P-36, a fast, long-range, all-metal monoplane fighter that was to be the basis of the P-40 Warhawk. Whereas, prior to the mid-1930s, despite the bold claims made by the protagonists of air power, its effectiveness was very limited, in contrast, from then to the early 1950s, aero-technology was relatively inexpensive, but potent enough to produce an age of mass industrial air power, provided investment was forthcoming.

The Soviet TB-3 was the first mass-produced, four-engine, all-metal bomber. Andrei Tupolev also produced the SB light bomber, which, with Nikolai Polikarpov's I-16 fighter, entered service in large numbers in 1934, being among the most advanced aircraft in the world. However, as a pointed instance of the rapid development of new types and capabilities, these planes quickly became obsolete. Seventy-six I-16s were among the 409 Soviet planes sent to Spain by June 1937, but they were no match for the early variants of the German Me-109 (B and C) that they encountered there. In response, the Soviets pushed forward the production of new aircraft, notably the I-22, I-26, and MIG-1 fighters, and the TB-7, DB-3, and Pe-2 bombers, but the fighters were no match for their German counterparts. In the Soviet Union, as in the capitalist West, there was a big aviation cult, lauding pilots such as Chkalov who flew over the North Pole in 1937.

The increasing size of aircraft also led to interest in the use of airborne troops. A number of powers, especially the Soviet Union and Germany, trained parachute and glider-borne units. From the late 1920s, the Italians made a major effort to develop such a capacity, and they had several parachute battalions. However, they never did a parachute drop in action, and they were used as elite infantry in the Second World War. The Soviets dropped an entire corps by parachute in 1935, but probably largely for impressing foreign observers rather than as a practical military operation. The Germans began training parachutists in 1936. There were also developments in air transport: in 1935, the Soviets moved a fourteen-thousand-strong rifle division by air from near Moscow to the Far East, a demonstration of an ability to respond to Japan, while in 1937–38 they practiced dropping artillery and tanks by parachute.

GERMANY

Under the 1919 Versailles peace settlement, German air power had been banned, although, following the Treaty of Rapallo of 1922, the Germans and Soviets had secretly combined on aircraft design and manufacture and on pilot training. After Hitler came to power in 1933, the Germans prioritized a new air force, the Luftwaffe, which was officially created in 1935, and they spent accordingly: about 40 percent of the defense budget in 1933–36. Air power appeared to offer both a counter to German fears of vulnerability and a way to embrace a modern technology that promised victory. There was a fascination with air power that, in part, reflected its apparent potency, but also the desire to take revenge on Versailles and to intimidate other powers. Air power was important to Nazi propaganda, as with Hitler's use of flight in his tours around Germany and Goebbels's film treatment of these tours.[10] Air power shaped German industrial and economic planning. Already, in March 1935, Hitler had told British ministers that his air force was the same size as that of Britain, which was a false claim, but one that indicated his drive. That October, the ambitious existing Luftwaffe program for expansion was stepped up.

However, the German air industry did not develop sufficiently to support an air force for a major conflict, while investment in infrastructure was inadequate. The Spanish Civil War (1936–39) also suggested to the Germans that large long-range bombers were not crucial: they used dive-bombers there, instead, and developed dive-bombing tactics. Seeking a strategic bombing force that could act as a deterrent, Germany had initially made progress in the development of the long-range bomber—the "Ural bomber"—but had only made prototypes. The capability to produce the engines necessary for the planned heavy bombers was lacking, while there were also shortages of key materials necessary for their production and use. Nevertheless, the Germans expected to have the four-engine He-177 (the first prototype flew in 1939) in production by 1940–41.[11] In the event, nicknamed the Flaming Coffin, the He-177 never came into full-scale production, it did not become operational until late 1942, and it was weakened by overcomplicated engineering. The failure of the He-177 led to the attempt to develop the four-engine bomber He-277, for which a few prototypes were built. However, it was not ready for testing until July 1944. There was also the Me-264 four-engine bomber, which also only saw prototypes being developed. The Ju-390 had six engines, but only two prototypes were built in 1943. This had been developed from the four-engine Ju-290, which saw service as a maritime bomber (sixty-five built) like the FW-200 Condor, developed from a passenger airliner, of which 276 were built. Both had multiple roles, including transport and reconnaissance, as well as being used as bombers and for maritime patrol. The lack of a large long-range bomber force affected the capability of German bombing during the Second World War.

More generally, there were problems with the availability of aviation fuel for the Luftwaffe, and with its training program. There was also a preference for numbers of aircraft as opposed to a balanced expenditure that would include investment in infrastructure, for example, logistical provision, especially spares. This preference owed much to the poor quality of leadership. Hermann Göring, a veteran of the air struggle during the First World War, became Germany's minister of aviation in 1933 and commander-in-chief of the Luftwaffe in March 1935. He was not interested in the less glamorous side of air power, and this helped to weaken the Luftwaffe in the subsequent war. Göring also was less than careful in his appointments. Ernst Udet, whom he made technical director, was overly interested in dive-bombing. Göring's concern for aircraft numbers helped to lead, in 1937, to the postponement of the four-engine bomber program, as it was easier to produce large numbers of twin-engine bombers.

Furthermore, German military doctrine and planning resulted in a lack of support for strategic bombing. Hitler's preference for quick wars, as well as the structure of the German economy, led to the search for a force structure that would make a success of combined operations focusing on a rapid attack, a system later described as blitzkrieg (lightning war). Strategic bombing was seen, instead, as a long-term solution in warfare. Blitzkrieg entailed no obvious requirement for a strategic bombing force.[12] Big "terror" bombing raids, as were practiced by the Germans, first in the Spanish Civil War and then, with greater force, in the Second World War, did not amount to sustained strategic bombing of the type used in the Allied air offensives on Germany and Japan.

Instead, the Germans became increasingly committed to air-land integration, with the Luftwaffe designed to provide both close air support and interdiction in support of land forces in order to enhance the possibility of obtaining a decisive victory and thus a successful strategic outcome. The Luftwaffe was to be employed as mobile artillery in order to provide tactical support at the front of the army's advance. Wolfram von Richthofen, chief of staff and then commander of the Condor Legion dispatched by Hitler to help the Nationalists in the Spanish Civil War, pressed for close coordination in both space and time and used the war to test and improve relevant techniques. The practice and phi-losophy of jointness was very important to blitzkrieg.[13] Alongside later criticism of the German failure to develop strategic bombing can come the contrary argument that the proper role of aircraft in ground support was grasped.[14] As in this case, differing modern perceptions affect the reading of the past.

Aircraft suitable for ground support were developed. First flown in 1935, the Ju-87, or Stuka, was more accurate than most aircraft, re-maining stable in near-vertical dives. This capability increased the Stu-ka's accuracy against moving tanks, although, in practice, fighting the Poles, the Luftwaffe in 1939 proved far more effective against static units. Organizationally, the Luftwaffe benefited from avoiding the RAF's division into functional commands, namely the separation into a Bomber Command and Fighter Command in 1936, and instead created Luftflotten (Air Fleets). Each of these contained different types of air-craft so that they could operate as multifunctional commands. More-over, antiaircraft units were transferred from the army to the Luftwaffe, thus protecting airfields.[15]

Germany was not alone in ignoring the post–First World War ban on military air power. The 1920 Treaty of Trianon did not allow defeated Hungary to have an air force. However, a secret military air arm was organized under the cover of civilian aviation clubs. The existence of the Royal Hungarian Air Force was revealed in 1938, and on January 1, 1939, it became independent of the army.

SPANISH CIVIL WAR, 1936–39

It is not clear that the conflicts that did occur were adequately analyzed. For example, the spectacular terror bombing of cities, such as Madrid (1936), Guernica (1937), Barcelona (1938), and Cartagena (1936 and 1939), by German and Italian aircraft sent to help Franco's Nationalists in the Spanish Civil War did not actually play a central role in the result of that conflict. These cities were civilian targets, but more was general-ly at stake. Thus, Cartagena and Barcelona were major ports, and the attacks on them were aspects of the attempt to prevent the Republicans from importing arms. The German destruction of the city of Guernica on April 26, 1937, was intended to destroy the morale of the Republican Basques and thus weaken their resistance to the Nationalist advance. Concerned about the world response to the bombing, the Germans and Nationalists sought to deny responsibility. The bombing of Guernica probably affected the resistance mounted when the Nationalists moved on to take the more important city of Bilbao in June. The bombing of refugees became an Italian specialty, notably those fleeing the city of Malaga in February 1937 and those fleeing toward Barcelona in the winter of 1938–39.

Terror bombing captured the imagination of many, sowing fears that the bombing of civilian targets would be decisive in a future war. This affected British thinking at the time of the Munich crisis in 1938 when confrontation with Germany led to the possibility of war. Indeed, British intelligence exaggerated German air capability. The resulting concentration on air defense was crucial for Britain in 1940, but some of the preparations for air attack led to a misapplication of scarce resources. Yet the impact of the bombing on the war in Spain, although deadly, was exaggerated. Moreover, as the Second World War was to show, Douhet and others had exaggerated the potential of bombing (as well as underestimating the size of bomber forces required) and underplayed the value of tactical air support. At the same time, as Thomas's report cited at the start of the chapter indicates, British observers in Spain did not see German and Italian air power only in terms of the attack on civilians.

The Italians sent 759 aircraft to Spain, the Germans about 700. In turn, the French sent the Republicans aircraft in the early stages of the war, while the Soviets provided them with 623 aircraft, notably Chato and Mosca fighters and Katiuska bombers. The Nationalists had a clear superiority. Aside from bombing cities, there were also attacks on Republican ground positions. At the Battle of the Ebro (July–November 1938), the last major Republican offensive of the war, the Republicans suffered from being seriously outnumbered in the air and lacked sufficient antiaircraft guns. As a result, their forces proved vulnerable to Italian and German aircraft, not least to their air attacks on the pontoon bridges built across the river. The Germans found that their use of aircraft required effective ground-air liaison and developed it—tactics that were to be important in the early stages of the Second World War. The war also saw developments in other fields such as air reconnaissance[16] and air transport. In August 1936, German Ju-52s and Italian

Savoia-Marchettis, escorted by He-51s and Italian CR-32s, transported
Spanish Nationalist troops from Morocco to southern Spain, providing
mobility and speed and overcoming the Republican naval blockade.

THE ISSUES OF BOMBING

In many countries, the ability to learn lessons from the Spanish Civil
War about the value of air support for ground forces was limited by
interservice rivalry and the nature of air force culture, notably the emphasis on strategic bombing, and a degree of reluctance in some quar-
ters to adopt an analytical approach. This was especially so in Britain
where there was a pronounced fear of air attack[17] and a major commitment to strategic bombing as a way to break the will of an opposing
population.[18] In November 1932, Stanley Baldwin, the previous (and
next) prime minister, had told the House of Commons that "the only
defence is in offence, which means that you will have to kill more
women and children more quickly than the enemy." Bombing was seen
as a way to avoid a military commitment to Continental Europe and the
political entanglements to which this would give rise. In 1936, Harris
pressed the case for bombers able to reach targets in the Soviet Union.
That year, when he resigned as chief of the (British) Imperial General
Staff, Sir Archibald Montgomery-Massingberd, an army man, wrote,

> I feel that the biggest battle that I have had to fight in the last three
> years is against the idea that on account of the arrival of air forces as
> a new arm, the Low Countries [Belgium, Netherlands] are of little
> value to us and that, therefore, we need not maintain a military force
> to assist in holding them . . . the elimination of any army commit-
> ment on the Continent sounds such a comfortable and cheap poli-
> cy . . . especially among the air mad.

Instead, he claimed that a war on the Continent would still be decided
on land,[19] a prediction that was to be proved correct in the Second
World War as far as Europe was concerned, but wrong in the war with
Japan.

There was resistance to the possibilities of ground-support operations on the part of those committed to strategic bombing. Indeed, RAF
bomber crews were not trained to operate over the battlefield. More-

over, the need to provide fighter escorts for bombers was not appreciated by the British or the Americans until they suffered heavy casualties in the Second World War.[20] The American B-17 Flying Fortress was heavily armed in the belief that it could defend itself, but the reality proved otherwise.

The focus on bombers offers a parallel to attitudes toward the inappropriate reliance on tanks alone in mobile warfare, rather than on mixed-arms forces and combined operations. A key point is the value of jointness. The history of air power suggests that much of its capability rested on being part of an integrated fighting system with an operational doctrine that relied on cooperation between arms and sought to implement realizable military political goals. The same was true of the impact of mechanization on land warfare. However, cooperation between ground-attack aircraft and tanks was limited because of ethos and practicality. Such cooperation required effective radio communications, as well as training and commitment. Moreover, both ground-attack aircraft and tanks tend to work independently if they aim to play to their strengths.

In France, there were significant disagreements on the strategic question, disagreements that adversely affected procurement, leading, in particular, to a failed attempt at multirole aircraft. There was an attempt to develop a strategic role for aviation, notably, in 1937, a drive to create an ambitious bomber force; but the powerful army staff was not prepared to support this pressure from the Air Ministry. Instead, tactical requirements prevailed. Rather than stressing strategic bombing, the French put the emphasis on reconnaissance aircraft and tactical roles. Despite some good aircraft, France lacked an air force to match that of Germany.[21]

The Soviet Union lacked an independent air force, but, despite weaknesses in relevant industrial capability, it had, thanks to the build-up of its aircraft industry from the late 1920s, the largest number of aircraft in the 1930s, as well as a strong aviation culture.[22] Furthermore, although the air force was largely an extension of the army, the Soviets had an interest in strategic bombing. The long-range TB-3 was intended as a deterrent against Japan. By the end of 1935, the Soviets had a 170-strong bomber force able to reach Japan and to threaten Japanese communications with Manchuria. However, the murderous purges of the military launched by Stalin in 1937 hit the air force hard. Yakov

Alksnis, the longtime head of the air force, was arrested in 1937 and executed in 1938. An extremely competent and effective manager, his loss had a severe impact on operational effectiveness. The purges were linked to a move by the Soviet air force from strategic capability to army support, although the Soviet Union had the largest number of multien-gine bombers until 1941.

Separate from this, it is unclear how effective Soviet air power might have been. A successful buildup required more than developing capability and the allocation of resources. As the Soviets did not have to fight, except for the limited case of Spain, until after the purges, there are two difficult counterfactuals: how would the Soviets have fought in 1936, or how would they have fought in 1941 if they had not suffered the purges? They were producing aircraft in quantities that were extraordinarily impressive, and when not overwhelmed by surprise, as happened at the hands of the Germans in 1941, quantity has a quality all its own. Their designs, however, were not world-beaters, and Soviet aircraft manufacturing had a mixed reputation as far as innovation and creativity were concerned. Moreover, as with their tanks, although the Soviets had an enormous force, only a fraction were of the most modern types: in 1941, 1,300 of the 8,300 in the five Soviet western military districts plus long-range aviation. Yet many of the German aircraft in 1941 were also older types, although that does not necessarily mean bad: the Me-109 held up very well, but not the He-111.

Both the British and the French devoted attention to fighter defense in the late 1930s, seeing this defense as a necessary response to German power, although the British Air Staff possessed scant evidence to support its belief that the Germans had plans for an air assault on Britain.[23] Concern about the Luftwaffe encouraged threat-based expenditure, as well as research and development, which ensured that the French air force won a bigger share than the navy or, still more, army in the increased defense expenditure in 1934–35. The weakness of the French air force was a contributory factor to vulnerability at the time of the Munich crisis in 1938, but, by 1939, France had 1,735 frontline aircraft. These included the Farman 222, which could carry an unprecedented load of bombs (over four tons), as well as the Dewoitine D-520, a well-armed fighter with an exceptional range. However, French fighters were not as fast as the Me-109. Although, after Japan, the most active user of aircraft in combat in 1935–38, Italy suffered from the mismatch between Mussolini's bold plans for a large and modern air force and the limitations of Italian industry, notably in engine manufacturing. Political favoritism in procurement was a major problem. Italy had the third-largest force of multiengine bombers in the world, but the emphasis in the war plan drawn up in late 1939 was on acting in conformity with the operations of the land army, not on strategic air warfare and concentrated bombing.[24]

In March 1934, Baldwin told the House of Commons that Britain would not accept inferiority in air power, and that July, a large majority voted in the Commons for a substantial increase in the size of the air force by 1939. While the War Office may have started rearmament efforts relatively late, the Air Ministry's rearmament program was already in play before 1936.[25] This was underscored by large British investments in the aircraft industry.[26] The British developed two effective monoplane fighters, the Hawker Hurricane and the Supermarine Spitfire. In November 1934, the Air Ministry had issued specifications for a fighter with improved speed, rate of climb, and ceiling, and with eight, not four, machine guns. The prototype Hawker Hurricane was ordered in February 1935 and made its first flight in November 1935. In December 1937, the Hawker Hurricane I entered service, beginning a new period of eight-machine-gun monoplane fighters that could fly faster than three hundred miles per hour. In March 1936, the prototype Supermarine Spitfire made its first flight, and the aircraft entered service in June 1938. It was the only aircraft to be in service before the Second World War and to remain in service after the war, albeit in a very different form that was almost an entirely different aircraft. At the 1936 Hendon Air Pageant, prototypes of the Battle, Hampden, Spitfire, and Wellington made their first appearances in public. In 1938, King Carol II of Romania visited the RAF airfield at Odiham, being shown around Britain's updated air force by the RAF's senior figures. This visit was filmed and distributed by British Pathé, to be shown in cinemas around the country. No pre-1935 designs were visible in the lineup displayed in the film. The formation takeoff presented in the film conveyed the sense of a powerful air force. Odiham was a new airfield, opened in October 1937 as a result of the 1936 expansion schemes.

In 1937, in a speech titled "Fighter Command in Home Defence," Sir Hugh Dowding told the RAF Staff College that the major threat to British security would be an attempt to gain air superiority in which the destruction of airfields would play a key role. This would leave the way clear for attacks on industry, London, and the ports. A system of defense was therefore the key necessity.[27] Alongside early-warning radar, Spitfires and Hurricanes were to help rescue Britain in 1940 from the consequences of devoting too much attention to bombing. At that stage, Britain had numerical superiority over Germany in single-engine fighters. In 1938, the Anschluss (German takeover of Austria) and the Munich crisis further encouraged an emphasis on air power in British rearmament, and by September 1939, the RAF had replaced most of its biplanes. In response to the German threat, new RAF air bases were built in East Anglia, Lincolnshire, and Yorkshire, and squadrons were moved there from elsewhere in Britain.

The 1939 Empire Air Day Souvenir Program contained a piece, "The Air Force Guards the Empire," by the chief of the Air Staff, Sir Cyril Newall. He presented the RAF as a "defensive force" forming a "sound system" of aerial defense.[28] At the same time, an air-based strategy for imperial defense faced major problems. First, given the dispersed nature of the empire and the range of aircraft types, such a policy would require a massive number of locally deployed squadrons. Second, even for 1940, there are huge question marks over whether the RAF had bombs of sufficient power to stop an invasion fleet. The Germans failed to stop British coastal convoys by air attack.

The emphasis on air power extended to the United States, where President Franklin Delano Roosevelt, who was increasingly conscious of the importance of air power, proved willing to support the sale of planes to the European democracies.[29] The French were keen to buy American aircraft, and in 1939 they purchased Martin and Douglas bombers. The Dutch also purchased Douglas-built aircraft.

Ethics were not to the fore when strategy was discussed by the military. There was some uneasiness about the ethical nature and practical consequences of strategic bombing against civilian targets. However, this uneasiness tended not to be expressed by air-power advocates who focused on the idea of a "magic bullet" promising victory without casualties at the front. In an undated memorandum that the catalog suggests is from 1925–26, but which contains a reference to a document of March 1930, Field Marshal Sir George Milne, the chief of the British Imperial General Staff, brought ethical issues about air power into organizational questions. He wrote of the highly organised and unscrupulous propaganda of the Air Staff . . . the separation of the Air Staff from the General Staff which prevents problems of defence being considered as a whole, and with a proper sense of proportion as to their cost . . . the Air Staff have found it necessary, in order to find support for their separate and independent existence . . . to devise a special form of so-called air strategy . . . there appears to be two principles or catch words upon which it is based . . . attack against the nerve centers of an enemy nation . . . and the moral effect of the air arm. In dealing with problems of war on a large scale against civilized countries the former term is usually employed. The objectives of such strategy are the centres of production—nominally of munitions, which, be it marked, is a term of very wide significance. In effect this new form of strategy takes the form of attack against civilian workers, including their women and children. The hitherto accepted objectives of land and sea warfare have been the armed forces of the enemy, and whether or no we as a nation are justified morally in adopting a military policy which is so totally at variance with the accepted dictates of humanity, there is no doubt that we should be the first to suffer if the next war were to be waged on such principles. [30]

Public responses to the threat of bombing varied. H. G. Wells's rewrite of *The War in the Air*, *The Shape of Things to Come*, was made into a film in which a world war begins in 1940 with terrifying air attacks on Everytown. Alongside alarm, there were calls for more bombers in order to provide deterrence through the threat of reprisals. There were also internationalist responses aimed at limiting the threat, not least, from the 1920s, the idea of an International Air Force under the control of the League of Nations. The Geneva Disarmament Conference in 1932–34, held under the auspices of the league, discussed such a force, as well as the abolition of bombing, and accepted a Czech proposal to prohibit the bombing of civilians. With reference to the conference, the RAF felt undermined by the willingness of the Foreign Office to accept limitations on air power. However, although these ideas continued to circulate, they lacked diplomatic traction. [31]

Instead, in the late 1930s, improvements in fighters began to undermine the doctrine of the paramountcy of the bomber. Thanks to the Rolls-Royce Merlin engines developed from 1932 and part of the major British advance in aero-engines, [32] British fighters, by 1939, could intercept the fastest German bombers. The introduction of radar on the eve of the war was another blow to the bombers.

LOOKING TOWARD THE FUTURE

The sense of the future as imminent repeatedly surrounded the discussion of air power. In part, this was because of the practicalities of new technology. Thus, the speed of aircraft posed great problems for antiaircraft fire, not least by challenging the processes used in ballistics. It was necessary to track rapid paths in three dimensions and to aim accordingly. Research in the United States was therefore directed at making operational what in effect was an analog computer. This research looked toward the development in the 1940s of cybernetics and the idea of systems that were human-machine hybrids.[33]

There was a growing interest in jet aircraft, rocketry, and space flight, especially in Germany, where the Verein für Raumschiffahrt (Space-Flight Society) was founded in 1927, and in the Soviet Union. There, Konstantin Tsiolkovsky (1857–1936) developed a theory of rocket flight that encouraged the use of liquid propellants for rockets. Other work led to the development of the Soviet Katyusha multiple rocket launcher, which was extensively used by the Red Army as a form of artillery during the Second World War.[34] More dramatic ideas focused on rocket flight. In his presidential address to the American Rocket Society in 1931, David Lasser discussed the potential of rocket shells, which could carry their own fuel, and of rocket aircraft flying at over three thousand miles per hour and threatening "an avalanche of death."[35]

Such ideas reflected and encouraged a sense of potential. They looked toward German hopes during the Second World War, including for long-range bombers, multistage rockets, space bombers, and submarine-launched missiles, which, it was planned, were to be used for attacks on New York City and Washington.[36] This technology appeared to offer an alternative to a German naval power projection that Allied naval strength precluded, and also seemed to be a way to hit the American home front and American industrial capability. More mundane ideas that indicated the excitement and inventiveness focused on air power included that of a streamlined gondola that was fitted into an aircraft and could be lowered and, while attached by a steel cable, maneuvered by a rudder and elevators. This, an American idea of 1936, was to be used to fire on criminals escaping by car.[37]

At a more practical level, Igor Sikorsky, the Russian inventor of the four-engine bomber in the early 1910s, who had emigrated to the United States in 1919, developed the first successful helicopter, the VS-300, in 1939. American interest in radio-control technology spanned the mediums, including ships and torpedoes, but also remotely piloted aircraft. Work became focused when the Naval Research Laboratory's Radio Division was established in 1923. Issues of practicality and funding were to the fore, but radio-controlled target ships became important in the 1930s and were followed by remotely piloted aircraft called drones. These were developed to act as targets, thus enabling the testing of antiaircraft fire.[38] However, the Germans were to make more progress with weaponizing radio-controlled devices. In 1938, they began the development of radio-guided gliding bombs, a precision weapon, which became operational in 1943.[39]

Far-reaching innovation was also seen in other fields. In 1930, Frank Whittle, a British air force officer, patented the principles that led to the first gas turbine jet engine, which he first ran under control in 1937. However, Whittle's engine did not generate much interest in the Air Ministry or the RAF: they saw it as something of an expensive novelty but with no practical use. He and two other former RAF officers formed Power Jets to develop the engine without government funding. His patent lapsed in 1935 because he was unable to afford the renewal fee, thereby allowing the patent to come into the public domain. The technology rapidly spread, with the Germans producing the first operational jet engine. The Germans, in 1939, and the Italians, in 1940, beat the British jet into the air.

The idea of a death ray, which was considered in 1935 by the new British Aeronautical Research Committee, was not viable; but a variation looked toward the very different idea of radar. With its capacity for long-distance detection of movement, radar developed rapidly. In 1904, Christian Hülsmeyer had first used radio waves to detect the presence of distant metallic objects. Thirty years later, the French CSF company took out a patent for detecting obstacles by ultrashort wavelengths, while, in 1935, Robert Watson-Watt published *The Detection of Aircraft by Radio Methods* and the Air Ministry decided to develop radar.

The following year, the American Naval Research Laboratory demonstrated pulse radar successfully.

In the Battle of Britain in 1940, the British benefited greatly from an integrated air-defense system founded on a chain of radar-equipped early-warning stations built from 1936 to 1939, but still incomplete at the time of the Munich crisis. These stations, which could spot aircraft one hundred miles off the southern coast of England, were linked to centralized control rooms where data were analyzed and then fed through into instructions for fighters. No other state had this capability at that stage.[40] The weakness of antiaircraft defenses enhanced the importance of the radar system, and this weakness led in Britain to the formation of a Balloon Command in November 1938.

PLANNING AIR WARFARE

More immediately, there was the development in the 1930s of a potential for air warfare that brought to fruition in planning, procurement, and training some of the ideas of the 1920s. At the same time, contemporaries found it difficult to make a realistic assessment about the potential. The conflicts of the 1920s and 1930s offered only limited guidance because they did not happen between equally balanced air forces, while rapid technological developments soon outdated experience. International crises increasingly involved much thought about the aerial aspect.

Thus, there was an air dimension in the Anglo-Italian crisis of 1935–36 over Ethiopia, although, in the event, there were no hostilities between the two powers. Nevertheless, the crisis showed the greater extent to which air power played a role in planning for war. Reflecting the dependence of strategic bombing on nearby airfields, the RAF proposed to bomb the industrial centers of northern Italy, notably Turin and Milan, from bases in southern France, assuming that France joined Britain. The British indeed were to do so in June 1940. There was also a need to protect British colonies from neighboring Italian colonies and, in turn, to permit attacks on the latter. As a result, the RAF moved aircraft to Egypt (against Libya), British Somaliland (against Italian Somaliland and Eritrea), and Malta (against both Libya and Italy). Fear of the vulnerability of Malta to Italian air attack led to the decision to withdraw the British Mediterranean Fleet to Alexandria in Egypt. The significance of air attack was such that the priority thereafter was to improve Malta's defenses against that rather than against bombardment or invasion. Matching their confidence that antiaircraft guns could protect warships, the British navy was certain that such improvement could be made, whereas senior airmen were convinced that sustained and heavy air attack could prevent safe use of the island and its naval base. This argument has been linked to the RAF's struggle for funds for Bomber Command.[41]

At the time of the Munich crisis in 1938, British intelligence and the Air Staff exaggerated German military capabilities. In practice, despite bold claims by Göring about its potential, the Luftwaffe lacked the training and range to launch a bomber offensive against Britain.[42] Similarly, the RAF in 1938 had only a few modern fighters, while its bombers were weak and its radar network was incomplete, and France was seriously short of new aircraft. Alongside widespread anxiety, indeed fear, there was a measure of skepticism about air power, with a degree of confidence in Britain's ability to withstand bombing; but, notably on the part of the "bomber barons" of the RAF, there was no lack of belief in the potential of bombing as such.[43]

Rearmament by the leading powers led weaker states to increase defense spending in the late 1930s. In doing so, they sought strategic outcomes of their own and procured aircraft accordingly. Thus, in 1936, the Dutch began the development of the Fokker TV bomber as a multi-engine aircraft able to patrol at height for several hours and capable of acting as what the French termed *croiseurs aériens* (air cruisers). These multirole aircraft were also designed for combat and reconnaissance, prefiguring modern aircraft. Seventy of the aircraft were ordered, but the concept was questioned in light of the improvement in single-seat fighters, and the Dutch changed in the winter of 1937–38 to a focus on fast fighters, notably the twin-engine Fokker GI and single-seat D-XXXI fighters, and ordered accordingly in early 1938.

OUTSIDE EUROPE

The global narrative for air power was more varied and complex. The Western empires continued to use air power, most dramatically with

Italy. Opposition to Italian rule in Libya was brutally suppressed in 1928–32, including with the dropping of gas bombs. This use of air attack was taken further in the Italian conquest of Ethiopia in 1935–36. Italian motorized columns were supported by about 350 aircraft, with large quantities of gas bombs dropped. As a reminder of the savagery covered by such remarks, the graphic eyewitness testimony, published in the *Times* of April 24, 1936, of Captain Brophil, who had organized the Ethiopian Medical Corps, is striking. His ambulance received its first victims of mustard gas bombs in the last week of December 1935:

> In nearly all cases those brought to the ambulance for treatment were civilians, the greater proportion being women and children burned in the exposed parts of the hand and face, blinded, choking, and gasping for breath. Many of these cases did not reach the ambulance until days after they were first burned, as they could only be brought for treatment at night, or early in the morning, on account of the constant bombing by Italians.

However, as with the case of civilian casualties during the Spanish Civil War, it is necessary to move beyond this horror in order to assess the impact of air attack. On the one hand, Sir Archibald Montgomery-Massingberd, chief of the (British) Imperial General Staff, saw the Italian invasion of Ethiopia as demonstrating the inability of a strong air force to ensure an early victory. Similarly, a memorandum circulated by the (British) secretary of state for war to Cabinet colleagues referred to "the failure of air bombardment to produce a decisive effect on the morale of the Ethiopians."[44] This was despite the serious Ethiopian weaknesses in aircraft and antiaircraft guns. The War Office reported on January 17, 1936, "The failure of air bombardment to produce a decisive effect on the morale of the Ethiopians had been a further surprise and disappointment to the Italians."[45]

Indeed, the same lesson was to be demonstrated over the following years in China, as clear Japanese air superiority and damaging deadly bombing with no concern for civilians did not end Chinese resistance. Nevertheless, the Italian air offensive in 1936 did play an important role, both in helping the land advance on the capital, Addis Ababa, and in weakening the cohesion of Ethiopian society, thus undermining its resistance.[46] The contrast with the situation in China underlines the need for caution on the basis of isolated examples, which has often been a problem with public discussion of air power, as well as with some of the analysis by commentators, both favorable and unfavorable.

Barring Japan, other imperial powers did not use air power on the scale of Italy because they did not launch comparable attacks, but it still played a role. This was true for both Britain and France. In 1930, the French employed aircraft to guide columns on the ground toward rebel concentrations in Vietnam, while in 1934 aircraft played a significant role in the last act of the conquest of the French Sahara, the capture of the oasis of Tindouf. Aircraft had already played a key part in French reconnaissance in the Sahara in the early 1930s, notably in ascertaining routes that motorized columns could follow, as well as in using air attack to subjugate the Anti-Atlas region in Morocco. In the 1930s, the improvement of aircraft performance and the creation of the *"echelon roulant d'accompagnement,"* which was a technical lorry support unit able to help aircraft flying over the desert, permitted the development of effective aerial support for ground operations.

Reconnaissance was the prime use of the RAF in opposing the Arab Rising of 1937–39 in Palestine, although there was also bombing and strafing, with the Fairey Gordon, a light day bomber, being used. As air officer commanding Palestine and Transjordan in 1938–39, Harris cooperated with the army and developed what he called the "air pin." Used earlier in Afghanistan and Iraq, this entailed pinning down villagers by the threat of bombing by patrolling aircraft until the army could reach the scene. In the face of the development of the Luftwaffe, Britain and France, however, had to consider the contrary requirements of home defense. Thus, relatively few aircraft were sent to France's colonies.

There were no such alternative commitments in the case of non-European powers. Aircraft played a greater role for these powers than had been the case in conflict in the 1920s. For example, air power was more significant in China in the 1930s because of the greater commitment by Chiang Kai-shek and also the strength of the Japanese air assault. In early 1932, when the Japanese deployment of troops to Shanghai met resistance, a Japanese air assault there killed numerous civilians. It did not, however, end the resistance. When Japan was not involved, the Guomindang government was able to use air power against its opponents, as in 1932 when rebels were defeated in Fujian Province and in December 1936 when forces advanced on the city of

Xi'an in order to free Chiang. He employed Americans and Italians as advisors in building air capabilities. This reflected the extent to which Chiang, like other Chinese Nationalists, was deeply committed to the idea of modernity. He himself was an army man. Air power appeared to compensate for the deficiencies of the Guomindang army, although it was not to do so.

In 1933, the British Chiefs of Staff Subcommittee referred to the Japanese air force as having "air equipment and a standard of training fast approaching that of the major European powers" and presented it as "the predominant factor in the air situation of the Far East."[47] Indeed, in 1937, Japan deployed about 1,500 planes at a time when only 87 of China's 300 aircraft were able to fly. Air power was used from the outset of the Sino-Japanese War, with the University of Tianjin, a prominent source of opposition to Japan, bombed in July 1937. As was to happen during the Cold War, there was intervention in this regional struggle from other powers. The Soviet Union delivered 297 aircraft to China in the winter of 1937–38. Flown by Soviet pilots, they began operating in defense of the capital, Nanjing. However, Japanese air power was greater, and this advantage proved important to Japanese advances in China. Nanjing fell in December 1937. Moreover, there was heavy Japanese bombing of positions at a distance from the battlefield. In 1939, once winter clouds and fog had ended, Chongqing, Chiang's next capital, proved the prime target. With no effective antiaircraft support or air cover, the city was badly damaged by a series of long-distance heavy raids by twin-engine bombers, raids which continued into 1940. This attempt to break Chinese morale, however, had no strategic or political effect.

Lessons were not drawn from the war. Japanese air superiority could not dictate developments on the ground. Not only did bombing fail to end Chinese resistance, but, also, the tactical impact of air power was limited. For example, the Battle of Shanghai in 1937 showed that Chinese losses made during the day could be regained at night when Japanese air power was less effective, a frequent experience. The vulnerability of ships to air attack was apparent, but these were isolated ships in confined waters. Having taken Shanghai, Japanese aircraft sank an American gunboat on the Yangtze River. Similarly, each side in the Chaco War between Bolivia and Paraguay in 1932–35, the largest-scale conflict in South America during the century, deployed aircraft, but they did not play a key role. Indeed, Bolivia, the defeated power, had the better aircraft.

Most second-rank powers tended to use their military not for international conflict but for the suppression of regional opposition. Air power could play a role and notably did so in South Asia. In 1935, in part with the support of its air force, Iraq suppressed a tribal uprising. In Afghanistan, later in the decade, British-supplied light bombers were used to help the army suppress rebellion.

The aircraft supplied to other powers were not the latest models. This was part of a more general system in which older aircraft were deployed in overseas empires. Thus, whereas in Britain the Audax, a speedy biplane built in 1932, was replaced in 1937 as a light bomber by the Fairey Battle (which, however, proved in 1940 to have serious performance deficiencies), the Audax continued in British service abroad, for example, in Egypt and Iraq. Adaptation to local conditions encouraged such usage.

In Persia (Iran), the air force was built up with foreign purchases, mostly from Britain, with the number of serviceable aircraft rising from 20 in 1930 to 145 by the end of 1934. American and Soviet aircraft were also purchased. Iran in 1941 had about 250 mostly obsolete biplanes and 10 modern American Curtiss P-36 Hawk fighters, most of which, however, remained in their packing. Due to a shortage of appropriate facilities and personnel, it proved difficult to maintain the air force, but the ruler, Reza Shah, an army man, was keen to increase his air strength. Near the capital, Tehran, he had the Shabbaz Aircraft factory built. Under British managers, the factory was formally opened in September 1936, and the first aircraft were produced there in early 1938. In contrast to the monoplanes being built in Europe, Persia's aircraft, however, were mostly biplanes and obsolescent. They did not compare with the aircraft deployed by Britain and the Soviet Union when they successfully invaded in 1941.

Aside from suppressing regional opposition, the military was also central around the world to the politics of coups, attempted coups, and threatened coups that became more common in the 1930s as economic problems caused severe political disruptions. In Chile, where an air force was created in 1930 from the previously separate army and navy aviation branches, the new force played a role in politics. In September 1931, it was deployed against a naval mutiny. About twenty aircraft failed to make any direct hits when bombing the warships and only caused three casualties, but the air attack combined with the government's uncompromising demand for complete surrender to cause an immediate and marked decline in the mutineers' morale. Thus, the bombing achieved its purpose. The mutiny ended. In 1932, the buzzing of the presidential palace played a role in repeated coups in Chile.

Air attacks were also employed in 1933 in the successful suppression by federal forces of a large-scale "constitutionalist" revolt in Brazil. The previous year, the city of São Paulo was bombed, demonstrating the strength and determination of the government forces in the face of provincial opposition. Although the effectiveness of the bombing was limited, it was regarded as displaying superiority and as a clear mark of sovereignty. The use of air power was therefore becoming increasingly common around the world. It was an adjunct of government and a key means of power. This looked toward its employment later in the century.

NAVAL AIR POWER

Improvements in the interwar years (1918–39) were particularly the case of the 1930s. New arrester gears were fitted, which helped slow aircraft down while landing on carriers, and, in addition, the equipment could be reset automatically, which was useful when more than one aircraft were landing. The hydraulically reset traverse arrester gear was in use by the British navy by 1933. Improvements in carriers and aircraft helped ensure that carriers, rather than seaplanes or airships, were seen as the way to apply air power at sea, and made it easier to envisage using carriers for operational and strategic ends. Naval air doctrine and tactics also advanced. The value of attacking first was understood, as what would hinder the chance of an opponent's carrier responding, notably as it was difficult for defenders to stop an air attack. Defending fighters and their control system lacked this capacity, while antiaircraft guns were of only limited value, not least in protecting such a big target.

There were some distinctly Japanese approaches to naval aviation. In particular, the Japanese navy focused not only on carriers but also on land-based bombers as an offensive force. These long-range bombers were capable of bombing and torpedoing ships, which was not the case with the American and British navies. This was partly because the Japanese navy thought it convenient to utilize the Pacific colonies it controlled, notably the Marianas, to provide air bases from which to intercept the advancing American fleet. Moreover, the Japanese navy enjoyed relative organizational autonomy in developing naval aviation as far as its army counterpart was concerned. While there was notoriously severe interservice rivalry between the army and the navy over budget, personnel, and resources, the Japanese navy was less restricted in terms of developing naval aviation, and less threatened by proponents of an independent air force, than the British and American navies were. This was linked to the extent to which the Japanese Naval Air Force was larger in size and better in equipment than the Japanese Army Air Force, a contrast with the situation in the United States.

However, Japanese naval aviators were mostly noncommissioned officers: officers comprised fewer than 15 percent of Japan's aviators. The Japanese navy initially tried to have an all-officer pilot corps, but it gave this up for fear of destabilizing the existing personnel hierarchy because a lot of aviators were needed. Instead, the navy introduced the Yokaren system, recruiting civilians between fifteen and seventeen in order to train sufficient noncommissioned officers to fill the lower ranks. This practice led to less organizational and political representation of aviators within the navy, which hampered the necessary transformation from a battleship-orientated navy to an air-centered one, although that was not the sole reason.

Britain and the United States had carrier fleets intended to compete with that of Japan. In contrast, Germany, Italy, and the Soviet Union did not build carriers in the interwar period, and France only had one, the *Béarn*, a converted battleship that was insufficiently fast to be considered an important asset. Moreover, there was concern about its vulnerability to shore-based Italian planes, which restricted its value in the Mediterranean. The Soviet emphasis, not on carriers but on shore-based aircraft, reflected the extent to which it was assumed by the Soviets that their naval operations would take place in the Gulf of Finland or otherwise close to Soviet-controlled coastlines.

Britain's carrier construction gave an important added dimension to her naval superiority over other European powers. In addition to the carriers in commission in the 1920s, four twenty-three-thousand-ton carriers, the *Illustrious* class, each able to make over thirty knots and having a three-inch armored flight deck, were laid down in 1937, following the twenty-two-thousand-ton *Ark Royal* laid down in 1935 and completed in November 1938. The 23,450-ton *Implacable* was laid down in February 1939, although it was not commissioned until August 1944.

British and American carrier and aircraft design diverged because of differing conceptions of future naval war. In the Second World War, the British armored-deck carriers proved less susceptible to bombs and Japanese kamikaze aircraft than the American wooden-deckers, as they tended not to penetrate the former. Japanese carriers also had wooden decks. The lighter-weight wooden decks were linked to the larger fuel capacity necessary for Pacific operations. Moreover, the wooden-deck carriers had capacity for more aircraft. In contrast, the British navy's most important task was protecting national waters and the major imperial trade route through the Mediterranean. Both tasks were well within the existing and forecast zones vulnerable to attack from land-based aircraft, notably from Italy. In the 1920s and 1930s, it was held that such aircraft would hold a major advantage over the slower and longer turning circle of carriers and the problems posed by headwinds for aircraft taking off and landing. However, that was not the key reason for armored decks. Instead, the British navy sought a line of carriers sailing parallel with, but farther away from, the battleships, which would be the primary ships to engage the enemy. The original carrier specifications called for the armor to stretch over both sides of the ship as protection against naval gunfire. Cost was the reason the side armor was dropped.

The organization of air power in the interwar period remains significant to debates about the role and capability of air power today. In the interwar period, this organization was linked to fundamental issues of strategic, operational, and tactical capability and conduct. Despite pressure from the Royal Navy, naval air power in Britain lacked a separate institutional framework. The RNAS merged with the RFC into the RAF in 1918. The RAF was primarily concerned with land-based airplanes and had little time for their naval counterparts. Indeed, in 1931, the RAF had pressed for major cuts in naval aviation. The decision to separate embarked aviation and its necessary shore support, but not land-based maritime air or aircraft procurement, from the RAF and return it to the navy was announced by the Inskip Award of 1937 and came into effect in May 1939.[48]

In France, the Air Ministry, established in 1928, gained nearly all naval air assets, and this helped ensure that plans for more carriers were not pursued there until 1938 when another one, the *Joffre*, was laid down. In 1936, the French navy had regained control of naval aviation. Nevertheless, more effective land-based aircraft in the 1930s affected the options for carriers, notably in the Mediterranean, and this lessened French interest in such warships while encouraging the British stress on making theirs defensible, the reason for armored decks. In Germany, the Luftwaffe took control over all military aviation, angering the navy, which had earlier developed an air capacity even though this was forbidden under the Versailles peace settlement. In the United States, there was a very different situation thanks to the Bureau of Aeronautics of the American navy created in 1921. The bureau stimulated the development of effective air-sea doctrine, operational policies, and tactics. American air-to-sea doctrine emphasized attacking capital ships. The number of aircraft in the American Naval Air Arm rose from 1,081 in 1925 to 2,050 in 1938, a larger figure than in the Army Air Corps. The United States had a third air arm in the Marine Corps. In the Netherlands, the navy was able to resist political pressure and maintain a separate Naval Air Service.

Aside from the construction and enhancement of carriers, there were also marked improvements in naval aircraft, notably as air frames became larger and more powerful in the 1930s, although carriers could not accommodate twin-engine bombers in this period. The Americans and British developed dive-bombing tactics in the 1920s and, subsequently, dive-bombers. However, they did not replace torpedo-bombers, aircraft that launched torpedoes. Torpedo-bombers were vulnerable to defensive firepower, but best able to sink armored ships.[49] Improved torpedoes were deployed. In 1931, the Japanese introduced the Type 91 Mod 1 antiship torpedo.

The emphasis on carrier attack should not crowd out other uses for naval air power. Many aircraft were employed at sea to help battleships spot the fall of their shells. They were launched from catapults on the top of turrets. Aerial reconnaissance was also crucial in the location of shipping.[50] A clear future for air power at sea was suggested by the British fleet reconstruction program of 1937, which aimed, by the late

1940s, to have twenty new battleships and twenty new carriers at the core of the battle fleet. From hindsight, the battleship appears redundant, but that was not how it seemed to contemporaries. Instead, it was believed that battleships could be protected against air attack, while carriers appeared vulnerable to gunnery, and thus to require protection, as well as being essentially fair-weather and daytime warships.[51]

CONCLUSIONS

The hope of air power in the 1930s was not matched by the level of technology necessary to deliver it. Some of the hopes, expectations, and fears were fantastical when it came to aircraft and what they might be capable of achieving. There was a particular blind spot when it came to antiaircraft defenses. Indeed, in response to the greater potential of air attack, air defense came to be a major issue in the 1920s and 1930s, with its own doctrine, technology, and organization. Under Hitler, the Air Defense League both trained Germans and took part in the militarization of society. Similarly, in the Soviet Union, as part of the total mobilization of society, preparations were made to handle the civilian reaction to air attack.[52] The French, however, who failed to match this effort, had a serious lack of antiaircraft guns as well as of civil defense. In Britain, there was acute concern about what air attack might bring.

Aircraft, both individually and collectively, were more potent than when the First World War had ended in 1918. At the same time, demonstrating the improved capability that both wars were to bring, the air forces available in 1939 lacked the strength that was to be deployed by 1945. Moreover, there were serious deficiencies in the range of aircraft available when war broke out in Europe in September 1939. None of the air forces had an effective purpose-built transport aircraft, and, with the exception of Japan, they did not have fast enough reconnaissance aircraft. In addition, there were significant problems in the design of some aircraft that had originally appeared promising.[53] It was far from clear what the next war would bring.

6

THE SECOND WORLD WAR

If they [the Japanese leaders] do not now accept our terms they may expect a rain of ruin from the air. . . . We are now prepared to obliterate more rapidly and completely every productive enterprise the Japanese have above ground in any city. We shall destroy their docks, their factories, and their communications. . . . We shall completely destroy Japan's power to make war. —Harry S. Truman[1]

The hitherto unprecedented scale, scope, and sophistication of air power during this global conflict reflected the manifold use of this power: in strategic, operational, and tactical terms, and affecting land and sea campaigning. Moreover, this use of air power demonstrated a responsiveness, indeed "quality," in terms of the rapid operation of, and improvement in, the action-reaction cycles of air power during the war. Already seen in the First World War, this process operated at a greater scale and range in the Second. The familiar coverage focuses on bombing, fighter escort and interception, and support for airborne forces, but there is also need to devote due attention to ground support, and to the role of air power in naval warfare, logistics, and communications. In particular, the integration of air power with land and sea campaigning proved instrumental in improving the effectiveness of both. In turn, the significance of antiaircraft practice increased, both that of aircraft seeking to block such activities and integration, and that of ground-based units.

Furthermore, the experience of being bombed and strafed was significant for the military and civilians. The latter experience became an important part of the collective memory of the war and of subsequent controversies. Bombing campaigns were indeed intended to produce an overwhelming impact on political opinion, most notably with the dropping of atomic bombs on Hiroshima and Nagasaki in August 1945 in order to knock Japan out of the war. This use of air power had a lasting cultural impact in the shape of a debate over how far it was necessary and appropriate.

The extensive use of air power reflected the length and range of the conflict, and the degree to which it involved a mobilization of the resources of societies. It was also possible to manufacture, supply, and man large numbers of aircraft, and in a variety of types, but without the high initial and ongoing costs that advanced electronics and other technological factors were to lead to by the 1980s. Technological changes did not relate solely to one model. The standardization of screw sizes, for example, was crucial to both speedy manufacture and easy repair, helping Britain greatly in 1940 in response to German air attack.

Thus, the characteristics of aircraft were particularly opportune during the Second World War. The major improvements made in aircraft and associated technology during the 1930s ensured that they were far more robust, potent, and useful than during the First World War; but, as yet, they were not overspecialized, and their specifications had not improved to a degree that was to limit and inhibit their use. The same situation was true of naval air power, of airfields, and of antiaircraft weaponry.

1939–40: GERMAN BLITZKRIEG

The first campaign in Europe, the rapid German conquest of Poland in 1939, demonstrated the use of air power in a campaign well suited to its impact. Tactical air power had three main missions: gaining or maintaining air superiority against enemy fighters, providing close air support for ground combat units, and interdiction—attacking the immediate supply and communications networks of enemy ground forces. The Germans were particularly good at the last. Greatly outnumbering the Poles in aircraft, the Germans, who began the war with a surprise assault, enjoyed the initiative, while the Polish fighters were outclassed by the Me-109. The Polish air force was rapidly destroyed, a crucial step in the German offensive. The Germans benefited from launching surprise attacks that destroyed some of the Polish aircraft on the ground, although the extent of these losses has been exaggerated, and many Polish aircraft were lost in aerial combat.

Subsequently, the rapid opening by the Germans of improvised airfields behind their advancing forces countered the short range of their aircraft and helped the Luftwaffe provide close air support, and this to a degree that was hitherto unique. In contrast to very poor relations between the Luftwaffe and the navy, those with the army were good. Aside from providing firepower, the Luftwaffe was strong in reconnaissance. The Luftwaffe was able to associate itself with the army's success and to present itself as largely responsible. German newsreels made much of the role of the Luftwaffe. Warsaw, the Polish capital, was heavily bombed, with about seven thousand people killed. Hitler liked to watch film of the bombing.

Unlike the German attack on Poland, Soviet control of the air did not help bring rapid victory in the Winter War with Finland in 1939–40, although the winter circumstances were far more difficult. The Finns and the Soviets were both equipped with obsolescent aircraft, but the Soviet air force vastly outnumbered the Finnish one and eventually employed at least fifteen air regiments. The Finnish capital, Helsinki, was bombed. The Soviets, however, relied on artillery, not air power, to blast their way through the Mannerheim Line, the main Finnish defense position. Artillery could deliver more destruction and was less dependent on the weather. This success led Finland to terms. Poor Soviet performance, including disproportionately heavy losses, was related to the rapid expansion of the air force at the expense of training. In the late 1930s, it was plagued with an inordinate number of training accidents trying to push so many men through pilot training in a short amount of time. Also, many men were assigned to pilot training without having requested it. Finnish airmanship was definitely superior.

The Germans proved more successful when they launched surprise attacks on Denmark and Norway on April 9, 1940. In the case of Denmark, the Germans made effective use of their air power against a weak resistance. Airborne troops of the Luftwaffe, including the first parachute assault, complemented the troops landed by ship and those advancing overland from Germany. Oslo, the capital of Norway, also fell on April 9: an amphibious landing was blocked in the Oslo fjord, but the

Germans compensated by airlifting troops to the airfield, which had been captured by airborne troops.

British and French forces were dispatched to oppose the German invasion of Norway, but a lack of adequate air cover left these forces vulnerable and contributed greatly to the German ability to seize and maintain the initiative and to overcome successive defensive positions. In an analysis of the campaign produced for the benefit of the British War Office, General Claude Auchinleck attributed the German victory primarily to air power.[2] The Ju-87 Stuka dive-bomber, although very vulnerable when fighting modern fighters, hit the morale of troops, not least due to its use of sirens attached to the bottom of the aircraft, the extreme angle of its descent, and the low height at which its bombs were dropped. The British navy was also shown to be unable to cope effectively with German air power, and a doctrine of reliance on antiaircraft fire was revealed as unsatisfactory. Admiral Sir Dudley Pound, the First Sea Lord, remarked, "The one lesson we have learnt here is that it is essential to have fighter protection over the Fleet whenever they are within reach of the enemy bombers,"[3] but that lesson was repeatedly to prove difficult to apply.

Invading the Netherlands, Belgium, and France on May 10, 1940, the Germans again benefited greatly from air operations. Both the Dutch and the Belgians were weak in the air, and the Germans swiftly gained and, crucially, used air superiority. One of the first glider-borne air assaults, and an exceptional piece of airmanship, was against the Belgian fort at Eben Emael. The capture of bridges by German airborne forces weakened the use of river and canal defenses, hit morale, and denied defense in depth. The crucial step in the conquest of the Netherlands was the capture by German paratroops of the Moerdijk bridge over the combined waters of the Meuse and the Waal some twenty-five kilometers south of Rotterdam. Air attacks supported the German advance.

However, the German use of airborne troops was only a partial success in the Netherlands. There, the German airborne troops generally failed in their attempts to take vital objects and airfields and were unable to capture either the Cabinet ministers or members of the royal family. About 350 transport aircraft were lost, and of about 7,250 airborne troops, nearly 2,000 became casualties or prisoners of war. Their dire situation may well have hastened the decision by Hitler and Göring to bomb the city of Rotterdam and force a quick Dutch surrender, although the Dutch army was poorly trained and its defenses had crumbled to land assault east of Utrecht. The destruction of much of the city center caused by the bombing of Rotterdam on May 14 was a brutal demonstration of what air attack could achieve. Some eighty thousand people lost their homes, and about six hundred to eight hundred were killed. The Dutch stopped fighting that day, and the surrender followed on May 15.

In part by concentrating their aircraft at critical places, the Germans also rapidly achieved air superiority over the French, inflicting heavy casualties on the French air force and then using their success to attack the French army, although there was as yet no direct radio communication between aircraft and ground forces. The Vichy Court of Supreme Justice was to hold the French Armée de l'Air responsible for defeat in 1940. Although a political judgment, it reflected the French failure to match the Luftwaffe in aircraft and doctrine. Most significantly, the French failed to prevent the Luftwaffe from assisting the German crossing of the Meuse River at Sedan on May 13. Even then, although assisted by the impact of Stuka attacks on French morale, Guderian's breakthrough was a standard infantry-artillery fight. What was new was the German tanks' ability to exploit the gains made by traditional arms. Air power largely played the tangential role of neutralizing French artillery in the rear areas.

In the face of German aircraft and rapidly deployed German antiaircraft guns, French air attacks failed to destroy the bridges across the Meuse the following day.[4] This failure highlighted both the inflated expectation of what air power could achieve and the difficulty of destroying bridges using aircraft. British aircraft also failed dismally in their attacks on French bridges. Maintaining the tempo of the attack, the Germans did not allow the French air force to regain the initiative, while the air force leaders lacked the necessary urgent response to a rapidly deteriorating situation. In particular, the leaders were unable to compensate for their initial deployment of their aerial resources across the entire frontier.[5]

The fall of France also involved the Germans fighting the British forces deployed in France as part of the alliance. The poor control of fighters against the Luftwaffe played a major role in the RAF's inability to inflict major damage, although the British fighters could hold their own against the Me-109. The German pilots had the great advantage of experience. Outnumbered, the RAF, with its focus on air conflict with the Germans, suffered from very poor coordination with the British army. As a result of this and of poor bombers, notably the Fairey Battle, the army lacked adequate close air support. Moreover, German air superiority prevented effective Allied air attacks on their advancing forces or supply lines. However, in large part thanks to the RAF, the Luftwaffe failed to prevent the evacuation of substantial Anglo-French forces from northern France, notably the beaches of Dunkirk, and this evacuation was crucial in providing Britain with the means to fight on.

BRITAIN UNDER ATTACK

The fall of France, which accepted German terms on June 22, 1940, left Britain vulnerable, as well as ensured that British air attacks on Germany would not be able to benefit from French airfields and friendly airspace. Instead, rapidly moved forward into France, Belgium, the Netherlands, and Norway, German airfields, notably in the Pas de Calais and Normandy, were now close to Britain, greatly cutting the journey time of bombers and allowing fighters to escort them. The situation was very different from previous occasions on which Britain had been threatened with invasion, most seriously by France under Napoleon in 1803–5. Then, British naval strength had provided security against invasion. In contrast, in 1940, the Luftwaffe was instructed to help prepare the way for an invasion, Operation Sealion, especially by driving British warships from the English Channel.

Instead, Luftwaffe commanders were increasingly concerned to attack the RAF and its supporting infrastructure in order to destroy the RAF and to prepare the way for reducing Britain to submission by a bombing war on civilian targets. This was a strategy that would put the Luftwaffe center stage, which was very much the intention of its commanders. In practice, however, a lack of clarity in the relationship between air attack and invasion affected German strategy. There was also a serious failure to prepare for a strategic air offensive, because the Germans, with their emphasis on tactical and operational imperatives, had not sufficiently anticipated its necessity. The Luftwaffe was primarily intended to act in concert with German ground forces, something that was not possible in the self-contained aerial battle with Britain.

In addition, the Germans suffered from a lack of well-trained pilots, and from limitations with their aircraft and tactics. Not only did the Luftwaffe fail to win the air-superiority contest in the Battle of Britain, but its medium and dive-bombers proved highly vulnerable to fighter attack and incapable of an effective strategic bombing campaign. Their bombers' load capacity and range were too small; and their fighters were too sluggish (Me-110), or had an inadequate range, affecting the time they could spend over England (Me-109). Moreover, operating near the edge of their fighter escort range, the fighters were handicapped by having to close escort the bombers. Furthermore, although the British had also lost heavily, the Luftwaffe had already lost many aircraft and pilots during the Battle of France. In a serious intelligence failure, the Germans underrated the size, sophistication, and strength of the defense and, in particular, failed to understand the role of British radar and its place in the integrated air-defense system. They devoted insufficient attention to attacking the radar stations and suffered from poor target intelligence. The British control system, with its plotters of opposing moves and its telephone lines, was an early instance of the network-enabled capability seen in the 2000s with its plasma screens and secure data links. In each case, the targeting, sensors, and shooters were linked through a network that included the decision maker.[6] In 1940, Germany had radar, but it was not yet available to help the Luftwaffe.

Initial German attacks on the RAF and its airfields inflicted serious blows, especially on pilot numbers. However, fighting over Britain, it was possible to recover RAF pilots who survived being shot down, while, contesting the battle it had planned for, and not needing to improvise as much as might have been the case, the RAF benefited from the support provided by radar and the ground-control organization, as well as from able command decisions, good intelligence, and a high level of fighting quality. Luftwaffe losses also reflected the vulnerability of bombers.[7] Moreover, despite issues with fuel supply,[8] the British outproduced the Germans in aircraft so that losses in fighters were quickly made good because of more efficient manufacture that drew on superior British engineering and management. The Germans did not devote enough attention to building aircraft, in part because their intelligence underestimated RAF strength. Fighter Command was helped by the repeated spoiling raids against German airfields mounted by Bomber Command, raids made more difficult for the Germans because the airfields were not protected by radar. Aside from the availability of radar for the British, it was difficult for German bombers to put British airfields out of action, not least as the wide, grassy strips that were a key element in the latter could not be wrecked, although hangars could be put out of action.

As a reminder of the multiplicity of factors involved, and the need to put explanations focused on air power into a broader context, the viability of Sealion before the onset of the winter weather was dubious even had the Germans achieved air superiority over southern England, while the lack of support from advancing land forces on the pattern of the German offensives so far, made such superiority harder to achieve. There were other British fighters further north and west in England, as well as the serious threat posed by the Royal Navy.[9] Moreover, Sealion lacked adequate planning, preparation, and resources, not least proper landing craft. The Germans had limited experience or understanding of amphibious operations, principally in the Baltic in 1917. The improvised nature of the German plans contrasted heavily with the detailed Allied preparations for the invasion of France in 1944. The Germans had also lost many warships in the invasion of Norway.

Nevertheless, however flawed the air assault was, victory in the Battle of Britain produced a significant boost to British civilian morale.[10] Moreover, the Battle of Britain served as a lasting account of valorous air combat and of the crucial role of air power. It did so not only for the RAF, but also for other air forces.

THE BLITZ

Fear about the consequences for the population of German air attack led to the mass evacuation of children (including my parents from the East End of London) when war broke out in 1939, as well as to the issue of gas masks, the preparation of a large number of cardboard coffins, and the implementation of blackout regulations. In the event, the German attacks did not come until the following autumn (by which time some of the 690,000 evacuated in September 1939 had returned), and they did not include gas attacks.

From September 7, 1940, the Luftwaffe bombed London heavily and repeatedly. The German word *Blitzkrieg* (lightning war) was shortened by the British to give a name to this terrifying new form of conflict: the Blitz. That day, 348 German bombers attacked. The inadequately prepared defenses were taken by surprise and failed to respond adequately. There were only ninety-two antiaircraft guns ready for action, and their fire-control system failed. The British fighter squadrons proved unable to stop the powerful air assault. Some 430 people were killed in the East End, where the docks on the river Thames were hit hard. This was what became a German strategy to starve Britain into surrender, in part by destroying the docks through which food was imported. Liverpool, Plymouth, and Southampton were also to be heavily attacked for that reason, as well as to deny the navy bases.

Another 412 people were killed in a night raid on London on September 8. It was only on September 11 that antiaircraft fire was sufficiently active to force the Germans to bomb from a greater height. Barrage balloons also forced bombers to fly higher, thus reducing bombing accuracy. In comparison with later figures, these casualties were modest, but they were far higher than those from individual bombing raids during the First World War.

From September 7 until mid-November 1940, the Germans bombed London every night bar one. There were also large-scale daylight attacks, as well as hit-and-run attacks. The attack on the moonlit night of October 15–16 proved particularly serious, with four hundred bombers active, of which only one was shot down by the RAF's forty-one fighters. The railway stations were hard hit, while Battersea Power Station was struck, as was the headquarters of the BBC (British Broadcasting Corporation). By mid-November, when the attacks became less focused on London, over thirteen thousand tons of high explosive bombs had been dropped on the city, as well as nearly one million incendiaries.

The German focus on attacking British cities in the Blitz from the autumn of 1940 was intended to destroy civilian morale by means of terror bombing. However, although there were occasional episodes of panic, for example, by the civic authorities in Southampton, as well as an increase in criminality, morale on the whole remained good, notably

among those who had not been bombed. This campaign continued the
Battle of Britain, but without an operational focus or the capability to
match its destructive purpose. Moreover, the attacks on British airfields
stopped.

London bore the brunt of the attack. There were also destructive
raids on other cities, including Coventry, an industrial center, with 449
bombers on November 14, and Southampton, a major port. Nighttime
air-defense techniques were poor, and, not least because of the absence
of precise aerial radar, it was hard to hit German aircraft once they
largely switched to night attacks in September 1940 in part in order to
cut losses. The German bombers almost always got through. Indeed,
relatively few German aircraft were shot down that winter, although
accidents and the winter weather led to many losses. By the late spring
of 1941, however, the British defense was becoming more effective
thanks to the use of radar-directed Beaufighter planes and ground defenses. From mid-November 1940 to the end of February 1941, eight
major raids were mounted on London. Thereafter, the focus was on the
ports, until May 1941 when the bomber forces were moved to prepare
for the invasion of the Soviet Union launched the following month. The
British bombing of Germany, notably the cities of Berlin and Mannheim, in late 1940 was on a smaller scale and inflicted much less damage.

In bombing London, the German high command had set out to
destroy civilian morale. In practice, there was an emphasis, in London
and elsewhere, on "taking it," forbearance, and making do, notably at
the docks, which continued operating. The German hope that the British people would realize their plight; overthrow Winston Churchill, the
anti-German prime minister; and make peace proved a serious misreading of British politics and public opinion. Instead, British intelligence
reports suggested that the bombing led to signs of "increasing hatred of
Germany," as well as to demands for "numerous reprisals."[11] The idea
that Hitler had to be defeated and removed was strengthened. There
was also a phlegmatic and fatalistic response to the bombing, one captured by the Listener Research Report organized by the BBC in 1941.
For social as well as political reasons, the air assault made the home
front far more significant. It became the focus of government effort, in
the shape of civil defense, and of activity by the public. The bravery of
the civilians was a key theme, a bravery in which women played the

central role. The emphasis on a stoical response to suffering was designed to preserve morale.[12] Similarly, the American bombing of North Vietnam was to have the effect of unifying the nation rather than destroying civilian morale.

Attempts to shelter from the remorseless bombing led many Londoners to seek refuge in the Underground system (the "Tube," or subway), where about 177,000 people were sleeping on the station platforms by late September 1940. There was a degree of social tension in the response to the bombing, as there was later to be in Italy in the face of Allied bombing. Thus, Londoners from the much-bombed working-class dockside district of Silvertown, where there was a lack of shelters, forced their way into the Savoy Hotel's impressive bomb shelter. Nevertheless, the government's theme of equality in suffering was made a reality by the Luftwaffe. Fortitude in the face of the Blitz became a key aspect of national identity; and the real and symbolic aspect of the assault on British civil society accentuated the sense of the entire country, including the royal family in Buckingham Palace, being under attack. This became a key theme in modern British public culture, indeed a central aspect of the democratization of the national heritage.

Film ensured that the Blitz was the first major episode of London's history that was captured dramatically for a wide audience. Photographs of St Paul's Cathedral surrounded by flames and devastation acquired totemic force, overseas as well as in Britain, including in the United States, where the British were making a major attempt to win support. Documentaries, including *London Can Take It* (1940) and *Christmas under Fire* (1941), spread film of the bombing. Moreover, the bombing had an impact on literature and poetry. Elizabeth Bowen's novel *The Heat of the Day* (1949), a tragic love story, has evocative descriptions of the atmosphere in the city while the air raids were in progress. Their lasting impact on writers was indicated by the number of novels in which characters were killed as a result, for example in the detective novels of Agatha Christie.

AIR-SEA WARFARE

Another assault on Britain was launched by German U-boats or submarines, which, as in the First World War, sought to starve Britain into
surrender. The RAF played a key role in resisting this assault. Most U-
boat "kills" of shipping were made by attack on the surface, which
rendered Allied sonar less effective. In contrast, aircraft forced U-boats
to submerge, where their speed was slower and it was harder to maintain visual contact with targets. On the surface, submarines operated
using diesel oil in engines that could drive the vessel three to four times
faster than underwater cruising, which of necessity was driven by bat-
tery-powered electric motors. This factor affected cruising range and
the number of days that could be spent at sea. Air power was the vital
element that reduced the killing power of the German submarine fleet
to the point that its effectiveness, measured by Allied tonnage lost,
decreased steadily.

Nevertheless, as a reminder of the significance of tasking or goals,
neither the RAF, which was interested in strategic bombing and theater
fighters, nor the navy, which was primarily concerned with hostile surface warships and was content to rely on convoys, hunter groups, and
sonar (of which there were very few sets) to limit submarine attempts,
had devoted sufficient preparation to air cover against submarines. In
addition, land-based aircraft operating against U-boats faced an "air
gap" across much of the mid-Atlantic, although Iceland's availability as
an Allied base from April 1941 increased the range of such air cover.
Again, as a reminder of choices, the British had used carrier-based
aircraft against U-boats at the start of the war, but the sinking of the
carrier *Courageous* by a U-boat ended the practice, and the remaining
fleet carriers were deployed against Axis surface warships. Moreover,
the demands of the bomber offensive against Germany on available
long-range aircraft restricted the numbers available for convoy escort,
while it took time to build escort aircraft carriers: the first entered
service in late 1941. Twenty-eight escort carriers were transferred from
the United States to Britain under Lend-Lease provisions.

At the same time, German air power had serious deficiencies in
affecting the war at sea, not least because coordination with the navy
was very poor. Despite Germany having conquered bases in western
France in 1940 from which long-range aircraft could threaten shipping

routes in British home waters, which was a potential lacking in the First World War, the Luftwaffe totally failed to devote sufficient resources, in aircraft or aviation fuel, to the Battle of the Atlantic against Allied shipping. The Luftwaffe was better at support for the army than for the navy, a contrast that reflected issues of personality among the leaders, but also the role of the army in German society, the Continental dominance of German strategy, and the extent to which support for army attacks fulfilled the Luftwaffe's image of activity.

The vulnerability of naval operations to air attack had been demonstrated even more clearly in the Mediterranean in 1941, notably with the German conquest of the British-held island of Crete in May. German air attacks hit the British navy's attempt to reinforce, supply, and, eventually, evacuate the island.[13] Carriers represented a major change to naval warfare in the First World War, but naval operations within the range of land were now vulnerable to attack unless air superiority could be gained. The British navy off Crete lacked air cover. Such vulnerability affected the rationale of naval operations, because the risk of a rapid and serious loss of ships, and thus of the loss of relative naval capability, was now far greater. Admiral Cunningham, the British commander-in-chief in the Mediterranean, observed, "You cannot conduct military operations in modern warfare without air forces which will allow you at least to establish temporary air superiority."[14] Indeed, General Thomas Blamey of the Australian army wrote about eastern Libya, "Cyrenaica is regarded as most urgent problem of Middle East as control to [the city of] Benghazi would give [British] fleet freedom of movement as far as Malta and advance air bases to allow cover of sea operations."[15]

These factors were to be underlined when the Japanese attacked in the Far East in December 1941, and were to affect the debate over the necessary prerequisites before the Allies could launch amphibious operations in Europe. The enclosed nature of the Mediterranean, all of which is close to land, accentuated the vulnerability of shipping there to air attack. The deployment of Luftwaffe units to the Mediterranean underlined this problem. German and Italian air attacks on Malta's harbor and airfields, and air and submarine attacks on British convoys supplying Malta in 1941–42, were central to an unsuccessful attempt to starve the British-held island into surrender. Spitfires that were delivered by carrier from March and, more successfully, May 1942 ensured that the air war over the island was won by the British that year.

GERMAN OFFENSIVES, 1941

On April 6, 1941, Germany attacked Yugoslavia and Greece. The attack on Yugoslavia included the terror bombing of the undefended city of Belgrade in order to cause heavy civilian casualties: over seventeen thousand people were killed. The British sent an expeditionary force to help the Greeks, but, with inadequate air support, it was swiftly pushed back. The tempo of the German advance, especially its rapid use of airborne troops and armor, brought a decisive advantage, as did the effective use of ground-support aircraft. The campaign culminated with the capture of the Greek island of Crete by German parachute and air-transported troops. This was a risky attack, as such forces were unable to bring heavy arms with them, a problem that was to affect the British airborne assault on Arnhem in the Netherlands in late 1944. However, on Crete, although it took heavy casualties in men and transport aircraft, the German assault force was able to gain the initiative from a poorly directed resistance, to seize airstrips, and to secure resupply by air. Glider troops tipped the balance during the assault on Maleme airfield, when they landed close to antiaircraft batteries, which they captured. The conquest of Crete was the first time a major objective had been taken by massed airborne assault, and the operation raised important questions regarding the utility of air power.

On June 22, 1941, Hitler launched Operation Barbarossa against the Soviet Union. Despite having the biggest air force in the world, the Soviets, greatly outnumbering but outclassed by the Luftwaffe, were less impressive. In part, this was because the Soviets suffered from a lack of good pilots, as well as the extent to which effective new aircraft had not replaced obsolescent models. The Soviets had no radar, and most of the aircraft lacked radio telephones. Their pilots were poorly trained, and their morale was low. The air force had been badly affected by Stalin's purges. Benefiting from surprise (unlike against the RAF in 1940), and destroying over 1,200 Soviet aircraft on the first day, the Germans rapidly gained superiority in the air and used it both to assist ground operations and to destroy ships of the Soviet Baltic and Black Sea fleets.

However, despite the priority placed on production for the Luftwaffe, one that hit the army hard, the Germans were short of the necessary aircraft, in part because the heavy losses suffered during the Battles of France and Britain had only just been replaced.[16] The Luftwaffe, moreover, now needed to maintain an air-defense (and attack) force to face Britain, to support German and Italian forces in the Mediterranean, to protect Germany from air attack, and to defend Norway and France, as well as to operate in the Soviet Union, none of them tasks that had to be fulfilled in early 1940. In addition, the German bombers lacked the necessary range and bomb capacity to be an effective strategic force on the Eastern Front. There were more serious problems arising from the space-force ratio, with the Germans not having the number of aircraft necessary in order to have a major impact across the very extensive range of the battle zone. Furthermore, as the Germans advanced, the Luftwaffe was forced to rely on improvised airfields and was affected by the general logistical crisis of Operation Barbarossa, notably the difficulties in bringing forward and maintaining supplies. The Luftwaffe found itself overstretched, and then fighting a war of attrition for air superiority that it could not win. The serviceability of its aircraft and airfields deteriorated.

The rapid Soviet revival of their air force, devastated in the initial German attack, was also significant. Much Soviet industry had remained beyond the range of German power, and this proved important to this revival. Moreover, there was an introduction of better aircraft, such as the YAK-1 (1940), YAK-7 (1941), MIG-3 (1941), LAGG-3 (1941), YAK-9 (1942), LA-5 (1942), YAK-3 (1943),[17] and LA-7 (1944). The Soviets also operated aircraft supplied by Britain and the United States, notably Hurricanes, P-39s, P-40s, and P-63s. In order to provide protection for their forces on the ground, the Germans therefore had to devote large numbers of aircraft to destroying Soviet aircraft. This again reduced the options of a bombing campaign.[18]

JAPANESE ATTACKS, 1941–42

Air power proved far more important to the Japanese attack on the United States, Britain, and the Dutch in December 1941 than it did in the German war on the Eastern Front. The key initial assault was the attack on December 7 on Pearl Harbor, the base of the American Pacific Fleet on the island of Oahu in the Hawaiian archipelago. The Japanese were encouraged by the example of the successful British torpedo aircraft attack on Italian warships in the naval base of Taranto on November 11, 1940, especially the technique of shallow running the torpedoes, an attack in which three Italian battleships were badly damaged by twenty-one carrier-launched aircraft. The attack on Pearl Harbor was a dramatic assault, but one that indicated the problems with achieving strategic results. A force of 353 aircraft from six Japanese carriers totally destroyed two American battleships and damaged three more, while nearly three hundred American aircraft were destroyed or damaged on the ground.

The attack, however, revealed grave deficiencies in Japanese (and American) planning, as well as in the Japanese war machine. Only 45 percent of naval air requirements had been met by the start of the war, and the last torpedoes employed in the attack were delivered only two days before the fleet sailed. The Japanese used Type 91 Mod 2 torpedoes, which, with their heavier charge, thinner air vessel, and antiroll stabilizers, were first delivered in April 1941. Modifications of aircraft to carry both torpedoes and heavy bombs were last minute, and there was a lack of practice. Moreover, the Japanese target-prioritization scheme was poor, attack routes conflicted, and the torpedo attack lacked simultaneity. The Japanese also failed to destroy Pearl Harbor. Because of the focus on destroying warships, there was no third-wave attack on the fuel and other harbor installations. Had the oil farms (stores) been destroyed, the Pacific Fleet would probably have had to fall back to the base at San Diego, which would have gravely inhibited American operations in the Pacific. The damage to America's battleships forced an important shift in American naval planning toward an emphasis on their carriers, the *Lexington*, the *Yorktown*, and the *Enterprise*, which, despite Japanese expectations, were not in Pearl Harbor when it was attacked.[19]

Air power proved important in the Japanese attacks elsewhere. The outnumbered British garrison on Hong Kong had only seven outdated aircraft, and the Japanese used air support to block interference with their supply routes by British motor torpedo boats based there. On the Philippines, the Japanese were able to destroy much of the poorly prepared US Far East Air Force on the ground at the outset. Having gained superiority in the air, the Japanese used it to attack American installations in the Philippines, seriously hitting morale and removing a threat to Japanese amphibious landings. The mobility offered by naval attack could be rapidly countered by air interference, but the potential of this interference was denied the Americans by the dominance provided by the initial Japanese air assault. Moreover, in the face of Japanese air power, the American navy was unwilling to risk the provision of the necessary support to oppose these landings. The navy argued that it would be impossible to relieve the Philippines by the time they had fallen to invasion. Air attack certainly gave the Japanese the initiative in their conquest of the Philippines, and proved important at the tactical level, providing the Japanese with mobile artillery, as with the effective attack in 1942 on the heavily fortified island of Corregidor in Manila Bay.

The successful Japanese invasion of British-held Malaya owed much to air power. The destruction of British aircraft on the ground accentuated the marked advantage the Japanese enjoyed in the number, quality, and use of aircraft. On December 10, 1941, moreover, eighty-five land-based Japanese naval bombers sank the battleship *Prince of Wales* and the battle cruiser *Repulse*, which had been sent north from Singapore to threaten Japanese landings on the east coast of Malaya. These were the first ships of these types sunk at sea solely by air attack, and their loss demonstrated the vulnerability of capital ships without air cover to enemy air attack. The lesson mentioned by Pound in May 1940 (see above) had not been applied. The use of Indochinese bases was critical, as it maximized the limited range of the Japanese aircraft. In this operation, the British were badly affected by poor naval command, as well as by poor coordination between the navy and the RAF. This was a systemic issue in air-sea coordination, as well as one specific to this campaign. Admiral Layton was subsequently to ask, "Was the preliminary work on naval aerodromes which was undertaken in 1941 (none of which ever reached completion) an unnecessary and unwise diversion of resources from the requirements of the RAF?"[20]

The Japanese then rapidly fought their way down the Malayan Peninsula, gaining airfields that they could use against the British forces, who had inadequate air support, not least from Buffaloes, which were wholly outclassed by Japanese Zeros and Oscars. The British were forced back to the island of Singapore, which was successfully invaded in February 1942. Under heavy attack and badly led, the garrison surrendered, a serious and humiliating blow. The threat of air attack on the civilian population of Singapore, a largely wooden city and therefore vulnerable to fire, was a factor in persuading the British commanders to surrender.

Similarly, aircraft were moved forward into captured airfields as the Japanese overran the Dutch East Indies (now Indonesia) in January–March 1942. The lack of adequate air power hit the defenders hard, including in the disastrous naval battles of the Java Sea from February 27 to March 1 in which five cruisers and five destroyers were lost. Other problems in these battles included a lack of shared intelligence, a complicated command structure, and the shortage of experienced fighter pilots. Dutch East India fighters had exhausted their strength in the defense of Malaya and had been overcome in Japanese air attacks on Java on February 19 and 27. The Japanese benefited in the battles of the Java Sea from air reconnaissance.

In addition, the Japanese bombed infrastructural targets from high altitudes, and the Allies had few means of preventing that. From January 11, Japanese paratroopers were successfully used in attacking targets on Sulawesi, Sumatra, and Timor. In April 1942, furthermore, Japanese aircraft from a force of five carriers sank two British heavy cruisers and a carrier, the *Hermes*, off Sri Lanka, as well as overcoming the island's air defenses.

With total air superiority, the Japanese had rapidly advanced in the first four months of the war. In part, Japanese success in the air was a matter of better aircraft. Thus, the navy's lightweight, readily maneuverable, and long-range A6M Zero fighter outclassed the American Brewster F-2A Buffalo and the Curtiss P-40. However, it was the use of aircraft, as part of an initiative-grabbing, high-tempo campaign, that proved more significant. In addition, the ability of the Japanese to move rapidly between targets was significant. Thus, the fall of Singapore enabled Japan to strengthen their air assault on Burma (Myanmar), where the British defenders had to rely largely on outclassed, if not obsolescent, American and British aircraft. However, losses over Burma were equal—Japan 117, Britain 116—in part due to the availability of experienced American pilots from Chenault's Flying Tigers.

Despite their operational skill and tempo, the Japanese, in a classic instance of strategic failure, lacked a realistic war plan and badly underrated American economic strength and the resolve of its people: the Americans were not interested in a compromise peace. Moreover, there were serious deficiencies in particular areas of Japanese doctrine, weaponry, and military-industrial infrastructure. For example, Japanese air power could not compete in the long term, not least because of coordination failures in its aero-industry. The Japanese also lacked a heavy bomber, while their aircraft were deficient in armor and self-sealing tanks. There were also insufficient mechanics to maintain the aircraft.[21] More significantly, the American Army Air Corps had already begun major expansion from 1939 as the war in Europe neared and then began.

The reality and capability of air power proved significant to the next stage of the Pacific War. On February 19, 1942, the town of Darwin was bombed, the first in a series of Japanese air attacks on northern Australia. These destructive raids were launched from four carriers and from airfields on Sulawesi and Ambon, parts of the conquered Dutch East Indies, notably those at Kendari and Amboina. The Japanese wished to seal off the island of Timor from Allied aid, as, without Timor, which fell on February 19–20, the Allies would not be able to send reinforcements by air to Java, which was invaded on March 1.

However, on March 17, American fighters arrived at Darwin, providing protection. Moreover, the Americans were able to thwart the Japanese attempt to mount an amphibious attack on Port Moresby in southeast New Guinea, from which Australia could be readily attacked. Having intercepted and decoded Japanese messages, the Americans were waiting in the Coral Sea for the Japanese fleet. This led, in the Battle of the Coral Sea on May 7–8, to the first battle entirely between carrier groups, one, in addition, in which the ships did not make visual contact. The Americans suffered serious losses, but the Japanese also suffered, notably in pilots, and, crucially, failed to persist with the operation, while American pilots acquired experience in attacking Japanese carriers. The battle demonstrated a serious problem with naval warfare, that of accurate surveillance, and also throws light on limitations of naval air power in this period. It was necessary to develop carrier warfare techniques, a formidable task because of limited prewar familiarity, although, by the mid-1930s, many American admirals had carrier experience. These techniques and doctrines had to include cooperation with other surface warships.

Naval air power proved crucial in the next stage of the Pacific War. The Doolittle raid, a symbolic American air attack on Tokyo on April 18, 1942, launched from the carrier *Hornet*, both raised American morale and encouraged the Japanese to act by demonstrating Japanese vulnerability. Admiral Isoroku Yamamoto sought a decisive naval battle, one intended to destroy the American carrier force, which he planned to draw under the guns of his battleships. The seizure of Midway Island was seen by the Japanese as a necessary preliminary.

The Japanese plan led, on June 4, to the Battle of Midway, a naval-air battle of unprecedented scale, one that, as with combined-arms operations on land, indicated the significance of integrated fighting, notably the combination of fighter support with carriers in defense, and of fighters with bombers in attack. While the ability to learn hard-won lessons from Coral Sea was highly significant, the dependence of operations on tactical adroitness and chance played a major role in a battle in which the ability to locate the target was crucial. The American strike from the *Hornet* failed because the fighters and dive-bombers were unable to locate the Japanese carriers. Lacking any or adequate fighter support, the torpedo-bomber attacks suffered very heavy losses. However, the result of these attacks was that the Japanese fighters were unable to respond, not least because they were at a low altitude, to the arrival of the American dive-bombers. In only a few minutes, three carriers were wrecked, a fourth following later; once wrecked, they sank. These minutes shifted the arithmetic of carrier power in the Pacific. Although their aircrews mostly survived, the loss of 110 pilots was especially serious, as the Japanese had stressed the value of training and had produced an elite force of aviators. The Japanese looked upon a carrier and its combat aircraft as an inseparable unit, the aircraft as the ship's armaments, much like guns on fighting surface craft. Once lost, the pilots proved difficult to replace, not least because of a shortage of fuel for training. More seriously, the loss of four carriers' maintenance crews could not be made up.[22]

The Battle of Midway demonstrated the power of carriers, but also their serious vulnerability. They were essentially a first-strike weapon, and their vulnerability to gunfire and air attack led to a continued stress on battleships and cruisers, both of which were also very important for shore bombardment in support of amphibious operations. Air power in the Pacific was seen as a preliminary to these operations, rather than as a war-winning tool in its own right. These warships, moreover, provided a powerful antiaircraft screen for the carriers, while the Americans also had eight antiaircraft cruisers in the Pacific. More generally, surface ships remained crucial for conflict with other surface ships, not least because, although there were spectacular losses, many battleships took considerable punishment before being sunk by air attack. In addition, battleships were still necessary while other powers maintained the type. Furthermore, until reliable all-weather day-and-night reconnaissance and strike aircraft were available (which was really in the 1950s), surface ships provided the means of fighting at night.

As with their plan for Midway, the Japanese continued to assume that battleship firepower would play a key role in a decisive battle, and this assumption led them to underrate carrier strength. Although the Japanese maintained an advantage in naval night fighting that caused serious American naval losses, Midway was followed by American successes in the Guadalcanal campaign in the Solomon Islands in the winter of 1942–43. The island of Guadalcanal was seen by the Japanese as the key forward base to cut off the American reinforcement and supply of Australia and New Zealand. The Americans invaded the island with the reinforced First Marine Division on August 7, 1942, but the Japanese defeated the Allied naval screening force off Savo Island on August 9. The marines were left dependent for protection on mostly marine Wildcat fighters based on Henderson Field, the airstrip within the marine defensive perimeter. These were inferior to the Japanese fighters that escorted both bomber attacks on the Americans on Guadalcanal as well as destroyers transporting Japanese troops.

A battle of attrition in the air, at sea, and on land eventually moved the American way, and the Japanese evacuated their forces in early 1943. The Japanese had lost over six hundred airmen, many well-trained pilots who could not be replaced, and the same was true of the air war over New Guinea. These losses contributed to an increasingly apparent aspect of the Pacific War, a decline in the quality of Japanese air power that reflected an inability to ensure good training for pilots, one that was to be matched by Germany. In the Guadalcanal campaign, moreover, the Americans developed a degree of cooperation between land, sea, and air forces that was to serve them well in subsequent operations.

AIR WAR IN EUROPE IN 1942

In contrast, although aircraft were heavily involved in the war on the Eastern Front, they did not play such a major operational role as in the war in the Pacific. Air superiority, nevertheless, could still be highly significant locally. Thus, in the German capture of the Kerch Peninsula in eastern Crimea in May 1942, the Soviet lack of adequate air-land cooperation was exploited by the Germans, who benefited from effective air support. There were also heavy German air attacks on the besieged city of Sevastopol that June. However, later in the year, the German bombing of the city of Stalingrad, which became the focus of the German offensive, helped make it a wrecked terrain that made it very difficult for the German attackers to conquer. Heavily bombed by the Allies, Monte Cassino in Italy and Caen in Normandy served the Germans in a similar fashion in 1944.

Once the Soviet counterattack, launched on November 19, 1942, had led to the encirclement of the German Sixth Army on November 23—nearly a third of a million men—in and close to Stalingrad, the Germans sought to provide sufficient supplies by air. This proved impossible. The Sixth Army needed 750 tons of supplies a day. Göring said the Luftwaffe could deliver 300, but on most days the army received fewer than 90, although on one day 262 tons were landed. Aside from lacking the resources, the Luftwaffe had no contingency plans for such an operation. Protests from the local Luftwaffe commander about the lack of necessary transport assets and infrastructure were overruled by Göring. During the operation, substantial units from Luftflotte 4 were withdrawn to deal with the Anglo-American Torch landings in North Africa. This did not help the airlift, although the very attempt to mount a large-scale airlift testified to the advances made by air power, while what was transported helped keep the Sixth Army alive, albeit at the loss of 495 transport aircraft. The failure of ground troops to break through the encirclement, which instead became stronger, led to the surrender of the army on January 31 to February 2, 1943.[23]

Air power effectiveness, meanwhile, increased in the Mediterranean war. Blamey reported to the Australian prime minister in September 1941 that air support had become a priority for Allied forces planning to attack the Germans and Italians in North Africa:

Great advance in this in last two months. Attitude Air Force here most co-operative. . . . All suitable air squadrons to be trained in army co-operation and joint control organization for field co-operation being set up. During operations specific air units to be allotted to military organizations under control army commander with air controller on his staff.[24]

The RAF in North Africa focused on unrelenting offensive action against German supply and communication lines. This in turn drew German fighters into attritional battles for air superiority that they could not win. The increased provision of air support for British forces from July 1942 proved highly significant for a recovery of morale by the British Eighth Army and also hit German and Italian morale.[25] Ground-based aircraft played the key role in the Mediterranean. In contrast, the British used two carriers on May 5–7, 1942, to cover the successful attack on Diego Suarez, the main port in Madagascar, which was held by the Vichy French. This attack was followed by the British conquest of the island, which was completed in November.

The range of air-power operations expanded in 1942 with the stepping up of the Allied bombing of Germany and occupied Europe, bombing that was designed to have a direct impact on the Germans and to meet Soviet pressure for action. Churchill insisted to the Soviets that the bomber offensive constituted a "Second Front" against Germany. A British strategic review of August 1941 had noted the consequences of British forces being unable to compete with the Germans in Continental Europe. The response of Britain, at that stage the operationally weaker power, was to seek strategic advantage from indirect attack, in the shape of bombing, blockade, and subversion, each of which was designed to hit the German economy and German morale:

Bombing on a vast scale is the weapon upon which we principally depend for the destruction of German economic life and morale. To achieve its object the bombing offensive must be on the heaviest possible scale and we aim at a force limited in size only by operational difficulties in the UK. After meeting the needs of our own security we give to the heavy bomber first priority in production.

Our policy at present is concentrate upon targets which affect both the German transportation system and morale. As our forces increase we intend to pass to a planned attack on civilian morale with the intensity and continuity which are essential for success. We be-

lieve that by these methods applied on a vast scale the whole structure on which the German forces are based can be destroyed. As a
result these forces will suffer such a decline in fighting power and
mobility that direct [British] action will once more become possible.

It was even mistakenly believed that these methods might be enough to
make Germany sue for peace.[26]

On the night of May 30–31, 1942, the British launched over 1,050
bombers at the German city of Cologne: 40 were lost. Although the
raid, which killed over 460 people, did not achieve all its objectives in
terms of the destruction of industry and morale, it indicated the ability
of the Allies to make a major attack on a German city and was seen as a
way to persuade the British public that the Germans could be hit hard.
Arthur Harris, appointed commander-in-chief of Bomber Command on
February 23, 1942, was determined to show the viability of RAF attacks
and to stop talk of ending bombing and allocating the bombers to help
the navy and the army. The raid saw the use of the bomber-stream
tactic, with bombers gathered in one stream in order to use mass to
counteract the power of the defenses.

However, for attacks to be sustained, it would be necessary to have a
major buildup in air power, in terms of not only the number of aircraft,
but also their quality, including their payload. The small bombers, such
as the Hampden I and the Blenheim, were not fast enough and had
poor defensive capabilities. Indeed, the concept of the small bomber
was not fully thought out. These aircraft were withdrawn from bombing
in 1942 and 1943, respectively. Britain lacked an effective bomber until
the advent of the Lancaster into operational service in March 1942. The
Stirling and Halifax bombers lacked the power and bomb load (twenty-
two thousand pounds) of the Lancaster. Similarly, there were long
problems with the conception, planning, production, deployment, and
use of British tanks, although by 1943 these had improved, as production was concentrated on fewer designs.[27]

As a sign of what was to come, most of the casualties in Cologne
were civilian. In attacking Germany, the RAF was supplemented by the
Americans (flying from British bases) from July 1942. The Cologne
attack was an exception, as most of the raids in 1942 were fairly small
scale. The cities of the Ruhr industrial region, notably Essen and Dort-
mund, were the main targets. The raids were important to the development of an effective ground-support system to support a bombing of-

fensive, as well as in the gaining of operational experience, a process necessary for the American and British armies and navies as well as for the air forces. The Germans, in turn, continued to bomb British cities, especially in the Baedecker raids, devastating, for example, the city of Exeter.

As a reminder of the varied use of air power, and the extent to which high specifications were not necessarily a key characteristic of its use, the RAF used aircraft to overawe crowds threatening strategic railways during the anti-British "Quit India" campaign in 1942–44.[28] This looked toward the governmental use of aircraft to overfly demonstrating crowds in Cairo during the "Arab Spring" in 2011.

AIR WAR IN 1943: EASTERN FRONT AND MEDITERRANEAN

In 1943, there were again contrasts between the significance of air warfare on different fronts, however intense it might be. On the Eastern Front, there was this intensity, but not an accompanying strategic significance. Thus, the successful German counteroffensive under Manstein in March 1943 benefited from the ability to defeat the Russians in the air, albeit at the cost of many aircraft, but this ability was not the key element. So also with the German Kursk offensive in July, which showed how, despite inflicting more losses on its opponents, the struggle in the air had moved against the Luftwaffe. Large numbers of Soviet fighters prevented it from gaining control of the skies, and, although German ground-attack aircraft inflicted much damage on Soviet forces, the same was true of their opponents. Moreover, there were improvements in Soviet aircraft, with the YAK-9U fighter, the LA-7 fighter, and the TU-2 bomber entering squadron service in 1943. At the same time, the Soviet focus on close air support ensured that there was no systematic attempt to destroy the Luftwaffe and obtain, as a result, broader air superiority.[29]

Air power also played a major role in the Mediterranean in 1943, although without being decisive. The Anglo-American invasion of Sicily on July 10 had been preceded by a thorough air assault during June, which had neutralized the Axis airfields and gained the Allies control of the air over the invasion zone. However, the use of airborne troops for the invasion proved difficult: due to strong winds, many of the gliders landed in the sea. Inexperienced and undertrained pilots were a problem, as was a lack of coordination with Allied naval forces who fired on the airborne armada, causing significant casualties and breaking up the cohesion of the transports and glider tugs. On Sicily, the airborne troops were scattered and without heavy weapons support. Moreover, the provision of effective air support for land operations proved hard to secure, both there and in continental Italy when it was invaded later in the year.

The successful evacuation of Messina by the Germans was a major failure in the Allies' campaign in Sicily. The Germans, over a period of six nights, finishing on August 16–17, evacuated nearly sixty thousand of their own troops, with most of their supplies, and a similar number of Italian troops. These forces were to take an important part in the defense of Italy. The narrowness of the Strait of Messina caused unpredictable currents, and the Allied naval commanders were reluctant to risk their ships in the confined area. The Germans also put in place a heavy concentration of flak batteries on both sides of the strait, and the flak batteries provided interlocking fire, which RAF pilots described as worse than over Essen. Although the Germans initially began their evacuation by night, they switched to daylight as their antiaircraft cover was so effective. Nevertheless, once obtained, Allied land control over southern Italy provided air bases, notably near Bari and Foggia, both captured in September 1943, that extended the Allied air assault on the German Empire, notably in the Balkans.

In contrast, the British inability to secure local air superiority over the Germans led to a serious British failure in the Dodecanese Islands campaign in the Aegean in September–November 1943. The establishment of garrisons on Leros, Cos, and the other islands was ill conceived, poorly resourced, and badly executed. This failure indicated the continued importance of air power, which, in this case, the Germans were able to deploy effectively, in part because of the greater flexibility brought by land-based air power. Operating at extreme range, the RAF, which lost 113 aircraft, was outclassed, and the army units, lacking effective air cover, suffered accordingly, while the British warships tended to keep to the dark.[30] British failure formed a striking contrast with American successes in the Pacific, where island targets were isolated before attack.

AIR WAR IN 1943: PACIFIC

Indeed, air power played a key strategic role in the Pacific. The time taken to defeat the Japanese on Guadalcanal in 1942–43, as well as the large number of islands they continued to hold, ensured that it would be necessary to focus American efforts carefully, a policy that required the identification of key targets. Thanks to increasing American air and sea superiority, a superiority that was dependent in part on new construction, it was easier to bypass Japanese bases, such as Rabaul on New Britain, which then could be isolated. Moreover, thanks to this superiority, the Japanese were less able to mount ripostes. Superior American interwar leadership development, based at the war colleges, and focused on the solving of complex higher operational and strategic problems, contributed to wartime successes. The American "twin drives" across the Pacific were a great military operational feat, and air power was central in them. Carriers played a major role in the island hopping, but so also did the creation and securing of airfields. They were important not only for their attack role, but also as part of the far-flung American command-and-control and supply systems. American and Australian operations in New Guinea depended heavily on air support, not least in the successful raids on the Japanese airfield at Wewak on August 17–18, 1943, after which Allied ground operations were rarely threatened.[31]

Whereas the Japanese had not introduced new classes of planes, the Americans had done so, and then produced the planes and their munitions in large numbers, and trained pilots accordingly. This process enabled the Americans to challenge the Zero, which had made such an impact in the initial Japanese advances. Now the Americans had the Corsair (which entered operations in February 1943) and the Hellcat (which entered operations that August), each of which outperformed the Zero. So also did the Lightning, a twin-engine aircraft in service from 1941. The Corsair and the Hellcat had powerful Pratt and Whitney air-cooled radial engines. In addition, their specifications included better protection, which enabled them to take more punishment than Japanese planes. The Japanese had designed the Zero with insufficient protection, in part because its light weight increased range and maneuverability, but also because the safety of their pilots was a low priority. The pilots themselves wanted the range and maneuverability over the protection: they were good samurai, and the samurai never used shields. When combined with the growing disparity in quality between pilots, a matter of numbers, training, and flying experience, it was clear that the Japanese could not compensate for growing numerical weakness in the air, though, with their emphasis on willpower, they were apt to believe they could.

Masters in aerial combat, American fighters were able to provide cover for their bombers, which, anyway, were better able than their counterparts in Europe to deal with opposition without heavy losses. In part, this was because, with far more territory to cover, the Japanese lacked a fighter defense system to match that of the Germans. The Japanese had a lower density of fighters and lacked the integrated nature of the German defense system, as well as its capacity to improve. Moreover, Japanese airfields were without protective radar, which weakened Wewak in 1943. It was easier to isolate island targets in the Pacific than in the Mediterranean: the American navy could concentrate force more effectively as a result.

AIR WAR IN 1943 AT SEA

In 1943, Allied air power was highly significant for the war against German submarines. The submarine bases and building yards in Europe such as Brest were bombed, but the value of these attacks was limited by the heavy fortification of the concrete-covered U-boat pens and bases, and by a lack of concrete-penetrating weapons. Attacking submarines at sea proved difficult: the RAF's capacity to navigate accurately over water was poor (too many missions ending as "Convoy Not Found"), while the RAF had equipped itself with a totally inadequate series of antisubmarine weapons.

In the event, air power in the shape of long-range aircraft was important to the Allied victory in the Atlantic. Already based in Britain, Iceland, and Canada, land-based American VLR (very long range) four-engine Liberators based in the (Portuguese) Azores were the key to closing the mid-Atlantic air gap in October 1943, and thus to denying submarines their safest hunting ground, which was to the west of the Azores. Air bases were established on the islands of Terceira and Santa Maria. They were subsequently to prove important American bases during the Cold War. Of the wartime airfields near where I live, Dunkeswell, built in 1941–42 for the RAF, was used by the US Navy from 1943 for long-range antisubmarine patrols and flew PB4Ys, a maritime version of the B-24.

Mass was a key element, and it demonstrated anew the ability of American industry to produce large quantities of all sorts of weapons. The number of aircraft deployed against submarines in the Atlantic rose from 595 in late 1942 to 1,300 a year later.[32] The availability of more aircraft meant that submarines could not safely sail from their French bases across the Bay of Biscay on the surface, and thus used up some of their supply of electricity, as the recharging of batteries had to be done on the surface, which made submarines increasingly vulnerable to air attack.

Furthermore, antisubmarine air tactics became more effective. Submarines were visible when they were below the surface if they were at insufficient depth. The snorkel, operational from 1944, enabled submarines to run their diesels and remain submerged, but not at sufficient depth to avoid detection from the air. A submarine just below the surface was visible from the air, so submarines operating in waters within the range of aerial antisubmarine patrols had to be either on the surface and maintaining aircraft watches continuously, or far enough below the surface to prevent detection from the air. More effective antisubmarine tactics by 1942 reflected improved synchronization with convoy movements, notably flying slightly ahead and on either side, and also incremental steps, such as better radar (and improved use of it), better searchlights, improved fuses for depth charges, the use of white paint that made it harder to spot aircraft, and enhanced maintenance. Much of this improvement stemmed from the application of the findings of British Coastal Command's Operational Research Station. British aircraft operating against submarines were under joint operational control, an important aid to effectiveness. The greater availability of escort carriers was also important. Aside from sinking submarines, the presence of aircraft was important in deterring attacks by them.

The Battle of the Pacific was primarily a carrier conflict, while that of the Atlantic was essentially a submarine war. In both, the ability to apply air power was crucial. Air power also helped limit the role of German surface warships. A clear demonstration of the vulnerability of warships to air attack was provided by the fate of the forty-two-thousand-ton German battleship *Bismarck*, which, having triumphed over a British intercepting force and sunk the battle cruiser *Hood*, was spotted by a flying boat and crippled by a hit on the rudder by a torpedo launched from a Swordfish biplane on May 26, 1941, after which she was sunk by surface warships. The torpedoing of the heavy cruiser *Lützow* by British air attack on June 12, 1941, ended the surface raiding of Atlantic sea routes. Concern about a possible British invasion of Norway and their vulnerability to air attack led the Germans to withdraw their major warships from Brest on February 12, 1942, although British attempts to sink these ships in the Channel and North Sea totally failed. Deception and the jamming of British radar achieved surprise, and effective German air defenses had been secretly massed to cover the breakout. A unified German command structure in this case was also important.

Norway became an important base for operations against British convoys taking supplies to the Soviet Union, but the serious inroads of German airplanes and, in particular, submarines were not matched by surface ships. The German battleship *Tirpitz*—sister ship of the *Bismarck*—which had sailed to Trondheim in Norway in January 1942, fell victim, after attacks by British bombers and midget submarines, to British bombing on November 12, 1944. The development of the twelve-thousand-pound (5,430 kg) Tallboy bomb, operational from June 1944, was crucial: two hit the ship. These heavier bombs also ensured that the RAF was able to inflict damage on the concrete submarine "pens" in Bergen, Norway. The twenty-two-thousand-pound (10,955 kg) Grand Slam bomb became operational the following March.

THE AIR ATTACK ON GERMANY, 1943

While Japan remained out of the range of regular and heavy American air attack, especially once the Chinese air bases initially used had been overrun by the Japanese in 1942, in an offensive deliberately launched for that purpose, Germany was under heavy air attack by 1943. Wartime factors accentuated the use of bombing, not simply the determination to employ available forces, but also the need to show domestic and international audiences that efforts were being made. A belief that the war being waged was a total one served to justify bombing, and, in turn, the latter was an instrumental demonstration that the war was indeed total. At the Casablanca Conference that January, the Americans and British agreed on what was termed the Combined Bomber Offensive, with the Americans attacking by daylight and the British by night. This was seen as a way to show Stalin that the Western Allies were doing their utmost to weaken Germany, and thus to aid Soviet operations. Similarly, the commitment at Casablanca to unconditional surrender by the Axis powers as a war goal was designed to reassure Stalin.

At Casablanca, it was agreed that the bombing should serve to destroy the German economic system and so hit German popular morale that the capacity for armed resistance would be fatally weakened. As most German factories were in cities, these goals were linked. Until the opening of the Second Front, by invading German-held France in 1944, this was the most effective way to hit at Germany. Although challenged by the strategic depth Germany enjoyed thanks to its conquests in 1940, strategic bombing was made more feasible by four-engine bombers, such as the British Lancaster, as well as by heavier bombs and thanks to developments in navigational aids and training.

The availability of large numbers of bombers reflected Allied industrial capacity, with American and British production of aircraft rising from over 70,000 in 1942 to over 120,000 in 1944. The Allies considerably outbuilt their opponents in the air. Numbers, however, were not the sole issue. The Allies also developed the ability to organize production so that it could be retooled quickly for improved marks and to ensure the production of a range of aircraft with different capabilities.

The first American raids deep into Germany occurred in February 1943 when the major rail marshaling yard at Hamm was attacked, finally with success on March 2. The Americans focused on daytime high-altitude precision bombing to hit industrial targets, especially ball-bearing factories. This reflected the unsuitability of the B-17 bomber for night flying and American criticism of the value of British area bombing. The British wished to destroy industrial targets, but the Butt report on night raids in June–July 1941 showed that they were not doing so. Accuracy was difficult with nighttime freefall bombing, and also, despite American bombsights, with daytime bombing, for there was no electronic navigation or target identification and no guided bombs. Instead, concerned about the daytime vulnerability of their bombers, the British focused, from March 1942, on nighttime area bombing. There was a similar contrast in the bombing of Italy by the Americans and the British.

Area bombing could lead to heavy civilian casualties, many of them factory workers, and this was seen by the protagonists of the policy, notably Harris, as likely to wreck German and Italian morale and thus their ability to continue the war. Cities were ranked on their economic importance as targets. Thirty-four to forty thousand people were killed in the British raids on Hamburg in July 1943, notably on July 28 as the result of a firestorm created by a combination of incendiary and high-explosive bombs. The impact was horrifying: those killed were either suffocated or burned to death. The raid, which followed the first firestorm, at Wuppertal on May 29–30, in which over 3,500 people were killed, badly affected German morale, leading to the partial evacuation of cities, including Hamburg and Berlin, and helped to bring about a marked increase in criticism of the Nazi regime.

Although the B-17 was a steady platform that could carry a large bomb load, precision bombing was not an easy alternative. Indeed, with bombs with lethal radii measured in a few tens of feet, a bombing tactic that involved bombardment squadrons all dropping simultaneously could not be accurately described as precision. Moreover, heavily armed bomber formations lacking fighter escorts proved far less effective, both in defending themselves and in destroying targets, than had been anticipated in interwar bombing doctrine. This conviction in the value of the bomber was partly responsible for a failure to push the development of long-range fighters sufficiently early. Prior to the introduction of long-range fighters, bombers were very vulnerable to interceptors. German day fighters learned to attack head-on because the top turret could not fire forward. B-17s were supposed to fly in box formations of four to provide mutual fire support, but, once the box was broken, the aircraft became easy targets. Diving steeply onto the formations, or attacking from above and behind, gave the fighters the edge. As a result, in a classic instance of the action-reaction cycle, a forward-firing chin turret with two remotely operated .50-caliber Brownings, the most defensive machine guns of any model, was added with the B-17G, introduced in July 1943.

Cripplingly heavy casualty rates occurred in some raids, notably the American ones against the ball-bearing factory at Schweinfurt in August and October 1943. Nineteen percent of the aircraft on the August 17 raid were lost, mostly to German fighters, and the factory continued to operate. The Germans had developed a complex and wide-ranging system of radar warning, with long-range, early-warning radars, as well as short-range radars that guided night fighters (which also had their own radars) toward the bombers. Indeed, the strength of the German resistance was a major reason, alongside bombing inaccuracy, inadequate intelligence, and poor weather, for the failure of the bombing to match optimistic prewar expectations.

Each was a significant factor. For example, poor industrial research greatly reduced the effectiveness of both British and American bombing. Although the locations of the head offices and major plants of most leading German companies were known, there was little or no knowledge of precisely what was made and where. Further, when the right city was known, it all too often was not known which industrial location made the most critical components or processed the critical materials. Thus, in the bombing of Darmstadt in 1944, what was presented as a large "chemical complex" to the north of the city and was attacked by the American Eighth Air Force was in fact producing routine pharmaceuticals and simple industrial-grade hospital equipment of no vital importance. In contrast, the Russelsheim plant of Adam Opel AG, a wholly owned subsidiary of General Motors, produced crucial connecting rods for diesel engines; but the American parent company did not know where the relevant plant was located within the huge complex, and "best guess" raids missed. Albert Speer quickly dispersed this manufacturing immediately on taking over direction of German industry. In addition, the attack on Schweinfurt involved a failure to understand the structure of the target company. This failure was also to be seen in the bombing of Japan. In the postwar period, in contrast, both Soviet and NATO forces made industry structure a priority intelligence task in preparing for a possible conflict.

The air war over Europe became attritional in 1943. There were problems with identifying the target, even in daylight and without anti-aircraft guns or enemy fighters, and accuracy remained heavily dependent on the skill of the pathfinder aircraft that preceded the bombers in order to identify targets. The technology to make precision bombing possible did not really exist. Despite improvements, the American Norden bombsight could not deliver the precision claimed. Indeed, until the advent of the smart bomb, which was used by the Americans from the Vietnam War (see chapter 8), "precision bombing" is a largely misapplied term. There were some notable exceptions, such as the British bombing of Amiens prison on February 18, 1944, by Mosquitoes in order to free resistance leaders, but this was a very low-altitude attack by a small number of fast twin-engine bombers. So also with the successful attack by Mosquitoes and American Mustang fighters against the Gestapo headquarters in Copenhagen in March 1945.

The needs of air defense ensured that much German military production was devoted to aircraft and antiaircraft guns (around 60 percent in 1943),[33] while Luftwaffe strength was increasingly concentrated in Germany, to the detriment of ground support, although much of the Luftwaffe continued to be employed on the Eastern Front. The protection of Germany from air attack reflected the concern about the prestige of the Nazi regime and the morale of the German populace that bombing gave rise to. Joseph Goebbels, the Nazi propaganda chief, sought to maintain morale in the face of bombing, not least by ensuring that the civil relief program worked well. The availability of more air power on the Eastern Front would have been operationally useful to Germany, but, given Soviet resources, it would not have had strategic effect there. In this respect, the contribution of the Allied air offensive to Soviet campaigning was very valuable, but not decisive.

A long-term emphasis on bombers, as well as the consequences of heavy aircraft losses from 1940 and a failure to increase aircraft production significantly until 1943, meant that the German fighter arm was weak. Moreover, the Germans suffered from being the focus of Allied attention. However, in response to the Allied bombers, German fighter-bombers and medium bombers were adapted to act as night fighters. Moreover, the Hamburg raid was followed by the development by the Germans of new night-fighting methods that were not dependent on radar. Radar-defense systems could be wrecked by the British use of "window," dropping strips of aluminum foil that appeared like bombers on the radar screens. In response, the Germans relied on radar guidance to the general area of British air activity, which "window" contributed to, and on visual sightings thereafter. This caused British losses to mount from the late summer of 1943. Furthermore, that autumn, German radar was adapted so as to be able to circumvent the impact of "window."

This action-reaction cycle was seen in other aspects of the air war. The British Lancaster bomber had a very advanced communications system for its time. Lancasters were fitted with the R1155 receiver and T1154 transmitter, ensuring radio direction firing. However, the Lancaster's H2S ground-looking navigation radar system, fitted from 1943, was eventually homed in on by the German night fighters' NAXOS receiver and had to be used with discretion. The H2S was supplemented by Fishpond, which provided additional coverage of aircraft attacking from beneath and displayed it on an auxiliary screen in the radio operator's position. Fishpond was designed to counter German night fighters equipped with upward firing cannon fitted in the fuselage so that they could fly parallel with the bomber but under it before shooting it down. Monica, rearward-looking radar designed to warn of night-fighter approaches, served as a homing beacon for suitably equipped night fighters and was therefore removed, while the ABC radar-jamming equipment could be tracked by the Germans, which led to heavy casualties. The development of radar was shown with the Village Inn, a radar-aimed rear turret fitted to some Lancasters in 1944. In November 1943, the RAF formed 100 Group (Bomber Support), which flew electronic countermeasures aircraft as well as operating night intruders in order to attack German night fighters, among many other activities all designed to reduce bomber losses.

Moreover, with OBOE, a targeting system first used in December 1941, and Gee-H, a radio navigation device introduced in 1942, the British developed accurate radio navigation systems, which ensured that weather, darkness, and smog were less of an obstacle to bombing. Gee, however, was limited to about 350 miles. It was the Pathfinder aircraft, which used OBOE, target makers, and H2S, that made the big difference by 1944, providing a valuable combination of technology and tactics. The last use of H2S was in 1993.

Meanwhile, Anglo-American bombing had had a heavy impact on Italy. About 60 percent of Italy's industrial capacity was wrecked. Around sixty thousand Italian civilians were killed in bombing during the war, which for Italy lasted from 1940 to 1945. Italian morale was badly affected, with the damaging attacks on the industrial centers of Genoa, Milan, and Turin in early 1943 leading to strikes and demonstrations for peace. There was anger about the government's inability to protect civilians. The Allies deliberately sought to encourage such atti-

tudes through the bombing and underlined this message through extensive leafleting.[34] The deficiencies of antiaircraft defenses and civilian
shelters contributed to this situation. The home front was close to collapse.[35] However, it was the Allied invasion of Sicily on July 10 that
precipitated Mussolini's overthrow by senior members of the military
and governmental leadership on July 25.

ALLIED GROUND SUPPORT, 1944

In 1944, it was again campaigning on land that was decisive in Europe,
while carriers provided a more significant role for air power in the war
against Japan, or, at least, in America's war. On the Eastern Front, both
the Germans and the Soviets employed air power principally in ground
support. Benefiting from a major rise in the production of aircraft, from
about fifteen thousand in 1941 to about forty thousand in 1944, the
Soviets had far more aircraft, while their tactical and operational effectiveness had improved. They were therefore better able to drive the
Luftwaffe from the battlefield. The Soviets focused on ground support,
complementing ground attack with close interdiction missions that hit
German mobility, whether reinforcing, or withdrawing from, the zone
of attack. The high German casualties that resulted from the integrated
use of air power may be referred to as tactical, but it had a strategic
consequence.[36] Operation Bagration, the advance through Belarus that
led to the destruction of Army Group Centre, was supported at the
outset, in June 1944, by over six thousand Soviet aircraft out of a frontline strength of thirteen thousand. The Germans, in contrast, had under
two thousand aircraft for the entire Eastern Front.

In turn, the rapid Soviet advance further south across the rivers
Dniester and Prut led to the surrender of Romania on August 23. The
loss of control over Romanian oil, the only significant source of nonsyn-
thetic oil in the German-dominated section of Europe, affected the fuel
that could be spared for the training of German pilots. The German
shortage of fuel encouraged the process by which members of the Luftwaffe were switched to deployment for ground warfare. In 1943, Romania had produced 2,406,000 tons of petroleum products for Germany, a
supply Hitler regarded as crucial. Italian-based American air attacks in
April–August 1944 destroyed most of the refineries.

Air power proved important in support of Anglo-American operations in Western Europe. In Italy, air power backed amphibious landings at Salerno in September 1943 and Anzio in February 1944. German counteroffensives could be stopped by air attack, although the weather was a key element in determining its effectiveness. General Alexander wrote about Anzio, "Given reasonable weather we should be able to break up any large concentration [German] counter-attack by switching on the whole of the Mediterranean Air Force, as we did at Salerno."[37] However, the Germans were rapidly able to repair bombing damage to rail links in Italy and to lessen the Allied advantage over Anzio by bringing in aircraft from Germany, France, Greece, and northern Italy.[38]

If by the time of the Normandy landings on June 6, 1944, D-Day, the Germans had lost the air war, this was a hard-won success, and German aircraft production actually rose to a peak in 1944.[39] The contrast with the earlier situation, like that, from the spring of 1943, in the Battle of the Atlantic against German submarines, was one of the reasons why the Allies were wise to delay until 1944 the opening of a Second Front by invading France. Only two Luftwaffe pilots fired shots in anger on June 6. German units treated aircraft as probably hostile, while Allied soldiers assumed that aircraft would be Allied. The contrast between the Luftwaffe's ability to threaten the British retreat from Dunkirk in 1940 and its failure to disrupt the Normandy landings was striking. However, on the following two days, the Luftwaffe did manage to put up more aircraft.

The Allied invasion of Normandy displayed an advantage of air power in the shape of delivering troops by parachute and glider landings. These troops proved important in securing the flanks of the Allied landings, notably by dropping American parachutists behind Utah Beach, on the western flank of the landings, and by British glider-borne troops seizing Pegasus Bridge to the east of the British landings. The botched American air drop was not helped by the aircraft being flown by crews who had no night-drop experience and by an unexpected bank of clouds, which made the pilots disperse widely for fear of collision. The drop was in many respects worse than the German drop on Crete in 1941. Nevertheless, what was remarkable about the dispersed troops on the ground was that the vast majority went about trying to fulfill their tasks even though they were often with men they did not know, which involved the need to resolve differing objectives. The disorganized nature of the air drop handicapped the German defense, as there were no coordinated targets to counterattack, while the Germans thought the attacks were over a much wider area than was the actual plan. The Americans took fewer casualties than were anticipated on Utah, in large part because the crucial fighting had already taken place inland.

However, the effectiveness of the parachutists owed much to the rapid advance of American troops from the landing sites, as the former lacked the necessary armaments to resist German armored attack. As yet, there had not been the development of helicopters, which were to provide the basis for new capabilities in vertical envelopment, ground support, and resupply. Had the Germans had massed armored forces available, the parachutists would have been overrun. Neither the American parachutists nor the British glider-borne troops on D-Day had any heavy equipment. It was only with the unsuccessful British airborne operation at Arnhem that September that 75 mm pack howitzers arrived by glider. Moreover, ammunition supply was a big problem for such operations. Only the huge Anglo-American drop across the Rhine in March 1945 was entirely successful. The problems of mass airborne drops had been learned the hard way.

On D-Day, much of the supporting firepower for the invasion force was provided by British and American warships. The bombers found it difficult to deliver the promised quantities of bombs on target and on time. The targeting of the German Atlantic Wall fortifications by warships and bombers was not as good as it should have been, so that many of the casemates and bunkers were not hit, while the Allies overestimated how effective shells and bombs would be against concrete, notably in the American assault on Omaha Beach. Steel-reinforced concrete, a composite material in which a three-dimensional lattice of steel has concrete poured over it, is very resistant to high explosives, and on D-Day, even direct hits by fifteen-inch shells and by one-thousand-pound bombs made very little impact on the structures, although the concussive effect of explosions was demoralizing to the occupants of the bunkers. Most gun emplacements that were put out of action by warships or bombers along the Atlantic Wall had their guns badly damaged rather than their concrete casements or bunkers destroyed in the action. Moreover, the defenders ran out of ammunition.

Despite Allied air attacks, both before and after D-Day, especially on bridges, attacks that the air force leadership regarded as a distraction from their air war on the German heartland, the Germans were able to reinforce their units in Normandy. Nevertheless, the delays forced on the German army by the air attacks both ensured that the Allies gained time to deepen their bridgehead and obliged the Germans to respond in an ad hoc fashion to Allied advances. When the German armor was eventually used in bulk, on June 29–30, it was stopped by Allied air attack. Allied ground-attack aircraft also played a role in wrecking the German tank counterattack launched through Mortain on August 7, 1944, although the defense by American ground forces, notably their artillery, was more important. On the earlier pattern of the Stuka on Allied forces, the rocket-firing Typhoon had a serious impact on German morale. Germans who were captured in Normandy said that the two main differences between fighting in Normandy and on the Eastern Front were, first, the lack of night operations in Normandy and, second, the ever-present threat from "Jabos": British and American ground-attack fighter-bombers. However, these aircraft inflicted less damage in practice. The accurate targeting of unguided rockets was very difficult against tanks, indeed against anything smaller than a train.[40]

The Germans were unable to challenge Allied command of the air over the combat zone and over the nearby communication routes, which therefore deprived them of reconnaissance. Intermediate-stage (between tactical and strategic) bombing had been developed by the British, using Wellingtons and Blenheims, and by the Americans, using B-25s and B-26s. This was seen in early 1944 in the bombing of Monte Cassino in Italy and of northern France.

The Normandy campaign also saw the successful use of close air support for Allied land forces, notably with the cab-rank system provided by the Second Tactical Air Force.[41] The effectiveness of Allied ground support owed much to the long-term process of gaining air superiority over the Luftwaffe, but there had also been improvements in doctrine and organization, including the use of air liaison teams with the army, as well as improvement in radio communications.[42] Allied aircraft were used in ground support, both against specific targets and for "carpet bombing." The latter was unsuccessful in the advance of British forces in Operation Goodwood, but more successful in the advance of American troops in the breakout from Normandy, Operation Cobra, in late July, although many of the bombs fell on American positions, killing numerous troops and delaying the start of the operation. Despite failures in coordination, as in Operation Cobra and the bombing of Monte Cassino, the Allies had become far more skilled at integrating their forces. However, air support could not prevent heavy casualties in ground fighting. The British field commander in Northwestern Europe, Field Marshal Montgomery, was to write in December 1944,

> Present operations in Western Europe in all stages have been combined Army/Air operations . . . the overall contribution of the Air Forces to the successes gained has been immense. . . . The greatest asset of air power is its flexibility. . . . The moral effect of air action is very great and is out of proportion to the material damage inflicted. . . . It is necessary to win the air battle before embarking on the land battle. . . . Technical developments in the air weapon continue apace and their possibilities are bounded only by the imagination. It follows that land operations are likely to be influenced more and more by air action. [43]

Allied ground attack proved so significant that, in December 1944, Hitler launched the counterattack that led to the Battle of the Bulge only when bad weather promised protection. This was a major contrast with the German offensive in 1940 when the Germans had wanted good weather in order to ensure air support, as well as to use parachutists and glider-borne troops in Belgium and the Netherlands. In turn, once the weather had improved in the winter of 1944–45, ground-support air attacks helped the Allies regain the initiative, and proved particularly important against German tanks. [44]

GERMAN ROCKET ATTACKS, 1944

Just as in the First World War, bombing increased in the later stages of the conflict, so air attacks on the economic capability and civilian morale of opponents were stepped up in 1944. The biggest change in weapon systems occurred with the beginning of rocket attacks by Germany. Ground-to-ground V-1s, launched at Britain from June 13, were followed, from September 8, by V-2s, which traveled at up to three thousand miles per hour, could be fired from a considerable distance, and could not be destroyed by antiaircraft fire as the V-1s could be. The problems encountered in hitting German bombers during the Blitz had led to the Anglo-American development of the proximity fuse. Widely used in the Pacific in 1943, the proximity fuse was responsible for the vast majority of V-1s shot down.

Large numbers of rockets were aimed at London, which was hit by 2,419 V-1s and 517 V-2s. Morale was badly hit. Other targets were also hit. More than 4,000 V-1s and 1,700 V-2s were fired at Greater Antwerp, reflecting the importance of its harbor for Allied operations, although the majority did not reach the port area, not least because of the bottleneck in the supply of rocket fuel as well as the limitations of the weapon. The casualties and damage inflicted by rockets led the British to devote particular effort to air raids on production facilities, as well as to capturing the launching pads in the advance from Normandy. This effort was an instance of the extent to which Allied bombing was devoted to far more than attacking German cities.[45]

The use of missiles reflected the inability of the Germans to sustain air attacks on Britain, as well as Hitler's fascination with new technology and the idea that it could bring a paradigm leap forward in military capability and satisfy the prospect of retaliation for British bombing.[46] Missiles, in fact, lacked the multipurpose capacity of aircraft. Moreover, their explosive payload was small. Because the rocket had to reenter the Earth's atmosphere, the nose cone heated up due to friction, which affected the payload that could be carried. Moreover, due to the lack of a reliable guidance system, the missiles could not be aimed accurately. The rush by the Germans to force the V-2 into service when the war was increasingly going very badly for them helped to lead to a high margin of error. The manufacture of missiles was symptomatic of the nature of the German war economy, with the harsh and murderous treatment of brutalized and malnourished foreign slave labor leading to high death rates.[47]

THE ALLIED AIR ATTACK ON GERMANY, 1944

Allied air attacks, meanwhile, had changed in intensity and method. Attacks on distant targets proved costly, reflecting the extent to which control and use of the air over Germany were difficult to gain. British night attacks on Berlin from November 18, 1943, until March 31, 1944, which Harris had promised would undermine German morale, led, instead, to the loss of 492 bombers, a rate of loss (5.2 percent overall; 9.1 percent on the final attack) that could not be sustained, despite a major expansion in the production of aircraft and the training of pilots.[48] The British raid on Nuremberg on March 30–31, 1944, led to the loss of 106 out of the 782 bombers. There was only limited damage to the city, and few German fighters were shot down. This led to the end of the bomber-stream technique of approaching the target, a technique that had exposed the slow, vulnerable, and highly flammable Lancasters to the cannon of more mobile German night fighters. The 20,224 British bomber sorties against German cities from November 1943 to March 1944 encountered formidable defenses, while the bad winter weather also caused serious problems.

However, the Allied air attack was stepped up that year as a result of the American introduction of long-range fighters. P-38s (twin-engine Lightnings), P-47s (Thunderbolts, which used drop fuel tanks), and P-51s (Mustangs, which also used drop fuel tanks) provided necessary escorts for the bombers and also enabled Allied fighters to seek out German fighters and thus to win the air war above Germany. This contrasted with the Luftwaffe's failed offensive on Britain in 1940–41: the Germans had lost the air war over Britain and had been unable to accompany serious devastation of Britain with the destruction or degradation of the British air force. Benefiting, as with tanks and other arms, from major economies of scale, the Americans were able to build large numbers of fighters: fourteen thousand Mustangs were built. Drop fuel tanks increased the range of aircraft, and in 1944 increasingly large tanks were introduced. The P-47, which entered squadron service in 1944, was the largest, heaviest single-engine fighter of the Second World War, and it could take a huge amount of punishment, which was a characteristic of many American aircraft. Fighter escorts could go all the way to Germany and take part in dogfights once there. The American engagement with long-range fighters was, for long, not matched by the conceptually more conservative RAF leadership.[49] This was an instance of the way in which the range of available resources and policies, which had grown greatly with large-scale air capability, created

THE SECOND WORLD WAR

particular demands on command-and-control skills and planning systems and therefore enhanced their role.

Whereas the Germans focused on a new technology, in the shape of rockets, the Allies benefited more from developing an existing technology by equipping long-range fighters with drop fuel tanks. The superiority of American long-range fighters to German interceptors was demonstrated in late February and March 1944, when, especially in "Big Week," major American raids in clear weather on German sites producing aircraft and oil led to large-scale battles with German interceptors, which could not avoid battle in these circumstances. Many American bombers were shot down, but the Luftwaffe also lost large numbers of aircraft and pilots as a result of the American policy of attrition. From 1944, the American fighters focused on seeking out the Luftwaffe, rather than on close bomber support.[50] There had also been heavy Luftwaffe losses over combat zones, notably on the Eastern Front.

Pilots were very difficult to replace, in large part because German training programs had not been increased in 1940–42, as was necessary given the scale of the war. This helped to ensure that, irrespective of aircraft construction figures, the Germans would be far weaker in the air. German aircraft construction was itself hit hard in these raids. Toward the end, the Germans, affected by the Allied bombing of synthetic oil plants, could not afford the fuel for training, while a lack of training time was also a consequence of the shortage of pilots. Fuel shortages had a similar impact on the Japanese. In mid-1944, Allied pilots received up to 400 hours of training, but their German counterparts received only about 110. The net effect was a lack of trained pilots comparable in quality to those of the Allies, a lack that led to a high accident rate, killing pilots and wrecking aircraft, and that particularly lessened the effectiveness of the Luftwaffe's night fighters.

In 1944, the Allied emphasis over Germany was, again, not on precision attack, which had proved difficult to execute, but on area bombing, with its attendant goals of disrupting the war economy and destroying urban life in order to hit morale and the workforce. This was clearly the policy of the RAF, and, although the United States Army Air Forces (USAAF) never officially switched to area bombing over Europe, its winter months campaigns often became area bombing operations in practice, not least as a result of targeting through the clouds using radar targeting, which proved far from precise. By increasing the target area,

area bombing also made the task of the defense more difficult. "V" raids, in which aircraft came in a succession of horizontal "V" formations to sweep a continuous path through the city, as employed against Darmstadt in 1944, proved devastating. The air force command, notably General Henry "Hap" Arnold, the commander of the USAAF, remained convinced of the strategic impact of bombing Germany and was less than supportive of other uses for heavy bombers.

The effectiveness, as well as the morality, of bombing has been the subject of considerable debate, and this was so, especially of the former, at the time. There is the question whether British Bomber Command underrated early assessments that stressed the limited value of the area bombing of German cities, and whether this attitude reduced the value of air attack and possibly led to a misuse of resources better devoted to ground or naval support. In January 1944, a group of scholars, asked by the USAAF to determine whether strategic bombing could force Germany out of the war by that spring, reported,

> Although the blockade and bombing have deranged Germany's economic structure, the German military economy has not been crippled at any vital point. . . . Although bombing has made a vital contribution to the ultimate defeat of Germany and although complete defeat cannot be achieved without an acceleration and intensification of bombing, it is improbable that bombing alone can bring about a German collapse by spring of 1944.[51]

These themes were also taken up for the public. J. F. C. Fuller, a former general and a notable British military commentator who was in favor of a negotiated peace, argued in the American journal *Newsweek* on October 2, 1944, that the bombing of Germany had not ended the war and had not cracked the morale and will of the German forces, and wrote of the "ineffectiveness of the Douhet theory." A fortnight later, he added in *Newsweek* that bombing had failed to paralyze the German high command.

Moral issues were raised by George Bell, bishop of Chichester, and by others, and have been pressed much more vigorously since.[52] The most frequently cited instance is that of "Dresden," a reference to the heavy casualties caused by the Anglo-American bombing of the city of Dresden on February 13–14, 1945, toward the close of the war, which is frequently mentioned as an Allied atrocity. However, the general con-

sensus at the time was that the bombing campaign was a deserved
return for earlier German air attacks (as well as current rocket attacks),
and also was likely to disrupt the German war effort and hit morale. As
far as the latter was concerned, the hopes of interwar air-power enthusiasts were not fully realized. During the war, most military leaders did
not argue that bombing alone could win. Instead, it was generally accepted that bombing should be part of an integrated strategy. Nevertheless, it was claimed that area bombing would cause heavy casualties,
which would terrorize the civilian population and hopefully put pressure on their governments, a revival of the British hopes of 1918.

The extent to which civilian morale was broken is controversial, but
it is possible that the impact of bombing on civilians has been underestimated by the habitual conclusion that the bombing did not end the war.
There was more to German resilience than Hitler's determination, and
the inability to stop bombing encouraged a sense that defeat was likely,
indeed was already occurring. A study of Nuremberg has suggested that
bombing was responsible for a serious decline in civilian morale from
1943, a process of social dissolution, and a matching crisis of confidence
in the Nazi Party.[53] Propaganda about the inability of Allied bombing to
damage targets within Germany was discredited. Whether these benefits justified heavy civilian casualties, and also a high level of losses
among Allied aircrews, is a question that has modern resonance given
current sensitivity about civilian casualties, but, by 1944, total war was
being pushed as precisely that. And anyway it was being waged by
Germany and Japan.

As a result, the concerns of contemporary military planners can best
be addressed in instrumental terms, with reference to the effectiveness
of air attack (a point also valid for Japan)[54] and to possible alternative
use of the resources devoted to it. The latter issue has attracted attention, as, indeed, has the question whether the German rocket program
represented an unwise allocation of resources that would have been
better devoted to air power or the search for a wonder weapon necessary to counter the losing tide. On the Allied side, there were alternative uses of air power, including different possible targets for heavy
bombers. As, however, there were serious practical and institutional
restrictions on any reallocation of resources, along with the economic
difficulties confronting a retooling of manufacturing, the feedback pro-

cess of judging policy could not be expected to work even had information flows been accurate and speedy—as is rarely the case in war.

Bombing was also advocated for the damage it could do to particular
targets, an approach that accords with modern doctrine. Despite the
limited precision of bombing by high-flying aircraft dropping free-fall
bombs, strategic bombing was crucial to the disruption of German communications and logistics, largely because it was eventually done on
such a massive scale, and because the targets could not be attacked by
any other means. Attacks on communications seriously affected the rest
of the German economy, limiting the transfer of resources and the
process of integration that is so significant for manufacturing. The reliance of European industry on rail was far greater than today, and that
increased its vulnerability to attack, because rail systems lack the flexibility of their road counterparts, being less dense and therefore less
able to switch routes. As critical points, bridges and marshaling yards
proved particular targets for attack. Air attack brought the SNCF (the
French rail system, then under German control) to collapse, followed
by the Reichsbahn (the German rail system). Damage was extensive
enough to preclude effective repairs, which indicated the potential for
increasing returns to scale in the air offensive. Its vulnerabilities ensured that the rail system was also prone to partisan attack in occupied
areas.

In addition, the oil industry and aircraft production were savagely hit
by Allied air attack. Such bombing directly benefited the Allied war
effort. It acted as a brake on Germany's expanding production of weaponry, which had important consequences for operational strength. For
example, thanks to bombing, the construction of a new, faster class of
submarine—type XXI—was delayed so that it did not become operational until April 1945. This was too late to challenge Allied command
of the sea; although even had it become operational earlier, it would not
have been in sufficient numbers to determine the struggle.[55]

Furthermore, from 1943, the Germans diverted massive resources
to antiaircraft defense forces, including much of the Luftwaffe itself. By
1944, more German guns were devoted to antiaircraft defenses than to
ground targets. These guns and aircraft, for example the 88 mm antiaircraft gun, which was also very effective against Allied tanks, might otherwise have made a major contribution on the Eastern and, later, the
Western Front. This is a counterfactual (what if?)[56] that it is impossible

to prove, not least because it assumes a ready response on the part of German decision makers, but it is not the less pertinent for that. Many of the military assets employed by the Germans in air defense were readily transferable—they were not fixed defenses—and, for that reason, their commitment to air defense and their nonavailability for transfer, whether permanently or even temporarily, was important. Far more German industrial capacity was used for aircraft and guns intended to oppose the Allied bomber offensive than for the manufacture of tanks. Moreover, this was an aspect of a more widespread focus. For example, the success of the British Dambusters' raid in breaching German dams near the Ruhr on the night of May 16–17, 1943, and thus in hitting the production of the hydroelectric power that helped industrial production, led to a major commitment of antiaircraft guns, labor, concrete, and additional resources to enhancing the defenses of these, and other, dams. This commitment resulted in a reduction in the availability of concrete and workers to improve the defenses of the Atlantic Wall against an Allied invasion of France.

The Allied air assault also played a role in the wider strategic equation. For example, once the Allies had invaded southern France on August 15, 1944, the holding of northern Italy was of dubious value to the Germans as it committed troops to an extensive perimeter, rather than the shorter line that would have been gained from relying on the Alps, a line that would also have taken advantage of Swiss neutrality. However, aside from Hitler's disinclination to countenance retreat, and his particular wish not to abandon Mussolini, there was also a justified concern that an Allied presence in Lombardy would facilitate the aerial assault on Germany by permitting a major advance of Allied air bases. Northern Italy itself was heavily bombed, notably the industrial cities of Genoa, Milan, and Turin.

The impact of the Second Front on the air war provided a salutary lesson. Part of the German air-defense system was lost as the Allies advanced in France and the Low Countries in 1944, and the major lack of depth of defense that resulted from the advance compromised the remainder of the defense. Furthermore, Allied bombers and escort fighters were now based in reconquered areas and were able to support the American and British heavy bombers based in eastern England. As a result, the bombing offensive on Germany that was launched from the autumn of 1944, as air support for the Second Front became less necessary, was far more intense and damaging than hitherto, while its destructiveness was further increased by the rise in the number of Allied aircraft.

More generally, the Allied air attack intensified economic disruption within Germany and sped up defeat. It affected not only Germany, which was far harder hit in 1944–45 than hitherto, but also her allies. For example, heavy bombing attacks on Bulgaria began on November 19, 1943. The raids, especially that of March 30, 1944, on the capital, Sofia, indicated clearly the shift in fortunes and encouraged a decline in enthusiasm for continued support for Germany. Bulgaria abandoned Germany in September, although the Soviet advance into the Balkans was far more significant in this than the bombing.[57]

WAR IN THE PACIFIC, 1944

In the Pacific, the Japanese were fooled by American strategy and deception. Having two simultaneous American drives created serious problems for the Japanese navy. Air power was central, and American carrier strength proved decisive. Having reconstructed their carrier forces after defeat at Midway in 1942, the Japanese had planned to destroy the spearhead of the advancing American fleet by concentrating their air power against it. In June, in the Battle of the Philippine Sea, American Task Force 58, with fifteen carriers and over nine hundred planes, was attacked by the nine carriers and four hundred planes of the Japanese First Mobile Fleet. However, located by American radar and benefiting from radio interception, Japanese air attacks, launched on June 19, were shot down by American fighters and by antiaircraft fire from supporting warships, with no damage to the American carriers. The following day, a long-range American air attack in the failing light sank or severely damaged three Japanese carriers. The Japanese carriers were protected by a screen of Zero fighters, but, as a clear sign of growing Japanese weakness in the air, this was too weak to resist the fighters escorting the American bombers. Although the Japanese still had a sizable carrier fleet, once again the loss of pilots and carrier-based maintenance crew was a crippling blow. This victory enabled the Americans to overrun the Marianas, a decisive advance into the Western Pacific and one that provided air bases for bombing Japan, notably the island of Saipan, conquered from June 15 to July 9.

At the Battle of Leyte Gulf of October 23–26, an attempt to disrupt the American invasion of the Philippines, Japan lost four carriers, ensuring that the invasion could continue. From October 25, during this battle, the Japanese employed kamikaze (suicide) aircraft against American warships: aircraft were flown into ships, making them manned missiles. Such attacks were a product not only of a fanatical self-sacrifice, but also of the limitations, by then, of the Japanese naval air arm. These attacks led in 1944–45 to the sinking of forty-nine ships, with another three hundred damaged, and were designed to sap American will. Initially, the percentage of hits and near misses was over a quarter, but the success rate fell the following spring as the Japanese increasingly relied on inexperienced pilots, while American air defenses improved, with more antiaircraft guns and also fighter patrols, notably Hellcats, which were dispatched miles from the fleet in order to shoot down outclassed Zeros. The Americans benefited from the large number of fighters carried by their numerous carriers and from the radar-based system of fighter control. Bomber attacks on Japanese air bases also helped. The Japanese lost about five thousand men in the kamikaze attacks. From April 1945, the Japanese also used Ohka (cherry blossom) flying bombs, powered by three solid-fuel rocket motors and launched from aircraft twenty-three miles from their intended targets. They had pilots but no propeller or landing gear, thus serving even more as manned missiles. About 750 were used, mostly in response to the American conquest of the island of Okinawa in April–June 1945, but only three American ships were sunk or damaged beyond repair as a result.

1945, EUROPE: JET AIRCRAFT

In 1945, total Allied control of the air in Europe reflected the extent to which the Luftwaffe had been outfought, while a lack of flying training and fuel had gravely compromised its capability. As at a smaller scale in Britain in 1940, a key element was the ability to replace losses in aircraft and trained crew, and the Allies proved superior in this to the Germans. Operation Bodenplatte (Baseplate) was the last large-scale strategic offensive mounted by the Luftwaffe during the war. The Luftwaffe intended to cripple Allied air forces in the Low Countries and to gain air superiority in the region. The Battle of the Bulge had been stagnant for some time, and Bodenplatte was intended to facilitate an advance of German forces. Repeatedly delayed due to bad weather and launched on January 1, 1945, the attack benefited from Allied complacency and achieved some success, destroying Allied aircraft on the ground, but could not win air superiority. In what proved a misconceived operation in which the flaws and problems of the Luftwaffe were fully revealed, the Germans lost many of their pilots. A lack of fuel and spares, as well as a lack of skilled pilots and a one-sided focus on fighters, was apparent.

Thereafter, the Luftwaffe continued to shoot down Allied bombers, inflicting serious losses, but the size of the bombing force was so large that the percentage of casualties was relatively low. In contrast, the percentage for the Luftwaffe was less favorable. Attrition had helped wreck the latter.[58] After Bodenplatte, whatever was left of the Luftwaffe had had even more limited training. Bombing continued to inflict great damage on Germany, which went on fighting.

The jet fighter arrived in service too late to affect the course of the war. In 1944, jets entered service: the British Meteor and the German Me-262. The tactics of the Me-262 posed serious problems. It could seize the initiative effectively, diving at high speed through the Allied fighter screen and continuing under the bombers, prior to climbing up in order to attack the bombers from behind. If, however, the Me-262 was involved in a dogfight, it was vulnerable, as it had a poor rate of turn. There were also efforts to catch it when even more vulnerable: on takeoff and particularly as it was coming in to land. As a result of these attacks, the Germans set up flak alleys along the approaches to the airfields. The Me-262 had slow acceleration with low thrust at slow speeds. About 190 Me-262s were lost in aerial combat, while no more than 150 Allied aircraft were shot down by the Me-262, though there is no consensus on these figures, which vary enormously. There was also separate work by the Germans on other jet aircraft: the Arado Ar-234, which was designed as a jet bomber and reconnaissance aircraft, and the Me-163 rocket aircraft, both of which saw operational use, and the Ju-287, a four-engine jet bomber, and the He-162, which did not see combat.

With 1,430 Me-262s built (only 564 in 1944), there were insufficient numbers to transform the course of the war, as well as a shortage of trained pilots, and design faults with the aircraft, notably problems with the turbines and poor engine reliability. As a reminder that use, as well as technology, was an issue, the German lead in jet-powered aircraft was, to a degree, squandered by Hitler. This was because of his preference that the Me-262 should not be used as an interceptor of Allied bombers, despite its effectiveness in that role, but, rather, as a high-speed bomber. Indeed, in June 1944, he ordered its name changed to Blitzbomber.[59] Underlining the extent to which wartime weaponry continued into the postwar world, the Me-262 was subsequently manufactured in Czechoslovakia, where it served in the air force as the Avia S-92 until 1951. Aside from the British Meteor, operational in July 1944, the American P-80 Shooting Star became operational in July 1945.

1945, THE FALL OF JAPAN

Japan was too weak in the air to protect itself against the American air assault. Initially, the American raids were long distance and unsupported by fighter cover, as fighter range was less than that of bombers. This situation led to American attacks from a high altitude, which reduced their effectiveness. The raids that were launched were hindered by poor weather, especially cloudy conditions; by strong tailwinds; and by difficulties with the B-29's reliability, as well as the general problems of precision bombing with the technology of the period. The B-29 had been initially designed to meet the requirements for a longer-range and faster bomber than the B-17. Due to America's entry into the war, the B-29 was rushed into production and, for quite some time, suffered from unexpected but frequent engine fires and other motor malfunctions. These, however, were sufficiently corrected to make it possible for the Americans to revise and carry out the massive bombing campaigns against Japan.

From February 1945, there was a switch to low-altitude nighttime area bombing of Japanese cities. The impact was devastating, not least because many Japanese dwellings were made of timber and paper and burned readily when bombarded with incendiaries, and also because population density in the cities was high. Fighters based on the recently conquered island of Iwo Jima (three hours by air from Tokyo), from April 7, 1945, could provide cover for the B-29s, which had been bombing Japan from bases on the more distant island of Saipan since November 1944. The Marine Corps defended its costly conquests on the grounds that carriers could not provide a base for aircraft of this size and for launching and adequately supporting air attacks of this scale. These attacks were designed to hit Japanese industrial production, in part by devastating the cities where much of it was based. The industrial working class was the target, alongside the attempt to mount precision attacks.

Weaknesses in Japanese antiaircraft defenses, both aircraft and guns, eased the American task and made it possible to increase the payload of the B-29s by removing their guns. Although the Japanese had developed some impressive interceptor fighters, especially the Mitsubishi A6M5 and the NIK2-J Shiden, they were unable to produce many due to the impact of Allied air raids and of submarine attacks on supply routes, and they were also very short of pilots. In 1944–45, American bombers destroyed over 30 percent of the buildings in Japan, including over half of the cities of Tokyo and Kobe. The deadliness of bombing was amply demonstrated. On March 9, 1945, 690,000 pounds of bombs were dropped on Tokyo in less than an hour, killing 87,793 people. The city smelled of burning flesh. An American invention (at Harvard in 1942), napalm, a thickened fuel, operated as a sticky gel that was used to deadly effect as an incendiary, destroying people and property.[60] Firebombing killed more Japanese than the atomic bombs.

Although the Japanese XIV Area Army on Luzon in the Philippines, where the Americans landed on January 9, had more than 250,000 troops, it had only about 150 operational combat aircraft to support them. These aircraft and their pilots could not match the Americans in quality, and most were destroyed by American carrier aircraft before the invasion. The Japanese army in Manchuria was also heavily outnumbered in the air when attacked by Soviet forces in August 1945, forces that benefited from airborne operations, for example at Harbin and Port Arthur, in advance of their ground units. The Soviets had about five thousand aircraft, the Japanese only fifty frontline ones.

At sea, kamikaze attacks could not alter the situation. They were responsible for much damage to American warships, but not enough to have a strategic impact. The Japanese sent their last major naval force, led by the battleship *Yamato*, on a kamikaze mission to attack the American ships off Okinawa, but it was intercepted by American bombers, and the *Yamato* and five accompanying ships were sunk on April 7.[61] In 1945, carrier-borne aircraft increasingly attacked Japan, dominated its airspace, and mined its waters. On July 24, for example, American and British carriers launched 1,747 aircraft to attack targets around the Inland Sea. However, the air assault was far more potent because of the heavier aircraft that could be launched from island bases.

ATOMIC BOMBS

The creation of the atomic bomb was indicative of the exceptional nature and scale of activity possible for an advanced industrial society. This was the product not only of the application of science, but also of the powerful industrial and technological capability of the United States, and the willingness to spend about $2 billion in rapidly creating a large nuclear industry. The electromagnets needed for isotope separation were particularly expensive and required 13,500 tons of silver.

At the Potsdam Conference, the Allied leaders issued the Potsdam Declaration on July 26, 1945, demanding unconditional surrender, as well as the occupation of Japan, Japan's loss of its overseas possessions, and the establishment of democracy. The threatened alternative was "prompt and utter destruction," but, on July 27, the Japanese government decided to ignore the declaration, which they saw as a political ultimatum. President Harry Truman wrote, "My object is to save as many American lives as possible."[62] He reportedly commented that he did not lose a night's sleep about the decision to use atomic bombs.

The air assault on Japan culminated in the dropping of atomic bombs on August 6 and 9 on Hiroshima and Nagasaki, respectively, the bombs landing very close to the aim points. As a result, probably over 280,000 people died, either at once or eventually through radiation poisoning. This transformed the situation by demonstrating that Japanese forces could not protect the homeland. On August 14, Japan agreed to surrender unconditionally. The heavy Allied losses in capturing the islands of Iwo Jima and Okinawa earlier in the year suggested that the use of atom bombs was necessary in order both to overcome a

suicidal determination to fight on, and to obtain unconditional surrender. The apparently inexorable process of devastation seen with the
dropping of the second bomb, on Nagasaki, had a greater impact on the
Japanese government than the use of the first. The combined shock of
the two bombs led the Japanese to surrender. The army had refused to
believe what had happened and still wanted to fight after Hiroshima.[63]
The limited American ability to deploy more bombs speedily was not
appreciated. No other bomb was available on August 9, although one
would have been about a week later. However, the Americans were
already considering the use of atom bombs in tactical support of a
planned landing on the island of Kyushu, which would have been the
first of the main Japanese islands to be invaded.

Moreover, had the war continued, civilian casualties would have
been immense. Aside from the direct and indirect consequences of air
invasion, the continuation of the conventional bombing campaign
would have been very costly, both directly and indirectly. Had the war
lasted to 1946, the destruction of the Japanese rail system by bombing
would have led to famine, as it would have been impossible to move
food supplies. Thus, as used in 1945, the atomic bombs were particularly destructive products of industrial warfare. They were employed as a
tool of limited war in order to achieve the total war goal of unconditional surrender without having to resort to a fight to the finish that would
follow an American invasion.

ETHICS

The devastation of Hiroshima and Nagasaki highlighted the question of
the ethics of air warfare. That questioning was to be one of the lasting
consequences of the Second World War, notably as criticism of bombing, and of war in general, rose from the 1960s. Particular criticism
focused on the bombing of Dresden in 1945. In turn, this criticism very
much reflected the ethical values and political needs of the postwar
world, rather than those at the time. Thus, the bombing of Dresden was
cited by the Soviet Union during the Cold War in order to castigate the
wartime record of Britain and the United States. German victimhood
became a theme intended to link the East German workers to the
Soviet Union.[64]

Bombing was not the sole activity that led to debate, both at the time and subsequently. In April 1943, Major General William Penney recorded lunch with Lieutenant General Carl Spaatz, the American commander of the Allied North Africa Air Forces, who had first seen action on the Mexican border in 1916:

> Discussion arose on rights or wrongs of shooting men who had baled [sic] out of aircraft and are on their way to earth or sea. Spaatz had heard that his boys had started it the day before in the Straits [between Tunisia and Sicily] chiefly owing to a report that they had received that the Boche [Germans] thought them soft and squeamish. Mary C's [Air Vice Marshal "Maori" Coningham, commander of the Desert Air Force] views were that the Boche did it regularly, ethics did not arise, and we should do it if the pilots etc were going to fall into their own lines or into the sea ie anywhere where they were not going to be eliminated as far as further flying was concerned. Spaatz and Kueter not so sure, again not on ethical grounds but on danger of diverting aircraft from their proper mission in order to protect their own pals who had taken to their parachutes. I always thought that there was some understanding that once . . . in a parachute drop you were immune. Entirely illogical and inconsistent with total war.[65]

RANGE OF AIR POWER

More immediately, the war demonstrated the range and variety of air power. For example, at a strategic level, the transport capabilities of aircraft were seen in the Anglo-American delivery of nearly 650,000 tons of matériel from northeastern India over the "Hump," the eastern Himalayas, to the Nationalist forces fighting the Japanese in China from July 1942 to 1945. This achievement represented an enormous development in air transport and in very difficult flying conditions, even though the individual load of aircraft was low by later standards.[66] Air-dropped supplies were important to the defensibility of British positions on the India-Burma border in 1944, to the advance of Australian forces in North Guinea the same year, and to the success of the Soviet invasion of Manchuria in 1945. The Germans and Japanese were not as well served by transport aircraft. Although the German Ju-52 did good service, it was not as good as the American C-47, which was produced in vast numbers and used in every theater. The C-47 was cheaper and easier to manufacture than the Ju-52. Another key capability was provided by aerial intelligence, which became crucial to Anglo-American operational planning.[67]

Unmanned flight brought together air power and artillery. Guided bombs and rockets were dramatic innovations but did not affect the course of the war. Accuracy was a major problem for the guided weapons developed by both sides.[68] The Germans employed Fritz-X radio-guided bombs against ships in the Mediterranean in 1943. Some were sunk, notably the Italian battleship *Roma* on the way to surrender to the Allies, while others suffered severe damage. The Germans also used the Henschel Hs-293 radio-guided glider bomb with some success against shipping. The Germans employed these bombs against bridges in Normandy in August 1944, but less successfully. Taking air warfare in a different direction, the United States considered the use against Japan of millions of suicide bats carrying napalm, but did not do so. After Pearl Harbor, the Japanese unsuccessfully sought to use incendiary balloons in order to set American forests alight.

More usefully, the air evacuation of the wounded and ill developed, such that the Allies evacuated over one million casualties by air in 1943–45. This was an aspect of air power in which women took a direct role, with over 5,400 female flight nurses in the United States Army Air Force's Medical Air Evacuation Squadrons.[69]

CONCLUSIONS

The scale of air power was extraordinary. At the beginning of 1945, more men were employed in Britain in producing bombers than as British infantry in Northwestern Europe. The United States produced not only over two hundred thousand aircraft, as well as the largest number of and most powerful aero-engines,[70] but also eighteen fleet carriers and eighty-six light fleet or escort carriers. So also with a new range for air power. The war against German submarines led to the building of many new air bases. They were developed by, and for, the Americans, in Cuba, the Dominican Republic, Haiti, and Panama, in order to oppose the destructive U-boat campaign in the Caribbean, as well as against U-boat operations in the Atlantic. Air bases were also developed to protect the Panama Canal. Based in northeastern Brazil, US Fleet Wing 16 patrolled against U-boats. American air bases in Brazil were also crucial to the movement of aircraft and shipment of arms to the Allies in the North African campaigns. Aircraft were flown from the United States (and shipped from Britain) to Takoradi in the Gold Coast (Ghana) and then, via Lagos and Khartoum, on to near Cairo. Similarly, the air base at Keflavik in Iceland was important to the American air bridge to the British Isles.

American air bases in Latin America and elsewhere familiarized a range of states with the regular use of military air power. American support was important in the development of the air force of Brazil, America's leading Latin American ally and the one that received three-quarters of the Lend-Lease aid sent there. The emphasis on air power also had institutional consequences, as in Argentina, where the air force was officially founded in January 1945, inheriting most of the Army Air Branch. Moreover, the use of American aircraft spread. This was also seen with the reequipping of the French military. By December 1943, French forces based in North Africa included ten fighter squadrons (five with American P-39s and P-47s, and five with British Spitfires and Hurricanes) and three bomber (A-35s and B-26s). In 1943, the Finns were sent about 160 Me-109Gs by Germany, and the surviving 102 remained in service until 1954.

The use of aircraft increased greatly around the world because so many states were involved in the conflict, including states not generally seen in that light. For example, in 1941, Persia (Iran) was invaded by British and Soviet forces. Aircraft were used for ground support, as when the British fought their way through the Zagros Mountains, and for bombing, as when the Soviets attacked Iranian barracks, including at Tabriz and Rasht, as well as air bases, such as Mashhad. The British also used paratroopers in this successful campaign.

An emphasis on the value of air power led to a stress on the acquisition and protection of air bases. This stress helped determine operational and strategic options. Thus, in 1944, the United States emphasized gaining control of islands from which raids could be launched against Japan. This was also an issue in Europe, Southwest Asia, and North Africa, with the occupation of Persia in 1941 seen as the basis for British air attacks on the important Baku oilfields in Azerbaijan if the

Germans seized them from the Soviet Union.[71] Similarly, the capture of southern Italy in 1943 provided a base for Allied strategic bombing, including, in 1944, heavy raids on the oil refineries in Ploesti, Romania. This focus on air bases looked forward to American and British priorities in the first two decades of the Cold War.

So also with the emphasis on oil, which included Italian raids in 1940 on the oil refineries in British-controlled Haifa and an unsuccessful attempt on two in the Gulf.[72] In turn, the Allied attack on fuel supplies and refining capacity was a major feature of the air assault on the Axis powers. Thus, on January 24 and 29, 1945, aircraft from four British carriers, their names redolent of British naval aspirations—*Illustrious*, *Indefatigable*, *Indomitable*, and *Victorious*—attacked Japanese oil refineries in Sumatra as well as their supporting airfields. The aircraft had to overcome Japanese interceptors as well as heavy flak, each a testimony to the importance the Japanese placed on oil, and succeeded in cutting production of aviation fuel in Sumatra as well as destroying many Japanese aircraft.

As far as the tactical, operational, and strategic levels were concerned, the war against German U-boats underlined the significance of combined operations in order to achieve success in the attack, and also in defense. In February 1943, Admiral Sir Dudley Pound, First Sea Lord in the British Admiralty, noted,

> At this moment we are doing all we can to produce super long-range aircraft so that we can cover the whole of the Atlantic from one side to the other as there is no question but that if you can put aircraft over the U-boats during the day, it prevents them getting into position for their night attacks. I am hoping very much that we shall be able to blast them out of their operational bases in the Bay of Biscay [in France by air attack].[73]

Combined operations, however, faced significant difficulties. In particular, close air support proved more difficult than tactical interdiction, a difficulty that affected the debate over their respective merits. Problems of inaccurate targeting and the vulnerability of tactical bombers to ground fire and opposing fighters limited the ability of aircraft to kill tanks and hit combat formations. The effectiveness of the Soviet use of the IL-2, the Shturmovik, a specialized ground-attack aircraft, depended on massive numbers (about thirty-six thousand were built) and a willingness to take heavy losses. Britain and the United States had entered the war not only with an exaggeration of what they could then achieve by strategic bombing, but also with weak or misguided tactical air doctrines that scattered aircraft in small units subject to ground commanders' orders. This resulted in wasteful attacks on minor targets and in continuous air cover for advancing units that proved of limited value against ground opposition. Unified tactical air command proved the solution, while the use of fighters as fighter-bombers provided aircraft that could defend themselves in dogfights and were also fast and maneuverable enough to heighten their survival rate in ground support and to deliver more accurate bombing against tactical targets such as bridges than medium and heavy bombers flying at high altitude ever could. This was an instance of the more general innovatory use of air power during the war. The varied needs of the conflict drove the pace of innovation.

The themes of combined air operations and ground support clashed with the idea of victory by air power alone through strategic bombing. This contrast continued to be a source of tension and indeed doctrinal confusion in the postwar world, one linked to the political and command tension associated with the desire for independent air forces. More generally, the use of air power in the Second World War set much of the tone for subsequent discussion and for the intellectual, emotional, and visual understanding of air warfare. This was particularly true of popular culture, as this conflict dominated war films. The influence, if not control, of the United States and Britain over much of the world of cinema in the quarter century after the Second World War underlined this point. In part, therefore, while the character of air power changed rapidly after 1945, notably with the development of jet capacity and atomic weaponry, and with the subsequent spread of missiles, the image of air power did not alter in a comparable fashion.

7

THE EARLY COLD WAR, 1946–62

The dropping of the atom bombs in 1945 subsequently dominated experience, imagination, and fears. The legacy of the Second World War, and notably of the strategic use of air power by the United States, was such that air attack, and the response to it, played a far larger role in discussion after the Second World War than had been the case after the First World War. In particular, air power was given an overwhelming role in preparing for conflict between the United States and the Soviet Union. For a time, the United States had the ability to devastate any country that threatened it, with no risk of retaliation. As the Soviet Union acquired a nuclear capability, an atomic war between the United States and the Soviet Union appeared likely, if not inevitable. Moreover, the best way to prevent such conflict seemed to be through the availability of a strong deterrent. For the United States, this deterrence focused on a powerful air force, one able to reach the Soviet Union and drop atomic bombs on cities and military facilities. This was the rationale for the establishment and independence of the United States Air Force (USAF). Alongside plans for the dropping of these bombs came plans for defense against such attacks. The former encouraged the latter in a reprise of the response in the 1930s to the threat from large-scale bombing.

These plans scarcely exhausted the subject of air power. Ambitions focused on air power, ambitions that had been developed in the Second World War, notably in the planning for victory against Germany and Japan, were sustained into the postwar world and influenced ideas and plans then, as was again to happen with the Cold War. This process was very clearly the case with the issue of the range of operations. Whereas these had been relatively modest in the case of the Anglo-American air war against Germany, Japan was a very different case due to the distance from Allied territory and, in this case, to Soviet neutrality until August 1945. As a result, very long-range bombers were required to attack Japan. Britain had no equivalent to the B-29 or the nascent B-36, but it intended to improve the range of Lancaster bombers with in-flight refueling. Britain proposed in September 1944 to deploy forty squadrons, half of them as tankers, against Japan, with the aircraft available for service in the summer of 1945. In July 1945, at Potsdam, the Combined Chiefs of Staff agreed that the RAF would contribute ten squadrons to the strategic bombing of Japan, a force to rise to twenty squadrons when airfields became available from December.[1] This force was not required in the event, but it testified to the willingness to plan for a long-range deployment in aerial force and to Britain's determination to maintain and use this capability.

Despite the absence of a total war of nuclear exchange, air power proved highly significant in local wars during the period from the end of the Second World War to the Cuban Missile Crisis in 1962. This was the case with wars between major powers, notably the Korean War (1950–53), as well as with counterinsurrectionary conflicts, such as those of the French in Indochina (Vietnam, Laos, and Cambodia) and Algeria, and with civil wars. However, the question of the use and potential use of air power in the period 1946–62 does not dominate academic attention for the postwar decades, those after the Second World War, because the 1960s were later to produce the imbroglio of American power in Vietnam, as well as the dramatically successful use of air attack by Israel in the Six-Day War in 1967. Nevertheless, in the 1960s, the increasing emphasis on ballistic missiles as their accuracy slowly improved was in fact making the aircraft element of air power less central as a strategic tool of great-power conflict. Indeed, of the period since the Second World War, the years 1946–62 were those most dominated by aircraft.

Many of the capabilities for missile attack were in their infancy, such as an understanding of high-altitude winds. Accurate aerial mapping was also incomplete. For example, in 1946, the British Colonial Office established the Directorate of Colonial (later Overseas) Survey and instructed it to map nine hundred thousand square miles of Africa within ten years, using aerial photography as well as ground surveys. The impressive expertise developed in photo-reconnaissance during wartime was deployed to map large areas previously surveyed only poorly. This capability was especially valuable in inaccessible terrain. Aerial photography could achieve precise results far more rapidly than ground surveys and was not dependent on local manpower, but it was still a slow process. Thus, in Malaya in the 1970s, much of the hinterland was still unmapped. Subsequently, satellite mapping was to be more significant and provided the basis for precise targeting data.

NUCLEAR DELIVERERS

The successful use of atomic bombs in 1945 in order to force Japan out of the war helped to ensure that American military planning thereafter was dominated by air power or, at least, was conducted with considerable reference to it. The prospect that any future attack on America or its allies could be countered by this means appeared to confirm overwhelming American strength and, in doing so, to counter the threat posed by the size of the Soviet army and the impressive successes and advances it had achieved in 1943–45. Indeed, nuclear armaments enabled the United States to demobilize much of its military after the Second World War rapidly, and thus, as the public wanted, to make the transition back to being a peacetime society. This was certainly the scenario envisaged by the air-power enthusiasts of Strategic Air Command (SAC), which was founded in 1946.

Their pragmatic defense of air power was linked to dreams of influence, if not glory, focused on aircraft. These dreams, developed in the interwar period, took on new energy as a consequence of the perception and presentation of the reasons for Allied victory in the Second World War.[2] This energy was linked to a fixation on technological progress and on the transformative character of air power. The United States Air Force, established on September 18, 1947, created an impressive public-relations machine, one that was far better than that of the army. Air power was very much linked to American popular culture.[3] As a further instance of the penetration of air power into American psychology, the Air National Guard was organized as a key reserve force. In Britain, the Netherlands, and elsewhere, Air Cadets were established for a similar purpose.

There was a pronounced and significant regional dimension in the United States, with the major political, economic, and cultural rise of California important to that of air power. Convair, Lockheed, Douglas, and North American aircraft manufacturers were all concentrated in Los Angeles County in Southern California. The large-scale components industry expanded this economic influence and regional focus.

However, even when the United States alone had the atomic bomb, from 1945 to 1949, its value as a weapon and a deterrent was limited. Despite claims that it was just another weapon, the bomb, and the prospect of its use, were insufficiently flexible and credible (in terms of military and political application, or acceptance of its use) to meet challenges other than that of full-scale war. Furthermore, in 1948, the United States had possibly as few as fifty atomic bombs that could be used. Indeed, American possession of the bomb, and, in fact, consideration of its use, did not deter the Soviets from trying to intimidate the West during the Berlin crisis of 1948–49 nor newly communist China from intervening in the Korean War in 1950. Moreover, in August 1949, thanks to a massive effort pressed very hard by the government and in part using convict labor, as well as to secrets obtained by espionage, the Soviet Union was able to carry out an atomic bomb test, much to the surprise of the United States. In response, preventive air-strikes against Soviet nuclear capabilities were seriously considered by the Americans, only to be discarded.[4]

The Soviet Long-Range Air Force had been created in 1946, and a long-range bomber, the TU-4, a copy of the American B-29, entered series production in 1948. Although obsolescent, it was capable of carrying nuclear bombs. The threat from the TU-4 was increased from 1950 because of the effectiveness of the new Soviet fighters, notably the MIG-15. In 1946, before the Cold War developed, the British had sold the Soviet Union crucial jet-engine technology, which helped the latter develop from a position of initial disadvantage, contributing to a whole range of modern weaponry such as fighters like the MIG-15.[5] The deployment of effective jet fighters produced the risk that bombers would only be able to reach their targets if they were escorted or had standoff missiles, the forerunners of cruise missiles.[6] Correspondingly, defeat in a struggle for air superiority might well lead to becoming the victim of nuclear attack.

Meanwhile, American strategic reliance on air power in the late 1940s was given a new energy. Concerns about Soviet plans, as well as surrounding what was for America a rapidly deteriorating position in East Asia, where the communists were winning the Chinese Civil War, most clearly from the winter of 1948–49, encouraged a massive expansion in military expenditure. This expansion was within the context of particular strategic assumptions that owed much to the specific nature of America as a war-peace society, one that sought to be the leading military power while enjoying the benefits of peace. Politically and socially, with no appetite for another foreign war, it would have been difficult to re-expand the army so soon after the Second World War, and air power provided a far more acceptable alternative.

A reliance on air power became an ideal norm for the United States. Moreover, an emphasis on the value of air power served to vindicate American conduct in the Second World War and, correspondingly, was supported by the positive legacy of that war. Thus, the justification of the bombing of Germany and Japan, a justification that in part rested on questions of ends and means, but also on after-action analyses, served to explain the need for strategic air power in response to the Soviet Union. Air power focused on the USAF and SAC, and the distribution of its aircraft reflected preparations for atomic war. B-29s capable of dropping atomic bombs, alongside bomb components, were deployed in Britain from 1950. The Americans could bomb the Soviet Union from Britain, whereas the United States was out of range of Soviet nuclear attack. In their targeting, the Americans proposed to focus on Soviet industry, although nuclear weapons were, in practice, area weapons focused as much on countervalue as on counterforce.

The stationing of the B-29s in Britain was a response to the Berlin crisis, in which, in 1948–49, the Soviets unsuccessfully blockaded West Berlin. This blockade was met by an Anglo-American airlift, an impressive display of air power, including during a bitter winter. A total of 278,228 flights, the majority American, supplied 2.3 million tons of supplies, enabling West Berlin to survive the crisis. The Soviets harassed the aircraft, for example firing flak nearby, but did not try to shoot them down. The flights ceased when air deliveries were greater than pre-airlift rail deliveries and it became clear to the Soviet Union that it was pointless to continue. After the use of the atom bombs, the airlift was the most decisive use of air power in history and altered world affairs. It signaled American military commitment to Europe in general and Germany in particular, and directly led to the creation of NATO (the North Atlantic Treaty Organization, founded in 1949).

The American airlift was organized from the massive Rhein-Main Air Base, just south of Frankfurt. This, America's leading air transport terminal in Europe, was of key significance for the American presence in West Germany. As a result, the roads focusing on Frankfurt were rapidly repaired and improved after the war. This was an instance of the important local impact and infrastructure of air power development right across NATO Europe, stretching to the north of Norway (for example, Bodø) and to the east of Turkey, both of which were aspects of a more general global situation.

A network of air bases, which attracted NATO infrastructure funding, was judged essential to American/NATO power as well as being its prime deterrence expression. The role of the bases in the Azores helped, for example, to explain why, although not a democracy, Portugal was a founding member of NATO in 1949. In 1953, moreover, the United States and Spain signed an agreement giving the Americans rights to establish air bases, although Spain, a Fascist dictatorship, was not invited to join NATO. The 1951 defense agreement with Iceland, a NATO member, ensured that the United States could use the base at Keflavik, which it, in turn, paid to develop. These and British air bases were crucial both to the resupply of American forces in NATO, and in providing strategic depth in the event of a Soviet advance into Western Europe that overran extensive territory.

The American network of bases was not restricted to NATO but was also seen in the zone where the Western Pacific met East Asia, notably in Japan and the Philippines, particularly on Okinawa. Subsequently, the air network spread, both as the key means of "containment" as that practice developed for responding to Soviet power and American fears, and, eventually, because of weaknesses in the British ability to sustain "containment" as the British Empire collapsed and Britain's economy hit repeated problems.

Air power was not restricted to SAC. There was a related development for the American navy in the shape of a fundamental move from battleships to carriers. Moreover, Britain was not only a base for SAC, but, like France, also developed its own atomic capability. Although allied in NATO, Britain sought to play more than a minor role compared to the United States. By January 1947, the British government had decided to develop a nuclear bomb, a policy regarded as necessary for Britain's independent security and, indeed, for independence in the face of the Soviet threat. At considerable cost, Britain became the third nuclear power, with a nuclear device detonated in 1952, although the first British practical atom bomb took longer. The first Valiant bomber designed to drop these bombs was delivered to the RAF in 1955, the Vulcan following in 1956, and the Victor in 1958.[7] Britain's nuclear capability not only deterred the Soviet Union, at least in part. It also guaranteed that the British could decide at what point the war would progress to a nuclear exchange, thereby ensuring American commitment. Britain was also an important base for the surveillance of Soviet activities, which even included, in 1956, high-altitude balloons equipped with cameras.

The extensive employment of air power in the Korean War (1950–53), and the extent to which it had proved necessary there to overcome Soviet MIGs, accentuated the American emphasis on air power, but this emphasis was primarily driven by the strategy of atomic confrontation with the Soviet Union. In 1953, indeed, use of the atom bomb was threatened by the Americans in order to secure an end to the Korean War.[8] Work on the superbomb or hydrogen bomb, in which a nuclear detonator heated hydrogen isotopes sufficiently to fuse them into helium atoms, releasing an enormous amount of destructive energy, was stepped up after the Soviet atomic test, being authorized by President Truman in January 1950, and was spurred on by the outbreak of the Korean War later that year. The American hydrogen bomb was first tested on November 1, 1952, producing an explosive yield of 10.4 megatons of TNT equivalent, whereas the bomb dropped on Hiroshima in 1945 had 15 kilotons and that on Nagasaki 20 kilotons. Massive destruction had apparently become easier and less expensive.

The ability of the Soviet Union rapidly to match the American development and deployment, first of atomic bombs and then of hydrogen bombs, led not to a decision to try to leapfrog to a new technology, nor to any serious attempt at mutual disarmament, but, rather, to an American attempt to be first and foremost. This, indeed, characterized American air power, and the American perception of air power in the

1950s helped to ensure that threats to this position took on an existential character. This was true not only of the Soviet development of the atom bomb, which led to a vigorous search for spies and traitors conducted among public hysteria, but also of subsequent concerns. These focused, successively, on the vulnerability of American airspace to Soviet jet bombers, an alleged "bomber gap" with the Soviet Union; on the ability of the Soviets to put a satellite into orbit, with Sputnik in 1957; and, subsequently, on a "missile gap" with the Soviet Union. Sputnik showed that the Soviet Union had an intercontinental ballistic missile capability, certainly in range, if not in accuracy.

Separately, and cumulatively, these concerns led in the United States to a sense of anxiety and to mutually supporting panics. There was a social dimension, of widespread public concern and associated preparations; a cultural dimension, with fear of the Soviets and the bomb, but also parables depicted in fiction and film, notably in science fiction; and a political aspect, with administrations accused by critics of being "soft" on defense and "the Soviets," and, allegedly, unwilling and unable to defend the country and its values. These charges were aimed by Republicans against the Truman administrations (1945–53) and by Democrats against the Eisenhower administrations (1953–61), but there were also criticisms voiced within the individual political parties. Indeed, the defense argument was one that was to be used in the long struggle over the identity and purpose of the American Right, as well as in bitter debates about what the Left stood for.[9]

In order to justify and fulfill its independent role, and to take the leading part in the Cold War, American air force thinking was increasingly dominated by strategic nuclear bombing. The only war that mattered was the conflict with the Soviet Union. The ability to strike at Soviet centers was seen as an effective deterrent, indeed as the sole counter to Soviet conventional strength, to the Sino-Soviet alliance negotiated in 1950 that followed communist success in the Chinese Civil War, and to the vulnerability of America's allies and interests. Strategic nuclear bombing was regarded as a war-winning capability and, subsequently, as a war-endurance capability. American vulnerability to a surprise attack led to the development of a second-strike capability, and hence the need for the "overkill" that provided guaranteed deterrence no matter who struck first.

Strategic nuclear bombing was thus seen as the essential purpose of American air power. This emphasis was given added force by the role of officers from SAC in the senior ranks of the Air Staff, by a fascination with aerial self-sufficiency and big bombers and missiles, and by the absence of a powerful drive for integrated warfare, which would have encouraged the development, instead, of doctrines for cooperation with the army and navy, and aircraft designed accordingly. The other forces were instead seen as largely irrelevant in a nuclear war.[10] The lack of this drive was related to the organization of the USAF into monofunctional commands. This reflected the pattern the RAF had established in 1936, and contrasted with the regional organization adopted by the Luftwaffe.

The expansion of its nuclear arsenal was America's first major experience of leading in a peacetime arms race. This expansion was a response to the major change in military capability and to the American sense of the tenuousness of victory in the Second World War. In the aftermath of the disaster year of 1942, which was still felt strongly, few in the United States in the early and mid-1950s believed in the inevitability of Axis defeat during the recent war. Moreover, the experience of surprise attack by Japan in 1941 made the possibility of a Soviet surprise attack more threatening. If the development of America's nuclear weapons spoke to its strategic weaknesses as much as its economic strengths, there were also more specific problems with American military structure and technology that encouraged an emphasis on nuclear weaponry. Until the deployment of the B-52 in 1955, American bombers had weaknesses.

Strategic nuclear bombing also played a major role in British air planning during the period. The bomber air bases were in eastern England, for bombing Leningrad (St. Petersburg) and Moscow (as they had formerly been used for bombing Germany), and in northern Iraq, for bombing industrial sites in Ukraine and southern Russia. This helped explain the strategic significance of Iraq to the containment of the Soviet Union, a role that was to be ended in 1958 when the pro-Western government was overthrown. From the British base in Cyprus, bombers could overfly Turkey, a NATO member from 1952, and thus threaten Ukraine.[11] This continued with the establishment of the Central Treaty Organization (CENTO) in 1955 when the nuclear threats against the Soviet Union expanded eastward to include bases in Iran and Pakistan.

In both the United States and Britain, the legacies of interwar air doctrine and of the "strategic" (i.e., war-winning) bombing campaigns of the Second World War were extremely important. In contrast, the value of close air support shown by Allied air operations in 1944–45, for example at Okinawa, was underrated, if not neglected. In the United States, TAC (Tactical Air Command), which was founded in 1948 as an equal to Strategic Air Command, was rapidly downgraded, and most of its aircraft were transferred to NATO and the Pacific.[12] This situation helped weaken the American military in the Vietnam War and also looked toward the subsequent emphasis on air power as a stand-alone or strategic tool, as in the Kosovo War (1999). However, it was argued that, had more of an effort been devoted to TAC, the effectiveness of the nuclear deterrent would be compromised, leading to the possibility of war with the communist bloc.

JET AIRCRAFT

Jet aircraft and their use developed rapidly after the Second World War. A problem with the early jets was the lack of acceleration from the engines at low speeds, which made dogfighting difficult. And if the throttle was applied too quickly at low speed, there was a danger of flameout. It was not until the introduction of reheat (the afterburner) in the early 1950s that the engines produced supersonic flow from the nozzles and supersonic flight became operationally feasible. An afterburner adds fuel to the air that has already passed through the turbine and burns it just before the nozzle, providing a huge amount of additional thrust. The speed made possible by jet engines, notably from the 1950s, posed new issues in training. In particular, the tactics of dogfighting had to change because of the higher speed of jets, which, it was thought, would render obsolete the sort of dogfighting seen in the Second World War. However, there was also an important degree of continuity. At the time, all fighters still used guns, not missiles, which, as yet, did not have reliable guidance systems. Higher speeds and g-forces when turning required greater emphasis on basic combat maneuvering, with attacks such as the high yo-yo or barrel-roll attack used to gain a firing situation behind enemy aircraft.

The process and problems of improvement were not simply those of a translation to jet power. For example, the continued problems of the B-29 with engine malfunctioning encouraged the USAF to begin modifications of its heavy bomber. The B-50, which first flew in June 1947 and became operational in June 1948, had a bomb-load capacity of nearly thirty thousand pounds, compared to the B-29's twenty thousand pounds, an increase that was due to an enlarged bomb bay, in contrast to the two smaller ones on the B-29. The B-29 was not designed for atomic bombs, and the August 1945 missions had involved impromptu, time-consuming modifications that the Americans, who had not yet successfully miniaturized the atomic bomb, did not wish to become involved with on a regular basis.

In contrast, the B-50 could carry these bombs. The aircraft also had an improved wing, which was attributable to a higher-quality aluminum sheet metal, as well as larger engines with turbochargers added (by Pratt and Whitney in East Hartford, Connecticut), a taller and broader tail for improved stabilization in view of the aircraft's extra weight, and a heavier-duty undercarriage to support this extra weight. In a major improvement to range, which had clear implications for strategic ambitions for air power, the B-50 was also designed to be refueled in the air, which the B-29 could not be; and, in the late 1940s, it flew missions above the Soviet polar north, including into Soviet airspace. However, the B-50 was an interim measure while deliveries of the B-47 were awaited. Delays in the delivery of the B-47 meant that the B-50 continued in service well into the 1950s.

When the B-50 became operational, the Soviet Union was still using Second World War interceptors, which did not quite have the ceiling that the B-50 did. This changed with the introduction of the Soviet MIG-15 jet interceptor, which had its first flight in 1947 and became operational in 1949. The first sorties were in early 1950 with the MIG-15bis, an all-weather interceptor version. This ensured a need for changing practice and improved specifications for the Americans. Moreover, the continual process of aircraft improvement, one greatly encouraged by rivalry for orders between competing manufacturers, was also significant. The Convair B-36, with six reverse prop engines and two underslung jet engines on each wingtip, had a longer range than the B-50, was somewhat faster and capable of somewhat higher altitudes, and was designed specifically to carry the atomic bomb from the start, whereas the B-50 was essentially a souped-up B-29, which was not so designed. The B-36 had an unprecedented range. Longer-range jet bombers, the B-47, with three jet engines on either side, and, in turn, the B-52 "Stratofortress," with its eight jet engines, put earlier bombers out of business. The B-36 was still basically a propeller-driven plane, and almost as vulnerable on that account, while the B-47 was intermediate, not long range. The B-52s, which entered service in February 1955, gave the United States an advantage in strategic air power, providing substance to President Dwight Eisenhower's policy of massive retaliation, and explaining why the air force received close to 45 percent of annual military spending from 1952 to 1960, while expenditures on the army and navy were markedly cut.

In the 1950s, encouraged by the Korean War buildup, jet fighter-bombers, such as the American F-84 Thunderjet, made their first appearance, and they came to play a major role, replacing more vulnerable Second World War–period aircraft, although the F-84 was no match for the MIG-15, which had low wing loading, could turn well, and was excellent in a dogfight. By the mid-1950s, the Americans had a profusion of test and mass-production fighters and fighter-bombers. Concern about Soviet bombers led to an emphasis on fighters able to achieve altitude quickly and shoot the bombers down, such as the American F-104, first flown in 1954. Like many aircraft of the period, it was based on experience gained in the Korean War. The Americans also deployed jet tankers (KC-135s) from 1957 to provide a significant increase in the range for the bombers. Meanwhile, ultra-high-altitude photo-reconnaissance aircraft, notably the American U-2, provided very long-range intelligence for strategic intentions and target selection. The notorious Gary Powers's flight took off from Peshawar in Pakistan and was en route to Bodø in Norway before it was shot down over Sverdlovsk. In 1964, the C-141 Starlifter entered service as the USAF's first all-jet-powered transport. With its four engines, it could carry 41,222 kg (90,880 lbs) or transport 154 troops.

Other states also acquired jet aircraft. The Royal Canadian Air Force (RCAF) acquired its first, the De Havilland Venom, in 1947, followed by the Canadian-built version of the American F-86 Sabre in 1950. The first Danish jets were the F-84 Thunderjets, American fighter-bombers acquired in 1951, followed by British Hawker Hunters in 1956, American Thunderflashes in 1957, American Sabres in 1958, American

Super Sabres in 1959, and American Starfighters in 1964. With the exception of the Hawker Hunters, the Mutual Defense Assistance Program (MDAP), whereby the United States gave its European allies military equipment in return for their increasing their military efforts, was dominant until the Danes acquired the Swedish Saab 35 Drakens in 1970. The Danes have really only ever chosen to buy the Hawker Hunters, the Drakens, and, in 1980, the American F-16s. The West German Luftwaffe relied heavily on American and Canadian aircraft, notably the F-84. Under the MDAP, in an Americanization that replaced British aircraft, the Dutch acquired Thunderjets, Thunderstreaks, Thunderflashes, Sabres, and Starfighters, as well as training aircraft, ground equipment, vehicles, radar systems, and training. Thunderstreaks and Thunderflashes were swept-wing, different-engine variants of the F-84; the Thunderflash was a tactical reconnaissance version. The F-86 Sabre was vastly superior to the F-84 Thunderjet. The quantities the Dutch acquired were considerable, including the aircraft for seven tactical squadrons, four air-observation squadrons, three night-fighter squadrons, and one transport squadron. The MDAP, which led to the Americanization of allied air forces, was ended in 1961.

By then, there was a very heavy reliance on American systems and models. For example, the use of American trainers and spare parts was highly significant. The development costs of aircraft from the 1950s onward became huge, which had a profound impact on the supply of advanced aircraft. Most European states stopped trying to develop their own aircraft, as it was cheaper to buy than to develop from scratch. Israel bought its first jets, Meteors from Britain, in 1953, followed by Ouragan (1955), Mystere (1956), and Mirage-3 (1963) jets from France. Japan acquired its first jet fighter, the F-86, in 1955. A total of 180 of them were imported from the United States from 1955 to 1957, but an additional three hundred were manufactured in Japan under license from 1956 to 1960. The F-104J Starfighter followed from 1962: 190 of the total 210 were manufactured in Japan under license. South Korea acquired its first jet, also the F-86, in 1955. The F-104 Starfighter was controversial with some NATO powers because it had a poor safety record, which was partly due to poor maintenance and pilot bravado. The Lockheed bribery scandal highlighted how the aircraft had been so readily taken up.

Despite the prominence of the United States, developments in aircraft manufacture were pressed forward in a number of states. In the late 1950s, Canada attempted to build its own supersonic interceptor, the Avro Arrow, but this project failed like the British TSR-2. Several test airframes were built but never tested with the intended Iroquois engine. The government deemed the project too expensive and canceled it. Suspicions of American influence ran high, as the Canadian government then purchased American interceptors and air-defense missiles. More generally, Americanization meant replacing British influence.

NATIONAL FORCE STRUCTURES

The development of distinctive air forces reflected historic factors as well as those specific to changing conjunctures and contingencies. The most important historic factors related to particular institutional traditions, but there was also the very varied experience of war. States that had been rapidly conquered, and by an opponent with a far more potent air force, such as Denmark, Norway, and the Netherlands in 1940, each victims of Germany, found it easier to justify both the development of a significant air force and membership in an alliance structure, in their case NATO, that brought the support of the United States, a superpower with the world's leading air force. At the same time, at the level of individual states, the particular configurations of air power reflected the interaction with the international environment, notably in the forms of threat perception and alliance dynamics; the significance of domestic policy, particularly financial constraints and industrial concerns; and the organizational policies of the individual military services.

While the United States focused very heavily on air power, seeing it as the key means for global power projection, other countries closer to the front line adopted a military profile in which air power played a smaller role. This prefigured the situation that was to be seen throughout the entire post-1945 period, both during the Cold War with the Soviet Union, which lasted until 1989, and thereafter. There were a number of reasons for this contrast, reasons variously centered on the United States or on other powers. In part, the technological and industrial lead and capacity of the United States was the key element, alongside the unmatched wealth of the state and country; its willingness to spend heavily on the military, and to borrow accordingly; and the strength of the military-industrial complex. In 1945, the American aircraft industry was the best placed in the world for manufacture, particularly for long-range aircraft.

This lead was sustained in part by the unprecedented postwar growth of the American civilian aircraft industry. This growth helped in the development of air-mindedness across a large continent and in the development of the related manufacturing plant, design skills, repair facilities, political linkages, and pilot experience. This process was especially apparent in Southern California, and that at a time in which the regional balance of political power was beginning to give more weight to the West, specifically to California. Although the British Comet, which went into commercial service in 1952, was the first jet-propelled airliner, it was affected by crashes that, for a while, were unexplained. Benefiting also from the economic, financial, and political muscle of the United States, it was to be the Boeing 707 that then dominated jet transport, becoming the aircraft of choice not only in the United States but also for many carriers throughout the noncommunist world.

No other country matched this combination. In Britain, there was an important tradition of air-mindedness, and a major civilian aircraft industry, while the RAF had played a major role in the war. The Battle of Britain of 1940 left an aura of heroism. However, the navy remained important to the national psyche and was still highly significant in the discussion of British strategy. Moreover, the war had exhausted Britain and left the state heavily indebted. Although air power was important for air defense and colonial policing, there was far less of a reliance on the air force than in the United States. British military planning in the late 1940s for the defense of West Germany against likely Soviet attack boiled down to a struggle between the army and the RAF for strategic supremacy, a struggle that was only resolved when each service settled upon a role that only they could perform.[13] Meanwhile, the Soviet Union built up an impressive long-range bomber force able to use atomic weaponry, but, on the pattern of the Second World War, it never lost its focus on air power, which remained that of assisting advancing ground forces, notably with close support but also with interdiction attacks.

More significantly, most European states feared invasion or insurrection, a fear seen either for the metropole (home country) or for the colonies, or for both. This fear encouraged an emphasis on armies. This emphasis, based largely on tasking and instrumental considerations, was accentuated by political concerns. Most states retained conscription, both to meet their military commitments and as an expression of citizenship. The last, motivated by concern about the values of a professional military, was designed in part to lessen the threat of coups. Thus, for example, for one or the other of these reasons, there was conscription in the Soviet Union, Britain, France, Italy, and, when it was re-armed, West Germany. Nearly independent states, keen to affirm identity, foster loyalty, and safeguard interests, also introduced conscription, as with Israel. At any rate, given the proximity of hostile forces, and the relative ease of training army versus air force recruits, such states put a major emphasis on their army. This process was encouraged by the extent to which independence frequently led to conflict, or the threat of conflict, as was the case, for example, for India, Pakistan, Israel, Jordan, Egypt, Syria, Indonesia, and Malaysia. These states, like those of Western Europe, feared attack and invasion by land in a way that the United States did not. Wars for them were very much won on the ground.

In states with a longer history of independence, armies remained the key element for political reasons focused on historical factors, citizenship, and the suppression of internal opposition. This was the case with the Latin American states, as well as Iran, Iraq, and Thailand. An emphasis on armies also accorded with the military-financial structure of most states, namely the consequence of their economies, public finances, and expenditure needs and opportunities. Most states were equipment poor and people rich because troops, notably if conscripted, were cheap, while cutting-edge equipment was expensive, had to be imported, and could be difficult to obtain and operate.

In China, where the communists gained power in 1949, having won the civil war, these political factors favoring expenditure on the army were focused by Mao Zedong's belief that the popular will could, should, and would defeat advanced technology as expressed, for example, by air power. Indeed, in the Chinese Civil War (1946–49), the side that was the weaker in air power, the communists, prevailed. Chiang Kai-shek, the Nationalist leader, was a big fan of air power, but he was unable to translate the strategic advantage offered by his monopoly of air power into decisive tactical and operational advantage. As is usually the case for troops whose side lacks effective air power, communist soldiers were scared of Nationalist air attack, a fear and psychological effect of air power that communist leaders felt they had to fight against. The communists made a point of acquiring and using antiaircraft guns when they could. They were employed at the siege of Changchun in order to hamper Chiang's airlift of food and other supplies to the city.

Nationalist air power could, and sometimes did, make a decisive difference, as with the third Battle of Siping in June 1947 in which Chiang used air power to help defend Siping against Lin Biao's attack. The communist attack ultimately failed, and Chiang praised the air force for its performance at Siping. However, there were also problems with Nationalist air power. These included poor coordination of air power and ground troops, and a lack of fuel and spare parts. In the last stages of the war in Manchuria, Chiang devoted a substantial portion of his air power to the fruitless task of keeping the garrisons in the cities of Shenyang and Changchun supplied, to this end flying aircraft out of Jinzhou and Beijing, airdropping grain and ammunition, and occasionally dropping handwritten orders from Chiang himself. This operation, which had all the hallmarks of Göring's forlorn attempts to resupply Stalingrad in 1942–43, coincided with the Berlin crisis in Europe. When ordering his troops to try to break out of Changchun, Chiang explained that continued airdrops of supplies could not be sustained because, due to the need to send fuel to Europe, the Americans could no longer keep his air force supplied. Air power, and the related fuel, was a key strategic resource, and one therefore that entailed crucial issues of prioritization.

Another limitation on Nationalist air power was that the communists learned how to keep its impact to a minimum. Theoretically, Chiang could have used air power to cut communist supply lines in the summer of 1948, as Lin Biao, a leading communist commander, was setting things up for the Liao-Shen campaign, a task that involved the transport of troops, artillery, and supplies from communist bases in north Manchuria south to Liaoning Province. However, totally debilitating attacks on such a supply chain are very difficult to achieve via air power, as American attempts on the Ho Chi Minh Trail during the Vietnam War were to show, and a lot more and better air power was applied to that operation. When Chiang's air force made rail transportation too dangerous, the communists used trucks. And when they wanted further to confuse the Nationalists, the communists switched back to rail, running trains at night and camouflaging them during the day. The ammunition cars were not put together in case they got hit.[14] At the same time, the nighttime rate of supply movements was lower.

Once the communists were in power, China quickly developed an air force as a branch of the People's Liberation Army (PLA). In January 1949, the Communist Party resolved to develop an air force within two years. A transitional administration structure followed in March, and the air force of the PLA was officially founded on November 11, 1949. Mao Zedong's interest in an invasion of Taiwan, which was still held by the Nationalists, led him to press the creation of an air force. The aviation industry followed from April 1951. With the help of Soviet experts, the Chinese first developed the capacity to repair aircraft and then began to develop their own aircraft industry. The successful trial production of the first trainer was achieved in 1954, the first fighter following in 1956. This, the Shengyang J-5, copied the Soviet MIG-17, while the first bomber, the Harbin H-5, which had its first test flight in 1966, copied the Soviet Ilyushin Il-28.

Aside from the Cold War, the development of air forces also reflected continuity from the former imperial experience, as well as that of the Second World War. This was seen in Malaya, where the Malayan Auxiliary Air Force was established in the mid-1930s as an adjunct to the RAF. This was followed, from 1940, by the Straits Settlements Volunteer Air Force and the Malayan Volunteer Air Force (MVAF), although, in 1941–42, the RAF and RAAF (Royal Australian Air Force) were the principal combatants in the unsuccessful war against Japanese invasion. In 1950, the Malayan Volunteer Air Force was revived in the Malayan emergency created by communist insurrection. In 1957, Malayan independence was followed by the Anglo-Malayan Defense Agreement, which provided for the defense of Malaya. Britain was to assist in expanding and training Malayan forces and was permitted to maintain its military bases. This led to the Five Power Defense Arrangement, in which British air power played a major role in providing security. In 1958, the MVAF was replaced by the Royal Federation of Malaya Air Force (RFMAF), initially under the direction of Air Commodore A. V. R. (Sandy) Johnstone, a hero of the Battle of Britain. In 1960, the first RAF air base in Malaya (established in 1941) was transferred to the RFMAF, with the Australians based at RAAF Butterworth at Penang and the British at RAF Tengah in Singapore, and with ground-based radars in both Malaya and Singapore. Initially, Malaya (then Malaysia) looked to Britain for its aircraft.

Varied national factors ensured that, whatever the examples set by the United States and the Second World War, air power was an add-on for most less powerful states. This situation was readily apparent in the institutional structure of militaries and in procurement policies. At the same time, the combined pressures of Cold War confrontation, the resulting arms race, the demands of alliance leaders, and the need to rearm in response to the spread of jet technology all led to greater investment in air power, investment that was made possible by economic growth or by acquiring aircraft at a cut price from allies. The combination of the economic "Long Boom" from 1945 to 1973 with the Cold War ensured the development of air power. The United States set the pattern within NATO, and the Soviet Union in the communist bloc. The American formation of an independent air force proved particularly important. Thus, in Portugal, where army and naval services had been separate, they were brought together in 1952 to create the Portuguese air force. This change arose from Portugal entering NATO, as a founding member, in 1949, and from the potent example of the American system. Similarly, the Danish air force did not become a service of its own until 1950, and the Dutch until 1953.

In the Netherlands, the immediate postwar organization reflected the imprint of the war years, notably the reconstruction plans made then with the RAF while the Dutch government was in exile in Britain. The British influence was clear in the organization of the air force (which in 1953 became an independent as opposed to an auxiliary force) and in the procurement of the British Meteor, a jet that was built under license by Fokker. The onset of the Cold War led to a stepping up of plans, with the combination of increased Dutch expenditure on defense and American aid providing the means. A determination to keep the United States satisfied was matched by concerns about the viability of the Dutch air industry. The latter played a major role, notably with the purchase of the Fokker F-27 transport aircraft in 1958, a decision made for economic reasons and despite the opposition of the Dutch air force and NATO. In the Dutch case, as in others, the individual national air force was set goals within the NATO context. Thus, at the time, the Dutch were not expected to prepare for strategic bombing, but rather for air combat above Germany, winning air superiority, conducting reconnaissance, and launching ground attacks, and also for maritime patrol. [15]

While American and, to a lesser extent, British influence was important in NATO, Soviet influence was significant in the communist bloc's Warsaw Pact. Thus, the Hungarian air force was reestablished in 1947 along Soviet lines. These patterns were also influential further afield. Thus, influenced by the United States, pro-Western Japan established an independent air force in 1954. In the Persian Gulf, air forces or army air force wings were established in Oman in 1959 and in Kuwait in 1961, the year of its independence.

AIRCRAFT FOR POLITICAL ALLIANCES

Aircraft were a tool for alliance building. Second World War aircraft, such as the Dakotas and Spitfires Egypt had, were replaced by jets. In 1955, the Soviet Union, through Czechoslovakia, agreed to provide two hundred MIG-15 fighters and fifty Il-28 bombers to Egypt. The MIG-15 was operated by other Soviet allies and sympathizers, including Albania, Angola, China, Congo, Guinea, Guinea-Bissau, Mali, Mozambique, North Korea, Romania, Syria, Tanzania, and Yemen, and was built in China, Czechoslovakia, and Poland. The more powerful and larger MIG-17 was built under license in China and Poland and was operated by many Soviet allies and sympathizers, including Albania, Algeria, Angola, Bulgaria, Congo, Cuba, Ethiopia, Guinea, Guinea-Bissau, Madagascar, Mali, Mozambique, Romania, and Syria. The MIG-21, which was first flown in 1957, was similarly distributed.

The United States transferred some aircraft based in Saudi Arabia in order to form the basis of its air force, which was established in 1950. Iran obtained American jet fighters from 1957, and, accordingly, their jet pilots trained at American bases. This encouraged the pilots to think about air power in terms of American doctrine. So also with the use of the T-37, the USAF's first purpose-built jet trainer. First flown in 1954 and introduced into the USAF in 1957, the T-37 was developed into an armed counterinsurgency aircraft equipped with bombs, gun pods, and missiles: the A-37. This was first flown in 1963, and the first operational use with the USAF was in 1967. The T-37 was flown by Chile, Colombia, West Germany, Greece, South Korea, Pakistan, Thailand, and Turkey; the A-37 by Chile, Colombia, the Dominican Republic, Ecuador, El Salvador, Guatemala, Honduras, South Korea, Peru, Thailand, and Uruguay. An older American aircraft, the T-33, which first flew as the P-80 in 1945, was used as a trainer or, with its machine guns, bombs and, later, missiles, for counterinsurgency missions by Bolivia, Canada, Ecuador, Greece, Iran, Japan, Mexico, Pakistan, Paraguay, South Korea, Thailand, Turkey, and Uruguay.

KOREAN WAR, 1950–53

The conflicts of the period indicated the value of air power. This was true both of wars between states and of counterinsurgency struggles. Despite the planning for conflict between the United States and the Soviet Union, the most important instance of the former was the Korean War. Beginning with an invasion of pro-Western South Korea by communist North Korea, this conflict rapidly broadened out as a result of an American-led United Nations (UN) intervention on behalf of the South, followed, later in 1950, by Chinese intervention in support of the North. In addition, the Soviet Union provided military backing, especially aircraft, for the North.

A key element, and one that established a hierarchy of military proficiency, was provided by air power. On the UN side, this overwhelmingly meant American air power, although there was also assistance from elsewhere, including British carriers as well as flying boats that were sent to assist with antisubmarine and antishipping patrols off Korea. Initially, the UN forces were heavily reliant on carrier air power because no airfields in South Korea could operate American jets, while many airfields there were lost to the rapid North Korean advance. Moreover, jets operating from American bases in Japan could only operate for fifteen minutes over South Korea, and that only by remaining at their optimum altitude of fifteen thousand feet. As a result, aside from carrier air power, which provided about one-third of the total air effort,[16] the subsequent UN advance north was critical as it ensured that bases were available in South Korea. On the communist side, the Soviet Union provided the key element, of both pilots and aircraft, from Manchurian bases north of North Korea, across the Yalu River in China.

There was a major transition in air power. At the start of the war, the Americans were flying P-51s and other propeller fighters, and the Soviet-trained North Korean and Chinese pilots were also flying propeller fighters, the Soviet-supplied Yak-9. As with much of the weaponry available in the early stages of the Cold War, this was a weapon from the latter stages of the Second World War: the Yak-9D, which entered squadron service in 1943, was followed in 1945 by the Yak-9U, which had a more powerful engine (1,650 horsepower as opposed to 1,260) and therefore a greater speed and range, as well as more weaponry. A formidable fighter, the Yak-9, in the hands of good pilots, was a match for the German Me-109 and even for the Focke-Wulf 190.

Rather quickly, both sides in the Korean War swung over to swept-wing jet interceptors, the Chinese using the Soviet-built MIG-15 and the Americans F-86s (Sabres), although jets were also shot down by propeller fighters. The Chinese and North Korean air forces were not well trained and lost far more heavily against the Americans than the several hundreds of Soviet pilots of the Manchurian-based "Group 64," who were flying MIG-15s. A combination of newer jets and training turned the balance of advantage and loss one way and another. Organizational factors were also important to American success over Korea. In particular, the rotation system employed by the Soviet pilots, the rotation of entire air groups on a specific training cycle, as opposed to the American rotation of pilots for individual preset tours of duty, greatly undermined their continuity of experience, and thus their effectiveness. The Americans were to confront this issue less successfully during the Vietnam War.

The war also saw the widespread use of helicopter medevac—the evacuation of casualties by helicopter—although there had been a limited use of helicopters for that purpose in the latter stages of the Second World War. The successful deployment of helicopters in moving troops into battle was seen with the First Marine Division in September 1951 and with the movement of the Indian army brigade charged with enforcing the cease-fire in the newly delineated Demilitarized Zone in Korea in 1953.

The impact of technology was qualified by a number of factors. Although the Americans were able to dominate the skies, with serious consequences for the invading communists, the absence of adequate command integration limited the American exploitation of this advantage, as did the weakness of tactical air support in USAF doctrine. The Americans lacked the necessary training and aircraft, not least because their jet fighters were designed for air superiority and, therefore, high-speed and altitude operations, and far less for ground support.

In tactical terms, the value of air support for the American army, notably at the time of the initial North Korean assault, did not diminish the heavy reliance on ground firepower in order to blunt Chinese attacks, understandably so given the damage that could be inflicted by artillery as well as the serious problems bad weather created for aircraft. When James Van Fleet became commander of the American Eighth Army in Korea in 1951, he insisted on each 105 mm howitzer being able to fire three hundred rounds per day, a rate that provided a greater impact at a lower cost than that from aircraft. More artillery fire avoided the reliance on weather seen with aircraft. The Soviet refusal to heed Chinese pressure for Soviet air support of Chinese ground forces was a major advantage for the Americans, as well as helping to limit the potential expansion of the conflict.[17] Conversely, there was no American pursuit of communist aircraft into the sanctuary of China and no use of atomic weaponry. These were deterrent threats, as was the availability of carrier air power to attack Chinese and Soviet targets. This was a bloody, limited war as both the United States and the communists also sought to keep the conflict nonnuclear.

Preferring to focus on strategic bombing, rather than ground support, preferences reflected in and drawing on its doctrine and aircraft, the USAF claimed that its conventional bombing had caused much damage in North Korea and helped lead America's opponents to accept the armistice in 1953. Heavy damage was certainly inflicted, for example, in 1952, to hydroelectric generating capacity with the successful attack on the Suiho dam complex. This left North Korea wholly dependent on China and the Soviet Union for electric power. However, the bombing, which included the firebombing of industrial cities in North Korea, did not break the stalemate of the last two years of the war. The USAF also devoted considerable effort to attacking North Korean supply lines, especially the rail links that provided supplies from China. Nevertheless, the USAF failed to inflict the anticipated logistical damage, not least because of the extent of opposition, both from aircraft and antiaircraft fire, as well as due to repairs and to the night movement of supplies, and as a consequence of the simple nature of the North Korean economy, one not reliant on the types of activity seen in wartime Germany and Japan. It proved impossible to isolate the battlefield by means of air power. In all these respects, the contrast between the hopes from bombing and what was achieved anticipated the situation during the Vietnam War, as the USAF again struggled to pursue a winning role. The contrast, however, did not lead American advocates of bombing to doubt its value.[18] Instead, their emphasis was on the political constraints posed by the fear of escalation, rather than on any intrinsic limitations of air power.

At the same time, the Korean War had seen an improvement in the use of tactical air power, with training on the job in air support, the production of appropriate aircraft and munitions, and the use of forward air controllers. Close air support was separated from the operational support of armies and came down to battalion and company level. New skills were brought to established requirements. In many respects, indeed, there was a repetition of the trajectory of ground-air support seen with the Americans and British in the Second World War. This trajectory reflected the extent to which commanders came from a SAC background, and the extent to which new aircrew were a feature of air warfare, notably after postwar demobilization. That lessons about the significance of air support had to be relearned was highlighted by a lack of emphasis on strategic long-range bombing comparable to the Second World War. The absence of this dimension highlighted the issues and deficiencies of tactical air power. Yet the war also showed the value of force substitution: of a massive number of troops by a far smaller number of aircraft.

The Korean War encouraged a more general buildup of air power across the board, because it not only greatly heightened Cold War tensions, but it also suggested that such tensions could result in a large-scale conventional war, and it led to renewed claims that air power was an effective element. In Western Europe, in part in response to America's worldwide commitments, NATO accelerated the buildup of Allied air forces so that the lesser powers moved their focus from air defense to the use of tactical air forces to blunt offensives and to buy time. However, the American emphasis and that of the RAF continued to be on strategic air power and a trip-wire philosophy, and there was a tendency to ignore the Korean War or to claim that it could have been waged more successfully had there been a reliance on such air power.

The reliance on SAC for war planning against the Soviet Union encouraged a reading from this situation to Korea.

After the cease-fire of July 1953, a team of all four American services toured South Korea to evaluate the effectiveness of tactical support and close air support of the ground forces. With expected dissent from the USAF, the evaluation rated the marines, who had their own air power, first and placed the USAF last. However, in the follow-up for appropriations and the development of strategic doctrine, the marines lost out. As a consequence, investment in aircraft and munitions continued to focus on long-range heavy bombers. Needs focused on these bombers dominated procurement, training, doctrinal discussion, and planning for the future of air power. The particular emphases were on American bombing with nuclear bombs and on the interception of similar Soviet bombers.

INSURRECTIONARY AND COUNTERINSURGENCY WARFARE

In some of the conflicts of the period, air power played a relatively minor role. Nevertheless, in general, air power provided armies resisting insurrections with significant advantages. This was the case both in Europe and farther afield. Within Europe, there was a ready availability of aircraft. The use of American-provided Helldivers played a major role in the success of government forces in overcoming communist opposition in the closing stages of the Greek Civil War in 1949.[19] In 1956, Soviet air attacks and helicopters supported armor in crushing popular opposition in Hungary.

Outside Europe, there was a widespread use of aircraft against insurrections. The surrender of Japan in 1945 left, in the former colonies of the Western imperial powers, a chaotic situation in which nationalists vied for control with the returned forces of these powers. This led to conflict, notably in the Netherlands East Indies (now Indonesia) and Vietnam. The British played a key role in restoring the authority of the Dutch and French, respectively, while refusing to reconquer these colonies. In east Java, in the Netherlands East Indies, in October 1945, the British deployed in the city of Surabaya, demonstrating their power with a flight of twelve P-47 Thunderbolts over the city. Fighting, however, broke out, and in November–December, British forces, supported by Thunderbolts and Mosquitoes, as well as warships, gained control after much difficulty. Air transport was a major RAF commitment. The British deployed one hundred aircraft and flew nearly twenty thousand sorties in the fifteen months they were in Java. In Vietnam in 1945, the British similarly found themselves in opposition to the nationalists, the Viet Minh, and, when the latter failed to comply and turned to violence, used aircraft to bomb and strafe their positions.

In the late 1940s, the Dutch used the Netherlands East Indies air force against nationalist opposition in Java and Sumatra, the two key islands in the Netherlands East Indies. However, although some Dutch air power theorists supported the idea of "colonial air policing," the means were simply never there. From 1946 to 1949, especially during the two so-called police actions[20] (in July–August 1947 and December 1948), the air force (the Army Air Corps) was mainly used in a conventional close air support/counterinsurgency role. For this task, two squadrons of fighter-bombers (mainly P-51 Mustangs) were usually available, but their operations were thinly spread across the vast archipelago. Some notable successes were achieved, but mainly against the (more or less) fixed positions of the Indonesian nationalists, such as airfields (destroying Indonesian aircraft) and coastal batteries. The most interesting offensive use of air power was the assault on Yokjakarta (1948) by commando-paratroopers, an example of modern combined-arms operations. Sukarno, the nationalist leader, was captured in this surprise raid. Although a political failure (the action cost the Dutch a great amount of international goodwill), the assault showed what the Dutch armed forces were capable of given the right tools. This fit into a pattern in which Dutch soldiers felt that they were generally being prevented by their political masters from going "all out" in their counterinsurgency war,[21] a common theme in such conflicts. Moving troops quickly was also a key role for the air force.

However, the Dutch were not able to defeat the Indonesians. After the second "police action," an eight-month guerrilla war then took as many Dutch lives as in the three preceding years. Spread thin, the Dutch were forced to face the fact that the only option was to get out. Talks started in August 1949, and a peace agreement was signed on November 2. Military issues played a role in the Dutch withdrawal, but so did strong American pressure on behalf of the nationalists, as well as

American urging that the Dutch focus on Europe, all of which was compounded by Dutch weakness after the Second World War.

In contrast, helped by greater political resolve, more resources, and weaker opposition, the British opposing communist insurrection in Malaya from 1948 to 1960 benefited greatly from the mobility, both in air transport and air supply, offered by helicopters and transport aircraft. Accurate intelligence was crucial, and the Auster spotter aircraft flew more sorties than any other type. Aircraft were also used to attack guerrilla targets—notably in support of land forces, proving especially useful when it was impossible to bring in artillery—and to drop propaganda leaflets. Air superiority stopped foreign insurgents from being airlifted in. The legacy of recent experience was significant. General Hugh Stockwell, who became army commander in Malaya in 1952, had commanded an airborne division in Palestine in 1947–48. Robert Thompson, a key advisor in counterinsurgency during the Malaya campaign, had been involved in air-supported irregular campaigning in Burma (Myanmar) during the Second World War. Australian and New Zealand aircraft supported the RAF, which was reinforced by jets and helicopters from Britain.

In Kenya, another British colony, the RAF provided a significant contribution in 1953–55 against the Mau Mau uprising of 1952–56, notably in 1953–54 in being able to attack the Mau Mau in areas beyond the reach of the army, especially in the distant forests around Mount Kenya and in the Aberdare Mountains. Lincoln heavy bombers were supported by Harvard transports. Mau Mau groups and supply dumps were attacked. Air power served in a number of respects to influence opinion, not least by demonstrating the strength of the government, and there was also broadcasting from the sky, which increased in scale in 1955. Leaflets were dropped in order to influence opinion, including five million in June 1955 alone. As part of the battle for opinion, care was taken to lessen civilian casualties by air attack through bombing and strafing. These attacks affected the insurgents' morale and broke up their groups. A photographic reconnaissance capability was also developed.[22] Air-supported forest patrols were important.

Air support, some of it carrier based, was also significant for the British in battling the EOKA insurrection in Cyprus. This was an environment that offered the British greater opportunities than in the cases of Malaya and Kenya, in part because there was far less tree cover, while the area of operations was smaller and aircraft were based more closely.

In Vietnam, the French in 1946–54 lacked the vastly greater air transport capability the Americans were to enjoy in Vietnam in the 1960s. As in Malaya, the dense foliage and heavy and low cloud cover of the region did not aid air operations. The French, however, were keen to deploy air support. French-flown British-supplied Spitfires were used to strafe and bomb Viet Minh positions when the Viet Minh refused to withdraw from the city of Haiphong in November 1946. In addition, hundreds of fleeing refugees were strafed and killed. Air power was particularly deadly when the Viet Minh launched mass attacks on French positions in the open areas of the Red River delta in North Vietnam in 1950–51. French aircraft used napalm among other weapons.

The French also sought to employ air power in order to achieve a mobility that would provide operational and, eventually, strategic effect. French air-mobile forces proved effective in operations in 1946–47, notably with parachute regiments deployed by Dakotas. At Nghia Lo in 1951 and Na San in late 1952, paratroopers attacked Viet Minh supply routes and thereby helped block their offensives. The Na San campaign involved a Viet Minh offensive against a fortified airfield which was kept open throughout the campaign.

In 1953–54, a forward base was developed by French parachutists at Dien Bien Phu near the border with Laos in order to protect native allies and the profitable opium crop, to threaten an invasion route into northern Laos, and to lure the Viet Minh into a major battle that, it was hoped, would enable the French to destroy them and hence negotiate from a position of strength. However, once Dien Bien Phu was attacked in March 1954, the French, then eleven thousand strong, were unable to clear the undergrowth sufficiently far out around their position, which was then heavily shelled. This prevented the French from landing aircraft. Instead, they were dependent on reinforcements and supplies dropped by parachute. These, however, proved insufficient in the face of the adroit and effective Viet Minh attacking tactics. Moreover, Dien Bien Phu was far from French air bases, which limited the effectiveness of air power, an effectiveness also affected by a shortage of radio navigation systems and by the difficult weather in the hill country.

The simplicity of Viet Minh logistics further lessened the options for French air power. The French, who had about four hundred aircraft in Vietnam in 1954, bombed the Viet Minh lines of communication, but the Viet Minh were always able to follow different routes. The United States considered intervening, as well as using nuclear bombs, but decided not to do so. The surrender of the French, their bases overrun, on May 7, 1954, led the French to abandon the conflict in Vietnam. The country was provisionally partitioned along the 17th parallel, a solution that neither communist North Vietnam nor pro-Western South Vietnam was happy to accept, but one that enabled the French to leave.

The action-reaction cycle so frequently seen with air power, as with other types of military activity, had been apparent in Vietnam. The Viet Minh made significant tactical and operational adaptations to French air power, including an increased reliance on night attacks from 1951, moving close to French positions in order to lessen the potential of air attack, employing sapper units against French airfields, and, from 1954, developing antiaircraft units.

In Algeria, the French faced an insurrection by the Front de Libération Nationale (FLN) from October 1954. From 1955, as the scale of FLN operations rose, the French increasingly complemented their static garrisons with pursuit groups, often moved by helicopters. These effective helicopter assault forces were stepped up in 1959, in large part in response to the introduction of significant numbers of large helicopters: Boeing Vertol H-21 helicopters, called *bananes*, which could fly entire units as well as light artillery. Eventually, the French deployed 175 helicopters, as well as 940 aircraft. The designation of large free-fire zones, cleared by forced resettlement, in which aircraft could bomb and strafe freely, increased the effectiveness of the aircraft. Unlike later insurgent forces under air attack, the FLN lacked antiaircraft missiles, while the terrain was far more exposed to air attack than the forested lands of Indochina. The indiscriminate character of the French use of strafing and bombing was all too characteristic of a failure to distinguish foes from the bulk of the population. French moves were often counterproductive in winning the loyalty of the latter. The helicopter-borne sweeps gravely damaged the FLN within Algeria, but the French were unable to end guerrilla action in what was a very costly struggle. Ultimately, France abandoned the struggle in 1962.

Algeria returned to civil conflict in 1992, as the FLN-ruled state proved unable to meet expectations, was perceived as corrupt and Westernized, and was certainly unwilling to respond to the popular will. The fundamentalist terrorists of the FIS (the Islamic Salvation Front) destabilized the state by widespread acts of brutal violence. In response, the government adopted the earlier techniques of the French, including helicopter-borne pursuit groups, large-scale sweep-and-search operations, and the use of terror as a reprisal. Success was only partial, but it was much greater than in the case of France in 1954–62. This contrast reflected the major difference in political context, rather than one in military means, and, correspondingly, the need in analysis to focus on the former.

Helicopters were a key aerial platform of the late 1950s and 1960s (and subsequently) as they offered the mobility that enabled troops to avoid ambushes on the ground. Moreover, helicopters represented the way in which air power was developing in different directions, as the range of specifications it offered increased. This increase enhanced the contrasting issues posed by the integration of air power.

Even if the effects of hostile air power could be countered, a lack of air power continued to handicap insurrections. Thus, in 1957, a rising by marines in the city of Cienfuegos against the Batista dictatorship in Cuba was suppressed by the army, with the regime using aircraft both to intimidate by overflying and to mount attacks on ground targets. The government had American surplus B-26s and Sea Furies. The Batista regime was less successful in its use of aircraft against the insurgents led by Fidel Castro in the mountainous Sierra Nevada range, a far more disparate target than the rebels in Cienfuegos.

On January 1, 1959, Batista fled Cuba and Castro took over. The following year, anticommunist exiles in Florida used aircraft to send supplies to opponents of Castro based in the Cuban mountains. In April 1961, President John F. Kennedy's failure to provide the necessary air support to a force of CIA-trained anticommunist exiles was blamed for the total defeat of their invasion at the Bay of Pigs. However, alongside this political decision, poor planning and stiff opposition were also highly significant in this failure. On April 15, American aircraft disguised with Cuban markings and piloted by Cuban exiles bombed Cuban airfields in an attempt to destroy the Cuban air force, but they had little success as the aircraft had already been moved and camouflaged. When the exiles landed in the Bay of Pigs on April 17, they met unexpected Cuban air attacks, which caused damage, notably the destruction of two ships, and confusion. The invasion continued the following day, and several B-26s, two manned by American pilots, flew over the Bay of Pigs from Nicaragua in an attempt to weaken the Cuban army and open the way for the landing of the necessary supplies for the stranded brigade. Most of the bombers were shot down, the supplies never arrived, and the exiles surrendered.

The slow speed, persistence, and low altitude that were appropriate for successful close air support aircraft in the COIN role required different specifications than fast jets. The piston engine A-1 Skyraider, the last piston fighter aircraft introduced into American service, was used by the French in Algeria from 1958. It proved very successful, operating with helicopter-borne rapid-pursuit forces against FLN infiltration. In the COIN role, over one thousand of these aircraft were to be used by the USAF, USN, and South Vietnamese in the Vietnam War. As is so often the case with aircraft use, this was a matter of specifications, but also of opportunities. The Skyraider was renowned for its massive payload, was also capable of nuclear tactical strike attacks, and had proved valuable in Korea for surviving massive damage from ground fire. There was also a massive surplus of these aircraft available because the A-1 Skyhawk light jet had replaced it in navy service in the late 1950s. The lesson of these wars was that air superiority provides the opportunity for success, but, certainly if misemployed, is no guarantee of success. Without air superiority, everything becomes more difficult, but air power is no panacea.

CONFLICTS BETWEEN STATES

Air power was also significant in conflict between states, notably as newly independent states struggled for territory and primacy in the aftermath of the retreat of imperial powers. Thus, in Kashmir in 1947, the transports of the Indian air force played a key role in airlifting Indian troops who prevented the loss of the region to Pakistani-supported raiders. Air power took a less central role as Israel successfully fought off Arab attacks in 1948–49 and again when it attacked Egypt in 1956. The Israelis were more effective than the Egyptians in aerial conflict, but in their ground-support tasks lost aircraft to antiaircraft fire.

Second World War surplus aircraft provided significant capability for independent states. Thus, both Egypt and Israel used British Spitfires while, by late 1949, Iran had obtained the P-47 Thunderbolt and the C-47 Dakota transport from the United States. The retreat of imperial powers and the provision of aircraft to independent air forces were linked to continued influence, notably in basing rights, training, and the provision of spares and maintenance. Thus, the Anglo-Ceylonese 1947 Defense Agreement allowed Britain to use the island's naval and air facilities in future emergencies. This agreement lasted until the 1956 Suez crisis led Ceylon (now Sri Lanka) to abrogate the agreement, which resulted in British planners placing a greater emphasis on carrier-based air power deployed in the Indian Ocean.

NAVAL AIR POWER

Naval air power was very much on display at the royal review of the British fleet on June 15, 1953, by the newly crowned Queen Elizabeth II. Five British fleet carriers, the *Eagle, Illustrious, Implacable, Indefatigable*, and *Indomitable*, were accompanied by two light carriers, as well as an Australian carrier and a Canadian one. At sea, indeed, the experience of the Second World War was taken forward in the strategic context of the Cold War. Initially, the carriers available reflected the situation in the closing years of the Second World War. Japan no longer had a fleet, while Britain and, far more, the United States benefited greatly from the building program during the conflict. The war ended as the *Midway*, the first of a new generation of three forty-five-thousand-ton American aircraft carriers, was completed. It was considerably larger than earlier carriers and had both increased aircraft capacity (144 aircraft) and an armored flight deck. The impact of air warfare was also shown by its carrying over 110 antiaircraft guns. The gunners contributed, with the air group, to a complement of 4,100 men. The *Midway*'s sister ship, the *Roosevelt* (known as the "Swanky Frankie"), was sent to the eastern Mediterranean in 1946 to bolster Western interests in the face of Soviet pressure on Greece and Turkey, and, from late 1947, there was at least one American carrier in the Mediterranean.

However, notably in competition with the other services, carriers initially struggled to define a strategic role. In 1949, the construction program of the American navy was rejected, and its major project, the supercarrier *United States*, was canceled in favor of the USAF plans for strategic bombing.

New issues and opportunities arose as a consequence of the introduction of jet aircraft and nuclear bombs. The first successful carrier landing of a jet aircraft took place on the British carrier *Ocean* in December 1945, while the Royal Navy operated Sea Vampires, its first jet, from 1947, and responded to the increased weight of aircraft by introducing steam catapults (first used in 1951) and angled decks (experiments began in 1952). The mirror landing system was first employed in 1953. All three were swiftly emulated by American carriers. The first launch of a nuclear-armed aircraft from a carrier took place from the American *Coral Sea* in 1950. As with the *Midway*, the naming of carriers after naval victories was significant, not least in reiterating narratives and establishing norms.

Ground-based air power became more potent as a consequence of the development of aerial refueling. However, although the USAF remained dominant, the apparent need for as wide-ranging a delivery of atomic bombs as possible ensured that the carriers were assigned strategic bombing duties, not least the use of a nuclear strike capability. The three ships of the *Midway* class accordingly had their flight decks strengthened. Authorized in 1951 and launched in late 1954, the *Forrestal* was the first American carrier to have an angled deck, which permitted two jets on two catapults to take off simultaneously. It was also the first American carrier to have steam catapults. The largest carrier hitherto in the American navy, the *Forrestal* was designed to accommodate large jets like the Douglas A-3 Skywarrior, a two-seater, two–jet engine bomber. The smaller A-4E Skyhawk, a single-seater introduced in 1956 and only retired in 2003, was also intended to carry nuclear bombs. As the aircraft carrying nuclear bombs required more fuel for their greater range and were therefore heavier, the catapults launching them also had to be heavier. The Soviet introduction of aircraft designed to attack American carriers was stepped up from 1954 when Soviet intelligence confirmed the presence on these carriers of nuclear weapons (bombs and Regulus missiles), as well as of aircraft able to deliver them.

Atomic ordnance was not used in the Korean War, but carriers took an active role in it, although far less so than in the Pacific War of 1941–45, as both sides had nearby land air bases. The communist powers lacked carriers, but, thanks to the Second World War, the United States and its allies had them aplenty. In addition to air combat, naval jets attacked ground targets, such as bridges over the Yalu River. The Americans dominated the scene, although the British Fleet Air Arm flew close to twenty-three thousand operational sorties, while one British light carrier was on station at any time during the Korean War, and two in 1952–53. Australia had commissioned its first carrier, *Sydney*, formerly the British *Terrible*, in 1948, and it saw service off Korea. France also deployed a carrier there, as well as using carriers off Vietnam against the Viet Minh. The scale of American naval air power was indicated by the number of F9F-2 to F9F-5 jets manufactured for the navy and the Marine Corps up to January 1953: 1,385 in total. By late 1954, the American navy had sixteen carrier air groups.[23]

Naval air power was also used by the British and French in attacking Egypt in the 1956 Suez crisis. The denial of the use of air bases in Libya, Jordan, and Iraq, hitherto friendly states, encouraged a reliance on naval power, as did the fact that carriers were closer than British bases in the colonies of Cyprus and (more distant) Malta, thus allowing British aircraft to replace their fuel and weapons load more rapidly. Alongside ground-based Canberras from Cyprus, aircraft from three British and two French carriers destroyed the Egyptian Air Force (EAF). Despite its modern jets, the EAF did not mount an adequate resistance to the bombing campaign, which ended up being successful, although it took three days to be completed, compared to one when the Israelis attacked in 1967. This destruction prepared the way for an airborne assault that included the first helicopter-borne assault landing from the sea: 415 marines and twenty-three tons of supplies landed by twenty-two helicopters from the British light carriers *Ocean* and *Theseus*. The after-action reports argued that the use of helicopters had been proven effective,[24] but that it would be extremely hazardous to enter a hot landing zone,[25] a conclusion that was to be disputed by the Americans.

Despite Suez, the value of naval air power was increasingly doubted in Britain, where the 1957 Defence White Paper, mirroring the preference for strategic missile operations, was issued only after a successful struggle by the Admiralty to save the carriers in the face of a minister of defense who regarded them as expensive and outmoded. The Chiefs of Staff reported that it was crucial to retain the Fleet Air Arm, as it offered a way to deploy air power in regions where ground-based air-craft could not be used, and concerns about adequate airfields, over-flight rights, and maintenance all played a role in this discussion.[26] Nevertheless, three of the light carriers were transferred to reserve, before being broken up in 1961–62, while a fourth became a mainte-nance ship.

Prefiguring developments in ground-based air power, there was an increasing contrast with sea-based air power, namely a marked differen-tiation between the policy and capability of the powers. While the Unit-ed States retained and developed its carrier groups, the British were the only other power to place a heavy focus on the distant strike capability brought by fleet carriers. Seeking to increase the ability of the fleet to operate without the support of bases, the Admiralty planned in the 1958–59 Naval Estimates for the continuous maintenance of a battle group centered on a carrier east of Suez. In 1960, the carrier *Victorious* joined the Far Eastern station, carrying several nuclear bombs and air-craft able to drop them. Subsequent British war planning called for the use of a carrier able to mount nuclear strikes on southern China, and for a second carrier to be deployed in 1964. These carriers were to comple-ment RAF aircraft based in Singapore. At the same time, there were significant changes in naval air power and in naval power as a whole. In 1960, *Devonshire*, the first British guided-missile destroyer, was launched. Guided missiles, albeit Sea Slug surface-to-air missiles, showed the way for a technology that would eventually give rise to cruise missiles, and offered an ability to hit targets faster and at less cost than with manned flight. The Soviet Union was to show particular inter-est.

Canada, which at the end of the Second World War had had the third-largest fleet in the world, ended its carrier presence in 1970. It had had one carrier operating consecutively from 1946: *Warrior* (1946–48), *Magnificent* (1948–57), and *Bonaventure* (1957–70). The *Bonaventure*, which had been the *Powerful* in the British navy, had an angled flight deck and operated Banshee jets. The Canadian navy also established a number of operational and training fixed-wing and heli-copter squadrons between 1946 and 1970. These carriers were not involved in any wars, other than training for a potential conflict with the Soviet Union. The *Magnificent* also transported Canadian troops and equipment to Egypt in 1956 when the peacekeeping United Nations Emergency Force (UNEF) was established.

Until taken out of service in 1968, the Dutch carrier, the former British *Venerable*, contributed to the NATO defense of the main sea lines across the Atlantic from the threat of Soviet submarines, served as a symbol of the importance and pride of the Dutch navy, and, in 1962, was sent to Netherlands (western) New Guinea, when military troubles with Indonesia were expected. However, when the Dutch bought the vessel, they did so because they envisaged the creation of no fewer than four carrier groups. In the end, they could not afford even one such group. After Netherlands New Guinea was lost to Indonesia, the carrier, a symbol of imperial grandeur, was quietly discarded and sold to Argentina. For smaller states, carriers offered emblematic as well as practical value. In 1961, India commissioned the *Vikrant*, originally intended to be the British *Hercules*, and in 1987 the *Viraat*, formerly the British *Hermes*.

At the strategic level, and led by the United States, there was the development of submarine-launched missiles carrying nuclear warheads. Submarines could be based near the coast of target states and were highly mobile and very hard to detect. In July 1960, the *George Washington* was responsible for the first successful underwater firing of a Polaris missile, and, the following year, the *Ethan Allen*, the first true fleet missile submarine, was commissioned. From 1964, American ballistic-missile submarines went on patrol on a regular basis. The capability of submarines had been enhanced by the development of nuclear power plants as a means of propulsion. By enabling submarines to remain submerged for far longer, this increased their range and lessened their vulnerability. Only the need to change crews made them come to the surface. Although more flexible, aircraft could not match their capability. The first nuclear-powered submarine, the USS *Nautilus*, was launched in 1952.

In December 1962, moreover, in what became known as the Nassau Agreement, the Americans agreed to provide Polaris for a class of four large nuclear-powered British submarines that were to be built. The Polaris A-1 had a maximum range of 1,400 miles, but it was replaced by the A-3, first test-fired in 1962 and deployed from 1964, which had a range of up to 2,880 miles thanks to newer synthetic materials, more powerful rocket engines, and greater size. The A-3 missile became operational on September 28, 1964, when the American submarine *Daniel Webster* began its initial operational patrol.

Meanwhile, naval air power developed in part in a counterinsurgency direction. British carrier-based Hellcats were used against targets in Java in late 1945. The British navy's first operational helicopter squadron was formed in 1952 in order to help antiguerrilla operations in Malaya. In 1960, *Bulwark*, formerly a light fleet carrier, was, after conversion, commissioned as a "Commando" carrier, able to carry a Royal Marine Commando unit; their arms, stores, and vehicles; the necessary assault craft; and a squadron of helicopters. In 1964, the British sent a carrier to Tanzania in order to help the government against a military coup: low-level flights by strike aircraft combined with the use of helicopter-borne troops proved crucial in restoring order. Conversely, in Uganda and Kenya, where loyal troops held the airfields, it was possible to fly in British troops to help their governments. Similarly, in 1953, a carrier had been sent to counter unrest in the colony of British Guiana (now Guyana).

In 1959, the tonnage of the Soviet navy exceeded that of the British for the first time, and thus became the world's second-largest navy. The Soviet naval focus, however, was not on air power. Indeed, the Soviets had no carriers at this stage. Instead, the emphasis was on submarines, which obliged the NATO powers to develop antisubmarine capability.[27]

THE SHADOW OF THE B-52

Theoretically, the Soviets possessed a capability to bomb the United States from 1953, using one-way missions, but the identification of long-range heavy bombers made the threat acute: the M-4 "Bison," which had four turbojets, in July 1953, and the TU-20 Bear, which had four turboprops, during the 1955 May Day parade. The assessment of threat varied, but USAF intelligence greatly stressed the threat, leading to the perception of a large "bomber gap."[28]

The American fear of Soviet bombers led to a stepping up of the American bomber program, to secret aerial reconnaissance of the Soviet Union, and, in a new strategic geography, to construction of early-warning radar systems in Canada designed to warn of Soviet attacks over the Arctic: the Pinetree Network in 1954, and the Distant Early Warning (DEW) and Mid-Canada Lines, both in 1957. The North American Air Defense Command, established in 1958, was important to the development of joint air-defense systems involving the United States and Canada. In order to attack over the North Pole, the United States had constructed a base at Thule in northwest Greenland in 1951–52, a base able to stage and refuel American bombers.

The SAGE (Semi-Automatic Ground Environment) Air Defense system, established in 1958, was a part of the investment in air defense. It involved the largest computers ever built and enabled prediction of the trajectory of aircraft and missiles. SAGE was an aspect of the key part of the Cold War in the development of American computer systems, with IBM and the Department of Defense playing central roles. The Internet was to be developed and funded by the Defense Department's Defense Advanced Research Projects Agency (DARPA) in order to help scientists using large computers to communicate with each other.[29]

The deployment of B-52 Stratofortress heavy bombers in 1955 upgraded American delivery capability, and a small number of aircraft appeared able, and rapidly, to achieve more than the far larger Allied bomber force had done against Germany in 1942–45. Equipped with eight Pratt and Whitney J57-P-1W turbojets, the B-52 could cruise at 525 miles per hour and had an unrefueled combat range of 3,600 miles, a payload of thirty tons of bombs, and a service ceiling of forty-seven thousand feet.[30] Using future missiles, such as the ill-fated Skybolt, the B-52s had a standoff range of as much as 1,500 nautical miles, greater even than the submarine missiles of the period. As a testament to its design, the B-52 is still in use.

Its capabilities, which were to be enhanced by aerial refueling, transformed the bombing threat in the late 1950s. Begun in 1958, constant airborne alert flights continued until 1968, when a B-52 carrying four thermonuclear bombs crashed in Greenland, although without any nuclear detonation. Deterrence appeared both realistic and affordable. It was hoped that these bombers would serve to deter both Soviet conventional and atomic attack, although doubts were expressed about the former. In December 1955, the NATO Council authorized "first use": the employment of atomic weaponry against the Warsaw Pact, even if the latter did not attack with such weaponry. This was a response to NATO's conventional inferiority. The B-52s were complemented by the four American supercarriers built in 1954–58, as some of their aircraft could carry nuclear bombs, albeit over much shorter ranges.

In the late 1950s and early 1960s, the B-52's guidance system, using radar navigation, was much more accurate than those on intermediate-range ballistic missiles (IRBMs) and intercontinental ballistic missiles (ICBMs), on which fusion warheads were mounted by 1959. It took some time, also, for the United States to make the transition with its ground-based missiles from the vulnerable, time-consuming, liquid-fuel missiles to the instantaneous, launch-on-command, solid-fuel missiles. This occurred in the early 1960s. Only when the United States developed a large submarine capable of firing large numbers of underwater missiles (the *Los Angeles* class of the early 1970s and the *Ohio* class of the mid-1970s) did the B-52s become apparently obsolete as nuclear delivery systems. However, in the meantime, they had been challenged by continual upgrades in Soviet jet interceptor technology, from the MIG-15 onward. In contrast, surface-to-surface missiles (SSMs), which were ballistic and went faster and higher, could not be shot down. There was only four minutes' warning for Britain (thirty for the United States) of attack: the nuclear-tipped Soviet medium-range missiles deployed in Eastern Europe from 1959 could readily hit Britain, and therefore the American air force bases there.

Alongside the strategic dimension, there was an emphasis on the modernization of tactical air power, notably with the deployment of "the second generation" of jet aircraft, such as the Hunter and the Thunderstreak, as well as on a new task: protection of nuclear weapons against a surprise Soviet attack. One aspect was the protection of nuclear bombers by keeping them dispersed and on Operational Readiness Platforms at the end of runways. In Western Europe, new all-weather aircraft were embedded in a new NATO Air Defense Ground Environment, an early-warning system that layered fighters, long-range nuclear missiles, and short-range tactical surface-to-air missiles (SAMs). Alongside defense against air attack, there was the deployment of fighter-bombers equipped with atomic bombs that were to be employed for attacking Soviet air bases, logistics, and ground forces. Meanwhile, the spread of tactical guided missiles provided a new dimension for the debate already raging over whether manned aircraft had a future. For a time, these missiles appeared to be the answer for providing air defense.

The accumulated size of NATO air forces was very great. Moreover, NATO served as an international alliance within which aircraft could be readily based and deployed across the Atlantic. The 1961 Berlin crisis led to a major American reinforcement of NATO, including Operation Stair Step, in which the Air National Guard deployed 216 fighters to Europe across the Atlantic. President Kennedy seriously considered using nuclear weaponry against the Soviet Union during the crisis.

CUBAN MISSILE CRISIS

The role of air power in the early Cold War culminated in 1962 with the Cuban Missile Crisis. Prior to the development of intercontinental missiles, the Soviet Union was more vulnerable to attack than the United States, as the United States had a far larger strategic bomber force, as well as nearby bases, for example, in eastern England; IRBMs in Turkey; and aircraft carriers. The Soviets had no such bases, nor carriers, which helped underline the shock caused for the Americans when Soviet missiles were deployed to newly communist Cuba. Soviet jet bombers capable of carrying nuclear weapons were also shipped there. The resulting crisis, in which American aerial surveillance played a key role, led to an American naval and air quarantine designed to prevent the shipping of further Soviet supplies, as well as to preparations both for an attack on the Soviet bases in Cuba and for the possibility of a wider war with the Soviet Union. Under the pressure of an acute international crisis, the difficulties of nuclear planning and command and control, as well as the political dimension of warfare, came to the fore.[31]

Strategic air power, drawing on America's overwhelming strength in the Caribbean as well as its superiority in nuclear weaponry, was an important part of the equation, with the Americans planning that operations against Cuba would focus on air attacks. General Curtis LeMay, the bellicose air force chief of staff and the key figure in the bombing campaign against Japan in 1945, pressed for the use of the USAF, including a preemptive military strike. Around the world, nuclear forces were alerted. However, the very prospect of all-out destruction through nuclear war may have prevented conventional military operations. The crisis did not only involve the United States. The Canadians provided air support, with the carrier *Bonaventure* joining the Canadian air force in patrolling Canada's operational area Westlant, off Newfoundland and Nova Scotia, for Soviet submarines. These were located and traced.[32]

The Cuban Missile Crisis encouraged a bifurcation in air power on the part of states with nuclear bombs. The strategic nuclear component increasingly focused on ground and sea-launched missiles, although air-dropped nuclear bombs continued to be needed. The prospect of nuclear war in 1962, by which time the United States had over 27,000 nuclear weapons, compared to 369 in 1950, as well as a perception of a lack of range in the American repertoire of response, led to the adoption, in place of the earlier doctrine of "Tripwire," of a policy of "Flexible Response," which focused on the possibility of gradual escalation, and an overwhelming need to buy time for political decisions to be made, a situation that boosted the role of air power. As the "Mutually Assured Destruction" of thermonuclear warfare became noncredible, so its replacement, "Flexible Response," depended on air power to enable a sustained campaign to be fought before a full release of thermonuclear weaponry was necessary. This policy, however, remained problematic in Europe, as NATO did not possess sufficient conventional land forces for such a gradual escalation. "Flexible Response" was designed also to offer an alternative to the devastation of high-tech conventional warfare, and to enable America to answer the challenge of communist "wars of national liberation." The emphasis on a range of responses helped not only to lead the Americans toward greater intervention in Vietnam in the mid-1960s, but also to determine the military means adopted at that time.

8

THE COLD WAR: THE MIDDLE PERIOD, 1963–75

For air power, the Vietnam War dominates attention in the middle period of the Cold War. This bitter struggle indicated the limitations of bombing, as well as its terrible devastation. The Vietnam War also saw the significant use of air power in tactical terms and in an attempt to achieve operational and strategic goals, as well as the elevation of systems of engineering, which was substituted for traditional definitions of war derived from Clausewitz and Jomini. The period was not important in the development of naval air power; but, at the strategic level, the shift from aircraft to missiles greatly gathered pace and thus transformed the geography of military power in the Cold War. However, air power still played a dramatic and important role in local wars around the world, notably the Arab-Israeli wars. So also did the development of antiaircraft weaponry, which proved particularly significant in the early 1970s, especially in the 1973 Arab-Israeli Yom Kippur War and in the insurrectionary struggles against Portuguese colonial rule in Africa. As a consequence, a focus on the Vietnam War can be misleading. Nevertheless, it is important to the discussion of air power, not least because the conflict played a major role in shaping debate about the value and ethics of air warfare, specifically bombing, which became the central issue in this warfare. Yet, it was dubious, given the poor weapon accuracy and the lack of training in nonnuclear war, whether air power was capable of delivering the effects sought. For example, in NATO planning, it was assumed that a sixteen-aircraft attack on a Warsaw Pact airfield might degrade the air base for only four to six hours but could cause NATO losses of up to a third of the attacking force.

THE VIETNAM WAR

Over half the $200 billion spent on the war by the United States went to air operations, and nearly eight million tons of bombs were dropped on Vietnam, Laos, and Cambodia. South Vietnam, where the Americans were helping the South Vietnamese resist North Vietnamese and Viet Cong attacks, became the most heavily bombed country in the history of warfare. This formidable bombing could have considerable tactical and operational effect, as when the offensive against the American base at Khe Sanh in 1968 was stopped in part by dropping bombs with an explosive power equivalent to that of five of the atomic bombs dropped at Hiroshima.[1] In this operation, the Americans benefited from the proximity of their airfields and carriers. There was no equivalent to the French failure at the remote Dien Bien Phu in 1954.

Air power, indeed, became a key tactical supplement to artillery, and far more bombs were dropped in South Vietnam than in the North. Insofar as air power was strategic, the prime strategic requirement was preventing the overrunning of American units in the South. Moreover, massive firepower capability was provided by slow-flying gunships, although the Viet Cong were proficient at entrenching in order to minimize their losses, as the Taliban were also to do in Afghanistan in 2002. Even elementary fighting positions will protect against many air attacks. In addition, the USAF lost heavily to ground fire. Ground attacks on twenty-three airfields by North Vietnamese and Viet Cong forces in their Tet Offensive in South Vietnam in 1968 were one testimony to the role of American air power, as well as to its apparent vulnerability.

There were also major American bombing offensives against North Vietnam. These were designed to fulfill operational and strategic goals: to limit Northern support for the war in the South and, strategically, to affect policy in the North by driving the North Vietnamese to negotiate, as well as to demonstrate American resolve and maintain South Vietnamese morale. These goals, however, were not fulfilled to the extent anticipated. In part, these failures may have been due to the political limits placed on the bombing of the North, especially Hanoi, and in

1965–68 the harbors, notably Haiphong, through which Soviet military assistance arrived. The bombing of North Vietnam, more generally, rested on a number of strategic flaws, notably that it would be possible to affect conduct there accordingly, that the missions could be sustained and would benefit the United States politically, that they offered a meaningful and productive display of resolve, and that bombing alone would act as an effective substitute for bombing combined with ground operations.

Political interference over targeting, for example, avoiding sites close to the border with China and (until June 1966) major population centers, and over the tempo of operations proved controversial, especially with military leaders. This interference, which still happens, violates the principle of military command. Criticism of this interference, however, was scarcely value free. Indeed, criticism varied in its cause, with the supporters of independent aerial campaigns in part responding to institutional justification and competitiveness, notably the claims of the USAF and its reluctance to focus on cooperation with the army.[2] Interference over targeting and over the pace of the air campaign owed much to the idea that a graduated air attack could be used to affect North Vietnamese policy. Moreover, there was a deliberate effort not to center the air offensive on making the civilian population the prime target. This reflected a reaction to public, political, and governmental moods that were different from those of the Second World War, and it was also a response to the international context: the United States was engaged in an explicitly limited war, one for which international support was far less than in the case of the Korean War.

However, the air war also raised more general questions about the effectiveness of bombing, at the strategic, operational, and tactical levels. Strategic doubts were not only voiced on the Left. J. F. C. Fuller, a leading British military theorist (and a former general), wrote to an American correspondent in July 1965, "Today your government and its military advisors would appear to have accepted the concept that the way to defeat Communism in Vietnam is by bombing when clearly the precepts garnered from World War Two should have told them that ideas cannot be dislodged by TNT."[3] Within North Vietnam, the bombing probably encouraged support for the regime and the war effort. There were also questions arising from the nature of the North Vietnamese economy and society, in particular the extent to which it would be possible to hit hard by bombing a subsistence economy that focused on agriculture. Insufficiently raised at the time, this point echoed Maoist ideas about the likely resilience of China if at war with the United States. In part, a strategic tool developed for conventional war against Germany and reengineered for war with the Soviet Union was used against a very different economy and society, while the strategy itself designed for war with the Soviets was not applied at all. As a result, the USAF struggled to find an appropriate strategy for the Vietnam War and found it easiest to hope that air power and bombing alone would settle the issue.

At the operational level, there were problems in conception and delivery. As a consequence of the long-term emphasis on strategic nuclear bombardment, the USAF was perhaps not sufficiently flexible to try alternatives. Indeed, in the Vietnam War, the Americans suffered from not working out an intermediate air-land strategy: their strategy had to be either strategic or tactical. This was epitomized by the use of what were basically jet fighters, a tactical means (outfitted for the purpose with bomb racks) to bomb Hanoi, the North Vietnamese capital (a strategic goal), throughout the Vietnam War. The failure of the marines and the navy to accept USAF pressure for operational cooperation in the shape of a single air-power controller, a turf issue, inhibited a consistent level of attack and thus minimized American capabilities and also prevented the sharing of lessons. This was but part of a more general failure of American preparedness, failure which encompassed inappropriate doctrine and aircraft, as well as inadequate command, coordination, and training. However, it is necessary to contextualize criticism. For example, albeit on a far smaller scale, Anglo-Australian bombing in the 1950s had achieved very little in counterinsurgency operations in Malaya.

In Operation Rolling Thunder, the air campaign launched in 1965, 643,000 tons of bombs were dropped on North Vietnam, the most intensive bomber offensive in countering any "war of national liberation," but without destroying the North Vietnamese war machine, the will to fight, or the transport facilities within North Vietnam that were the major target.[4] Military targeting policy was against an enemy industrial capacity and war-fighting capability, but North Vietnam's effective industrial capacity was located in China and the Soviet Union. President Johnson believed he was signaling to North Vietnam via frequent bombing pauses and the withdrawal of certain target sets. The North Vietnamese regarded the limitations on targeting as weakness and exploited the opportunities, while at the same time portraying the Americans as bloodthirsty imperialists conducting a campaign that was ineffectual.

As perhaps should have been expected, the air offensives launched against the Ho Chi Minh Trail, notably from 1969, failed to stop the movement of troops and supplies along it from North to South Vietnam. The bicycles on which the North Vietnamese relied heavily were not an easy target, while the Vietnamese use of camouflage was exceptional and the "trail" difficult to hit and readily repaired. Moreover, when one area of the "trail" had been cratered, the North Vietnamese simply used a different one.

Moreover, Soviet surface-to-air missiles, supplied to North Vietnam from April 1965, inflicted heavy, and visible, casualties on American bombers, as did the agile MIG-17s and MIG-21s. As a result, the cost to the United States, both militarily and politically, of using air power was pushed up. Ultimately, more than 83 percent of the USAF's total combat losses were to ground fire. As an instance of the competitive advantage of technology, the Americans used electronic jamming in order to limit attacks on their aircraft by missiles and radar-controlled guns, only for the North Vietnamese to aim at the jamming signals.[5] As a consequence, countermeasures aircraft were an essential element of any American attacking force, and international interest in such capability increased. Prisoners taken from American aircraft that were shot down gave the North Vietnamese a valuable negotiating card that was also used very effectively in the struggle to influence American domestic opinion.

The range of capabilities offered by air power was demonstrated by the greatly increased use of helicopters by the Americans. Although the period of the Vietnam War is not generally seen in terms of innovations in air power, in practice they were considerable. Guided munitions attract the most immediate interest in terms of technology, but there were also significant organizational developments. In 1962, Robert McNamara, the secretary of defense, ordered a new look at the army's mobility requirements, leading to the establishment of the Army Tactical Mobility Requirements Board, or Howze Board after its president. The board's 1962 report led to the development of new tactical doctrine and operational capabilities, and the redrawing of service boundaries. The focus was on helicopters and air-mobile units as the basis for army aviation, and, although these are usually understood in terms of the requirements of the Vietnam War, in fact they were independent. The emphasis was on tactical, not operational, purpose, with helicopters accordingly placed in the existing transportation and artillery branches of the army.[6]

Helicopters were important in supplying positions, as a mobile artillery, and in applying the doctrine of air mobility. Airlifted troops, notably the new First Cavalry Division Airmobile, a successful large-scale air assault force, brought mobility and helped take the war to the enemy. The operation mounted into the Ia Drang valley by the nascent Air Cavalry proved to be a bloody learning experience for both sides. The Americans, who deployed many inexperienced, often conscripted, soldiers in the lower ranks, sought to prove the "air-mobile" concept, but went into landing zones that were easily predictable and were ambushed, as were their reinforcements. The ensuing battle was costly for both sides, and only the extensive use of close air support and the gallantry of the helicopter crews in flying in supplies and taking out the wounded saved the Americans from being overrun. The Americans managed to inflict heavy casualties, mainly due to close air support including the extensive use of napalm, and they considered they had won a victory. More generally, the Americans became ever more dependent on helicopters, while their opponents altered their tactics, not least their vulnerability to effective close air support.

Helicopters served to insert units and then to support them. The Americans flew about 36,125,000 helicopter sorties during the war, including 7,547,000 assault sorties, in which machine guns and rockets were used, plus 3,932,000 attack sorties. Their initial success led to somewhat inflexible tactics, and their relatively low speed made them vulnerable to attack from the ground. Over 2,300 were shot down, while many others were lost to accidents. Nevertheless, helicopters had become more reliable, more powerful, and faster than in the 1950s, and their use helped to overcome guerrilla challenges to land supply and communication routes.[7] They were survivable, compared to the jet-fuel-propelled Blackhawks of today, and Hueys were also easier to repair and get back in the air. Helicopters were also used to recover downed aircrews. In response to ground fire, helicopters able to suppress ground opposition were developed. These helicopter gunships enjoyed a formidable arsenal, notably with guns able to fire rapidly and with computer targeting and infrared night vision.

Aside from their attack functions, helicopters were also crucial in a logistical context made complex by the absence of front lines. Isolated American positions required aerial resupply, including airdrop in a fashion that had not been necessary in the Second World War or the Korean War. AirLand (landing aircraft and unloading them) was a more effective means of delivering supplies, but required a landing zone while also exposing the aircraft that did land to enemy fire. Due to the latter, the Americans ended the use of C-130s to resupply Khe Sanh in 1968 when it was besieged and, instead, switched to airdrop. The emphasis on survivability permitted a development of relevant tactics for airdrop.

As in other conflicts, there was a learning curve. This could be seen with the North Vietnamese use of antiaircraft weaponry, which limited, in particular, the safety of low flying and thus affected the vertical space of the aerial battlefield, compromising a major aspect of air power. The introduction of handheld SAM-7s threatened American airdrops in support of the besieged garrison at An Loc in 1972, leading the Americans to focus on high-speed low-altitude airdrops, a method with limited accuracy. However, there was also increased effectiveness in the American delivery of air power, reflecting improved technique as well as weaponry. This was seen in 1972, both in opposing the North Vietnamese Easter Offensive in the South and in the Linebacker II bombing offensive against the North, the latter of which displayed clear political will.

Greater effectiveness in 1972 owed something to bombing North Vietnamese harbors, but it was also due to a marked improvement in American air capability that reflected both the displacement of earlier doctrine, in response to the varied needs of the Vietnam War, and also the use of laser-guided bombs. The latter compensated for earlier limitations of accuracy in bombing caused by flying at high altitudes above deadly antiaircraft fire.[8] Indeed, as with other weapon systems, such as the tank, the bomber did not come into its own until the advent of smart munitions. When the Americans had earlier tried to hit bridges in Vietnam, they had largely failed despite many raids. A single bomb, a direct hit from a Paveway I laser-guided bomb dropped by an F-4

Phantom on the Thanh Hoa Bridge, a key link on the supply route from China, on April 27, 1972, achieved an effect that numerous sorties had failed to achieve during Operation Rolling Thunder. The bridge was subsequently hit twice more with Paveways. Thus, irrespective of the skill of the pilots, the bomber was only as good as its ordnance. Although precision-guided munitions, whether camera guided or laser guided, are much more expensive than unguided iron bombs, the cost once adjusted for hit rates was lower. Also in 1972, the Americans benefited from advances in ground-based radar technology, which helped in the direction and defense of B-52 strikes. Indeed, the establishment of radar positions became part of the geopolitics of the war, notably with Site 85, a long-range radar control station at Pha Thi in Laos. Designed to assist air attacks in North Vietnam, this position was established in 1967, but captured in 1968.[9]

In 1972, in response to the North Vietnamese Nguyen Hue campaign (to the Americans, the Easter Offensive), the Americans launched the Linebacker I air campaign of May to October 1972. Waged in large part by fighter-bombers, this campaign, which to a great extent was an interdiction one, hit the North Vietnam supply system, cutting the movement of supplies to their forces. The conventional nature of the force that had invaded the South, including Soviet-supplied tanks and trucks, made American air attacks more devastating than those directed against the Viet Cong had been and had a major impact on the conflict on the ground. The enhanced effectiveness of American air power in 1972 was due not only to North Vietnamese operational and tactical goals and methods, but also to a marked improvement in American air capability. This both hit North Vietnamese logistics and was also very useful in close air support, notably against tanks. American air power thus lessened North Vietnamese military options, and to a greater extent than in the mid-1960s. The vulnerability arising from North Vietnamese methods was matched in 1973 when the Egyptians advanced into the Sinai beyond the range of antiaircraft cover and were then hit hard by Israeli air attack. At a different level in 1972, helicopter-fired wire-guided missiles hit attacking North Vietnamese forces hard. The failure of the Easter Offensive led the North Vietnamese to revert to a mixture of guerrilla and conventional operations, rather than focusing on the latter.

In 1972, air power was increasingly significant in the Vietnam War, not only thanks to increased accuracy, but also because of an American wish to limit and, finally, end the ground commitment. Thus, in another instance of the way in which air power acted as a substitute for troops, air power made up the difference as the Americans reduced their force numbers in South Vietnam, and provided a key context in which a compromise peace could be negotiated. Air power had not led to American victory, but it played a major role in preventing defeat in the 1960s and early 1970s. The Linebacker II campaign from December 18 to 29, 1972—heavy, frequent, and accurate B-52 raids on North Vietnam, notably on the transport and oil supply systems—helped lead (to some commentators) North Vietnam to agree to the Paris Peace Agreement signed on January 27, 1973. At the same time, as so often with air power, for example in Bosnia in 1995 and Kosovo in 1999 (see chapter 10), other factors also came into play in securing this agreement, for example, Chinese pressure on North Vietnam.

Moreover, it is important to note that strong North Vietnamese air defenses limited the effectiveness of all the raids. In the Hanoi Military Museum, one of the large-scale dioramas relating to the struggle for independence is devoted to the offensive, which is described as "the Dien Bien Phu of the Air." The North Vietnamese saw it as a great strategic victory. The discrepancy in interpretation is instructive. Strategic Air Command (SAC) deployed B-52s based in Guam and Thailand to mount the raids. They were supported by "Wild Weasel" electronic warfare aircraft, as well as escort fighters. The attacks, initially planned by SAC staff based in the United States, rather than local air staff, were characterized at first by unimaginative and predictable tactics. The bombers were directed to fly along well-established routes up the Mekong Valley before turning to attack Hanoi. This gave the North Vietnamese air-defense system plenty of warning and allowed them to allocate targets to their antiaircraft missile battalions. The North Vietnamese had studied the operational behavior of the B-52 and had provided detailed guidance to their air defense. The bombers attacked the same targets and used the same entry and exit flight paths. They were directed to bank steeply away after releasing their bombs, which was standard operating procedure to avoid the effect of blast when dropping nuclear weapons but was quite unnecessary. Moreover, it had the effect of negating the forward-facing and downward-facing jamming

devices built into the aircraft. Adjusting their tracking and firing procedures, the North Vietnamese shot down many aircraft before American
tactics were changed. On December 26, a mass attack on Hanoi from
multiple directions, without rolling away after bomb release, overwhelmed and destroyed the air defenses, leading the North Vietnamese
to return to the negotiating table. Civilian morale, however, was given
an enormous boost by the sight of B-52s being blown out of the sky.
The North Vietnamese felt they had fought back successfully. Nevertheless, the determined use of air attack played a pivotal role in enabling the Nixon administration to use air power to extricate itself from
an unpopular war. At the same time, the North Vietnamese accepted
the treaty because they knew that further suffering was pointless and
the Americans were departing. [10]

The Vietnam War had seen the rise of specialist helicopter gunships,
the use of gunships from converted AC-47s and AC-130s, and specialized electronic countermeasures (ECM) pods carried by aircraft such as
the F-4 ("Wild Weasel" Thunderchiefs), whose sole job was countermeasures on bombing raids. These aircraft carried missiles for attacking
active radar on the ground in order to suppress SAMs. They operated as
part of the new tactics for bombing targets that involved strike groups
with large numbers of aircraft that were not bomber tactics seen in
Linebacker 1. The war saw the rise of the weapon systems officer
among aircrew. Dogfighting as understood in the Second World War
had changed because of the speed of flying and the use of air-to-air
missiles, although there could be overconfidence in these missiles.

The war also saw intense use of the Lockheed SR-71 Blackbird. In a
program initiated in 1964, the plane first flew in 1966 and remained in
service until 1998. A total of thirty-two were built. At the height of the
Vietnam War in 1972, the Blackbirds, which could fly at Mach 3 and
outrun any missile, were flying weekly reconnaissance flights over
North Vietnam, Laos, and southern China. However, unlike modern
reconnaissance platforms, the Blackbird lacked a data download link
(they were not made then), which meant that it could not send real-
time intelligence to battlefield commanders. Other developments included air-dropped scatter mines; submunitions (smaller munitions carried in a casing such as cluster bombs); electronic countermeasures to
defeat radars, antiaircraft artillery, and missiles; the rise of satellite intelligence; and the tactical use of drones (unmanned aerial vehicles).

The drones were derived from the Ryan Fire Bee target drone, which was adapted, with the Ryan Model 147 series, to provide reconnaissance. They brought back high-resolution photographs and avoided pilot loss. From 1964 until their last combat flight in 1975, the USAF One Hundredth Strategic Reconnaissance Wing flew 3,435 Ryan 147B reconnaissance drones over North Vietnam and surrounding areas. About 554 were lost to all causes. Drones also served to check Chinese air defenses. Experiments were also carried out to develop drones further for combat operations.

In part thanks to an excellent North Vietnamese propaganda campaign, hostility to the war in both the United States and elsewhere focused in large part on the bombing. There was opposition to the bombing of civilians, to area bombing, and, as an extension, to the use of air power, as immoral and ineffective. This opposition increased with time and particularly affected the public response to the Linebacker II attacks. In the Netherlands, usually a NATO hawk, leading politicians took part in an antiwar protest after these attacks, as they also did in neutral Sweden. In turn, this opposition affected the perception of earlier bombing, notably the Allied bombing of Germany and Japan in the Second World War.[11] In the reassessment of bombing, the pressure of current events was matched by that from more general social and cultural trends. Here, the focus in the West was on a less deferential society and a less nationalistic culture. Related to this came a conviction that morality, rather than national interest, was a, even *the*, key context, and that national interest could not define morality. An antiwar component was an important aspect of this cultural shift.

The events of 1975, when a new North Vietnamese offensive rapidly conquered South Vietnam in the absence of American intervention, provided an instructive contrast to developments in 1972. However, that interpretation can place an excessive weight on air power, because the conquest also reflected the contrasts in fighting quality and determination between the combatants in 1975, as well as more specific flaws on the part of much of the South Vietnamese military leadership and officer corps, notably a mistaken strategy. The last had been apparent with the unsuccessful South Vietnamese invasion of Laos in 1971. At that time, the Americans provided air and logistical support (taking heavy losses of helicopters and crew) but could not determine the situation on the ground, a lesson for subsequent commitments, notably the situation planned for Afghanistan. Similar points arise in the case of Cambodia. An American–South Vietnamese ground invasion was launched in April 1970 to destroy communist bases there after bombing had failed to do so. The "incursion" succeeded in the short term, with the Americans providing military aid and air support for the government of General Lon Nol, which had seized power in March 1970. Air operations continued until 1973, but, in 1975, the guerrillas of the Khmer Rouge, the Cambodian Communist Party, overcame the Lon Nol government.[12]

The Vietnam War was also a period in which commercial air travel increased, both in the United States and in the West, in large part due to the economic growth of the 1960s and to greater opportunities. Aircraft specifications improved, with the 1960s bringing more powerful engines and the wide-body design seen most successfully with the Boeing 747, the original jumbo jet, an American development. First flown on February 9, 1969, the 747 was introduced for commercial service, by Pan American, on January 22, 1970. The relationship between these developments and military air power was at once direct, in the sense of technology sharing, but also tenuous, in that criticism of the practice of bombing was readily compatible with air travel for pleasure.

THE ARAB-ISRAELI WARS

A very different impression of air power from that in Vietnam was gained from the Six-Day War in 1967. Israel mounted a preemptive attack on Egypt in order to deal with the growing aggression of its unpredictable ruler, Colonel Gamal Abdel Nasser. The Israeli assault began early on June 5 with Operation Moked, a surprise dawn attack on eighteen Egyptian air bases, launched by planes coming in over the Mediterranean from the west, in other words not from the direction of Israel. Lulled into a false sense of security, the Egyptians, who, like the Americans in December 1941, had failed to take the most basic precautions in protecting their planes on the ground, lost 286 planes in just one morning, including all thirty Tu-16 heavy bombers. As a reminder that air power depends on a whole series of structures and systems, the heavy bombing, in addition, of Egyptian runways reduced the usefulness of Egypt's remaining planes. In order to make the scale of destruction conceivable, Nasser falsely claimed that the Americans and British had been responsible for the air assault.

Gaining air superiority rapidly proved crucial to the subsequent land conflict. Egyptian ground forces, badly affected by Israeli air-to-ground attacks, were defeated in the Gaza Strip and the Sinai Peninsula. Egyptian tanks proved particularly vulnerable. Desert terrain is especially suitable for air power. The Sinai is devoid of all vegetation and most other features suitable for cover and concealment. Jordan joined in on June 5 on the Egyptian side, only to have its air force also destroyed by the Israelis. Benefiting greatly from air superiority, Israeli ground forces subsequently overran the Jordanian-ruled West Bank. The same fate later affected Syria, with the Golan Heights overrun. Its air force had been hit hard in attacks on its air bases on the first day of the war.

The winning of air superiority thanks to the initial surprise attacks, a superiority confirmed in subsequent air-to-air battles, had proved crucial to success on the ground, not only due to the actual damage inflicted, but also thanks to the disorientation and demoralization imposed on Arab forces. This disorientation and demoralization greatly enhanced the impact of Israeli mobility, notably by tanks, while close air support strengthened their firepower, not least in the absence of sufficient artillery support. Retreating columns of Egyptian tanks were attacked in the Sinai passes and destroyed in a manner similar to that of the British air attacks on Ottoman Turkish forces at Wadi el Fara in 1918. Israeli morale also benefited from their aircraft being highly visible. In combination, the tactical victories fed into operational successes that had a strategic consequence. This was more significant than any result that could have resulted from a strategic air offensive against Arab capitals. The Israelis were not equipped or trained for such an offensive, but it would not have had a strategic impact. That came, instead, from the defeat of Arab forces and the seizure of key territories.[13]

The Israeli air assault attracted the study of Western air forces, not least because it was dramatic, successful, and more accessible than the 1965 war between India and Pakistan. Moreover, the Six-Day War contrasted with the Vietnam War, a conflict that was not only unsuccessful but also apparently had little to teach second-rank air powers. Against this background, and that of a shift to missiles, the Six-Day War could be used to vindicate air strength and air attack. The war also demonstrated that results could be obtained without resorting to atomic weaponry. The tempo of the Israeli air assault was totally different from that of the Americans in Vietnam, but the circumstances and environment contrasted greatly. Opposing air forces were not located in a remote sanctuary and were accessible for the Israeli aircraft to attack and destroy, and this greatly enhanced the understanding of an effective role for air power. Moreover, in large part due to different military cultures, political and strategic circumstances, and terrain, the North Vietnam military did not prove to be disoriented by air attack as that of Egypt was.

The public impact of the Six-Day War was important, as it provided an acceptable account for air power, one that offered a reprise and modernization of the 1940 Battle of Britain, bringing the latter and the account into a postcolonial world, one of jet aircraft and technicolor. The image of an underdog triumphant as a result of air operations proved attractive, albeit underrating the role of Israeli ground forces. That the Israeli air attacks were not launched on civilian targets was very important in providing a contrast to the more deadly, slower, and less successful nature of American air operations in Vietnam. One operated as the antithesis of the other.

With time, Israel's reputation as a state was to be compromised, notably on the Left and in much of the Third World, while its air force was to find it difficult to avoid civilian casualties when it attacked guerrillas based in urban areas. This compromising, however, did not lessen the impact of the Six-Day War on air-power professionals. Furthermore, they were interested in how Israel overcame subsequent challenges. This process was enhanced because, to many American commentators, Israel became an acceptable way to view American air power as successful—a process that owed much to the Israeli acquisition of American aircraft—and thus served as an alternative to the Vietnam War, or as a way to drive home lessons alleged to derive from that war.

In 1968, the United States decided to provide Israel with F-4 Phantom jets, an important step in the definition of the Arab-Israeli struggle in terms of the Cold War. This provision was a response to the Soviet Union rearming Egypt and Syria and to the mixed Israeli success against the Egyptian air force (and supporting missiles) during the "War of Attrition" along the Suez Canal in 1967–70. Israel pressed for Phantoms because the dogfights with the Egyptian air force in late 1967 and

1968 were producing losses of 2.5 to 1 or less in favor of the Israelis, a ratio that was not acceptable to them. From 1969, there were heavy Israeli air attacks on Egyptian missiles and artillery on the west side of the canal. From January 1970, Israel responded to continuing Egyptian attacks along the canal by launching air attacks deep into Egypt. The Soviet Union, in response, deployed air and air-defense units to Egypt, including MIG-21s, SAMs, and the ZSU-23-4, a self-propelled vehicle with radar-guided quad 23 mm machine guns mounted in a turret. They offered a formidable air-defense capability and were supplied to Syria as well. These units were deployed at least in part to improve the Soviet capacity to keep tabs on the American Sixth Fleet in the Mediterranean.[14] By the summer of 1970, Soviet-manned planes and missile sites were in conflict with the Israeli planes, with both sides losing planes. A truce was declared on August 7. There was also conflict with the Syrian air force during this period.

Air power proved important anew when large-scale conflict resumed in the Yom Kippur War in 1973. Egypt and Syria began a surprise attack while Israeli forces were largely at home for the Yom Kippur religious holiday. As a sign of the significance and possibilities of air attack, the Israeli chief of staff tried to convince Prime Minister Golda Meir to agree to a preemptive air strike, but she, fearing international opprobrium, refused to attack first. Egypt, instead, launched a successful surprise air attack on Israeli forces on the afternoon of October 6, 1973. Arab planning relied heavily on the new, highly mobile SAM-6s and ZSU-23-4s, which were cleverly integrated and coordinated with their initial assaults. Syrian forces also advanced. Initial land successes by the Arabs meant that Israeli aircraft had to be diverted from the air-superiority battle against both aircraft and SAMs to blunt the tank thrusts, especially the Syrian ones on the Golan Heights. Intervening against Egyptian forces that had successfully crossed the Suez Canal into the Israeli-occupied Sinai, Israeli planes on October 8 suffered heavily from the Egyptian use of effective Soviet SAM-6 ground-to-air missiles, which destroyed more Israeli aircraft than Egyptian aircraft and conventional antiaircraft guns combined. Up to October 9, the IDF had lost 55 of its 330 combat planes, with another 55 not being fully operational. Confronted by initial losses and possible calamity, the Israelis loaded nuclear weapons onto their aircraft.

However, once the Egyptian armor had advanced beyond the range of ground-based radar and static SAMs into the Sinai, it was badly mauled. Many of the advancing mobile SAM and antiaircraft batteries were destroyed by ground fire, thereby giving the Israeli air force freedom to act. The Israelis also benefited from using electronic countermeasures. Having suffered from basing their doctrine on the Six-Day War, and having not taken note of the improved capability of SAMs, the Israelis eventually prevailed, both in the air and on the ground. At sea, both sides deployed missile boats. As with carriers in the Second World War, the emphasis there was on accurate first strike. In addition, electronic countermeasures against missile attacks were important.

In the conflict with Syria, the Israeli suppression of Syrian SAM batteries proved crucial. This was achieved on the morning of October 9, which allowed the Israeli air force to provide the necessary close support to ground forces, which, as a result, were able that day to recover the territory on the Golan Heights lost on October 6. By the end of the war, the Israelis were able to attack targets within Egypt and Syria, notably airfields.

Air power was important to the wider international context in 1973. In response to the Soviet airlift of weaponry to Egypt and Syria, the (more distant) United States rushed supplies to the Israelis by air, in part via their air base in the Azores. Initially, the United States agreed to provide one hundred Sidewinder air-to-air missiles, which Israel had ordered before the war, but not to deliver the combat aircraft Israel sought while the fighting was continuing. These aircraft would ensure replacements for Israeli losses but would compromise American relations with Arab allies, as well as having to be taken from the American military inventory. There was, indeed, justified concern that the Israelis would lock the United States into a very difficult international situation by means of arms supplies. Israel, however, did less well in the early stages of the war than the United States had anticipated.

As a result, and encouraged by public pressure and the Soviet airlift, Nixon agreed on October 11 to provide forty Phantoms. The Americans failed to find a carrier ready to lease planes to transport them, and the problems Israel encountered in its operations led to instructions to the USAF Military Airlift Command to deliver supplies directly to Israel rather than, as originally discussed, handing them over to Israeli planes in the Azores, which would have been less compromising politically. C-

141 Starlifters and C-5 Galaxies were used, the first arriving at Ben-Gurion Airport at Tel Aviv in Israel on October 13. Alongside ammunition and tanks, Phantom and Skyhawk planes were delivered in a massive airlift, which Henry Kissinger reported would involve a plane landing every fifty minutes.[15] Phantoms were flown across the Atlantic ready for combat. They were turned around and launched on operations within an hour or two after delivery. In contrast, all the material sent by sea arrived only after the war was over.

AIR WARFARE

Conflicts between states were relatively uncommon in this period, but, when they occurred, air power played a significant role. Combat air power, however, did not play a role in the brief war between India and China in 1962, a topic that still causes controversy in India. The Chinese wanted a limited conflict. As the initiators, in terms of direct military action, they could set the tone, and they eschewed use of the People's Liberation Army Air Force (PLAAF). The Indian army and air force were woefully ill equipped and ill prepared for this war. In particular, their lack of helicopters and forward airstrips left their forward troops totally exposed. Although they did not have air bases in Tibet, the Chinese were operating on the Tibetan plateau close to a military road that was designed for all-weather operations. They were well equipped and supplied and acclimatized to the high altitude. Communications between the Indian plains and the border were very difficult. India conducted some airlift missions, but Pandit Nehru, the Indian prime minister, fearing Chinese bombing of Calcutta and other urban areas, did not want to expand the war to the air despite the IAF (Indian Air Force) having excellent bases in north and east India. Nehru's attempt to limit war helped ensure a limited defeat, but defeat it was. In the desperate days before the Chinese declared a unilateral cease-fire, Nehru asked for direct intervention by American air-defense batteries and fighter and bomber squadrons, but the war ended almost as soon as this request was made. The United States subsequently supplied transport aircraft to the IAF and ground equipment for Indian army mountain divisions, but not the air-defense items Nehru initially envisaged when it seemed the Chinese might bomb Calcutta or march into the Indian plains.

In 1962, an Indonesian-based rebellion in Brunei by the "North Borneo Liberation Army" led to a major British naval response, including the deployment of the carrier *Albion* and the landing of troops by helicopter. The rising was swiftly suppressed but was followed by broader-ranging Indonesian attacks on Malaysia in 1963–66, the so-called Confrontation. The British, Australian, and New Zealand forces that supported Malaysia benefited from complete command of air and sea, the navy providing aircraft and helicopters as well as necessary maintenance for both naval and RAF helicopters. Carriers provided crucial platforms. Helicopters were important for attacking targets on the ground and for moving and supplying troops, notably to block Indonesian raids. Although the (British) Wessex helicopters, which were the workhorses of the campaign, were equipped with rocket pods, their gun sights were nonexistent. Pilots drew rudimentary aiming marks onto their windscreens with chinagraph pens. They were not in any sense "gunships" on the American model in Vietnam, but were invaluable for moving 105 mm pack howitzers into forward firebases close to the border and for keeping them supplied. These guns provided fire support for the patrols along the borderline. Moreover, British units were inserted by air into Indonesia. Planes from the British carriers *Victorious*, *Ark Royal*, *Hermes*, and *Centaur* and the Australian carrier *Melbourne* both provided supporting air strikes and acted as a deterrent against Indonesian escalation. Javelins based in Singapore provided air cover, on one occasion destroying a transport aircraft attempting to insert insurgents. The situation was held until a change in government in Indonesia in 1965 led to a transformation in policy there and to successful negotiations.

On the Arabian Peninsula, Saudi air power was used to support the royalist side in the civil war in Yemen, where the republicans, who seized power in a coup in 1962, were backed by Egypt. The Saudis purchased British planes. The Egyptians used their aircraft for bombing, ground attack, and air mobility, as with the capture of the town of Sadah after paratroopers had seized a runway on which troops could be landed. The Egyptians also developed the use of helicopter-borne aerial resupply for their forces. The Egyptian capability to take the initiative did not, however, lead to an ability to obtain victory, for, unless occupied, territory could not be retained. The repeated Egyptian bombing of royalist bases in Saudi Arabia did not end the struggle. In the end, a compromise was negotiated in 1970.[16] In 2015, Saudi planes again bombed Yemeni targets.

In the brief 1965 war between India and Pakistan, the two air forces were heavily engaged. The Pakistan Air Force (PAF) was able to inflict greater casualties despite being smaller. This owed much to the technical superiority of the PAF's F-86 Sabres over the IAF's Hunters and Mysteres. Crucially, the F-86s were equipped with Sidewinder air-to-air missiles. The Indian Gnats, which lacked missiles, proved to be extremely maneuverable and enjoyed some success as a result. Aircraft losses on the ground rather than in air-to-air combat were significant. The PAF also used its small force of Canberra bombers, but not effectively. Hercules transport aircraft were used unsuccessfully as improvised bombers. In contrast, the IAF made effective use of British-supplied Canberra bombers flying at extremely low levels. Operating close to its bases, the PAF had the advantage of effective radar coverage, which, like the Sidewinders, was supplied by the Americans. The PAF continues to see this conflict as an underdog's success, and the war plays a major role in the PAF's lasting account that it is martially and technically superior to the IAF. Whether or not this is justified is another question, but the air force historians of each country focus on fighting the other air force.[17]

Unlike in the 1965 war, in the 1971 war, the IAF was able to gain air superiority easily over East Pakistan, which was hardly surprising given Pakistan's impossible strategic situation in the east. The PAF stationed only one squadron of Sabres and a few support aircraft in Dacca and understandably concentrated its units in West Pakistan. India had benefited from turning, after 1965, to the Soviet Union as its arms supplier of choice. By the 1971 war, India's fighter squadrons had been re-equipped with MIG-21s and also had missile batteries and comprehensive radar coverage. The PAF's preemptive strike against the Indian airfields in west India on December 3, a counter-air operation, failed because, in comparison with the Six-Day War, the Pakistanis lacked the combat effectiveness of the Israelis, while the Indians were more competent than the Arabs. Over the skies of West Pakistan, the IAF won the subsequent attrition war. The IAF fighter bombers were crucial to repelling a Pakistani tank advance in the Rajasthan desert toward Jaisalmer, the Battle of Longewala. The IAF had greater reserves, while the PAF was affected by the inadequate supply by the United States of spare parts for its Sabres and Starfighters, although the war was so brief that there was hardly time for much resupply.

The Indian invasion of East Pakistan in 1971 was marked by an effective use of air power. The Indians conducted a paradrop in East Pakistan and made good use of transport helicopters in crossing a major river en route to Dacca (now Dhaka) from the east. The cooperation between the Indian army and air force was more a result of senior officers having personal relationships than of institutional arrangements. Indeed, one of the prominent aspects of both the 1965 and the 1971 wars was the generally poor coordination among the armies, air forces, and navies on both sides. Nonetheless, in 1971, air power helped India win the ground campaign, and speedily, which was necessary in order to prevent international pressure on behalf of Pakistan by the United States and China. Despite some Indian strikes on Dacca, both sides generally avoided civilian targets in both 1965 and 1971.[18]

In 1967–70, the Nigerian Civil War involved Nigeria in conflict with Biafra, a separatist protostate. The Nigerians benefited from overwhelming numerical superiority, including in the air. Nigeria was armed by Britain and the Soviet Union. Frequently ineffective, Nigerian air attacks were unable to determine the conflict on the ground, where Nigerian armored vehicles proved more useful. However, air power was significant in terms of links with the outside world. Unlike the Viet Minh and the Viet Cong, the Biafrans were swiftly cut off from foreign land links, and this exacerbated their lack of food and military supplies. The Biafran air force consisted of five small piston-engine Malmö MFI-9 MiniCOINs, a trainer on which rocket pods and machine guns were mounted. Under a Swede, Count Carl Gustav von Rosen, they attacked airfields between May 22 and July 9, 1969, destroying or damaging several Nigerian aircraft used to attack relief flights, including MIG-17s and three of Nigeria's six Il-28s. The hard-pressed Biafrans finally collapsed after their airstrip at Uli was overrun in 1970, severing their only remaining supply link.[19]

Air power tended to be more significant in shorter conflicts, as in September 1970 when Syria invaded Jordan. The Syrian Fifth Division was hit by air strikes after it broke through Jordanian positions. The division included the Sixty-Eighth and Ninety-First Tank Brigades, with more than two hundred T-55s. Although they were under the command of the PLO, the tanks were crewed by Syrians. The Jordanian air force's Hunters destroyed a large number of tanks, leading to a loss of morale and contributing to their withdrawal. The Syrian air force was not used, as there was a serious threat of Israeli intervention if it had been, as well as two American carrier battle groups off the Lebanese coast. King Hussein of Jordan asked Israel for assistance, and an overflight by four Israeli Phantoms allegedly helped persuade the Syrians to withdraw, but this is contentious. In turn, air superiority, airlift, and close air support were all important when Turkey swiftly and successfully invaded and overran northern Cyprus in 1974, a step that precipitated the fall of the Greek military government, which had backed union between Cyprus and Greece. For a time, it seemed as if the whole of Cyprus might be overrun, including the sovereign British military bases where nuclear weapons were deployed in support of CENTO. However, the RAF rapidly deployed a powerful F-4 Phantom detachment, and the Turks halted before the British bases.

Air power remained significant in counterinsurgency warfare, as in eastern Congo in 1964–65, where CIA-provided aircraft and mercenaries helped General Mobuto's troops suppress opposition.[20] So also did the movement of Belgian paratroopers by American aircraft. The role of air power was also seen with the British in Aden (subsequently South Yemen) and with the Portuguese in their African colonies. Helicopters proved important in operations in Aden. For example, they played a key role in support of the capture of the rebel stronghold in the inaccessible Wadi Dhubsan in 1964. However, their position undermined by a failure to sustain local support, the British withdrew from Aden in 1967.

The Portuguese had faced insurrections in their African colonies (Angola, Mozambique, and Guinea-Bissau) from 1961 but mounted a formidable resistance. They were helped by aircraft and helicopters, which enabled them to overcome the problems of movement on land, including ambushes and mines. Nevertheless, the introduction of Soviet surface-to-air SAM-7s changed the situation tactically in the early 1970s, as well as powerfully contributing to the sense that the Portuguese had lost the initiative. A left-wing revolution in Portugal in 1974 was followed by the end of colonial rule.

In a campaign redolent of the air control of the 1920s, from 1973, Soviet heavy machine guns hardly affected the ability of Oman and its

British and Iranian allies to use planes and helicopters to help suppress the insurrection in Dhofar, although a change in methods was necessary before success was obtained in the mid-1970s. The use of SAMs came too late to make a significant impact on the campaign, which culminated in a major offensive that severed the supply route to Yemen. Air power, although limited in scale and sophistication, was critical to the success of the government forces, providing ground support, resupply, and the air transport essential to the hearts-and-minds campaign: medical teams, livestock, and water-drilling equipment were flown into the mountainous and inaccessible interior. In more propitious military circumstances, Iranian antiaircraft cover helped the Kurdish rising against Iraq in 1974–75.

Air power could also play a significant role in the politics of coups. However, in general, events on the ground were more decisive. For example, under General Qassem, who ruled Iraq in 1958–63, the heavily fortified Ministry of Defense compound was the center of government, protected by about two thousand troops. When Qassem was overthrown, the compound was attacked from the air before being besieged. Having surrendered, Qassem was killed.[21] In 1973, the presidential palace in Santiago, Chile, was strafed by attack jets as part of the military coup under General Pinochet that seized power there on September 11, 1973. At the same time, the palace was surrounded by tanks and had to be seized by ground forces.

NAVAL AIR POWER

The United States remained the foremost naval power, and carriers continued to be the key element, one furthered by the decline of the battleship. From the 1950s, American carriers were assigned strategic bombing duties in the event of war with the Soviet Union. Their carrier-based strategic nuclear bombers were followed by the British with the nuclear-strike-capable Blackburn Buccaneer.

The emphasis, however, was on the nonnuclear use of carriers. The most extensive use was during the Vietnam War, when the carriers proved especially useful. The carriers were able to provide a nearby safe base for American air operations over both North and South Vietnam. Improvements in supply methods since the Second World War, including resupply from other ships, ensured that the carriers were able to stay at sea for longer than hitherto. During most of 1972, no fewer than six American carriers were on station, and, that summer, an average of four thousand sorties were flown monthly, although the absence of hostile submarines provided a mistaken impression of the general invulnerability of carriers:[22] now shore-to-ship missiles are an effective additional threat. Although the carrier-based planes lacked the payload of the large land-based planes, especially the B-52s, they provided significant firepower, both in support of ground operations in South Vietnam and in attacking North Vietnam. Moreover, when, in April 1969, President Nixon decided that the Vietnam commitment precluded the bombing of North Korea after an American electronic reconnaissance aircraft was shot down, he nevertheless resorted to a show of strength with a carrier task force. The American army commander in Vietnam, Creighton Abrams, refused to send any helicopters.[23] In 1971, Indian Sea Hawks and Alizes from the carrier *Vikrant* (formerly the British *Hercules*) conducted attacks on shore targets in East Pakistan and laid mines in some of the key harbors.

Carrier warfare, however, was in retreat during these years. In part, this was because, aside from submarines, the Soviets focused on missile cruisers. The Soviets also supplied Styx missiles, employing radar homing, to their allies, and the Egyptians and Indians successfully used them against Israel and Pakistan, respectively. For new naval powers, missiles, rather than expensive aircraft, were the key. Nevertheless, in late 1970, as an important enhancement of their naval capability and aspect of power projection, the Soviets began to construct the aircraft carrier *Kiev*. This was referred to as a cruiser, as the Montreux Convention forbade the passage of carriers between the Black Sea and the Aegean. Coming into service, the *Kiev* was essentially a very large anti-submarine helicopter platform, with a complement of Yak-35 Forger V/STOLs (vertical/short takeoff and landing aircraft) for ground attack and local air-defense. Indeed, the *Kiev* was essentially a larger version of the *Invincible* the British laid down in 1973. Not as effective as the British Harrier, the Yak-35 encountered many problems, particularly with its two lift engines and main propulsion engine. Its weapon load was negligible, and it finally went out of service in the 1980s, which left the three carriers of the *Kiev* class without a core weapon system. Against American submarines, the Soviets deployed the smaller *Moskva* class of helicopter carriers equipped with dipping sonars and nuclear-tipped antisubmarine missiles.

In part in response to Soviet naval activity but also as a result of American prompting, the Japanese revived their naval air power in the shape of the Maritime Self-Defense Force. This focused on antisubmarine warfare as an auxiliary force to the American navy. There was investment accordingly in helicopters operated from destroyers and in land-based patrol aircraft to chase Soviet submarines.

The British meanwhile had abandoned their attempt to emulate the Americans by building a class of three large strike aircraft carriers. The first, the planned fifty-three-thousand-ton CVA-01, which would have been the first carrier to be built in Britain since the Second World War, was canceled in February 1966 as part of Britain's retreat from "East of Suez." It was then envisaged that, after the existing carriers, with their distant-strike capability, came to the end of their service, which was projected to be in the 1970s, British naval air power would amount essentially to helicopters and short-range aircraft designed to act against Soviet submarines in the North Atlantic. The V/STOL aircraft, which for Britain meant the Sea Harriers, did not require fleet carriers,[24] and an ability to support amphibious operations with large fleet carriers no longer appeared necessary. The *Victorious* was sold in 1969, and the *Eagle* went into reserve in 1972 and was broken up in 1978, leaving only the *Ark Royal*. The light fleet carrier *Hermes* was converted to a helicopter carrier in 1971–73. The first British carrier designed for antisubmarine duty and equipped for operating V/STOL aircraft, the sixteen-thousand-ton *Invincible*, was laid down in 1973. With a big deck carrier, the *Ark Royal*, and large amphibious platforms, the British had advantages over the Soviet Union, but they were outmatched in tonnage, manpower, and nuclear submarines. France maintained a large carrier presence, commissioning the 32,780-ton *Foch* in 1963. In contrast, judging it unaffordable, Canada withdrew its last carrier from service in 1970, a major practical and symbolic blow.

The emphasis of naval air power was now therefore on the United States, which, from 1969, in response to Soviet naval development, concentrated on planning for naval conflict with the Soviets, rather than on attacking the Soviet Union itself. The focus was on being able to destroy Soviet naval power in battle and in its home waters. This led to a stress on big carriers and large submarines, both intended to attack the Soviet fleet. American dominance of air power was most clearly demonstrated at sea. In turn, the Soviets deployed nuclear-armed missiles and torpedoes on their submarines in order to attack American carriers.

THE STRATEGIC DIMENSION

In the case of the United States and the Soviet Union, as well as of the second-rank nuclear powers, notably Britain, France, and China, the direction of strategic air power was toward missiles and away from aircraft. The deployment of nuclear-armed B-52 heavy bombers in 1955 had upgraded American delivery capability so that a small number of aircraft were able, and rapidly, to achieve vastly more than the far larger Allied bomber force had done against Germany in 1942–45. Nuclear bombers were flexible: they could be held up to a day in orbit, retasked and refueled, or recalled just before they were due to launch their weapons. These aircraft were upgraded by the use of standoff missiles, such as Hound Dog, Blue Steel, and the planned Skybolt, enabling a nuclear missile to be fired at long range for area suppression before closing in on a particular target with free-fall nuclear bombs.

In a mutually supportive "triad" of capability, B-52s were seen as a second wave: the more vulnerable manned bombers followed as a second wave the less vulnerable and speedier land-based and submarine-launched missiles, each of which appeared to permit a more sophisticated management of deterrence and retaliation. Submarines were harder to detect than aircraft and could be based near the coast of target states. In the 1960s and early 1970s, these weapon systems were developed, and new weaponry was deployed. Thus, in 1970, the United States deployed Minuteman III ICBMs equipped with multiple independently targeted reentry vehicles, which enhanced strike capacity. The launch time of land-based intercontinental missiles was cut by developing the Titan, which had storable liquid propellants enabling in-silo launches. Aircraft acting as strategic bombers in a nuclear conflict were, in contrast, slower and more vulnerable. Similarly, unlike spy planes, which could be shot down, satellites were sufficiently high to be invulnerable, and therefore offered the possibility of frequent overflights and thus of more information. However, such a capability required many satellites and was therefore very expensive. Many of the high-definition satellites needed to be in low Earth orbit, where the decay rate is high. For this reason, they were kept on ground alert. The most advanced aircraft of its day was the American Lockheed SR-71 Black-bird, a high-altitude reconnaissance plane. Made of titanium and able to fly at great height and speed (eighty thousand feet at Mach 3.0), this amazing aircraft was overtaken by the development of satellites and the parallel development of high-resolution cameras, which used the whole width of the electromagnetic spectrum.

AIRLIFT

Although the logistical capability of air power was constrained by political factors, air power could be used to move large numbers of troops more rapidly than ships. The first American troops to arrive in South Korea in 1950 in response to invasion by North Korea did so by air from Japan, which was then under American occupation. In 1958, Britain flew troops into Amman, the capital of Jordan, when its government appealed for help against possible attack by radical Arab states. This airlift was given fighter air cover. In 1961, troops were initially flown into Kuwait airport when Iraqi invasion was threatened. RAF and naval aircraft were also sent. In response to disorder in the Dominican Republic in 1965, the United States airlifted twenty-three thousand troops in less than two weeks.

In turn, considerable Soviet airlift capacity was demonstrated in re-supplying Egypt and Syria during the Yom Kippur War in 1973, and in Angola in 1975, helping to thwart a takeover by pro-Western forces. Air power, indeed, was very significant in supporting pro-Soviet Cuban intervention in Africa: in Angola, Ethiopia, and elsewhere. As a consequence of the role of airlift, airports became points of key importance: Soviet tanks were flown into Czechoslovak airports, notably Prague airport on the night of August 20–21, 1968, when the Czechoslovakian reform movement was forcibly ended. The Antonov-12 and Antonov-22 transport aircraft used were able to move tanks as well as troops. First flown in 1965, the An-22 could carry a cargo of 80,000 kg (176,350 lbs). At the same time, the Warsaw Pact intervention into Czechoslovakia underlined the significance of ground intervention: the United States at the time could have airlifted no more than 10,000 troops per day from North America to Europe, whereas the Warsaw Pact moved in 250,000 troops within twenty-four hours. The Soviets knew of this weakness.

Alongside the availability of suitable aircraft and political approval, the outload capability was also important. Often, even today, for example with humanitarian help in Nepal in 2015, numbers of massive aircraft can arrive with tons of cargo and many personnel, but if they cannot be handled and then deployed off the base to the area of need, the whole system becomes clogged up and nothing moves.

AIRCRAFT PROCUREMENT

The 1960s and 1970s saw an increase in the number of independent countries. Most established an air force, just as they created national flag carriers for civilian flight. For example, Singapore established an air force, the Singapore Air Defense Command, in 1968, initially with two Cessnas and with systems inherited from Britain. As the new states lacked aircraft manufacturers, certainly for military jets, they were dependent on receiving these planes from those few states that manufactured them. This ensured that air power became a key element in the trade in military hardware and, as such, an important element of the Cold War. The Cold War protagonists supplied planes, maintenance, and training in order to create and sustain links. This was true within military alliances, notably NATO for the West and the Warsaw Pact for the Soviet bloc, but also as these protagonists sought to win support in the "Third World," particularly in the newly independent states. Thus, Australian surplus CAC Sabre fighters were delivered to Malaysia between 1969 and 1972, while the Soviet Union supplied MIGs to India, including, eventually, the sophisticated 25, 27, and 29 types. Singapore acquired British Hawker Hunters and Strikemasters, as well as French Alouette 3 helicopters. Initially, Singaporean airmen had to be sent abroad to train, while foreign-seconded and contract personnel were brought in for maintenance. Training abroad was a key aspect of air activity for second-rank powers and also helped to establish an international hierarchy in practical and symbolic, institutional and personal ways.

The United States dominated NATO aircraft production. In 1965, Britain decided to purchase the American F-111K in order to fill the gap after the cancellation of the projected British TSR-2 strike reconnaissance plane able to deliver a tactical nuclear weapon, a plane that was over budget, late, and affected by the Labour government's determination to cut defense costs. The purchase of the F-111K, in turn, was canceled by that government in 1968 as the result of a further defense review made necessary by financial crisis, and the F-4 was bought as a stopgap, first for ground attack/strike, and then as a follow-on fighter.

Alongside the crucial political and military "push" factors in encouraging arms supplies came others in the shape of aircraft industries, both with spare capacity and needing volume sales in order to reduce or spread costs, and governments seeking to protect these industries. On top of this, the rapid change in jet types, as technology was updated in an intensely competitive race, ensured that there were jets, no longer at the cutting edge, that could be passed on. There was also the question of particular types of aircraft. Thus, the American-designed Northrop F-5 Freedom Fighter was supplied to Asian (South Vietnam, Thailand, and the Philippines) and South American states as a capable, easy-to-maintain competitor for Soviet fighters. As an instance of American manufacturing range, together with the supporting industrial and technological dominance, the F-5 was supplied without compromising America's advantage in higher-tech aircraft, such as the F-15, which was first flown in 1972. Carriers could also be passed on. Thus, the British *Venerable*, built during the Second World War, was sold to the Dutch in 1948, before being taken out of service by them in 1968 and sold to Argentina, where it was renamed 25 *de Mayo*. Its movements were a factor in the Anglo-Argentinian 1982 Falklands War.

The net effect was a dramatic increase in air power in the Third World. In turn, as individual states gained advanced aircraft, so local rivals sought the same. This was seen in particular in the Middle East. For example, Iraq sought and obtained Soviet and French planes to counteract the American ones acquired by Iran. The strategic significance of the Middle East was enhanced by the great-power competition that increased there from the late 1960s, as well as due to the greater importance of Middle Eastern oil. Oil producers were to spend heavily on aircraft. Abu Dhabi created an air force in 1968, Qatar in 1974, and Bahrain in 1977. The largest producer, Saudi Arabia, bought British

Lightnings in order to match Egyptian purchases before buying Tornado bombers under the Al Yamamah deal and F-15 air superiority fighters from the United States. Recent orders include the F-15 Strike Eagle, as well as Typhoon fighters. Saudi Arabia is now the fourth-largest
defense spender. The maintenance and training package with Britain
lasted decades, proved extremely beneficial to both parties, and laid the
firm foundations of a modern air arm in Saudi Arabia. A similar British
agreement with Oman proved equally successful.

In Iran, a major oil exporter, the air force, which became a separate
service in 1955, benefited from the support of the Shah, Muhammad
Reza, a pilot who enjoyed flying. There was marked expansion from the
acquisition of the F-5 Tiger in 1965 and the F-4 Phantom in 1968. The
air force grew from 75 combat aircraft in 1965 to 200 in 1968 and over
420 by 1978, fielding some of the most modern American equipment.
American technology (including air-to-air missiles and guided bombs)
and doctrine played a key role, and the air force was reconceptualized
from air defense and close air support to becoming the main strike arm.
From 1970, the air force gained the highest priority in a defense budget
swelled by rising oil revenues. The Shah's brother-in-law, Muhammad
Khatami, the head of the air force, ensured governmental support. Iran
became the only foreign state to purchase the F-14A Tomcat, an
American swing-wing fighter equipped with very long-range Phoenix
missiles: it acquired seventy-seven. The air force also acquired twenty-
four tankers for in-flight refueling, as well as seventy large jets to provide transport, and, by 1978, had a personnel of one hundred thousand,
compared to seven thousand in 1965. The other services also obtained
air power. The navy acquired P-3 aircraft to spot submarines in and
around the Strait of Hormuz, as well as 46 helicopters, in part for
antisubmarine warfare, while the army aviation command had 220
American helicopter gunships and nearly 400 other helicopters for
troop transport and other functions. However, there was a lack of the
skilled personnel necessary to maintain the aircraft, as well as serious
deficiencies in training.[25]

The provision of aircraft became more fluid in this period, as links
with former providers, notably former imperial powers, were challenged. Thus, Malaysia turned to Europe and, eventually, Russia, rather
than Britain. The major British arms manufacturer, BAE Systems, was
very much involved in the Pergau Dam affair of 1988–94, when devel-

opment aid was offered to Malaysia in exchange for the purchase of arms, particularly the Tornado F-3 fighter. Eventually, however, the MIG-29 and the Sukhoi Su-30 were obtained from Russia, largely in a form of barter for palm oil. Estranged from the Soviet Union, Romania and Yugoslavia combined on the Avioane IAR-93/SOKO J-22, a ground-attack fighter that first flew in 1974. Seeking to reduce reliance on the United States, France and West Germany cooperated on the Alpha, a trainer as well as ground-attack aircraft that first flew in 1973. A total of 504 had been built by 1991. The plane was also operated by states in which France had influence, namely Belgium, Cameroon, the Ivory Coast, Morocco, and Togo, as well as by Egypt, Nigeria, Portugal, and Qatar. Japan began developing indigenous jet aircraft in 1967, with the T-2, a trainer, flying from 1971 and the F1, a ground-attack fighter based on it, flying from 1975.

States affected by embargoes also sought to develop their own production. Copying a French design, Israel produced the Kfir fighter, first flown in 1973 and entering service in 1975. In turn, Israel sold the Kfir to Argentina, Colombia, Ecuador, and Sri Lanka and helped embargoed South Africa produce the Cheetah, which also copied a French design. The Cheetah entered service with the South African air force in 1986. South Africa had already produced the Impala Mk1, Mirage F1, Mirage III, Alouette III, Kudu OM4, Impala MR11, and Puma SA 330, and, in 1990, was to follow with the Rooivalk CSH2-XPM attack helicopter. The South Africans also produced air-to-air missiles. India's anxieties about being cut off by supplier sanctions, combined with its anti-imperialist desire for independent, unfettered defense decision making, led New Delhi toward stressing coproduction attempts to develop its own aircraft industry.

CONCLUSIONS

Alongside the issues arising from the nature of war and the varied capabilities and limitations of air power, it is instructive to emphasize the complexity of the global context. China dropped a nuclear bomb successfully from a Harbin H-5 bomber in 1968. Similarly, although later, in India and Pakistan, aircraft were to be the primary means of delivery for the first years of nuclear weapons capability. However, in

China, as elsewhere, the emphasis was to move to missiles. Yet, at the same time that the strategic significance of air power was declining in the face of the reliance on missiles to deliver nuclear weaponry, there was a far greater reliance on air power in regional struggles due to the spread of jet aircraft. This spread counteracted the effect of the concentration of manufacturing capacity, providing a clear contrast with nuclear weaponry, which only spread to a limited extent. Thus, in 1966, the J-7, a version of the MIG-21 built under license by China, first flew. The J-7, and variants, were to be operated by China's allies, including Albania, Myanmar, Pakistan, Sudan, and Tanzania, as well as by other states seeking an inexpensive plane: Bangladesh, Egypt, Iran, and Zimbabwe. China's H-6 was a copy of the Soviet Tu-16 built under license. China's breaking away from Soviet links was shown with the J-8, a fighter first flown in 1969 that had an indigenous Chinese design even if influenced by Soviet patterns.

Moreover, the spread of jets ensured that aircraft played a major role in regional conflicts, as well as being a factor in the counterinsurgency struggles of the postcolonial world. Suffering air attack was perceived as threatening the viability of regimes, not least by demonstrating weakness and raising the possibility of unrest. This was the case with Israeli strikes against Egypt in the War of Attrition and against Syria in 1973.

At the same time, leading powers invested in new aircraft in an attempt to achieve and maintain a capability edge. Thus, the United States commissioned the F-15 in order to counter claims made on behalf of the MIG-25 Foxbat (first flown in 1964), including an ability to fly at over three times the speed of sound and with unique agility. The defection to Japan of a pilot with a MIG-25 in 1976 showed that these claims were widely exaggerated, although it was indeed very fast. The two aircraft that the Israelis were unable to engage when they overflew their nuclear reactor at Dimona in 1967 may have been MIG-25s.[26] As well as being generally robust, the F-15, with its look-down, shoot-down radar capability, was superior as a weapons platform. Its avionics were based on vacuum tubes. This gave the plane advantages in that it was not susceptible to damage from the electronic pulse emitted by a nuclear detonation. The MIG-29, which came into service in 1983, proved more agile than the faster MIG-25.

Electronic warfare provided a key reason for new investment. American losses in bombing North Vietnam, notably in 1972, and Israeli losses in the Yom Kippur War led to an appreciation that SAM systems had become highly potent and could greatly affect bombing (as in the Second World War) and play a major role in an expanded struggle for air superiority, which they had not greatly done hitherto. As a result, much greater effort was to be put into electronic countermeasures, including radar detection, as well as into suppressing SAM defenses. This priority affected research and procurement, both of aircraft and of munitions, and these led to the significantly enhanced capability that Israel displayed against Syria in air conflict in 1982 and that the United States was to show against Iraq in 1991. "Wild Weasel" F-4Gs, Prowlers, and, most recently, F-16CJs, mostly equipped with high-speed anti-radiation missiles (HARM), could now swiftly fire at and destroy any radar that was transmitting, thereby thwarting any SAM launch or tracking.

However, investment plans for new and existing aircraft, munitions, and infrastructure were affected by the problems in the global financial system seen with the ending of the Bretton Woods system in 1971, and with the downturn in the global economy following the dramatic hike in oil prices by OPEC after the 1973 Yom Kippur War. Among states that did not export oil, this downturn reduced government revenues and thus the funds available for new investment. In some Western states, there were also hopes that the détente of the mid-1970s would reduce the need for such investment. The likely trajectory for air power was far from clear.

9

THE LATER COLD WAR, 1976–89

In the last period of the Cold War, hopes of détente in the mid-1970s were replaced by a marked buildup in tension in the Brezhnev era of the early 1980s, followed by the unwinding of Cold War tensions from 1985 under Gorbachev. Air power continued to be important, both in the Cold War and with reference to the other struggles of the period, many of which were linked, directly or indirectly, to the Cold War.

COLD WAR CONFRONTATION

Air power remained central in preparing for conflict between the United States and the Soviet Union, which encouraged a stress on advances in weaponry, training, and doctrine. At the level of full-scale war, the focus was on standoff missiles, and these were of significance at intercontinental, intermediate, and tactical ranges. At each range, these missiles and their nuclear warheads were seen as potentially decisive. At the combat-ready level, the first Soviet SS-20 missiles were deployed. These were highly mobile and more accurate missiles, armed with nuclear warheads, that were designed to be used in conjunction with conventional forces in an invasion of Western Europe. The West responded with the deployment of cruise and Pershing missiles capable of carrying nuclear warheads.

However, there was also renewed interest, certainly on the NATO side, in the possibility of a conflict that would not become a nuclear or, at least, full-scale nuclear war. This interest helped lead to an emphasis on an enhanced air power able to wage conventional warfare. This emphasis was encouraged by the development, in the 1980s, of a maneuverist strategy on the NATO side and by the increased use of smart weapons. These included air-to-air, air-to-ground, and ground-to-air missiles; guided bombs; and electronic measures and countermeasures.

The American Sidewinder missile illustrated the development of weapon types. The AIM-9L was the first "all-aspect" version of the Sidewinder heat-seeking missile. It could even be fired almost head-on, which opponents were unprepared for. Previous variants had to be fired from less than forty degrees off the target's tail, which required the fighter to maneuver hard against the adversary to get behind him. First used in combat by the Americans against two Libyan-flown Soviet-made Su-22s in 1981, and successfully so, this version of the Sidewinder was employed by the British in the Falklands War of 1982. Despite the appalling weather conditions and the fact that many missiles were fired on the edge of their range envelope, the AIM-9L had an approximately 80 percent kill rate and was responsible for shooting down nineteen Argentinian planes. Sidewinder missiles also helped the Israelis overcome the Syrian air force in conflict over Lebanon in 1982. Meanwhile, the accuracy of bombing was revolutionized by laser marking systems, which guided bombs to their targets. Whereas the NATO requirement was for half of all unguided bombs to hit within 140 feet of the target, with precision target marking 90 percent of bombs impacted within 3 meters. Pilots launched bombs into the "cone" of the laser beam in order to hone in on the reflected light off the target. Laser markers could be operated independently from the bomber, either by aircraft or from the ground.

New military capabilities accentuated uncertainty and encouraged tension. In 1977, the Americans tested a neutron bomb, an "enhanced radiation weapon" that was supposed to have low radiation persistence. This bomb was intended to incapacitate Soviet tank crews and was not, despite Soviet propaganda to the contrary, for use against Soviet cities, where it would cause vast numbers of casualties. The rationale for using the neutron bomb was a confession of weakness that not only could conventional arms alone not stop a Soviet armored attack into West Germany, but that the Americans were reluctant to use standard tactical nuclear weapons, knowing that the Soviets would retaliate with them (if they had not used them before), and everything would escalate into the strategic domain. The Americans were trying to hammer out a new battlefield doctrine between conventional response (and conventional warfare including enormously lethal biological and chemical weapons) and standard tactical nuclear weaponry.

In the 1980s, a new, maneuverist, what we now call AirLand doctrine was implemented by NATO in order to aid planning for a mobile defense of Western Europe in the event of Soviet attack. This doctrine and planning was linked to the post-Vietnam revitalization of the American military, a revitalization that involved a process of transformation, or at least redirection, so as to focus on conflict with the Warsaw Pact rather than to prepare for another Vietnam-style conflict. The presentation of the example of Israeli success in the Yom Kippur War of 1973, and the doctrine of AirLand Battle deployed in 1982 by the American army's Training and Doctrine Command (TRADOC), led to a stress on the integration of firepower with mobility in order to thwart the Soviet concept of "Deep Battle." There was a change in the doctrine of the American army from the defensive mind-set of "Active Defense" to the offensive AirLand Battle, of which the air component, especially with the integration of Apache attack helicopters, was integral in defeating and counterattacking a Soviet offensive in Germany. The key component in implementation was the creation of world-class training centers at the National Training Center (NTC) in the California desert, the Joint Readiness Training Center (JRTC) in Louisiana, and the Combined Maneuver Training Center (CMTC) in Grafenwehr, Germany. The creation of an opposing force (OPFOR) using Soviet doctrine was a critical element in the training.

Proposing an effective synergy between land and air, and an intermediate, operational level between the tactical and the strategic, AirLand Battle doctrine was designed to permit the engagement and destruction of the second- and third-echelon Warsaw Pact forces, at the same time that the main ground battle was taking place along the front, a doctrine which suggested that NATO would be better placed than had been argued to throttle a Soviet conventional attack in Europe. AirLand Battle proposed high-tempo and offensive campaigning, with the gaining of air superiority employed in order to provide effective interdiction. This was very different from the already significant advances in air-ground coordination with regard to tactical air support. These advances benefited from practices evolved in Vietnam as well as in NATO training. Forward air controllers had better equipment than their Second World War predecessors. As a result of the Vietnam War, the USAF underwent a major makeover. High agility was restored in aircraft like the F-16 and F-15, and crews were trained against simulated Soviet "aggressor" squadrons, who were experts in Soviet weapons and tactics. Greater emphasis was given to new doctrine, and smart weapons and stealth capabilities were developed.

The doctrine of AirLand Battle led to a focus on the modernization of conventional weaponry, with the Americans spending heavily in order to maintain a qualitative advantage and to ensure that their emphasis on firepower over manpower remained valid. New weaponry played a major role in the doctrinal, strategic, operational, and tactical reevaluation of the period. In part, this modernization was a question of an enhanced aerial component for the army. Thus, the Blackhawk helicopter, introduced in 1979, was followed, in 1986, by the Apache attack helicopter, equipped with radar and Hellfire missiles. There was also a more ambitious role for the USAF as part of what was seen as a wide-ranging, technologically advanced spectrum of attack. Advances stemmed from airplane stealth technology; look-down, shoot-down, air-to-air radars; and the enhancement of air combat resulting from improvements in heat-seeking short-range missiles and their improved, radar-guided, long-range counterparts. While ground radars are limited by hill shadows and a radar horizon of about thirty miles, the introduction of AWACS (airborne warning and control system) aircraft, which, from 30,000 feet, could detect aircraft out to 400 miles and could track even low-flying aircraft out to the radar horizon at 250 miles, gave the United States and NATO for the first time a clear picture of the entire air battle space.

These and other advances were combined with those in related aerial fields to ensure that aircraft had formidable war-fighting capabilities. For example, specifically designed for air superiority, the F-15 (first flown in 1972) and the F-16 (first flown in 1974) each had supreme aerodynamic performance and a thrust-to-weight ratio of greater than one, which enabled the aircraft to accelerate while maneuvering or climbing. Although aerodynamically unstable, computers provided excellent high-g maneuverability, which was greatly enhanced by sophisticated airborne radars, operated by "hands on throttle and stick" controls, together with head-up displays that permitted great situational awareness and highly effective engagement. The enhancement of capabilities and integration of air computers was important given American leadership in electronics, as well as marked Soviet deficiencies. Thus, the F-15 and F-16 each had computer-aimed 20 mm M61A1 cannon. Although the computers reduced the workload of pilots, the complexities of tactics and the battle space meant that the latter were still significant. For example, greater speed and thrust-to-weight ratio, as well as aerodynamic advances in Soviet fighters, ensured that pilots had to understand their comparative "energy envelopes." All the while, American, Belgian, Dutch, Italian, and West German F-15s and F-16s were also equipped to carry theater nuclear weapons in the shape of B-61 gravity bombs,[1] while British Phantoms and Jaguars also had this capability so that conventional defense was underpinned by a range of nuclear options. Israel used F-15s and F-16s in its successful 1981 attack on the nuclear reactor being built at Osirak by Iraq, an important strategic use of air power that prevented Saddam Hussein from processing fissile material presumably for the "Super Gun" he was building in order to bombard Israel.

The aircraft of other powers were also upgraded. Thus, first flown in 1982, the Mirage 2000 replaced the Mirage-3 and Mirage-5 in French service. Whereas they each had a payload of 4,000 kg (8,818 lbs), the Mirage 2000 had a payload of 6,300 kg (13,890 lbs), with the D model having terrain-following avionics as well as fixings for precision-guided weapons. The Mirage 2000 was also operated by Abu Dhabi, Egypt, Greece, India, Peru, Qatar, and Taiwan. Foreign sales played a key role in financing developments. The low-level penetration role for fighters, designed to minimize Soviet air defense effectiveness by ground hugging, was seen with planes like the British Tornado, first flown in 1974 and operated by Britain, West Germany, Italy, and Saudi Arabia. It was equipped with runway-cratering bombs and mines, such as the JP-233, and was intended to attack Warsaw Pact airfields.

American ambitions were bold and far flung. The "Star Wars" program, or Strategic Defense Initiative, outlined by President Ronald Reagan in a speech on March 23, 1983, was designed to enable the United States to dominate space, employing space-mounted weapons to destroy Soviet satellites and missiles,[2] although it is not clear that the technology would have survived Soviet disruption techniques.[3] Below that level, the United States planned to employ stealthy attack aircraft and long-range precision standoff weapons such as the air-launched cruise missile (ALCM) and the ground-launched cruise missile (GLCM) that caused such controversy in Europe when it was fielded. Laser-guided projectiles and programmed cruise missiles would inflict heavy damage on Soviet armor, while advanced aircraft, such as the F-15 and F-16, would win air superiority and also attack Soviet ground forces. Stealth technology would permit the penetration of Soviet air defenses, obliging the Soviets to retain more aircraft in air defense, and would make their nuclear deterrent vulnerable to a first strike and thus affect the strategic balance. Coordination would be made possible by computer networking, a new generation of spy satellites with six-inch resolution, AWACS aircraft, and the Global Positioning System (GPS), planned for introduction in the early 1990s.

The feasibility of this new hardware was not tested in practice against the Soviet Union, which at the same time was deploying advanced MIG-29s, MIG-31s, and Su-27s, as well as SAM-10s, SAM-11s, SAM-12s, and SAM-13s, which were more mobile and accurate than earlier models. The Soviets had also learned from the Syrian defeat by Israel in 1982.[4] Rapid victory, employing American 1980s doctrine and technology in the war with Iraq in 1991, the First Gulf War, did not necessarily indicate the likely outcome against the far more powerful Soviet Union, although it was a microcosm, as the Soviet Union employed similar aircraft and a similar relatively untrained conscript force. Soviet observers at the NTC in the late 1980s quipped that the OPFOR performed Soviet doctrine better than any force they could muster. The Soviets also relied on unwilling Warsaw Pact allies who might not have fought well. By 1989, Soviet military capability was a shadow of its former self. Nevertheless, there remained the need to respond to the resources, methods, and resilience of any Soviet attack, which would have included the use of their long-range bombers, notably the Tu-22 Backfire, the Tu-95 Bear, and the Tu-160 Blackjack. However, American planning arguably was overreliant on the potential of air power.

The Americans repeatedly sought to embrace the possibilities of change. Thus, the tiltrotor, an aircraft able to life into the sky vertically but then fly like an ordinary plane, was developed as a faster and longer-range replacement of the helicopter, primarily for the marines, but also for the USAF, navy, and army. However, grave difficulties in the technology, high overruns, delays, and the impact of defense cuts repeatedly hit the program. The V-22 Osprey finally entered service in 2007.[5]

REGIONAL WARS

Air power played an important, but very varied, role in the regional wars of the period. After the fall of the Shah in the Islamic Revolution in Iran in 1979, Iraq attacked Iran in 1980. This launched a struggle that lasted until 1988, the longest conventional war of the period, and one that involved more combatants and casualties than other conflicts of the time. The Iraqis planned to use the same methods as those employed by Israel against Egypt in 1967: a surprise air attack to destroy the opponent's air force, followed by a tank offensive. However well conceived the operational plan, the Iraqis proved incapable of executing it. The surprise Iraqi attack on ten Iranian air bases on September 22, 1980, failed because of inadequate targeting, a lack of adequate expertise, and a lack of precision equipment. In addition, most Iranian airfields were at the edge of Iraqi range, and Iraqi pilots had scant combat experience. The rigid operational control exercised by the Iraqi dictator Saddam Hussein proved mistaken. That day, 192 Iraqi aircraft took off at noon, but a mistaken focus on targeting Iranian runways rather than strafing unsheltered aircraft lessened the damage done, as did the failure of many bombs to land. The effective Iranian air defense was also a factor, while, learning a lesson from the Israeli attack on Egypt in 1967, many of the Iranian aircraft were held in hardened shelters.

The failure of the Iraqi attack ensured that the Iranian air force survived and, with over two hundred aircraft launched, many of which were up-to-date American-supplied aircraft such as Phantoms and F-14s, was successfully able to attack Iraqi air bases the next day and its oil facilities on September 25. These attacks hit the financial underpinnings of the Iraqi war effort. In turn, the Iranian Army Aviation deployed its American-supplied Cobra helicopter gunships, over sixty of which were equipped to use TOW (tube-launched, optically tracked, wire command data link) antitank guided missiles. These inflicted serious losses on Iraqi tank advances, which led Iraqi commanders to command more cautiously, thus helping the outnumbered Iranian army units. In turn, Iraq deployed Gazelle helicopter gunships against Iranian tanks.

In subsequent operations, for example the recapture of the city of Khorramshahr on May 24, 1982, the Iranians benefited from their use of helicopters, which were able to fire heat-seeking missiles against Iraqi tanks, and from the employment of Soviet-supplied SAM-7 shoulder-launched short-range surface-to-air missiles.

The Iran-Iraq war demonstrated the complexity of the relationships between major powers insofar as aerial capacity was concerned. Iraq was supplied by the Soviet Union and France, both seeking influence, and the first using the war to test out new weaponry. The United States had assumed that the withdrawal of its advisors after the Islamic Revolution that overthrew the Shah would mean that Iran would not be able to sustain its American-supplied weapon systems, but it was proved wrong at least for a while. The war began with the Iranian air force more technologically advanced than that of Iraq and less affected by revolutionary chaos than the latter had assumed, and these factors remained the case for the first year or so. The release, by the new regime, of newly imprisoned pilots and specialists proved significant in maintaining Iranian effectiveness.

Stasis on the front line led to Iraqi air attacks on Iran's oil installations and shipping in order to undermine its finances. The Iraqis used French Super Frelon helicopters, as well as, from 1983, Super Extendard aircraft, and, from 1985, Mirage F-1 aircraft, all firing Exocet missiles. In turn, Iran's Phantoms attacked tankers carrying Gulf oil. From 1984, in the "war of the cities," Scud missile and aircraft attacks were mounted indiscriminately on each other's cities. Iraqi attacks led much of the population of Tehran to flee the city in 1988. The Iranians, meanwhile, as a result of the American embargo, suffered increasingly from a shortage of spare parts, notably missiles. By war's end, most Iranian aircraft lacked fully functional avionics, including adequate radars.

The Iraqi and Iranian militaries displayed a major shortcoming of most regional forces, namely a lack of operational logistics and planning. The militaries were/are only capable of fighting one battle and then have to stop and refit and plan the next advance. Cultural factors play a role, but most of the issue stems from a lack of capacity.

The Israeli army had benefited from close air support in its invasion of southern Lebanon in 1978, an invasion in which the PLO's infra-structure was destroyed. The Israelis had responded to their heavy losses in 1973 by fielding new antiradiation missiles of the Shrike and HARM types and by developing a new doctrine and training designed to suppress SAM defenses. This served them in good stead in 1982 when they invaded southern Lebanon anew. The Syrian SAM batteries failed to act as a deterrent, despite being a new Soviet system of SAM-6s, SAM-8s, and SAM-9s and being manned by Soviet advisors. The Syrian occupying force initially fought well. However, their nineteen missile batteries in the Bekaa Valley in eastern Lebanon (installed in 1981) were knocked out on June 8–9, 1982, in what became known as the "Bekaa Valley Turkey Shoot." Moreover, their air force was badly pummeled by Israeli aircraft directed by AWACS, armed with American-supplied Sparrow and Sidewinder missiles, and supported by electronic countermeasures. The Syrians lost about sixty-four aircraft, with no Israeli losses. The Sidewinders proved highly reliable.

The Israelis benefited from an important qualitative advantage. The MIG-21s on which the Syrians relied were far from cutting edge and contrasted with the Israelis' American-supplied F-15s and F-16s. The Syrians were also outnumbered in aircraft three to two. Moreover, the American-supplied Sidewinders and Sparrow radar-guided missiles out-matched the Syrians' AA-2s. The Israelis also benefited greatly from a clear superiority in control and communications, with many Syrian air-craft receiving no effective warning from the ground and being unaware that they were targeted. Aside from skill and training, this involved the use of American-supplied AWACS aircraft, the E-2C Hawkeye. First flown in 1960 and originally designed for carrier operations, this aircraft had been enhanced as electronics improved. The Hawkeye, an airborne radar platform able to manage aerial combat, had not been used in previous Israeli operations. It provided accurate information on all Syr-ian air movements and could guide Israeli fighters onto the Syrian MIGs where they were blindsided. Moreover, Syrian communications and radar systems were jammed. The Israelis also used drones as de-coys, simulating the radar signature of aircraft so that the Syrians acti-vated their SAM radars and fired against them. Drones, which the

Israelis had been testing from the early 1970s, also provided effective intelligence material as well as carrying laser designators that could guide air-launched laser-guided weapons.

In turn, Israeli individual and cumulative advantages were magnified by Syrian disadvantages, a process so often crucial to capability. Syrian training, tactics, and technology, including control systems, were inferior. For example, the Syrians failed to move or camouflage their SAMs. The Syrian ground forces proved highly vulnerable to Israeli attack once it was bolstered by clear superiority in the air. The Israelis also relied on helicopter support for their integrated advancing units of armor/infantry/artillery and engineers. The following year, in contrast, lacking surprise, as well as adequate knowledge of the local situation, an American carrier-based attack on Syrian sites in the Bekaa Valley lost two aircraft to unsuppressed Syrian fire. The French separately launched carrier strikes in 1983, while the British carried out show-of-force attacks over Beirut. However, Western sensibilities over involvement in such operations were clearly demonstrated by the successful suicide attacks on Allied forces in Beirut in 1982, when three hundred American marines were killed in their barracks. This showed the political vulnerability of boots on the ground, and President Reagan immediately ordered the removal of all American ground forces from the area. This encouraged a subsequent shift to air power, which offered involvement with far lower political costs.

Later in the decade, the Israelis had to withdraw from Lebanon. This was in part because they faced Hizbullah, a determined guerrilla force, difficult to fix as a target but able to respond with small surface-to-air missiles to Israeli air power. However, the more significant factors were political and strategic: strong international opposition to Israel's presence there and the serious consequences of the commitment for Israeli military manpower.

Air power also played a significant role in conflict in Africa, delivering close air support as well as force at a distance in a way that had political and military impact. In East Africa, a secessionist dispute over the Somali-populated Ogaden region of Ethiopia became a violent part of the Cold War. When Soviet-armed Somalia attacked Ethiopia in 1977, not least with MIG fighters and Il-28 bombers, the Soviets armed Ethiopia in return for abandoning its American ally. Aside from Cuban troops, the Soviets provided Ethiopia with air reconnaissance and airlift, as well as a commander, General Petrov. Having gained air dominance and used it, in January 1978, to attack Somali supply routes, Petrov launched assaults, supported by air attacks. Firm resistance near the town of Jijiga led to the use of airborne attacks, with parachutists assisted by helicopter troops, which enabled the attackers to overcome the tactical strengths of the Somali position. Victory was followed by the Ethiopian reoccupation of the Ogaden.

Soviet-supported intervention in Angola was less successful because South African air cover helped UNITA as it struggled against the Cuban-backed communist government of post-Portuguese Angola. Conversely, in the winter of 1987–88, a UNITA and South African siege of the southern city of Cuito Cuanavale failed. The South African inability to maintain air superiority during the siege, and more generally by this stage, was a major development. The establishment of communist, pro-Soviet governments in Angola, Guinea-Bissau, and Mozambique was followed by their air forces being equipped with Soviet aircraft, as that of Cuba had earlier been. Similarly, Laos and Vietnam acquired the MIG-21, and Ethiopia the MIG-17, MIG-21, and MIG-23.

Thanks to oil wealth spent on Soviet arms, Colonel Gaddafi, the dictator of Libya, had, by the mid-1980s, built up a military that included 535 combat aircraft, including the MIG-21 and the MIG-23. Libyan intervention in neighboring Chad in 1983 and 1987, in order both to pursue a territorial claim and to support protégés, was thwarted, however, by mobile Chad forces backed by French aircraft that enjoyed air superiority and that attacked Libyan ground forces. American aerial surveillance provided the French with valuable intelligence. Conversely, in southern Sudan, air power proved less effective in a counterinsurgency role, as the ground-to-air missiles of the separatist Sudan People's Liberation Army made the aerial resupply of government garrisons, such as Juba, hazardous.

The sponsorship of terrorism by the Gaddafi regime led to Operation El Dorado Canyon. This entailed the bombing of targets in the capital, Tripoli, as well as near the city of Benghazi on April 15, 1986, by American F-111s flying from British bases, supported by aerial refueling, as well as carrier-based planes. The bombing demonstrated Libyan vulnerability but, although it destroyed his tent, failed to kill Gaddafi, in part probably because of warnings provided by the government of Malta, whose airspace was overflown. In the long term, the bombing seems to have restrained him, at least in part.[6] However, it also led to Gadda-fi's sponsorship of aerial terrorism, with the placing of a bomb on an American civilian aircraft that exploded over Lockerbie. This foreshadowed the terrorist attacks in 2001.

American attacks in the Caribbean reflected different uses of air power. In Operation Urgent Fury, the island of Grenada was seized in 1983, in part by the rapid deployment of parachute and helicopter assaults as well as an amphibious assault. However, there was a serious reconnaissance failure. Moreover, without a joint force theater commander, or adequate preparation, the operation saw inadequate interservice coordination (as well as a measure of acrimony), which led, despite the rapid seizure of both airports, to delay as each service fought its own war, and to most American losses being due to "friendly fire." These problems had been remedied by 1989 when, in Operation Just Cause, the government of Panama run by the drug-smuggling General Noriega was overthrown by an American invasion. In this case, joint operations worked well, while new weapons, including the AC-130 gunship, performed successfully. The Goldwater-Nichols Act of 1986 forced the military into joint operations, with interservice cooperation from education to training to command and control. Air officers now served on army staffs and vice versa.

The strengths and limitations of air power were also shown in Afghanistan. The Soviets were able to overthrow the government in December 1979, in part by the use of airborne troops, notably in the capital, Kabul. In turn, the Soviets were interested in developing a major air base at Shindand near Kandahar, from which the entrance to the Gulf could be threatened. Moreover, the Soviets employed air power, including airborne special forces, against subsequent resistance. Aerial resupply helped isolated Soviet garrisons, while aircraft escorted convoys. The Soviets used their Sukhoi ground-attack aircraft, including the most recent, the Su-25 Frogfoot.

The Soviets did not deploy sufficient air power for the difficult tasks posed by Afghanistan and its society, geography, remoteness, and natural camouflage—a country in which they also had too few troops. Each remark, however, mistakenly assumes that they could have succeeded if only they had more, when there is no basis for such a conclusion. Given Soviet domination in the air, the Afghan guerrillas benefited from 1986 by receiving American shoulder-fired ground-to-air Stinger missiles and their British counterpart, the Blowpipe. These missiles brought down Soviet helicopter gunships and aircraft, forcing them to fly higher. This cut the effectiveness of their ground support and bombing and left garrisons beleaguered. Soviet morale collapsed as isolated garrisons were attacked and destroyed with few survivors. In 1989, the Soviets withdrew, although the limitations of Soviet air power were only part of the equation. Imperial overstretch was a key factor, as was the willingness of the Gorbachev government to change policy. However, the main issue was the failure to develop a homegrown government that the Afghans would support.

The Soviet presence in Afghanistan, combined with Soviet arms supplies to India, led the United States to provide assistance to neighboring Pakistan. Its elderly air force was modernized with the supply of forty F-16s, although the United States refused to supply AWACS aircraft. Moreover, Pakistan became dependent on access to American spares and maintenance.[7]

The Americans also provided assistance to allies facing guerrilla opposition. In El Salvador, the Reagan administration sent helicopter gunships as part of the aid to the right-wing junta resisting the Farabundo Marti National Liberation Front (FMLN). The war revealed some of the weaknesses of counterinsurgency strategies, including the problems of using air attacks to ensure civil peace, problems also matched by other forms of military activity. The identification of targets was far from easy.

Air power and airborne troops were also significant in conflicts within states. These could involve foreign intervention, as in 1978 in Congo, when Belgian and French paratroopers supported by American and French air transport helped suppress a Cuban-backed invasion of the province of Shaba. In 1988, the Indian air force delivered paratroopers to quell a coup in the Maldives. However, these conflicts did not need to involve foreign troops. Thus, in Northern Ireland, the British army made extensive use of helicopters in order to support isolated garrisons and to overcome the problems of the ambushing and booby-trapping of units on the ground by the terrorists of the Provisional IRA. In Afghanistan, in 1978–79, prior to the Soviet invasion, the communist government faced rebellions from late 1978, including a serious rising in the city of Herat in May 1979. These rebellions were met with the colonial-era remedy of "pacification" by bombing.

In Southern Rhodesia (now Zimbabwe), the white-minority government used air power as an increasingly important aspect of its counterinsurgency struggle. The Rhodesian air force provided bombardment as well as transport to support attacks, from 1977, on insurgent bases in nearby Mozambique and Zambia, notably the attack on the base at Chimoio in Mozambique. For this attack, the Rhodesians used forty-two helicopters and about thirty-five ex-RAF Hunter aircraft, although the arms embargo Rhodesia experienced ensured that these aircraft could not be replaced or modernized. These attacks inflicted heavy casualties on the insurgents. The South African Defense Force was to launch comparable attacks on insurgent bases in the 1980s.

The South Africans had loaned helicopters to the Rhodesians, as well as providing some direct helicopter support for Rhodesian attacks on insurgent bases in 1979. Helicopters were also acquired from Israel. The availability of shoulder-mounted SAM defenses posed a problem for such attacks. Not only insurgent bases were attacked. In 1979, Rhodesian raids destroyed ten bridges in Zambia in order to maintain Zambia's dependence on Rhodesian rail links and thus lessen the possibility of hostile acts. Alongside air and helicopter attacks, paradrops from Dakotas were common as a means of taking the fight directly to the insurgents.[8]

NAVAL AIR POWER

Naval air power remained dominated by the United States. The Soviet Union continued to rely on land-based long-range bombers and reconnaissance aircraft. One large (sixty-five thousand ton) fleet carrier, laid down in 1983 as the *Leonid Brezhnev*, did not enter service until 1990 when, as communism ebbed, the ship, instead of being named after a communist leader, was called the *Admiral Kuznetsov*. The major American defense buildup under the Reagan administration included a continued emphasis on a blue-water navy and its strike capacity. In 1982, in the Northern Wedding naval exercise, American carrier battle groups approached close enough to the Kola Peninsula to be able to launch aircraft with a full bomb load able to attack the Severomorsk naval base and then return. During the period, American naval reinforcement of NATO became a cornerstone of Northern defense. The commander Carrier Striking Force was to have deployed across the Atlantic with an American marine corps, in the teeth of Soviet opposition. In 1991, at the end of the Soviet Union, it had five carriers compared to thirteen American ones, the numbers excluding helicopter carriers. Most powers, however, lacked a carrier capacity and used land-based weapons, both missiles and guns, in attempts to affect the situation at sea. For example, in the Iran-Iraq war of 1980–88, both sides used Silkworms, the Chinese-manufactured copy of the Soviet Styx missiles, more properly known as the HY-2 Hai Ying (Sea Eagle).

In Britain, in 1978, *Eagle* was broken up, while the last large fixed-wing aircraft strike carrier, *Ark Royal*, was decommissioned, and in 1981, *Bulwark*, the veteran "Commando Carrier," was laid up. That year, the defense review, *The Way Forward*, implied that the navy was not concentrating on what should be its core mission, which was identified as antisubmarine warfare in the NATO area, and, instead, that there was an anachronistic emphasis on the surface fleet. Instead, unexpectedly, need was found when, on April 2, 1982, Argentina successfully invaded the Falkland Islands, a British Overseas Territory in the South Atlantic. As a result of the shift from large fleet carriers, the expeditionary force the British then sent lacked a large carrier, and therefore, crucially, airborne early warning of attacks. Configured for operations in the Eastern Atlantic, the British certainly suffered from the lack of an AWACS capability. However, the expedition had two smaller carriers, *Hermes* and *Invincible*. These were equipped with Sea Harrier fighter-bomber V/STOL aircraft, a process aided by the fitting of a "ski jump" ramp to assist take off, the first of which was tested in 1976. This ramp permitted fuel savings and increased payloads. The Sea Harrier became operational on carriers in 1980.

Conversely, the Argentinian carrier *25 de Mayo* had not been refitted to operate the Super Etendard aircraft Argentina had just bought from France. Moreover, the sinking by a British submarine of the heavy cruiser *General Belgrano* led the Argentinians to withdraw their carrier to base. Nevertheless, in the face of Royal Naval weakness, Argentinian air power was almost decisive, with a small number of aircraft coming close to inflicting crippling losses. Bombs and French-supplied Exocet missiles led to the loss of six British ships. Another eleven were damaged, while thirteen bombs hit ships but failed to explode, as they were released too close. Had these bombs exploded, it would have been impossible to continue the operation. British losses showed that ship-borne antiaircraft missile systems, in this case Sea Darts and Sea Wolfs, were not necessarily a match for determined low-level aircraft attack, and revealed a lack of adequate preparedness on the part of the navy, which had no effective airborne early warning and had to rely on missile systems not hitherto tested in war. However, the Argentinians did not sink the two carriers that were positioned for their protection far to the east and provided vital air support (but not superiority) for both sea and land operations.

Designed for antisubmarine warfare in the North Atlantic, the car-riers' Sea King helicopters and twenty Sea Harriers, as well as reinforc-ing RAF Harriers, nevertheless did well, both in combat air patrols and in close air support roles. The American supply of 12.5 million gallons of highly refined aviation fuel, as well as Sidewinder missiles, was signif-icant, as was the provision of real-time Internet-style satellite-based communications. The Sidewinders offered an important edge in aerial conflict. With a sensitive laser fuse, they were far less susceptible to early detonations when close to the ground. Whereas Argentinian mis-siles required radar lock-on through the time of flight, the Sidewinder 9L was a launch-and-leave missile with an excellent detector that could quickly acquire the target and be used even at fleeting targets flying away over land.

Aerial refueling permitted an eight-thousand-mile round-trip British bomber attack on the runway at Port Stanley on the Falklands on May 1. This raid, which demonstrated the capability of air power to strike over global distances, was both an important symbolic act, albeit one that was expensive, and an operation that cratered the runway and destroyed infrastructure. The raid led Argentina to deploy two squad-rons for the defense of Buenos Aires and demonstrated the vulnerabil-ity of Port Stanley as a forward base. As a result, the Argentinian air force was dissuaded from basing its fighter-bombers at Port Stanley and attacking the British carriers. Instead the aircraft had to operate from mainland bases, which put them at the limit of their operational range over the Falklands. Subsequent air attacks on Port Stanley by Harrier and Vulcan aircraft were met with heavy ground fire by radar-con-trolled cannon and missiles, but the success of this fire was limited. Overall, ground- and sea-based antiaircraft systems were not decisive in preventing air attacks, although they had an adverse effect on tactics, which reduced the effectiveness of those air attacks.

Landing on the Falklands on May 21, the British, despite lacking control of the air, outfought the Argentinians, who surrendered on June 14. The campaign on land was affected by a shortage of ammunition for the British field artillery due to a lack of helicopters available to ferry it forward. The earlier loss to Exocet attack of the *Atlantic Conveyor*, a British merchantman carrying eight helicopters, had a major impact on the pace of the campaign, as there were no usable roads.

This conflict represented an interesting evolutionary point in the development of air power, notably with regard to missile systems. The war saw the commitment and use of essentially post–Second World War technology, alongside the employment of modern and emerging technology by both of the combatants. It was also the last conflict for which the reporting of the media could be, and was, controlled in the conflict zone. The range of aerial warfare employed included long-range bombing, using both missiles and old-style "iron bombs"; air attacks on shipping, using both; air-to-air dogfights; aerial reconnaissance; close air support of ground forces; extensive sophisticated antiaircraft gun and missile systems; the massive employment of transport aircraft to support the landing force from the forward operating air base on Ascension Island, which, as a result, on June 1, was the busiest airfield in the world; and the first extensive tactical use of satellite communications. Air-power operations from the sea, using carriers, were opposed by aircraft operating from land bases, and both sides utilized in-flight refueling. There was also the employment of civilian aircraft in a military role. Throughout the conflict, the new aircraft operated alongside the older equipment.

The possession of Ascension Island, with its large runway, communication facilities, and limited harbor facilities, at roughly the halfway point between Britain and the Falklands, was an essential element in the effective mounting and support of the amphibious task force. Aside from its crucial role in transport and as a refueling base, Ascension also served as a base for antisubmarine air-patrol cover for the ships, as well as for long-range bombing and air-to-air refueling.

The success of the Harrier helped settle the debate in favor of V/STOL aircraft. They had been criticized for being short range and for having a limited weapons load, modest endurance, a lack of real combat capability, and the need for a forward deployment that created onerous defense responsibilities. However, the Falklands War showed that, with the right pilots and weapons, the Harrier was highly effective in combat. As such, it provided a key support for air and sea operations while offering a flexibility and mobility in operating off rough-field air strips that other ground-support aircraft lacked. The Harrier was to encapsulate integrated air operations and to be significant, not only in the aerial repertoire of the last stage of the Cold War, but also in the subsequent expeditionary warfare and operations of the 1990s and 2000s, including British operations in Iraq (1991, 2003), Sierra Leone (2000), Bosnia, Kosovo, Belize, and Afghanistan. The American role was important in the development of the Harrier, notably in procurement for the marines, in weaponry, and in helping to improve specifications.[9]

The Falklands War encouraged a reexamination, in Britain and elsewhere, of the case for naval air power. *Invincible* had been about to be sold to Australia in early 1982 but was retained. *Invincible* was to have replaced *Melbourne* (formerly the British *Majestic*), which had entered Australian service in 1955. When the latter was decommissioned in 1983, this was the end of fixed-wing aviation in the Australian navy. *Hermes* was sold to India in 1986 and commissioned in the navy as the *Viraat* the following year, but *Ark Royal*, another V/STOL carrier given a famous carrier name, entered British service in 1986. However, the most important and costly British naval commitment was to the sixteen-thousand-ton *Vanguard* class submarines armed with Trident, the replacement to Polaris. Four were laid down in 1986–93. After the war, Phantoms were deployed alongside Harriers to deter Argentinian ambitions, with both operating off AM-2 runway matting at Stanley. The war led Britain to develop Mount Pleasant Air Base in the Falklands in order to provide a facility for permanent rapid air deployment against the possibility of future Argentinian attack.

PROCUREMENT

Many of the characteristics of air power, notably tasking and related doctrine, planning, procurement, and training, continued to reflect the distinctive strategic cultures of individual states. A good example was that of Western European states that were not members of NATO or its

THE LATER COLD WAR

military structure, notably Sweden, Switzerland, and France. Neutral in the Cold War, Sweden, nevertheless, aimed to be able to defend itself against the Soviet Union. This led it to have the fifth-largest air force in the world in 1991—425 indigenous combat aircraft—as well as to operational planning for defense, including a forward-oriented defense-in-depth, and to a reliance on producing its own aircraft, such as the J-35 Draken, an interceptor; the Saab 105, a ground-attack aircraft; and the JA-37 Viggen, a multirole fighter, which appeared in 1955, 1963, and 1967, respectively, and was lately armed with British radar-controlled Skyflash missiles. The Draken was also flown by Austria and Finland, both neutral, as well as by Denmark, a neighbor.

Such a reliance was also seen elsewhere. In Taiwan, AIDC, a local manufacturer, began by building American F-5s under license, but continued in 1975 by beginning work on the AT-3, a trainer and ground-attack aircraft first flown in 1980. Sixty were built for the Taiwanese air force, followed by AIDC's Ching Kuo, a multirole fighter, first flown in 1989, that was developed from 1982 after the United States refused to sell fighters to Iran: Taiwan was concerned about the consequences of American rapprochement with China. Other allies felt able to rely on American planes. In 1979, an American C-5A Galaxy delivered the first batch of five F-5s to Singapore, taking the air force of the latter into the modern age. The F-15, an air-superiority fighter, was operated by Israel, Japan, and Saudi Arabia. Aside from such provision of aircraft, the process of assembly under license provided a way to gain employment and to lessen costs. Chile did so with the A/T-36, which was the Spanish C-101, a trainer and ground-attack aircraft first flown in 1977. In contrast, Honduras and Jordan, which lacked the capacity to assemble aircraft, bought them from Spain.

CONCLUSIONS

The varied use of air power was again to the fore. As in earlier periods, it is too easy to forget the tactical, operational, and strategic potential of airlift, as at once a deterrent and a facilitator of power. In particular, Soviet airlift capacity increased greatly in the 1970s and 1980s with the development of long-range heavy-lift transport aircraft. First flown in 1982, the Antonov An-124 Condor had a wingspan of 73.7 m (240 feet,

5 inches), was the world's largest aircraft, could carry a cargo of 150,000 kg (330,700 lbs), and could hold 451 passengers. It held world records for payload, altitude, and distance, and its rugged design made it possible to use a wide range of airfields. Its payload exceeded that of American rivals, notably the C-5 Galaxy, first flown in 1968, which could carry 118,387 kg, and the KC-10 Extender, which began operating in 1981 and could carry 110,945 kg. The Soviet transport fleet had been supplemented in 1971 when the Il-74 Candid was first flown. It had a payload of 52,000 kg and could carry 140 troops.

The number of Soviet transport planes rose to six hundred by 1984. This capability offered the Soviets an ability to "leapfrog" American containment plans, and at a considerable scale. Indeed, the Caribbean island of Grenada acquired strategic significance as a result of the development of the airport at Point Salines by the Cubans as an airlift base, with a nine-thousand-foot runway, able to support their interests in Africa. Concern about this capability helped to explain the American invasion of Grenada in 1983. In turn, the Americans also developed airlift, although handicapped by serious bureaucratic infighting within the USAF and between it and the army.[10] As another instance of intervention, India used transports escorted by fighters to drop humanitarian supplies in northern Sri Lanka before intervening in 1987, and also deployed Hind attack helicopters to support the operations there of the Indian Peace-Keeping Force (IPKF) from 1987 to 1990. Throughout the period, much political capital was gained by the use of airlift in disaster relief.

For the United States, the Soviet Union, and other powers keen to project their power, air bases remained of essential and strategic importance as they permitted such projection. They were also important in providing a network for containment strategies. Thus, in response to an increase in the number of Soviet bombers entering Icelandic air space in the early 1980s, en route into the North Atlantic, the Americans increased the number of fighter jets at Keflavik from twelve to eighteen.

Very differently, the American development of cruise missile technology both offered a radical new capability and provided a new means for existing weaponry. The B-52s were given a new lease on life by being equipped with ALCMs, a long-range subsonic nuclear or conventional missile with high accuracy, and a low radar cross-section.

More profoundly, aircraft continued to grasp the imagination and to suggest a particular potency. In part, this was because missiles were not associated with individual bravery, and thus masculinity. Moreover, the limitations of air power were not to the fore among most public commentators or, certainly, as far as popular culture was concerned. Instead, alongside ethical doubts about strategic bombing, a heroic idea of aerial conflict, one focused on fighters and aerial interception, continued to prevail. This was the case both for the leading military powers, as with the popular American film *Top Gun* (1986), and more generally. This focus was an important aspect of air-power culture both within the military and the public. The 1980s saw a shift in USAF circles from a bombing high command to a fighter high command. Since then, in most, if not all, air force establishments, the fighter pilot is the alpha male, and his fighter aircraft is the totem of the tribe. Most air force commanders have a background as a fighter pilot. This background no more encouraged caution than the former mastery of the "bomber barons."

10

AIR POWER AND THE REVOLUTION IN MILITARY AFFAIRS, 1990–2003

In 1997, five hundred American paratroopers embarked in North Carolina, flew 6,700 miles, and jumped into Kazakhstan and Uzbekistan in Central Asia. This was a dramatic display of new global aerial capability in the shape of the range made possible by aerial refueling and the possible consequences at this range. A sense of infinite potential in the new American-dominated world appeared practical as well as relevant. Moreover, theories of air power played a crucial role in the supposed Revolution in Military Affairs and related Transformation of the 1990s and early 2000s, and in the surrounding discussions. In part, these theories and discussions drew on the Western use of air power in this period, notably against Iraq in 1991 and, to a lesser extent, 2003, and in Afghanistan in 2001. These episodes opened up the question about how far the doctrine and practice of air power really matched, or the extent to which there was a contrast. This issue was highlighted by consideration of the limitations of air power, notably, but not only, in the Kosovo crisis in 1999. Meanwhile, a very different discussion about the nature and future of air power arose with reference to the extensive use of unmanned cruise missiles and UAVs, and resulting questions about the continued relevance of manned air power.

IRAQ, 1991

A sense of the potential of the new was captured by the Gulf War of 1991, a war that was a response to Iraq's conquest of Kuwait in 1990. America led an international coalition to oblige Iraq to withdraw from Kuwait, an obligation that meant the prospect and eventual use of force. Due to unpracticed command and control (a result of misguided headquarters reductions during the post-Vietnam drawdown), as well as a lack of enabler units, it took six months to build up a capacity to attack with sufficient assurance to guarantee success. This was a period fraught with risk had Saddam Hussein attacked the buildup in Saudi Arabia. However, although commanded by the US Centcom, the significant contribution by NATO states meant that command systems and procedures were rapidly harmonized. Deployment to Saudi Arabia and the Gulf provided the first major instance of the process by which states that had been used to operating many of their aircraft from established home bases instead had to contribute to a series of expeditionary campaigns, and to adapt their aircraft and institutions accordingly, especially to the heat and sand of the desert. There were also important implications for personnel due to operating in the heat and under a nuclear, biological, or chemical threat.

In the initial stages of the Gulf War, F117A stealth aircraft with precision-guided bombs and cruise missiles were employed, notably by the United States, to open the door. The global capability of long-range air power was dramatically demonstrated with the opening attacks on Iraq coming from B-52 aircraft armed with conventional ALCMs flying directly to Iraq from Barksdale Air Force Base in Louisiana. Although aircraft from twelve countries were involved in the major air offensive that began on January 17, 1991, with 1,300 combat sorties that night, the Americans were central to the offensive, which involved forty thousand attack sorties and lasted for thirty-eight days. The possibility of long-range air power was dramatically demonstrated with attacks on Iraq from Barksdale Air Force Base in Louisiana. The air offensive, though, was never designed to persuade Saddam Hussein to evacuate Kuwait, which could have proved a strategic triumph for air power. Nevertheless, this offensive succeeded militarily from the outset in inflicting serious damage by overcoming the sophisticated Iraqi antiaircraft system, a system put in place in part due to the conflict with Iran.

His expenditure based on oil revenues, Saddam had used French and Soviet technology to produce an integrated system in which computers linked radars and missiles. This system was advanced for the day and was an enormous improvement on that used in North Vietnam in the 1960s and early 1970s. The destruction of this system, with only one aircraft lost (to an Iraqi MIG-29), on the first night of the air offensive was a triumph not only for weaponry, but also for planning, which made full use of the opportunities presented by the Allied weapons while outthinking the Iraqis. For example, borrowing an Israeli method successfully employed against the Syrians in 1982, the Americans used decoys to get the Iraqis to bring their radars to full power, which exposed them to attack by high-speed antiradiation missiles.

The use of stealth and precision in 1991 ensured that it was practicable to employ a direct air assault aimed at overcoming the entire Iraqi air system, rather than an incremental rollback campaign. Moreover, the situation on the ground was totally transformed. As a consequence of the air assault, Iraqi forces were to be short of supplies, their command-and-control system was heavily disrupted, and their morale was low. In addition, the battlefield was isolated, with all bridges across the Tigris and Euphrates Rivers destroyed.[1] In part, this air campaign drew on the ideas of Colonel John A. Warden III, who suggested a "five-ring model" of the modern state, each ring linked to a level of activity and a category of target. By attacking the strategic center, it was argued, the regime could be defeated. The command-and control-system, at once political and military, was regarded as crucial. Warden saw this approach as leading to the paralysis of the Iraqi military system, what, indeed, was later to be termed "strategic paralysis."[2] However, as mounted, the bombing campaign included a focus on all rings apart from the population, including the Iraqi armed forces as a whole. The Americans were confident that one of the rings would decisively collapse. Virtually all communications were rendered unusable, although it is not clear that "strategic paralysis" was imposed on the Iraqi regime. Saddam Hussein was forced to carry out his council meetings in a Winnebago caravan. As a targeting method, the systems approach proved adequate, but when raised to the level of strategic success, it was flawed, as virtually no amount of damage would persuade Saddam to evacuate Kuwait. Instead of treating the nature of war, as Clausewitz had, as the complex interaction of policy, emotion, and chance, systems warfare focused on pieces of a design that supposedly, if neutralized, would bring down the whole. Certainly, the political consequences were limited. The Iraqi government did not fall, and, as anticipated, it proved necessary for the coalition to launch a ground offensive.

Launched on February 24, 1991, the ground offensive benefited greatly from air support. Moreover, this was a full-spectrum support, including satellite surveillance, cruise missiles (288 fired), and guided bombs, as well as Patriot antimissile missiles used against Iraqi attacks.[3] American Pioneer drones acted as battlefield intelligence-gathering platforms. The American navy deployed four carriers in the Gulf, but their sortie numbers were smaller than those of the air force. In addition, the debilitating tensions seen in the Vietnam War were present anew. The navy resented the extent to which the air force's Air Operations Center rejected their target nominations and subverted the targeting process to get its ends.[4] However, compared to earlier conflicts, notably the Vietnam War, there was, as a result of the Goldwater-Nichols Act, unified control over air operations, with a single air commander: the Joint Force Air Component commander, responsible only to the Joint Force commander.

Large-scale air attacks ensured that Iraqi ground defenses had been left disorganized, isolated, and ineffective before the coalition ground attack began. The psychological impact, heightened by the bomb, leaflet, bomb approach, was considerable, as seen in the numbers who surrendered (87,000) and deserted (150,000), as opposed to the fewer than 10,000 who were killed. The possibility of mounting a cohesive and coordinated defense had been destroyed. This was more significant than the extensive destruction of equipment that had been achieved, highly important as that was.[5] Indeed, as tactical and, still more, operational effectiveness depends on such coordination, air power proved particularly effective. The Iraqi forces lost the ability to move, and thus to respond and to reinforce. The destruction of Iraqi communication systems was linked to the total failure of the command system. Indicating the unique ability of air power to provide attack in depth, these results were obtained not only at the expense of the front line of Iraqi formations, but also throughout the theater. As a result, there were no units in the rear that could be readily brought forward to replace or reinforce those at the front. Seventeen bridges across the rivers Tigris and Euphrates were destroyed.

Aside from the value of the prior air attack, air support proved highly important once the ground attack had been launched. Aircraft and helicopters were able to inflict considerable damage on Iraqi tanks: A-10s with armor-piercing cannon and Maverick missiles, and AH-64 Apaches with Hellfire missiles, as well as F-111s operating as deep-interdiction aircraft carrying out what became known as "tank plinking," the laser-guided attack on individual tanks, one by one. The impact induced a terror that led Iraqi gun crews to flee their guns when attacked from the air. The A-10 is armed with the GAU-8/A Avenger rotary cannon, which fires depleted uranium rounds at 3,900 rpm. Bombing by B-52s, a plan designed for strategic bombing but here used against tactical targets, had the same psychological effect. Iraqis described the air bombardment as like having to deal with three earthquakes a day. Bombing was followed by leafleting warning of the need to run away and then by more bombing. The cumulative effect of air power was helping to achieve strategic effect on the battlefield, which was different from the argument that it could secure strategic decision away from the battlefield by separate operations.

Despite the rapid victory, the American doctrine of AirLand Battle proved, like most military concepts, more difficult to execute, in planning and training, than to advance in theory. This gap in part arose from the problems of synchronizing air and land forces under fast-moving combat conditions, problems that led to deaths from "friendly fire," including 33 of the 143 American battle fatalities. In the Second World War, the bombing of friendly troops, as well as antiaircraft fire directed at friendly aircraft, was not uncommon, but it became an issue in the Gulf War because of public concern, which was made worse by the military's willingness to make bold claims about the precision of its technology. There was a widespread, but flawed, belief that error, both human and technical, had been eliminated, except where someone acted incompetently. In part, the revulsion toward war and violence that affected much of Western opinion from the 1960s onward was at stake. There was a willingness to support what were perceived as just wars, but even in that case, "blue on blue" casualties seemed pointless, possibly precisely because these were wars of choice rather than of necessity.

Important parts of the Allied military did not employ the advanced weaponry that was becoming available. For example, the Americans used 9,300 precision-guided munitions, which indeed did much of the damage, but most of their aircraft were not equipped, nor their pilots trained, for the use of these munitions. Instead, they employed unguided munitions, which made up over 90 percent of the aerial munitions employed, and over a fifth of these "dumb" munitions were dropped by B-52s. This use of unguided munitions was in spite of the precedent set by the extensive and effective use of the more expensive precision-guided munitions in the Linebacker campaigns in Vietnam in 1972. At the same time, in part this was a question of using the appropriate weapon against the right target, with cost playing a major role. The situation was to be different against Iraq in 2003, by which time modern and modernized aircraft were dominant. Similarly, in 1991, although the Americans had developed stealth aircraft, most of their planes lacked this expensive capability. Moreover, some high-tech weaponry, such as the British JP233 runway-cratering bombs and the American Patriot missile, did less well than was claimed at the time. However, helped by the nature of the target and terrain, target acquisition and accuracy were effective, the pace of the air attack was maintained, and this attack was successfully employed to affect operations on the ground.[6] Air power was given a definite boost.

Allied air forces, including those of Egypt and Saudi Arabia, played a role in the war, but it was very much secondary to the United States, which lost twenty-five of the thirty-one Allied aircraft shot down. Moreover, some air forces, such as that of France, proved ill prepared in 1991, although they contributed to the total of 2,700 aircraft deployed by the Allies. The deficiencies revealed in 1991 encouraged a degree of transformation, as in the case of France. In this process, the shrinking defense budgets that followed the end of the Cold War as a "peace dividend," and which also reflected economic problems in the early 1990s, posed problems, lessening new procurement, yet also encouraging the retirement of old aircraft and a reduction of personnel.[7] The number of bases was cut, and foreign agreements were renegotiated accordingly. Thus, the American government decided to remove its eighteen F-15s from Iceland, as it was no longer concerned about Soviet flights. In the face of Icelandic opposition, it was agreed, in 1996, that a minimum of four be retained. A changing attitude to the strategic significance of particular locations was seen with the removal, after the September 11, 2001, attacks, of Iceland, Greenland, and the Azores from the list of areas seen as vital from the perspective of American continental defense. In 2004, the American navy's P-3 Orion patrol reconnaissance planes were withdrawn from Iceland.[8]

Such transformation was also seen with air forces that had not been involved in the Gulf War, such as those of Denmark and Sweden. These air forces followed closely the course of the war and responded accordingly. Both the Danes and the Swedes procured precision strike capabilities, enabling Danish planes to take part in the 1999 Kosovo campaign. The Dutch, who did not provide aircraft for the attack on Iraq, although they did help in ancillary roles, finally retired their dated NF-5 in 1991, and cut the number of their F-16s, while upgrading the latter so as to have a force of 108 modernized F-16s by 2004, supported by two KDC-10 tanker aircraft.

American influence meanwhile spread greatly with the end of the Cold War as ex-communist states applied to join NATO and acquired American planes. Interoperability was a key element. For example, from 2006 the most modern version of F-16s were delivered to Poland. With the fall of East Germany, the Luftwaffe acquired a fleet of MIG-29s. Now surplus Soviet-era planes were sold by Russia, but they proved unattractive to most purchasers, in part because there was scant confidence in spares and maintenance for them, but also because Russia did not significantly invest in upgrading capability. At the same time, the Russian Sukhoi aircraft were impressive and had good avionics. Thus, the radar of the Su-30 enabled it to track several other aircraft at once, as did that of the Tornado F-3.

Alongside expenditure, public and political reluctance to spend money had a major impact on air forces, as in 2010 when Switzerland postponed the decision to replace its aging F-5 Tigers. More seriously, in South Africa, a cut in defense spending of over 50 percent in real terms between 1990 and 1999, alongside serious disruption during the transformation accompanying and following the end of the apartheid regime, seriously hit training, with a lack of funds causing a shortage of fuel that slashed flying hours. Only nine C-130s were operational, which affected air mobility. In 1999 the government decided to buy nine light fighters to replace the Cheetahs, with an option on nineteen more, which contrasted with the original tender for thirty-six.[9] The 1990s also saw savage cuts in Russian military expenditure.

1992–2000

The 1991 Gulf War was followed by a reliance in the United States on air power, with a powerful direction that had consequences for, and, in turn, drew on, tasking, doctrine, and procurement. The success of precision weapons in the Gulf War encouraged their wholesale adoption, along with the procurement and improvement of planes and the training of pilots accordingly, as well as ensuring increased demand for in-time information. The tactical impact of such weaponry encouraged a strong sense of operational possibility, with the latter seen as having strategic effect. Bombing now appeared to its protagonists to guarantee victory without the risks and devastation of nuclear warfare. The precision versus area bombing question of the Second World War appeared to be settled in favor of a true prospect of the former.

Moreover, delivering apparently assured results with fewer planes, and thus for less cost, although often leading to hollow forces in reality, seemingly offered military possibilities that could address political needs. This prospect drew on the attitudes underlying "air policing" of the 1920s but extrapolated it onto a global scale that met hopes of a "new world order," as declared by President George H. W. Bush in 1991 with reference to driving the Iraqi invaders out of Kuwait. The Americans and British, the traditional states focused on long-range air power, felt themselves particularly responsible for this order. In a re-conceptualization of deterrence, there was a forward policy of intimidation and coercion, one in which the threat of air assault was regarded as crucial. This reliance was related to a "mystique" of air power in the United States, of aerial combat and space as new frontiers for Americans to conquer.[10] Alongside the appeal of air power as a military means came a political convenience and reliance in support of its employment, indeed frequent employment,[11] not least because the contentiousness and vulnerability of "boots on the ground" were avoided. Air power appeared to offer an easy means to win.

Thus, after Saddam Hussein in 1991 had successfully used helicopter-borne assault forces to suppress Shiite opposition in southern Iraq, there was the long-term use of Allied air power to prevent Iraq from rebuilding its military. However, the over three hundred thousand sorties flown proved an expensive commitment that had only partial success. Policing the "no-fly zones" declared over much of Iraq, a policing led by the United States and Britain in which Saudi Arabia and Turkey played a role, was easier than influencing developments on the ground. Furthermore, launched in response to the Iraqi refusal to allow in UN inspectors to assess their weapons program, the Anglo-American Desert Fox bombing campaign in December 1998, in which smart bombs accompanied 415 cruise missiles, was not regarded as a success in terms of ensuring the desired outcome. Indeed, it provoked Iraqi intransigence, with Saddam announcing that coalition aircraft would be attacked in the no-fly zones. The same was true of the American air assault in August 1998 against Osama bin Laden's terrorist bases in Afghanistan. The Sudanese chemical weapons plant attacked by cruise missiles later that year was in fact producing antimalarial drugs, an error that revealed the issues posed by unreliable intelligence, an age-old problem. More positively, Allied air power helped stop Saddam from attacking the Kurds and also gave notice that Iraq could not resist Allied air power, a lesson well learned by 2003.

In 2001–3, drones came to play a role in policing the no-fly zones over Iraq, but the Iraqi air force combined with ground-based defense units began to attack them, destroying a drone. This led to the arming of some drones with air-to-air Stinger missiles. This process culminated, just before the 2003 war started, with Stinger missiles being fired at two Iraqi MIGs in the first drone air-to-air battle.

Meanwhile, the Americans had encountered notable difficulties as well as successes with air power. On October 3, 1993, the shooting down of two American helicopters in a raid on a warlord in Mogadishu, Somalia, where United Nations forces had been deployed in what was a "failed state," ensured that, in a battle played out in the full glare of a media campaign, the Americans lost the initiative. In the subsequent fighting, helicopters provided vital cover as well as dropping water for troops trapped on the ground, but they could not evacuate the troops, which had to be done by ground forces the following day. Although a relatively minor clash, and one that should have been factored in, the operation was perceived as a failure by the relatively risk-averse Clinton administration, which decided to withdraw all American forces from Somalia. In a very different context, and benefiting from much better intelligence, the Israelis assassinated hostile Palestinians from the air, as in 2000.

When Yugoslavia collapsed as a state after the Cold War, all branches of the military were purged of officers who were not loyal to the essentially Serbian attempt to keep the country united. In practice this meant that many, but not all, non-Serbs were retired or dismissed. The weaponized aircraft stationed outside Serbia were seized, leaving behind only a handful of trainers, transports, biplanes, and helicopters. Yugoslavia had an aircraft manufacturer at Mostar in the former republic of Bosnia, but the factory was dismantled in 1992 and much of the tooling removed to the Utva works in Pančevo in Serbia. The most modern plane, the G-4, mostly ended up in the Federal Yugoslav (i.e., Serbian) air force, where it was upgraded to carry Maverick missiles and to act more effectively as a ground-attack aircraft. Its predecessor, the G-2, also a ground-attack aircraft, was used by both Croats and Serbs.

Conflict between Croatia and Serbia was followed by a bitter civil war within Bosnia. This civil war led to attempts at international peacemaking, including, in Operation Deny Flight, the UN creation of a no-fly zone over Bosnia in 1992. However, the Bosnian Serbs, the major cause of destabilizing aggression, were unwilling to respond to the peacemaking requirements of the United Nations Protection Force. The Serbs violated the no-fly zone and bombed villages lived in by Bosnian Croats and Muslims, and they used helicopter assault to capture villages that were then "ethnically cleansed."

In response, in 1994, NATO launched its first combat action, one that was to be heavily dependent on the United States, although with other NATO powers involved, including Britain, the Netherlands, and Turkey. Italian air bases on the other side of the Adriatic Sea, from Ariano to Gioia del Colle, were crucial. In this case, as more generally, NATO forces were well prepared and moved smoothly into a combined campaign. Coalition activities encouraged a greater degree of interoperability between aircraft and also between air forces, as well as the standardization of operating procedures, although there were also serious problems in agreeing over targeting criteria, notably in attacks that sought to protect NATO nationals on the ground in Bosnia and that might endanger civilians. The first air strike was on the airfield of Udbina, which served Serb forces in both Croatia and Bosnia. Udbina was a major communications hub in the service of the Croatian Serbs. The airfield was disabled on November 21, 1994.[12] However, the initial air strikes on Bosnian Serb forces proved limited in number, affected by extremely restrictive rules of engagement, and largely ineffective. The UN controlled air operations, and, although Bosnian Serb ground raids were seen on a daily basis, NATO aircraft were not allowed to intervene, only report. The Serb use of ground-to-air missiles obliged NATO aircraft to fly high or to avoid known SAM sites, which affected targeting.

Moreover, the Serbs were able to continue to use their air power and move their forces around. Thus, there was an "overlapping" of air power, one that may become more significant in the future as miniaturized, inexpensive drones give weaker forces an ability to use air power irrespective of the greater strength of a major state.

In 1995, in contrast, there was a greater commitment of air power. This reflected the inability of the United Nations Peacekeeping Force to keep the peace and, specifically, prevent Serb attacks on the UN safe areas. The refusal of the Bosnian Serbs to agree to stop bombarding the Bosnian capital, Sarajevo, led to NATO air strikes against a Bosnian Serbian ammunition dump, but these limited strikes did not prevent an escalation of the crisis. Moreover, UN peacekeepers were held hostage by the Bosnian Serbs as "human shields" in order to deter further attack. In July 1995, after that crisis was resolved, the UN safe area of Srebrenica was overrun, and over seven thousand Bosnian Muslim men were slaughtered. NATO flights failed to stop the fall of Srebrenica, nor indeed to affect Serb conduct.

NATO anger, combined with the danger of more massacres, led to the American decision to launch an air campaign if the remaining safe areas were attacked. A deadly mortar attack by Bosnian Serbs on Sarajevo's market triggered Operation Deliberate Force. This was intended not only to deter further attacks on the safe areas, but also to destroy Bosnian Serb military offensive capability, and to ensure that the situation on the ground helped the Croats and Muslims as negotiations neared. These varied goals meant air operations near the safe areas, as well as more distant attacks on the Bosnian Serb Army (BSA). The prelude was the destruction of the BSA air-defense system. Soon after, the bombing switched to what was intended as a calibrated means to bring the Bosnian Serbs to the negotiating table. In hitting the communications of the BSA, the NATO air attack lessened their mobility and their command-and-control capability. Moreover, the BSA were denied aerial support. American Reaper drones monitored troops and helped seek targets. However, a lack of political support for wide-ranging bombing meant that NATO ran out of agreed targets to hit, although this was not known by the Serbs.

In the event, the Bosnian Serbs agreed to stop offensive operations around Sarajevo in return for an end to the bombing. Eventually the Bosnian Serbs accepted a settlement in November 1995, the Dayton Accords. NATO air attack had played a role, as had diplomatic pressure, but American-supported ground military action by the Croats and Bosnian Muslims was possibly more significant. They acted as de facto ground forces to NATO's campaign, while, conversely, NATO supplied air power to indigenous ground forces. The Croatian army's early August 1995 Operacija Oluja (Operation Thunder), in which it destroyed the Serb insurgency in Croatia, was along similar lines: NATO took out Serb C-2 capabilities and air defenses, and the Croats overran Serb ground defenses. The Croats had also acquired some older fighter aircraft by then, in part from Germany and the United States. The threat of American ground invasion was also a factor.

In turn, in Kosovo, an autonomous region within Serbia, the Serbs used tactics of "ethnic cleansing" (i.e., brutally driving people out) against the majority ethnic Albanian population, most of whom were Muslims. In response, NATO turned to air power as the weapon of first resort. On March 24, 1999, a seventy-eight-day bombing and cruise missile assault, Operation Allied Force, was launched. Cruise missiles were fired from naval vessels and from B-52 bombers. The operation helped lead to a Serb acceptance of terms on June 6, followed by Serb withdrawal and the acceptance of a cease-fire.

Both at the time and thereafter, the success of the air campaign was a matter of considerable controversy, not only on its own terms but for what it might show about the potential of air power. That year, George Robertson, the British secretary of state for defense (and later secretary general of NATO), publicly scorned commentators who warned about the difficulty of winning the Kosovo conflict by air power alone, and about the contrast between output (bomb and missile damage) and outcome. Some commentators proclaimed the campaign as one won by air power alone[13] (a view that continues to be held within the USAF) and, in that, as a fundamental change in the nature and development of military capability. Dramatically different weaponry was on show, notably stealth aircraft and satellite-guided cruise missiles. The American

F-117A Nighthawk stealth fighter, the planning for which had begun in 1975 with the plane flying from 1982, was matched by the newer B-2 Spirit stealth bomber. The most expensive aircraft yet to enter service, the B-2 program was cut back by Congress as part of the 1990s' defense cuts. The B-2 could be armed with cruise missiles, joint direct attack munitions (JDAMs), penetration bombs, and nuclear weapons. Alongside USAF assets, there was an important provision of naval air power, both from Tomahawk cruise missiles and from planes mounting strike missions and serving as forward air controllers for the air force planes. Drones were used to designate targets by means of lasers.

A reliance on air power certainly suited President Bill Clinton, who was highly risk averse and reluctant to accept the prospect of casualties, let alone the use of ground troops. Indeed, the initial instructions for the campaign had included no loss of aircraft.[14] Clinton's attitudes ensured that he adopted not only a reliance on air power but also an incremental approach to its use, one that was similar to that unsuccessfully attempted, at a much greater scale, by President Johnson in the Vietnam War. It was hoped that a small initial level of attack would yield results, but there was no real understanding of how, and with what consequences, this was to happen, and no politically approved coherent campaign plan. The Bosnia campaign was held up as an example, but with a reluctance to commit to any ground dimension.

In practice, the means available, initially about 120 strike-capable aircraft and fewer than fifty daily bombing sorties for the first week, were inadequate for the bold (and confused) tasks outlined by Clinton and other politicians, let alone for the short timescale offered. The conduct of operations did not match the policy goals or the asymmetry in commitment, with the Serbian government seeing the issue as one of national survival. Moreover, declaring an air power–only effort meant that the limitations of its use defined the Allied threat. This problem was exacerbated by the difficulties, as a result of political vacillation and disharmony, of achieving NATO agreement on daily air-tasking orders, while the aircraft were also constrained by rigid rules of engagement. As a result, the flexibility of air power was greatly compromised. There was no surprise factor in the initial attack nor in its progress, a situation that was to be repeated in air attacks against ISIS in Iraq and Syria in 2014–15.

The use of air power in Bosnia in 1995 had already amply demonstrated the problems of managing an air assault when the alliance responsible was divided about its application, as well as resolved to avoid its own casualties and to inflict as little collateral damage as possible. The NATO air attack in 1999 suffered the loss of only two aircraft (and no fatalities), but took far longer to achieve its goals than had been anticipated, both privately and publicly. Serbian resolve was repeatedly underestimated. Moreover, the subsequent Serbian withdrawal from Kosovo revealed that NATO estimates of the damage inflicted by air attack, for example to Serb tanks, had been considerably exaggerated. The Serbs benefited in practice from the limitations of NATO intelligence information and its serious consequences for NATO targeting, and from the severe impact of the weather on NATO air operations, a large number of which were, as a result, canceled or weakened. Laser-guided weapons require largely cloud-free skies in order to lock on and thus work. Like the 1991 Gulf War, in which winter conditions had caused problems, weather remained a very important factor in air operations, one overlooked in much of the technological triumphalism offered by commentators. Supposedly all-weather aircraft proved, in practice, to have more limited capability.

Moreover, although the Serbian high- and medium-altitude antiaircraft systems proved ineffective, the shoulder-fired missiles of Serbia's MANPAD (Man-Portable Air Defense Systems) curbed NATO's willingness to mount low-altitude flights and thus to be effective in ground attack. Apache attack helicopters were not employed and A-10 Warthogs only to a limited extent. There were ten thousand NATO strike sorties, but the Serbs, employing simple and inexpensive camouflage techniques that took advantage of the mountainous terrain, the wooded cover, and the cloud cover, including the use of decoys, preserved most of their equipment. It is probable that Serbian forces could have continued to hold out despite the bombing, although fears of future losses as the weather improved in summer may have been a factor in encouraging the Serbian government to settle.

The United States provided the foremost contribution in 1999, and France the second. Other NATO powers that took part included Britain, Denmark, and the Netherlands. Italian air bases were again crucial, notably Amendola, which, farther south than the bases used for operations over Bosnia, was more appropriate for Kosovo. In addition to land-based planes, carriers took part, including the French *Foch* (commissioned in 1963) and the British *Invincible*. NATO certainly demonstrated its viability in orchestrating the air assault. Nevertheless, the report produced in 2000 by the (British) National Audit Office on British operations in 1999 depicted major problems with the RAF. On cloudy days, the planes were unable to identify targets and were grounded, which, ironically, prevented an excessive depletion of bombs like that suffered by the Americans with cruise missiles. Bombs were far more costly than in the past, and, because of defense cuts, there were also fewer of them. Moreover, many bombs mounted on aircraft were unable to survive the shock of takeoff, while heat and vibration damage affected missiles.

In addition, the NATO air offensive did not immediately prevent the large-scale expulsion of Kosovars from their home, a brutal expulsion that badly compromised the success of Operation Allied Force. Indeed, the Serbian ethnic-cleansing campaign, Operation Horseshoe, increased as the air attack was mounted, with the Serbs freed from restraint and increasing the size of their force in Kosovo. In turn, this ethnic cleansing led, in April, to an expansion of the NATO air attack to include targeting "strategic infrastructure," an expansion for which, with 150 strike-capable aircraft by this stage, there were insufficient aircraft.

A continued sense of the failure to achieve objectives quickly ensured that, after the NATO Summit on April 23–25, there was a substantial escalation, including an increase in the number of strike-capable aircraft deployed (to four hundred) and in the daily strike mission rate, and a loosening of the rules of engagement, including permitting targets of opportunity. The pressure on Serbia increased greatly, with more frequent attacks on war industries and logistics, and a focus on oil refining and storage, electricity generation and transformation, and bridges. On May 2, over 70 percent of the population was blacked out as a result of short-circuiting electrical systems in attacks on five transformer stations. This assault was typical of the high rate of accuracy of bombing missions, although, on other occasions, misplaced assumptions about accuracy were heavily challenged by a series of mistakes that involved civilian casualties. Moreover, the use of cluster bombs was controversial, as was the serious environmental damage that arose from attacking oil installations.

The Serb withdrawal from Kosovo in 1999 may have owed as much to a conviction that a NATO land attack was imminent, as well as to the withdrawal of Russian support, while the role of the Kosovo Liberation Army should not be discounted. Indeed, the Kosovo crisis suggested that air power, as so often, would be most effective as part of a joint strategy, rather than as a strategic tool alone. Rather than thinking in terms of binary divides, ground and air threats were not totally separate, as the possibility of a ground invasion encouraged a concentration of defending forces that made them more vulnerable to air attack. Furthermore, although the damage to the Serbian army from air attack was limited, the devastation of Serbia's infrastructure, in the shape of bridges, factories, and electrical power plants, was important. This devastation greatly affected the financial interests and morale of the elite, as well as the functioning of the economy and the morale of the population, in each case encouraging pressure for peace. Thus, in this case, there was a marked contrast between the limited tactical and operational impact of air power, and its possibly more effective strategic consequences, a contrast that, to a degree, matched John Warden's ideas of rings of attack.[15]

Air power was not only used by Western powers. Russia made much use of bombing and aerial ground support during its wars with Chechen separatists in the north Caucasus in 1994–96 and 1999–2000. The capital, Grozny, was captured in 1995 after intensive artillery barrages and bombing.[16] However, under Boris Yeltsin as president from 1991 to 1999, there was a marked lack of expenditure on the Russian military, which, indeed, was not protected from the economic meltdown of the period. As a result, pilots had very little training, and operational effectiveness decreased. This trajectory paralleled the situation in South Africa and captured the degree to which air power required sustainability.

In 1999, there was good cooperation between the IAF and the Indian army during the Kargil war with Pakistan, although there were also many recriminations thereafter. This, the first time the IAF had been used in combat on the mainland subcontinent since 1971, was an important political message about Indian capability, whatever the battlefield impact. The use of air power was part of India's effort to tell Pakistan, and the larger international community, that the incursions were not simply another minor border scuffle. This was also a message to the Indian population that the government was determined, as well as a morale boost to the soldiers on the ground. Indian planes were forbidden from crossing into Pakistani air space, although there was fatal fire on them from the ground, while the IAF destroyed the Pakistani forward logistics base at Muntho Dhalo. The PAF maintained combat patrols only on its side of the border, and there were no air-to-air engagements. As with NATO targeting in Kosovo in 1999, this restraint underlined the extent to which the use of air power was greatly affected by political limitations.[17]

In Zaire (Congo), the 1996–97 Rwandan invasion led to the use of air power by Zaire for both air mobility (flying in reinforcements and equipment) and bombing (for example, of the town of Bukavu). This activity encouraged the Rwandans to attack airfields, as at Kisangani. The Rwandans, in turn, used small aircraft (De Havilland Twin-Otters and a Britten-Norman Islander) to move supplies and commanders. Zaire, the combatant with the stronger air power, was defeated in a conflict decided by rapidly advancing Rwandan ground forces.[18]

A degree of uniformity in state air power owed much to aircraft being built under license in other states. For example, the Aermacchi MB-326, an Italian trainer and ground-attack aircraft, was built under license in Brazil and South Africa, as the AT-26 Xavante and Atlas Impala, respectively. The plane was also flown in 1999 by Argentina, Australia, Paraguay, Togo, Zaire, and Zambia, while the MB-326K, a single-seat version, was flown by Dubai, Ghana, Tunisia, and Zambia. The more powerful MB-339C, the armaments of which included Sidewinder and Maverick missiles, was flown by Argentina, Eritrea, Ghana, Italy, Nigeria, Peru, New Zealand, and the United Arab Emirates, while Malaysia had a specialist antiship version. A different form of uniformity came from sharing in developments in capability and matching characteristics. For example, the Russian Sukhoi Su-30 Flanker C added a precision attack capability to the air-to-air capability of the Su-27 Flanker, thus matching American developments.

At sea, the Russians decommissioned all their carriers bar the *Admiral Kuznetsov* during the 1990s. The Su-33 was designed to operate from the carrier. In 2001, the nuclear-powered, forty-one-thousand-ton French carrier *Charles de Gaulle* entered service, six months after the older *Foch* was decommissioned and sold to Brazil. America's use of its dominant position at sea was demonstrated in 1996, when two aircraft carrier battle groups were utilized in the Taiwan Straits crisis in order to thwart China's coercive diplomacy. The Chinese climbdown led to their determination to develop antiship capabilities.

AFGHANISTAN

In 2001, the United States unleashed its air power against the Taliban regime in Afghanistan when it refused to hand over al-Qaeda leaders following the September 11 attacks on New York and Washington. Launched on October 7, Operation Enduring Freedom proved an effective attack, one facilitated by American Special Operations Forces and USAF forward air controllers, who played a crucial role in calling down and guiding large-scale American close air support. Unused to protecting themselves from such attack, and in terrain much of which, being flat and treeless, provided only limited cover, Taliban forces in the north of Afghanistan were heavily battered. Indeed, the regime's fall was seen as a success for American air power and was widely proclaimed as a demonstration of a paradigm shift in the means of waging war.

The air power deployed included carriers (the *Carl Vinson* was the first coalition asset to conduct combat operations); B-52 bombers; B-2 "stealth" bombers; extensive aerial refueling, which enabled planes to fly very long missions; Tomahawk cruise missiles from warships in the Arabian Sea; AC-130 gunships; unpiloted drones providing reconnaissance or firing Hellfire missiles; and CBU-130 "combined-effects munitions," which spread cluster bombs. The availability of dual-mode, laser and GPS guidance for bombs increased the range of precision available. Moreover, the air assault benefited from the effective and, crucially, rapid management of information from a number of sources, including forward air controllers and ground-based GPS devices. GPS coordinates could be programmed in the bombs while they were airborne, providing enhanced flexibility in "time-sensitive targeting." In-flight targeting helped air power operate as a readily responsive part of the multiple-source information-based warfare the Americans employed. Drones played a major role in the development of time-sensitive targeting. Greater accuracy ensured that the weight of bombs required could be cut, which affected payload and flying distance. In addition, the absence of hostile air power and effective antiaircraft fire was important to American effectiveness. In that respect, Afghanistan was a target that was less challenging than Iraq or Serbia. In 2001, the Americans were able to use helicopters to lift troops into combat from ships in the Arabian Sea to Kandahar in Afghanistan, a distance of 450 miles. There was a measure of coalition support, including from Britain, Denmark, France, and the Netherlands.

American capability illustrated the development of air power. Directed by secure and extensive communication systems, aircraft that could fly from the United States to bomb targets halfway around the world, refueling in midair en route, were very different from what Britain (in 1919) and even the Soviet Union (in 1979–88) could throw at Afghanistan, as was the degree of aerial surveillance. Indeed, the weaponry would have been the stuff of fantasy for earlier generations. The flexibility of air power was demonstrated by the B-52s. Originally designed for international strategic strikes, they were successfully armed with joint direct attack munitions so that they could provide effective close air support in Afghanistan.

As an aspect of the synergistic combination of different factors, the Taliban, however, ultimately had to be overcome on the ground by rival Afghan forces. In doing so, the lack of coherence of the Taliban regime and the porosity and changeable nature of alignments in Afghanistan were important to the war's outcome. Certainly, the American air assault helped switch the local political balance within Afghanistan. Air power was also important in specific instances, for example, on November 9, on the approach to the important northern city of Mazar-e Sharif from the south, when B-52s were required to overcome Taliban defenses, which included multiple rocket launchers.

The air assault had a considerable impact on the operations in northern Afghanistan in November 2001. However, the impact lessened in the ground operations launched by Afghan and Allied forces against Taliban and al-Qaeda survivors in Tora Bora (December 2001), and in Operation Anaconda, south of Gardiz (March 2002). This decline in effectiveness, which underlined the already known limitations of air power for suppressing insurgents,[19] was attributed to poor American command decisions, as well as to the Taliban's ability to respond to air attack by taking advantage of camouflage and the cover of terrain features, notably caves.[20] This decline in the effectiveness of air attack matched the British experience in the 1920s and 1930s. Helicopters provided important fire support and lift for the Afghan forces during Operation Anaconda, but unescorted low-flying helicopters took damage from ground fire, notably rocket-propelled grenades, to which they proved highly vulnerable. Many from the Taliban and al-Qaeda escaped due to a lack of close air support.

IRAQ, 2003

The Iraq campaign of 2003 brought the optimism about air power to a height, although it was ordered that all air operations would solely be in support of the ground campaign, with no independent use of air power. As in 1991, Iraqi air defenses were rapidly suppressed by an American-led coalition, one in which, due to fewer allies and improved American air effectiveness, American air power was even more dominant than in 1991, although it had to confront Turkey's refusal to permit the use of bases there. Badly damaged in 1991, the Iraqi air defenses had subsequently been weakened by the enforcement of the no-fly zone and by sanctions, which had limited their repair. The Iraqi air force did not contest control of the air but, instead, buried its aircraft. Had it not done so, it would have faced a high level of Allied air-to-air effectiveness. Nor did Iraq use its Russian-supplied cruise missiles. However, the air assault encountered problems, notably with the "deep attack" of the Eleventh Attack Aviation Regiment. The Iraqis were prepared, at least at that juncture, for a long-range air attack. Compared to 1991, they camouflaged their assets better and hid them next to buildings. The Iraqis also turned bright lights on to interrupt the aviation equipment of the Americans, who suffered losses in the attack.

American air power was the key element in destroying Iraqi artillery and armor and in bringing a dominance of reconnaissance. The speed and sophistication of American networking was such that about 80 percent of sorties were redirected after launch (provided with their target or new targeting after taking off), compared to about 20 percent in 1991 and about 43 percent in 2001. Such redirection was particularly useful against targets of opportunity, notably military units, as opposed to strategic targets. The Americans made particular use of JDAMs, which employed GPS to make conventional bombs act as satellite-guided weapons, converting dumb bombs into smart munitions. This capability was an important addition to the improvement in American air power that characterized post-Vietnam developments. The GPS system is superior to infrared and laser guidance systems, which can be disrupted by poor weather conditions; JDAMs are not affected by poor visibility or bad weather, although sandstorms are an issue. With accurate targeting, it was possible to use air power effectively and, in turn, to contribute to its reputation for effectiveness. About 70 percent of the aerial munitions employed by the Americans, mainly the one-ton JDAM, were "smart" (guided) rather than "dumb" (unguided), in contrast to 10 percent against Iraq in 1991. In turn, the RAF, which went up from 15 percent to 85 percent guided munitions, used Storm Shadow in 2003. This combined a considerable standoff range; a high degree of accuracy, aided by en route navigation systems; and a weapon able to penetrate reinforced concrete, such as that used to protect bunkers.

The Americans also benefited from the use of helicopter gunships, especially the impressive AH-60 Apache, and from Predator and Global Hawk UAVs (drones), while the British used Phoenix UAVs. Able to operate in high-threat areas close to targets, drones could provide accuracy in intelligence acquisition and targeting. This proved highly significant in the hunt for Iraqi mobile missile launchers. Drones are particularly valuable against targets that can be engaged with small warheads, rather than large missiles, and because they can operate at a level of tactical control below that of larger air assets.

Despite sandstorms, many of Iraq's Russian-built tanks were destroyed by air attack, notably by JDAMs and by the A-10, which was able to fire 4,100 armor-piercing bullets a minute from its seven-barrel 30 mm rotary cannon. The integration of air power and land maneuver generated an overwhelming tempo that provided the Iraqis with problems to which timely response proved impossible. An attacking force far smaller than in 1991, and with far more terrain to cover, took relatively few casualties in achieving its goals, despite not enjoying the conventional margin of advantage of attackers over defenders. The attackers obtained most of their indirect fire capability and support from aircraft rather than artillery.[21]

There was more specific support for particular operations, such as the Anglo-American helicopter attack on the Al Faw Peninsula the first night. This benefited from the preliminary bombardment of known Iraqi positions by American F-18s dropping JDAMs and American AC-

130 gunships. Airborne surveillance and control was important to this and other operations.

A less prominent instance of air-supported force projection occurred in June 2003. The French sent troops to eastern Congo as part of a multinational peacekeeping force with the support of French aircraft in French bases in the former colonies: at Ndjamena in Chad and Libreville in Gabon. Matching the American pattern at the global scale, France used air bases in former colonies, such as Djibouti and the Ivory Coast, in order to maintain influence and support military intervention. In the 2000s, this network was extended to include, in the United Arab Emirates, France's first base outside its former empire.

REVOLUTION IN MILITARY AFFAIRS

The rapid overthrow of the Iraqi government, an overthrow achieved with few Allied casualties, encouraged much favorable comment on American air power, specifically ideas associated with John Warden,[22] and, more generally,[23] the success of the American understanding and use of the Revolution in Military Affairs (RMA). Variously defined and explained, the RMA was a product of cultural and political assumptions in the 1990s and early 2000s. Andrew Marshall, director of the Office of Net Assessment in the Department of Defense, launched one interpretation in the late 1980s. It was in common use in the 1990s and found a strong advocate in Admiral William Owens, vice chairman of the US Joint Chiefs of Staff from 1994 to 1996. After 2001, Donald Rumsfeld, the secretary of defense, supplanted the RMA as the catalytic politico-military term of the day with "transformation," a term with still wider and more diffuse meanings. An assertion of Western, more particularly American, superiority, the RMA was a product of a belief in, indeed ideology of, mechanization that had long been important to American military thought. This focused on aircraft, the key demonstration of capability in a machine age. The potency of these machines was employed to demonstrate worth, strength, and superiority,[24] and, indeed, more effective aircraft entered operational service in the late 1990s and early 2000s, including the French Rafale and the American F-22 Raptor. Older aircraft were replaced. Thus, Italy replaced the American F-104 Starfighter (first flown in 1954) with leased Tornado F-3s.

It was crucial to Americans that the RMA was an American-led, indeed validated, military revolution, as it apparently underlined America's position and character.[25] Moreover, in line with the "American Way of War" and strategic culture, the RMA met the American need to believe in the possibility of high-intensity conflict and of total victory, with opponents "shocked and awed" into accepting defeat. It appeared possible to avoid both the costs of attritional victory and the frequently ambiguous and qualified nature of modern victory, let alone the risk of defeat. The 1991 Gulf War suggested that the relationship between air and ground forces was changing, and thus that further change could be obtained. Key elements appeared to be the ability to suppress enemy air defenses, to locate ground targets, and to deliver munitions precisely.[26] The use of stealthy attack aircraft able to penetrate opposing, integrated air defenses apparently moved the dialectic of offense and defense.

Aside from continued faith in the possibility of victory through air attack alone,[27] and of an air power–only strategy,[28] air power was also reconceptualized as playing a key role in a joint warfare considered in terms of what was presented as a matrix of networks of sensors, information processors, and shooters. "Network-centric" or "netcentric" warfare was the goal, as it was believed to take military capability to a new level of effectiveness.[29] This approach represented a way to shape technological developments. The opportunities for action, command, and control achieved by aggregating sensors, shooters, and deciders offered the opportunity of achieving a precise mass effect from dispersed units, and thus minimizing their vulnerability. "Information dominance" was a key aspect of the prospectus, one that simultaneously shortened and made more accurate the American decision cycle while lengthening and making less accurate that of America's opponent. "Shock and Awe" was advanced as a concept in 1996 to describe a rapidly effective paralyzing air offensive using precision weaponry and networked intelligence. This idea focused even more on information dominance than Warden had done.[30] The term was to be much used in the media to describe the 2003 invasion.

There was also an emphasis on cheaper, unmanned platforms or drones, intended to replace reconnaissance and attack aircraft. Whether termed "unmanned aerial vehicles" (UAVs) or "remotely piloted vehicles" (RPVs), these platforms were designed to take the advantage of missiles further by providing mobile platforms from which they could be fired or from which bombs could be dropped. Platforms do not require crew and thus can be used without risk to the life and liberty of personnel. As a consequence, these platforms can be low flying and enjoy enhanced accuracy, as the risk of loss of pilots to antiaircraft fire has been removed. These losses, and the problems they posed, not least the prospect of hostage-type situations with the pressures they entailed, contributed to the priorities for a new type of air power, entailing new moral issues.

The logistical burden of air power is reduced with unmanned platforms, as is the cost, as these platforms, although costly to buy and control, are less expensive than manned counterparts, and there are savings in pilot training and use, despite the need for ground pilots. Unmanned platforms are more compact and "stealthy" (less easy to detect and intercept), while the acceleration and maneuverability of such platforms are no longer limited by g-forces that would render pilots unconscious, although there are still the constraints posed by the materials used. In 1999, unarmed drones were employed extensively for surveillance over Kosovo in order to send information on bomb damage and refugee columns. However, this capability was also a weakness. Real-time data linking enabled the picture to be distributed even into the offices of the highest officials, encouraging political interference, which could have dire consequences.

In Afghanistan from 2001 and Iraq from 2003, armed drones were used as firing platforms. This was not a robotic weapon but a sophisticated firing platform controlled from a distance, one that offered a marked enhancement of capability at the intersection of artillery, air power, and ethics. This distinction between robotic (i.e., supposedly autonomous) weapons and firing platforms controlled from a distance has been continuously misrepresented by antidrone campaigners and the media for years.

The capability of unmanned platforms is enhanced by designing them to work within systems that benefit from satellite information transmitted instantaneously. Thus, the RMA, in some respects an air-power ideology, was one that represented the extension of the latter into space. As such, the RMA suffered from the more general problems of air-power ideology, namely the tendency always to find strategic value in its use, a process linked not only to institutional need but also to the determination to assert control over the chaos of the battlefield.[31] As an instance of a more general process, belief in the extreme accuracy of smart bombs encouraged commanders to plan and order attacks on small targets not much bigger than the average miss distances of such munitions, thus causing civilian casualties.[32] Conversely, smart munitions not only targeted specific buildings but could be seen to do so by the civilian population as in the First Gulf War. Thus, the potential morale effect was as great as a mass of bombs from the sky.

The conflicts of the 1990s and 2000s demonstrated the more general point that some air-power advocates tend to underrate its deficiencies tactically and operationally and to exaggerate the ability to obtain strategic goals through using air attack. This was to become clearer in the aftermath of the American interventions in Afghanistan and Iraq. From a different perspective, the spread of atomic weaponry also acted as a constraint on the use of air attack to obtain such goals. In 1998, both India and Pakistan test-fired their atomic bombs.[33] More generally, the extent to which in the 1990s air power was assigned tasks it could do, in short "the permissive circumstances of its employment," led, in practice, to a misreading of the true extent of its potential and its limitations.[34]

11

A COMPLEX REALITY, 2004–15

The aftermath of the conquest of Iraq in 2003 led to a fall, in many circles collapse, of confidence in the RMA, as hopes of a speedy success ran into the sands of an escalating and very public crisis of disorder and opposition. The persistence of an Iraqi insurrection proved a serious problem for the American occupiers and resulted in a new focus, in the American military and elsewhere, on counterinsurgency operations (COIN). This focus was linked to a widespread criticism of an earlier American triumphalism, a criticism that centered on political failure but that also involved criticism of the utility of air power.

The new focus, and the accompanying criticism, created pressure to define an expanded role for air power. This pressure provided a background within which the subsequent use of air power was considered and, in turn, deployed in debates about best practice and concerning plans for the future. There was a search for an air-power doctrine related to counterinsurgency.[1] It is instructive that Sebastian Ritchie, the official historian at the Air Historical Branch of the British Ministry of Defence, published *The RAF, Small Wars and Insurgencies* (2011). In practice, air power had to deal with asymmetric threats from the outset, with each side searching for new capabilities and opportunities, but these threats now became especially relevant, rather than as a footnote to a concern with symmetrical challenges.

COIN operations in Iraq and Afghanistan indicated the value of air supremacy in providing a freedom of movement by air as well as offering offensive air support, both aspects of the more general asymmetric advantage that was enjoyed as a result of air power. The Afghan and Iraqi commitments saw the employment both of strategic airlift (moving forces to the theater) and of its operational and tactical counterparts. Air mobility was particularly significant due to problems with ground movement and to a growing emphasis on information-driven operations, notably raids on insurgent safe havens. Moreover, the key to COIN is excellent and timely intelligence, especially if insurgents camouflage themselves among the population, and aircraft could provide this. Air reconnaissance, using sophisticated visual and radar sensors, supplied vital details. For the insurgents, innocent civilian deaths are effective weapons in the coercive campaign, but, for the West, deaths are failures in the "hearts and minds" campaign. There is also need for an understanding (which is mostly absent) of what the effect will be of a particular strike—physical, political, and psychological.

There were also improvements in weapons technology. An upgrade to JDAMs, which included a terminal laser guidance system (LJDAM), enabled the bomb to hit a moving target and was first used in American operations over Iraq in 2008. Such weaponry combined with network-enhanced capability permitted a speedy response to asymmetric enemies in the fleeting moments when they revealed themselves, generally before an attack.

However, alongside attempts to adapt air-superiority fighters, such as the British Typhoon, so that they could focus on all-weather ground attack, operations in Iraq and Afghanistan also revealed a lack of flexibility on the part of "fast jets." This problem reflected the more general problems with targeting light infantry irrespective of advances in surveillance and weaponry.[2] In response, the USAF searched for a modernized turbo/piston engine aircraft with modern sensors and standoff capability that could "get down and dirty" and "hug the weeds" in order to provide COIN capability as it was really required. One of the options proposed was to produce a "cloned" A-1 Skyraider, with new materials, weapons systems, and avionics, as it was seen as able to absorb ground fire, to carry weaponry, to "loiter over the battlefield," and to operate from rough airstrips. Thus, there was pressure for aircraft with many of the characteristics of helicopters without their clear vulnerability. Air attacks were a key means in the killing of insurgent leaders. On June 7, 2006, Abu Musab Al-Zarqawi, the leader of Al Qaeda in Iraq, was killed in a bombing raid. As a very different aspect of the "War on Terror," aircraft such as the Gulfstream executive jet were also used by the CIA to transport prisoners across the globe, enabling them to be moved, by "extraordinary rendition," in order to circumvent legal protection in the United States.[3]

In Afghanistan and Iraq, ambushes of NATO and American forces led to a dependence on helicopters for mobility and logistics, as well as firepower, which was also provided by fixed-wing aircraft. However, there were only limited numbers of aircraft, and there was only so much air power could achieve, especially, but not only, in bad flying conditions. As a result, it proved difficult to gain the initiative. Insurgents contested the Allied use of air power, not by having an air force, but by antiaircraft fire, attacks on airfields, and the use of propaganda about casualties.[4] Moreover, the insurgents lacked a fixed leadership, a clear governmental structure, and an infrastructure to provide targets. As a consequence, the language employed by John Warden about a living system, the brain (leadership) of which should be hit by air attack, was inappropriate. So indeed were the very ideas of "strategic" air power, other than in terms of power projection and as part of COIN operations. Air power in all its forms had been the key facilitator for the whole operation, but in the end it was just one part of the carrot and the stick of politics and war.

Nevertheless, although they were difficult to counter or strike at, air power was useful in the struggle with amorphous bands of guerrillas. Airborne reconnaissance and surveillance proved particularly valuable, notably Joint Surveillance and Target Attack Radar System (JSTARS) aircraft. In addition, the tactical integration, by the United States and its allies, of air power and ground operations in Afghanistan and Iraq was frequently impressive.[5]

ISRAEL

One of the more dramatic instances of pressure to rethink military methods was provided by the fate of the Israeli attack on Hizbullah in July 2006. In response to Hizbullah's consolidation of its power in southern Lebanon, and to attacks mounted from there, Israel blockaded Lebanon and launched a limited, but large-scale, invasion of southern Lebanon that month, combined with extensive aerial attack involving over four thousand air strikes, focused in particular on Hizbul-lah's rocket sites. This offensive, however, proved misconceived and poorly executed. The Israelis planned for a guerrilla war, but, instead, Hizbullah switched to more conventional operations. The inadequacy of the "netcentric" systems approach to warfare, with its targeting of nodes and specific systems of the adversary in order to cause the whole to collapse, was revealed, notably not taking into account the human or chance elements of war. Israel subsequently jettisoned the theory. In 2006, Israeli tanks failed to repeat earlier successes. Moreover, far from providing a coercive outcome, one that could cement or offset the re-sults of the invasion, the Israeli air assault was unable to crush resis-tance. Instead, it wracked a degree of devastation on Lebanon's civilian population that challenged Israel's international reputation and helped to ensure that Israel lost the propaganda war.

In response to the Israeli attack, Hizbullah fired about five thousand rockets indiscriminately against cities, dramatically confounding Israel's capacity for deterrence. In the face of Hizbullah's view of civilians as targets in this campaign, close to a million Israelis moved south, away from exposed frontier areas, or took shelter in air-raid shelters. Haifa, the key city in the north, was particularly exposed. Public criticism rose, but civilian resolve was not crushed. In 2006, Israeli air power proved unable to end rocket attacks from Lebanon, although a large percent-age of the long-range Hizbullah rocket systems, which were supplied by Iran, were destroyed. In the aftermath, Hizbullah built up an even stronger rocket capacity. Missiles also affected Israeli naval power. In 2006, the corvette *Hanit* was hit by a radar-guided C-802 missile fired from southern Lebanon. Three years later, Hamas fired missiles at Is-raeli warships that were bombarding Hamas positions in the Gaza Strip.[6]

Israeli commentators calculated that, by 2012, Hamas had fired maybe twelve thousand missiles from Gaza. Israeli air and air-sup-ported land counterattacks on rocket squads in the Gaza Strip, includ-ing a sustained air and land attack in 2014, failed to end these attacks. Israel took aim at Hamas leaders but was accused of indiscriminate bombing. Hamas, in contrast, just fired rockets indiscriminately. Mean-while, with American assistance, Israel had developed an "Iron Dome" antimissile system over its major cities, a system that proved effective against Hamas missiles in 2014. The firing of missiles against Ben-

Gurion Airport reflected the extent to which it was crucial to Israel's international links.

The Israeli use of cluster munitions during the 2006 war encouraged international criticism of these dispersed warhead munitions, many of which, with delayed fuses, did not explode at the time, leading to later civilian casualties. Norway led a postwar attempt to ban their use, and in 2010 the Convention on Cluster Munitions entered into force, although many powers chose not to sign, including the United States and Israel.

Meanwhile, the Israeli air force continued its process of upgrading in order to provide a cutting-edge capability within a tough financial environment. The reduction of platforms, now judged obsolete, was a key element in the new acquisition program. Thus, F-4 Phantoms and A-4 Skyhawks were cut in the mid-2000s in order to make way for the F-16I Soufa (Storm), which had a key advantage in being a multirole fighter. Israel made use of the Heron, a UAV equipped with air-to-ground missiles, from Operation Cast Lead (December 2008–January 2009) against Hamas onward.[7] Hamas had no qualms in sheltering their rocket launchers next to mosques or hospitals, and the detection of most rockets only after launch gave the terrorists time to flee before the arrival of any air attack. On November 14, 2014, in response to incessant rocket attacks from the Gaza Striip, the IDF launched Operation Pillar of Defense, a widespread campaign against terror targets in Gaza. During the operation, the Israeli air force targeted terrorist targets throughout the Gaza Strip, resulting in significant damage to Hamas infrastructure.

SUDAN

Sudan spent part of the money raised by oil exports on a major military program including MIG-29s from Russia. Less speedy planes were deployed when the government made extensive use of aircraft in its brutal struggle to impose control over tribal groups and peripheral areas. From 2003, the government was threatened by a serious rebellion in the Darfur region of the west of the country by the Sudan Liberation Army, which complained of the oppression of non-Arabs by the government. In response, in 2004, the government used its regular forces, including infantry moved in trucks and Russian-supplied aircraft, in order to support a brutal Arab militia. Villages were destroyed in a scorched-earth policy designed to deny the rebels shelter. Aircraft were also used to attack larger tribal bases, such as Shangal Tobay in 2011. The same techniques were employed elsewhere by the Sudanese military, for example in the province of Southern Kordofan in the early 2010s. Moreover, once South Sudan became independent in 2011, Sudan employed aircraft in sustained border clashes with it, both for ground support and for bombing.

LIBYA

NATO intervention in Libya in 2011 threw a different light on air power, although, yet again, limitations at the strategic level arose and greatly offset operational and, even more, tactical advantages. Moreover, this intervention provided an instance of the degree to which the ready ability to deploy and use air power, and its apparent qualities of speed, accuracy, and low exposure to casualties, encouraged a reliance on force that was unwise, and which was hailed as proof that air power was sufficient to bring about strategic results. What was originally the establishment of a no-fly zone intended to protect civilians in accordance with a UN Security Council Resolution became a drive to overthrow Gaddafi, which provided a strategic goal. The selection of targets reflected this. The brakes on the employment of force and on subsequent escalation that might otherwise operate did not do so, although the NATO coalition lost members as a result of the move to support regime change, with Norway, in protest, withdrawing its six F-16s. Moreover, the international consequences in terms of angering Russia were serious.

The rebellion against the Gaddafi regime was greatly aided by the NATO intervention. It helped counter the advantages enjoyed by the Libyan military: these included air cover, but also tanks, artillery, and training. American "stealth" bombers were central to Operation Odyssey Dawn, the original, highly damaging assault on the Libyan air force, much of which subsequently defected to Malta. The Americans also played a vital role in the initial cruise missile attack on Libya's Russian-supplied air defenses, as well as in air-to-air refueling, reconnaissance, and intelligence provision. American aircraft also flew civilians out of Libya, reducing the risk of hostages. However, for domestic political reasons within the context of domestic political pressure for withdrawal from the conflicts in Iraq and Afghanistan, America did not wish to be seen to provide the lead element, although about 70 percent of all air-support sorties, such as AWACS, were provided by the Americans. Much air support for the rebellion was from Britain and France, operating from Italian air bases and the French carrier *Charles de Gaulle*, but also using air refueling. American and Italian carriers also played a role. Other NATO powers that provided support included Belgium, Canada, Denmark, the Netherlands, and Norway, but not Germany. Non-NATO powers, including Jordan, Sweden, Qatar, and the United Arab Emirates, also helped the air campaign, which lasted almost eight months.

Despite the major problems these attacks faced, due to a lack of reliable reconnaissance information, they first countered Libyan army units and then seriously damaged them, for example destroying tanks, as well as the Libyan navy. It took a long time to prevent the Libyan army from launching attacks, and there were concerns that the lengthy operation had failed or become attritional. Initially too small, the commitment did not succeed as originally anticipated. Nevertheless, after a sizable escalation, the air umbrella provided crucial support for the Libyan insurgents. In the key operation, the insurgents eventually advanced to capture the capital, Tripoli, and to overthrow the regime. NATO air reconnaissance detected Gaddafi's flight, and the militia then hunted him down. The Libyan intervention suggested that, as with Afghanistan in 2001, air power would be most effective as part of a joint strategy,[8] although, in Libya, the situation on the ground was more propitious than in Kosovo in 1999. However, the new regime soon faced serious problems with independent militias and insurrection, problems it could not control. Air power had masked the problems of Islamists on the ground.

SYRIA

In a larger-scale, and apparently similarly intractable, civil war, that in Syria which began in 2011, air power was largely used by the Assad regime, which was supplied by Russia and Iran. The bombing by the regime of rebel-held areas, such as the cities of Aleppo and Homs, was especially indiscriminate. Barrel bombs—oil drums packed with explosive and shrapnel, and dropped on residential areas from aircraft and helicopters—proved particularly deadly. The regime also used missiles against civilians. They were responsible for a particular outrage, the killing of over 1,400 people as a result of the regime's employment of sarin gas in the Damascus suburb of Ghouta on August 21, 2013.

This slaughter, an American "red line," led to consideration of crossing an American-led response that would have included cruise missiles and bombing, provided by the United States, Britain, and France, but, in the event, first Britain and then the United States and France pulled back.[9] The diversity of air power was further demonstrated in the Russian use of reconnaissance drones in order to provide the Syrian army with accurate information on their opponents to help in targeting. The significance of air bases as sites of power and control was demonstrated in 2012 when the Syrian government fired Scud missiles for the first time from the An Nasiriyah air base, a key site near Damascus, against the rebel-held Sheikh Suleiman base near Aleppo.

Similarly, airports are major sites for operations elsewhere. This was particularly true of Bagram and Kandahar in Afghanistan (former Soviet air bases), and of Baghdad and Basra in Iraq. To support the International Security Assistance Force (ISAF) deployed in Afghanistan, Kabul International Airport was reactivated and rebuilt in early 2002, permitting the use of C-130 and An-124 planes and the operation of an air bridge. From January to July 2002, thirty-eight thousand tons of freight, four million liters of fuel, and twenty-eight thousand personnel were moved in support of ISAF via the airport.[10] The African Union Mission in Somalia established in 2011 has its main base adjacent to the airport in Mogadishu, the capital. Similarly, IFOR and SFOR headquarters were at Camp Butmir, Sarajevo. Air bases are key to operations.

The crisis in Syria threatened to lead to border conflict with neighboring Turkey, which backed the insurgents, notably after Syria shot down a Turkish F-4 Phantom reconnaissance plane in June 2012. There was talk then of a safe zone for insurgents within Syria, as well as of a no-fly zone in Syria designed to limit government air attacks there; but, aside from the political commitment, the maintenance of such zones would have required a formidable effort by the Turkish air force. It would have been necessary to suppress Syrian air defenses, a major task, as well as to overcome Syrian air power. Instead, Turkey, in 2012, successfully obtained NATO Patriot missile batteries able to intercept aircraft and missiles, including the cruise missiles Russia had supplied to Syria, although, in the event, no attack was launched. This NATO mission was a political sign rather than a military necessity.

RANGE OF USE, 2013–15

Air power was widely applied in this period in order to seek to influence developments on the ground. Air attacks were directed against civilians, for example in the Sudanese bombing of villages in the rebellious region of Darfur, but also against military targets. The two were sometimes difficult to distinguish when using aircraft against guerrilla movements, as in the Aceh region of Sumatra in 2003–5, when the Indonesian government employed ground-attack aircraft and parachutists against the Gerakan Aceh Merdeka (GAM, or Free Aceh Movement) separatist movement. In 2013, there was French intervention in Mali against insurrection by the Tuareg in the north, whose advance south in late 2012 had taken them near the strategic airport at Sevare. French air attack provided the best means to assist the Malian and West African forces, who then pushed back the Tuareg. Other NATO powers provided air support. These included Britain and Denmark, the latter showing how NATO operations repeatedly brought the air forces of relatively minor powers into operational activity. The United States assisted France with refueling, while Algeria permitted France to use its air space, which is always an important aspect of acquiescence or help, but one usually underplayed in public discussion. Aerial refueling became a more significant aspect of air activity in the 2000s and 2010s both for this reason and due to the greater importance both of expeditionary warfare and of long-range operations.

Coalition warfare increasingly became the prime means of air activity, although the degree of commitment varied. Thus, Singapore deployed KC-135 tankers, C-130 transports, maritime patrol aircraft, and drones in coalition operations in Iraq, Afghanistan, and the Gulf of Aden in the early twenty-first century, but not its F-15s or F-16s in combat roles. Transport aircraft, which simply need to take off and land, are easier to integrate with other coalition aircraft than fighters unless the latter use updated technology. The strategic significance of the Gulf and of North Africa ensured that air bases were sought in relevant areas, including Abu Dhabi and Djibouti. From the latter, American aircraft attacked Islamic fundamentalists in neighboring Somalia.

In 2014–15, air attacks by a number of powers, including the United States, Britain, Canada, Denmark, France, the Netherlands, Jordan, Abu Dhabi, and Saudi Arabia, were used to assist the Kurds and to shore up the Iraqi government as they reeled from attacks by the rapidly advancing forces of the Islamic insurrectionary movement, ISIS. These limited air attacks proved successful up to a point, not least because the attacks on ISIS units and leaders benefited greatly from the reliable intelligence provided by reconnaissance. Coalition aircraft also attacked ISIS targets in Syria. Aircraft from the United Arab Emirates attacked oilfields in Syria that had fallen into the hands of ISIS.

However, as with other struggles, the situation on the ground proved dangerous as well as decisive, and there the situation was less positive. This was also true of Iraqi air attacks on ISIS forces; of air attacks on Boko Haram by Nigeria, Niger, and Chad; of Libyan air attacks on Islamic insurgents; of Pakistani air attacks on Taliban opponents in the North-West Frontier Province; and of Turkish air attacks on Kurdish separatists. In March 2015, when Iranian-trained Houthi rebels overran much of Yemen, a coalition of Sunni Arab states led by Saudi Arabia and including its Gulf allies, Egypt and Jordan, deployed nearly two hundred aircraft to wipe out the Houthi air force and attack Houthi targets, including the al-Anab air base from which the successful Houthi advance on Aden was supported. The Americans, who, until the Houthi success, had used Yemen as a base for drone strikes against Al Qaeda in the Arabian Peninsula, provided the coalition with intelligence and logistical support. However, at the time of writing (September 2015), the Arab coalition has failed to achieve its goals on the ground. The multiple role of American air power was seen not only in the frequent use of American planes but also in training. Thus, the Libyan air force was headed by the American-trained Saqer el-Jarroushi.

Insurrectionary forces did not tend to have access to air power, although in Sri Lanka, the Tamil Tigers (LTTE) had a small "air force" that launched a few high-visibility raids, including an attack on Colombo airport. This won considerable publicity but had no real military consequences, indeed even less than that of the Biafran air force during the Biafran rebellion of 1967–70 (see chapter 8). In contrast, the Sri Lankan air force had a significant role in the civil war. The army won the war, but the air force played a useful part in ground-support strikes, reconnaissance, and the airlift of supplies to the Jaffna Peninsula, thus bypassing ambushes. In 2014–15, the ability of Syrian insurgents and of ISIS to operate captured aircraft became a matter of contention. There is no sign that they can be used to any purpose, but the seizure of air bases, such as Ghardabiya in Sirte, Libya, by ISIS in May 2015, caused alarm.

A key element of military development was that of tactical air mobility. The helicopter had demonstrated its value clearly from the 1950s, but, in the aftermath of the Cold War, notably with the growing emphasis on COIN, there was a renewed stress on the potential offered by the flexibility of helicopters, both in the airlift of troops and in the provision of fire support. American-produced Apache armed helicopters were particularly significant in the latter, having been acquired by Britain, Egypt, Greece, Israel, the Netherlands, Saudi Arabia, and the United Arab Emirates. First flown in 1961, the Chinook, also American, was acquired by Argentina, Australia, Britain, Canada, Greece, Japan, Iran, Italy, Libya, Morocco, the Netherlands, Singapore, South Korea, Spain, Taiwan, Thailand, and Turkey. Chinook and Cougar transport helicopters, and Apache armed helicopters, were acquired by the Dutch in the 1990s as the helicopter fleet was expanded in order to meet the new needs and opportunities provided by the establishment of an AirMobile Brigade in 1992. Other powers, including Singapore, created similar forces. In 2014, India and Russia reached agreement on building advanced helicopters in India, while Pakistan pursued discussions to buy Russian Mi-35 attack helicopters. Pakistan had used armed air power extensively for COIN in Swat and in the FATA from 2009, unlike India, where the military are less powerful, which has followed a far more cautious path.

DRONES

The pace of development, in particular, the issues posed for the United States by the "War on Terror," and the opportunities offered by the massive increase in the American defense budget, helped to ensure that UAV technology matured rapidly. Attacks on insurgent leaders increasingly made use of drones, for example, in Afghanistan, Lebanon, Pakistan, Somalia, and Yemen. Drone attacks increased greatly under President Obama (2009–17), from 9 in Pakistan in 2004–7, when George W. Bush was president, to 117 in 2010. Moreover, the frequency of attacks was employed to signal intentions, as in 2014 when Pakistani attempts to rally domestic support for a new policy toward the Taliban were eased by the marked lessening of these unpopular American attacks. Pakistani governments secretly made available bases for American drones and helped provide targeting information, and yet they sought to cover their domestic base by criticizing the attacks when civilians died.

Drone specifications rapidly improved. The twenty-six-foot American-produced Predator, with its operating radius of four hundred miles, flight duration of up to fourteen hours, cruising speed of eighty miles per hour, and normal operating altitudes of up to fifteen thousand feet, could be used in areas contaminated by chemical or germ warfare, an aspect of their D-3 tasking for dangerous, dull, and dirty tasks. Britain, France, and several other NATO nations shadowed the American employment of the Predator, which rapidly evolved into the Reaper with an up to forty-two-hour endurance and the capability to carry Hellfire missiles, laser-guided bombers, and even JDAMs.

The use of drones of all sizes spread swiftly, both with increased use of drones where they were long established, for example, in Singapore where the first squadron was founded in 1984, as well as in states that had not hitherto had drones. During the 2006 Lebanon crisis, both Israel and Hizbullah employed drones, with the Israelis making particularly marked use of them as an instance of their aerial dominance and attack capacity. Hizbullah's drones had been provided by Iran. In 2008, the Russian-backed breakaway region of Abkhazia claimed to destroy seven reconnaissance drones sent from Georgia (the Caucasus republic, not the American state); Israel had provided them. It has also sold drones to other powers, including Russia and Turkey. In 2010, Singapore sent a UAV Task Group to Afghanistan, providing information to

American and Australian forces on the ground.[11] In 2012, an Iranian-supplied Sudanese drone was allegedly shot down over the rebel province of Southern Kordofan, while, in the early 2010s, India's paramilitary forces deployed drones as part of their large-scale action against Maoist insurgents known as Naxalites: India has some indigenous types and some from Israel. The United Nations deployed drones to observe rebel groups in Congo, a development in UN ideas about acquiring intelligence. Malaysia developed drones for use in coastal surveillance. In the 2010s, Britain and France began a joint development of combat drones, while, in 2014, Britain unveiled the Taranis, a prototype fighter-bomber drone. Allies, such as South Korea, bought American drones. In December 2013, the Dutch decided to buy four Reaper drones and the associated ground stations. Japan has resolved to acquire drones by 2019, but not to build its own. In 2014, Russia, which had lagged behind in drone development, bought a number of Israeli drones, which were used to guide separatist artillery fire in eastern Ukraine, complementing the use of missiles against Ukrainian planes. In 2015, the Pakistani army announced that it had test-fired Barq laser-guided missiles from an indigenously developed drone and claimed that it had hit stationary and moving targets.

The increasing use of ever more sophisticated drones suggests that they will come to play an ever bigger role, and this featured importantly in American political debate in 2015 over defense plans and expenditure. Drones, however, are more expensive to buy and operate than is often appreciated, as many of the delicate sensors and weapons systems replicate those already deployed in other aircraft. Moreover, loss rates have been relatively high, with operational problems restricting the employment of drones: in Iraq in 2003, there were problems with the unusability of American drones due to high temperatures and also issues arising from the cloud base, as well as vulnerability to ground fire. There is also a limitation in the bandwidth spectrum available for control and data transmission, such that the number of drones that can be employed in an area is limited.

By the early 2010s, researchers were trying to teach drones to follow human gestures so that they would be able to respond to the directions of deck handlers and thus use aircraft carriers. Israel and the United States, moreover, were active in the field of small-scale drones designed to mimic the characteristics of bird flight. The European Neuron project, in which France plays a major role, seeks to provide a supersonic, stealthy, combat drone capable of delivering nuclear weapons. Remotely piloted fighter aircraft have attracted attention. It is unclear how revolutionary unmanned vehicles will become, but the theme of change is very much to the fore. At the same time, the continued vulnerability of drones to competent air defenses is worth noting, a vulnerability enhanced by their being relatively slow. This issue affects their use across the spectrum of conflict: air superiority, over both other aircraft and ground defenses, is required.

The ethics of drone use, specifically of killing without risk and at a distance, as well as its legality, notably in crossing international borders, has attracted considerable attention.[12] The rules of engagement are far more complex and constraining than suggested by criticism in terms of "death by PlayStation," but the latter criticism is frequently deployed, not least when arguing that drones somehow depersonalize killing and make it "easy." Instead, posttraumatic stress disorder rates among American and British drone operators are similar to those among the pilots of manned aircraft.[13]

NEW AIRCRAFT

Revived competition among the great powers from the 2000s encouraged the development of more advanced aircraft types, as well as the purchase of more of existing types. Particular emphasis on aircraft purchase was seen in the Middle East and in East Asia, fueled, respectively, by oil production and economic growth, and encouraged by international competition and related fears.

Alongside the need to replace aging aircraft such as the F-16, which, for example, entered Danish service in 1980, improved specifications ensured an attempt to develop types that would cover a range of needs. This led to the biggest military program in history, the American F-35 Joint Strike Fighter, which was the latest in a series of projects for a single aircraft for that function. An earlier example was the TFX of the 1960s, which became the F-111 built by General Dynamics while the carrier variant, the F-111B, was canceled. The initial research and development contract and production contract for what became known as the F-35 were signed in 1996 and 2001, respectively, and, in that period, it appeared to have a lot to offer and to be value for money. The F-35 was designed as a comparatively inexpensive tactical aircraft intended to achieve air superiority and as a ground-attack tool. The F-35 was also seen as at the cutting edge in technology, as it was planned with the "stealth" capability that defeats radar recognition as well as with advanced software and sensors. Designed to replace at least four other types in service, the F-35 was intended as the central American fighter for the next half century, as well as the basis for allied air forces.

It was planned that the United States would purchase 2,443 F-35s, ensuring that, alongside orders from allies, at least three thousand could be ordered from the outset. This bulk order was intended to produce major economies of scale, both in procurement and in subsequent maintenance and support. In doing so, it was planned to counter the great expense of producing and delivering new aircraft. These costs were such that the very economic viability of air power had diminished, notably as measured in the number of firms and countries able to manufacture aircraft, as well as the number of countries capable of supporting a significant state-of-the-art air force. The sheer cost of new aircraft precludes their acquisition by most states, thus maintaining a degree of air asymmetry. As a result, coalitions of interest were required for the production and introduction of new aircraft, as with the F-35 or the Eurofighter Typhoon fighter. In large part for geopolitical reasons of strategic alignment, Japan settled on the F-35 in 2011. Australia, Britain, the Netherlands, and Norway are other purchasers. The size of the RAF, however, has been greatly affected by defense cuts, with the number of fast jet squadrons falling from sixteen in 2004 to twelve in 2010 and then, under the 2010 Strategic Defence and Security Review of that year, to seven. As a result of fiscal pressures, Britain will take far fewer F-35s than the 137 that had been originally planned.

Deliveries of the F-35 to air forces were supposed to start in 2010, but, by the summer of 2011, the date for entering service had been postponed to 2016. Problems stemmed from the oversophistication, stealth, and multiplicity of variants. Moreover, as a prime instance of defense inflation, the average price of each aircraft had nearly doubled, from $81 million to $156 million, and total program costs had risen to $382 billion. The cost of operating and sustaining the aircraft has also risen significantly, ensuring that the F-35 would be far more expensive than the aircraft it was intended to replace. The scale of America's fiscal crisis, which, in part, is due to expensive wars in the 2000s, made this unacceptable. Although a lesser factor, the cost of highly trained aircrew is also considerable.

Moreover, changes in the strategic environment and the nature of weaponry make the effectiveness and hence the value of the F-35 increasingly questionable. Its air combat maneuvering capability seems less than current aircraft, and there is doubt about its "stealth" capacity and its related ability to cope with the most modern air-defense systems that it may have to face. Range is also an issue. The United States has nearby bases from which to confront the Soviet Union, Iraq, and Iran, for example, in Abu Dhabi in the Gulf for the last. In contrast, the range of about six hundred miles is less helpful in opposing China, whose deployment of new aircraft, including Su-30 MK2 fighters and JH-7A fighter-bombers, increases its challenge at sea.[14] Moreover, the development and deployment by China of antiship missiles able to challenge American carriers, notably the DF-21 intermediate-range (1,500 km) ballistic missile fitted with a maneuvering terminally guided head containing an antiship seeker, poses a major problem. As a result, the carriers may have to operate well to the east of Taiwan, in other words beyond the range of the American navy's F-35s. The new anticarrier technology has led to a call in the United States for doctrinal flexibility in defining the role of carriers as they cease to be the clear supreme arbiter of (American) naval power.[15] This problem is pertinent for other F-35 states, especially Britain, whose F-35B variants have even shorter range, exposing its new carriers to danger against any opponent with the DF-21 missile. Obsolescence of the F-35 was further underlined by planned developments for rival weapon systems, both drones and hypersonic cruise missiles.

In addition, the F-35 indicated classic problems that need to be borne in mind when discussing effectiveness. The F-35's anticipated costs and performance were compromised by being expected to fulfill many roles, which in turn led to an overly complicated design. This was an aspect of the cost context, as high costs led to a preference for long-term use and a multimission capability able to respond to different operational requirements. In particular, the F-35 was intended for the American air force, replacing its F-16s and A-10s, as well as for the navy, providing a conventional takeoff and landing version (the F-35B) to replace its F-18s, and also for the marines, to replace their AV-8B jump jets with a short takeoff and vertical landing version (the F-35B). Aside from its much more limited range and payload, the last caused particular problems, both with structure and propulsion, and was placed on "probation" in 2011, although it subsequently came out of it. In turn, the carrier version, the F-35C, caused difficulties with the location of its arrester hook, which was determined by the plane's radar-avoiding stealth design, proving, however, inadequate for catching the wire on landing. Moreover, there are difficulties in integrating and test-ing the complex software that runs the F-35's electronics and sensors. In 2011, test flights were stopped when a defective valve in the power system was discovered.[16]

This was part of a crisis of system failures that saw the F-22 Raptor also grounded after a defect was found with its oxygen system. Indeed, the F-22, a truly stealthy aircraft, has been beset by problems since it began to enter service in 2006. In turn, the F-35 may prove to be an expense too far and an entirely unnecessary system. Indeed, the loss of all, or part of, the program was mentioned in late 2011 as a possible outcome of defense cuts,[17] but the program was not abandoned. The cost also led to the facetious forecast that, by 2054, the United States would be able to afford only one combat aircraft, although the cost of the Department of Defense was easily overshadowed by the debt creat-ed by social programs. At any rate, the fate of the F-35 reflects the rapid rise of obsolescence, but also the abiding issues, for air power, as for other branches of the military, of confusion in goals, limitations in func-tion, and changing tactical, operational, and strategic parameters.

The capabilities of Western aircraft became more of an issue be-cause of the maiden flights of competitor fifth-generation fighters: the Russian Sukhoi T-50 (PAK-FA) in 2010 and the Chinese Chengdu J-20 in 2011, the latter intended to replace Russian aircraft in Chinese ser-vice. These aircraft are designed to be stealthy, agile, aware, fast, and lethal, and thus fifth generation. India (which had taken delivery of the Su-30 MK1 fighter-bomber in 2002) and Vietnam are believed to be export customers for the Sukhoi T-50, thus helping in part to cover the development costs. These aircraft threaten to make obsolete conven-tional third- and fourth-generation fighters that lack stealth technology and, in particular, to weaken the West's air power advantage by chang-ing likely key ratios in air combat. The T-50 is scheduled to enter service in 2016, but may not do so until 2020. In parallel with their development, both the Chinese and the Russians further affected the possible capability of the air power of other states by developing large and effective forces of surface-to-air missiles, notably the Russian SAM-20 and the Chinese HQ-9. In 2014, Russia agreed in principle to the sale of the S-400 air-defense missile system (which has a range of four hundred kilometers) to China, as well as the Su-36 aircraft. In 2015, it agreed to provide an advanced air-defense missile system to Iran.

Meanwhile, the number of states in the 2010s that invested in new fighters indicated the continued significance of this platform. Thus, Denmark, in the 2014–17 Defense Agreement, has undertaken to replace its fleet of aging F-16 fighters, its largest defense procurement program in a generation. Similarly, at the end of 2013, having participated in the development phase of the F-35, the Netherlands decided to replace its sixty-one F-16s by buying thirty-seven F-35s: their order for the first eight was placed on March 26, 2015. The number the Netherlands can afford has dropped as the unit cost soared. Norway has ordered fifty-two F-35s. In contrast, Canada has pushed back plans to replace its F/A-18 Hornets. It bought 138 in 1982–88, but only about half were flying by the mid-2000s. Given the need to operate up into the Arctic, discussion in Canada focuses on the need for a reliable two-engine versus a single-engine aircraft, and over the need for a large fleet given technological advances, specifically the use of drones. Other states did not turn to the United States for planes. Zimbabwe, for example, has about forty-five older, combat-capable Russian and Chinese fighter aircraft. Egypt, India, and Qatar agreed to buy the French Rafale. In 2015, Argentina negotiated with Russia to lease twelve long-range "Fencer" bombers with which they could threaten the British position in the Falkland Islands.

The importance of specialized bombers was highlighted by the reintroduction of long-range patrol flights by the Russian air force's strategic bomber fleet, notably into the North Sea in 2014. That year, NATO intercepted Russian aircraft near its borders over four hundred times, more than four times the number in 2013. In 2015, Russian "Bear" bombers, without clearance or communication, flew down the English Channel, disrupting civilian flights. Such sorties were designed to test defenses, to carry out intelligence gathering, and to exert political pressure. At the same time, the Russian aircraft were frequently obsolescent, or at least far from cutting edge. Ironically, Russia may

wake a sleeping American military and economic giant and thus ultimately thwart its own buildup. There is much American economic capital sitting on the sidelines that could be invested.

Cost was a key element in deciding whether to purchase new aircraft
such as the F-35. The more complex the systems, the more costly they
are, especially when they do not work as predicted or when other problems arise. This is true of the F-22 and the F-35, and will remain true
for all future fast jets and, indeed, any modern weapon system. Part of
the problem is how the projects are costed in the first place and the
timetable that is imposed for development and deployments. These
problems are exacerbated by the increasing sophistication of the aircraft
systems. Aside from affecting new projects, cost ensured that aircraft
were not upgraded as necessary if they were to match developing capabilities. This was true of the F-16s of most Eastern and Southern European states in the 2000s.

The questions over the F-35 in part arise because of the cost. However, the notion that all aspects of such a complex system can be got
right the first time, the common view among politicians and the public,
is misplaced, and the solutions are not easy to find because of the
complexity of the systems. The main question is how any aircraft will
perform in combat environments, and the answer will depend on many
factors besides its technical specifications. The hardware cannot be isolated from the real world in which it operates. Then the question of how
one aircraft performs against another is as much about the ability and
training of the pilot as the capability of the aircraft.

The course of air-power inflation has vindicated the 1942 argument
of Nicholas Spykman, a prominent American geopolitician who contributed to the notion of containment, that only large states would be able
to sustain air-, sea-, and land-based warfare.[18] Defense expenditure was
again under particular pressure in the 2010s, as a result not only of fiscal
problems arising from the economic downturn of the late 2000s but also
of a widespread popular reluctance to spend on the military. By 2014,
the official NATO figures on military expenditure indicated, alongside a
guideline (to the United States an unfulfilled commitment) of 2 percent
of GDP, that the United States was spending 4.4 percent, Canada 1
percent, and the European NATO powers an average of 1.6 percent.
The latter included France with 1.9 percent, Germany (the largest
economy) with 1.3, Italy with 1.2, and Spain with 0.9. Britain struggled

to maintain 2 percent, although in 2015 the new British government committed itself to this percentage until 2025. The real average for the European NATO powers may have been closer to 1.3 percent. Meanwhile, cost, as well as the wish to cut imports, encouraged India to press forward with the development of indigenous aerospace technology.

Alongside the issue of maintaining existing aircraft as opposed to introducing new ones, came that with reference to munitions. For example, B-61 nuclear gravity bombs, which are designed to be dropped by B-2 bombers, were refurbished in the 2000s. However, the prospect of extending the life of the tactical version has been compromised by the question of whether the F-35 will have that capability as the F-16 does.[19]

CHINA AND JAPAN

The development of Chinese air power is a consequence of its economic strength and its political ambitions. This development, in mass, technology, and modernization, poses major problems for other East Asian states, as well as for the United States. In particular, there has been an exacerbation of the vulnerability of Taiwan, notably to an initial precision bombardment that would degrade its defenses, making it vulnerable to an assault. China has had a long time to plan, prepare, and train for such an attack, not least by gaining intelligence, and Taiwan's proximity to China makes the task of defense harder. In response, renewed interest in the concept of the AirSea Battle began to percolate from 2011–12. Many in the Pentagon, not necessarily the air force, had become convinced that the overwhelming emphasis on COIN left the air force not ready for major conventional operations against a peer competitor such as China. The systems that had been developed, especially the current fleet of UAVs, were seen as inadequate for a "forced entry" operation against China, which had developed an "anti-access/area-denial" philosophy. While the navy was in many respects the senior partner in the development of the AirSea concept, many of the traditional claims from the army and marines resurfaced in criticism of the air force.

Air and maritime vulnerability and preparedness have also been identified as key issues in recent Japanese defense policies. In November 2013, China unilaterally declared an ADIZ (air defense identification zone), over the East China Sea beyond its territorial waters, that overlaps with Japan's own zone. This requires all foreign aircraft entering the zone to submit flight plans. Moreover, the number of Chinese unidentified flights, for which Japan scrambles fighters, has increased dramatically in the last four years, supplementing the long-standing need to scramble against Russian bombers, although there have only been a few actual violations of Japanese air space. Since July 2013, Chinese military aircraft have conducted long-range flight operations over the Pacific, with Y-8 early-warning aircraft and H-6 bombers flying through the Ryukyu island chain, part of Japan, which includes the American bases on Okinawa. The Chinese also constructed air bases on atolls and islands they claim in the South China Sea, islands they built up.

In response to Chinese steps, Japan increased its defense expenditure and decided, in 2012, to purchase the F-35 as its next-generation fighter. It had long wanted the F-22, but the United States had imposed a de facto ban on its export. Japan is also developing its own stealth fighter. Japan's indigenous air industry has not been as active as its shipbuilding industry. It tends to procure aircraft from, or jointly develop them with, the United States. Developing aircraft engines has proved a real difficulty for Japan, which is increasingly challenged by the need to maintain industrial expertise amid fewer orders for military aircraft. This is a problem that also faces other states, and one that underlines the significance of arms sales. The Japanese decision in 2014 to relax its long-standing ban on weapons exports and codevelopment was made in part to lower the cost of procuring advanced systems. Moreover, Japan's air capabilities have been fundamentally limited by several self-imposed restrictions springing from Japan's post-1945 commitment to pacifism. One is aerial refueling capability, which has only recently begun to be addressed, and slowly. In addition, Japan does not maintain bomber aircraft, or jet aircraft carriers, as opposed to helicopter carriers, notably the *Hyuga* and the *Izumo*. Carriers are banned under the constitution because they exceed the requirements of self-defense and provide the ability to attack other countries. Delivered in March 2015, the *Izumo* was a "helicopter-carrying destroyer" according to the government, and did not have the hangars or engineering facilities necessary to service fixed-wing aircraft, nor the catapults needed to launch them.

Nevertheless, the *Izumo* was as big as Second World War carriers; could take the V-22 Osprey, which Japan intends to acquire; and could be modified to launch V/STOLs, notably the F-35B.[20] After the Cold War, it was argued in Japan that the navy focused too much on antisubmarine warfare and that a more balanced force was required. By the 2010s, however, in response to the rapid increase in the quality and size of the Chinese submarine force, the emphasis on an antisubmarine naval aviation capability had been reaffirmed.

As a consequence of Chinese expenditure and of international disputes, notably over the East and South China Seas, other regional powers also sought to develop their air power. Malaysia, which also claims part of the disputed Spratly Islands, plans to replace its MIG-29s, due to retire in 2015, with thirty-six to forty new fighters. Moreover, China's buildup and actions affected America's deployment of aircraft in the Western Pacific. Thus, the island of Guam was upgraded from 2006 as a central strategic operating base, the upgrading including hardened storage facilities for B-2 bombers as part of a continuous bomber presence there. American commanders were clear on the deterrent capability that the stealthy B-2s were intended to offer against a China that currently has no means to engage them.[21]

In part in response to China, India is investing heavily in a new generation of combat aircraft. This was linked to the air force's reluctance to support the army and, instead, to its determination to secure a deep-strike strategic role. The prospect of the latter, however, was challenged by both Pakistan and China possessing nuclear capability. The army's alternative, "Cold Start," a limited nonnuclear war in which, with close air support, the army operates near the frontier, has been downplayed by the air force. Thus, on a long-standing pattern, the Indian services remain ready to fight different wars. The air force offers neither the deterrence of its nuclear rocketry nor the ability to pursue local advantage seen in integrated operations with the army.[22]

Both China and India have spent enormous amounts of time, resources, and intellectual capital attempting to develop their capabilities. In many countries, the focus on air power has been oriented toward prestige rather than capability, but China and India are each intent on developing a force that can go to war and be successful. They are attempting to learn from Western powers, wrestling to integrate space, cyber, missile, and other capabilities, and questioning what types of capabilities they need as rising powers. For both countries, the Soviet/Russian model has lost its earlier appeal, but, in many respects, they remain tied to aspects of that model due to the systems in their inventories. Both China and India have spent a great deal of their time over the past two decades learning and applying lessons to develop their air forces. This is an important development because these are two independent air forces not closely tied to either the United States/NATO or, as previously, Russia. Their ability to break out and develop new concepts and capabilities may present some surprises in the future, particularly in terms of influencing other non-Western air forces.

Operating in response to the danger of attack by North Korea rather than China, South Korean air power in 2013 still relied on massive American power projection while including 600 helicopters with the army, 60 helicopters or patrol aircraft with the navy, and 420 fighters, 60 ISR aircraft, 40 air-mobility aircraft, 190 trainers, and 40 helicopters with the air force. That year, the Korean-made FA-50 fighter/attack aircraft was deployed.

NAVAL AIR POWER

Naval air power remained dominated by the United States. In 2008, the United States had eleven operational carriers, a number that could surge to fifteen or sixteen as a result of drawing on the powerful reserve fleet. Each carrier strike force is a key element of power projection. The United States in 2008 also had ten carrier wings. Despite talk of reducing the number of carriers and wings, the carrier capability remains robust and a reminder of the continuing close relationship between American power and naval strength. The launch, in 2009, at Newport News, of the *George H. W. Bush*, the last of the nuclear-powered *Nimitz* class carriers (which displaced seventy-eight thousand tons), was a testimony to the American defense economy and the willingness to spend money on the military. Work has started on the *Gerald R. Ford*, the first of a class of four carriers, each of which is estimated to cost $13 billion to build (up from $11.2 billion in 2009). The aircraft are to be launched by electromagnetic catapults.

Carriers, moreover, remained important to American power projection and in operational terms. In 2010, the *George Washington's* involvement in large joint naval exercises with South Korea in the Yellow Sea demonstrated an American military commitment against North Korean aggression. In 2012, the *Abraham Lincoln*, supported by five other warships, sailed through the Straits of Hormuz in order to underline the right of passage under international law, and thus to repel any Iranian threat to the export of oil from the Gulf. In practice, American army ground-based air defense in the Gulf states permitted the navy's freedom of movement by providing an air-defense umbrella. In 2014, the *George H. W. Bush* from the Gulf and the *Carl Vinson* from the Red Sea played the key role in airstrikes against ISIS targets in Iraq and Syria.

Other states also sought to develop carrier capacity. "An aircraft carrier is a symbol of the country's overall national strength as well as the competitiveness of the country's force." This 2008 declaration by Colonel Huang Xueping of the Chinese Defense Ministry[23] reflected the extent to which military power was a matter of image as much as lethality. Yet, there were also particular strategic needs. The deployment of American carrier battle groups to protect Taiwan from Chinese threats, notably in 1996, underlined China's determination to develop its naval air power. The sea trials in 2011 of *Liaoning*, China's first carrier, a Soviet-era *Kuznetsov*-class carrier bought from Ukraine, intensified speculation about strategic rivalry with the United States. So also did the carrier's first launch and recovery of J-15 fighters in 2012, and the tensions when it was deployed in the East China Sea in 2013. China plans to increase the size of its carrier fleet.

For smaller powers, carriers imply great-power status. Their procurement is heavily based on considerations of status and image. Under the 2010 Strategic Defence and Security Review, Britain retired the serving aircraft carriers and the remaining four Maritime Patrol and Joint Force Harrier squadrons, which, however, weakened its ability to intervene in Libya in 2011, a point made at the time. Britain is building two sixty-five-thousand-tonne carriers, the *Queen Elizabeth* and the *Prince of Wales*. For long, it looked as though one would be sold or placed in reserve because of the cost of running two. However, in 2014, Britain announced that it was planned that both would become operational. This decision can be regarded as political and institutional, in the shaping of meeting assumptions about great-power status, rather than reflecting a sensible response to the vulnerabilities of carriers, notably to swarm missile attacks. In this respect, they become too valuable to hazard, and thus uneconomic. Moreover, expenditure on the carriers threatens to leave little money for other new warships.[24]

Other countries also maintained or increased their carrier force. Resources will continue to be a key issue. The announcement by Vladimir Putin in July 2008 that Russia would build five carriers, each to be the basis of a carrier group, lacked credibility, not least due to a lack of shipyards. Moreover, the frequent repairs required by the *Admiral Kuznetsov*, the sole Russian carrier, indicated the problems of maintaining capability. When, in 2007, the carrier was sent into the Atlantic and then the Mediterranean, as part of the first deployment of major Russian warships since 1995, it was escorted by two tugs in case of need. The dramatic fall in the price of oil in 2014–15 affected Russia's ability to sustain its naval plans, including claims that by 2020 it would have 6 carrier groups, 800 new aircraft, and 1,400 new helicopters. However, Russian defense expenditure is steadily rising, as is its determination to have hegemonic power over its neighbors.

In 2014, India had two carriers on active service, one the formerly British *Hermes*, slated for decommission in 2015, and one the rebuild of the Soviet *Gorshkov*, commissioned in 2013, with another, a new *Vikrant*, launched but several years from commissioning, and a fourth planned. Italy had two in 2014, and Brazil, France, Russia, Spain, and Thailand each had one. In October 2010, France sent a carrier strike group led by the nuclear-powered carrier *Charles de Gaulle* to the Indian Ocean. This provided an air presence in Afghanistan and the Indian Ocean and paid a port visit to Abu Dhabi as a key element of a new French strategic engagement with the region. In 2011, that carrier played a successful role in NATO operations over Libya, and in 2015 in operations against ISIS in Iraq. Although it is small by comparison with American nuclear-powered carriers, the *Charles de Gaulle* is still an impressive, although somewhat unreliable, vessel. Its air group includes twelve Rafale fighters, two Hawkeye early-warning aircraft, light and medium helicopters, and nine Super Etendard strike aircraft. However, its replacement is proving politically difficult due to the cost, and it is likely that France will not build another nuclear-powered carrier. Aircraft carriers were not the sole element. In 2014, France blocked the sale to Russia of two *Mistral*-class helicopter carriers capable of supporting amphibious operations.

The use of carriers addressed some of the issues posed by the deployment of fast jets to foreign air bases, notably the support and security of the host nation, overflight permission, and logistical capability. However, as a classic instance of the problems of insufficient mass and problematic resilience, problems more generally facing the slimmed-down air forces of the early twenty-first century, one carrier is not enough to maintain round-the-clock capability. This is especially so if the carrier is under repair, which was an issue for the *Charles de Gaulle*, as it had persistent serious difficulties. Ordered in 1986 and laid down in 1989, the carrier was launched in 1994 but not commissioned until 2001. There were problems with propellers and the rudder, while the nuclear power plant was refueled between September 2007 and December 2008. In 2014, the United States (which needs carriers on station) had three on operations and one more en route to a patrol area, with the others on training missions or being maintained or refurbished. Britain requires two carriers in order to keep one ready for action. There has been talk about Anglo-French cooperation to address the problem.

The apparent significance of carriers rose in 2013–14 as tension over Chinese expansionism in the East and South China Seas increased. At the same time, these interlinked crises, notably that between China and Japan over the East China Sea, indicated the extent to which conventional naval air power was supplemented by other forms and factors, particularly the role of missiles, whether land or sea based. The extent to which Chinese-based missiles and submarines might inhibit American action on behalf of Japan became a key issue in military calculation. In October 2013, the United States agreed to base surveillance drones and reconnaissance aircraft in Japan so as to patrol waters in the region. At the same time, not all states that could afford it pursued a carrier capacity. Thus, the Australian Defense White Paper of 2009 sought a capability for land-attack cruise missiles deployed in guided-missile destroyers. Twenty-four new helicopters are to fly off two new amphibious-landing ships.

CONCLUSIONS

As with other branches of the military, the "lessons of air power" were very much affected by the perspective provided by the crises of the moment. These crises offered differing insights depending on whether the focus was on state-to-state confrontation or on counterinsurgency warfare. Thus, those who focused on the latter, and on asymmetric threats as a whole, could be skeptical about the value of all, or some, fast jet fighters, carriers, and nuclear weapons.[25] However, air power provided much of value for both state-to-state confrontation and for COIN, not only at the operational and tactical level but also in international power politics. The operational and tactical dimensions were clear in the case of the war between Russia and Georgia in 2008, in which, as a result of each being part of the former Soviet Union, both sides used Su-25 ground-attack aircraft. Despite Russia having more aircraft, it initially failed to win air supremacy, had five aircraft shot down, and lacked the air-land communication that the Georgians enjoyed.

In this and other cases, arguments for a strategic value for air power were possibly less than convincing in the late 2000s and early 2010s. Perhaps as a result, in the early twenty-first century, there have been almost no major theoretical innovations or developments in air power. Practitioners today are more centered on method than outcomes. In the United States, it is striking to realize that, notably in the *Air and Space Power Journal* and other Air Force publications intended to reflect new ideas, the thinking, instead, tends to be based on technologies, geography, operating processes, and other nontheoretical perspectives. Air power was largely built on a set of promises and possibilities about what it could deliver in the future. There is considerably less of that today and no single thesis to anchor new thinking. At the same time, Russian and Chinese policies suggest continuing strategic opportunities for air power. Moreover, whereas in the past the flexibility of air power meant that the aircraft for contingency operations could easily be found from within the high-technology force, the converse is not true. Aircraft designed solely to help ground forces in bushfire wars will have limited value against the deep targets of well-armed opponents.

Separate from discussion over the effectiveness of air power came that over its morality. The proportionality, practice, and ethos of bombing attracted particular attention.[26] This was true of air operations past and present. Whereas Britain's Fighter Command enjoyed good postwar coverage due to its key role in defeating German air attack in the Battle of Britain in 1940, the treatment of Bomber Command was more ambivalent. It proved easier to commemorate the underdog and the defender of 1940, even though the individual bombers that subsequently attacked Germany were highly vulnerable. In Germany, after decades in which suffering from Allied bombing was overshadowed by German war crimes, there was an emphasis, notably from the 2000s, on German casualties, and thus on the alleged iniquities of Allied bombing. A focus on the bombing, and on Germans as victims, offered many a way to deal with the legacy of Nazism, as well as to provide a history for a new, reunited Germany.[27] Many (although far from all) Germans are disinclined to consider adequately Germany's wartime role in beginning terror bombing; its willingness to move to use rockets simply fired against civilian targets, notably Antwerp and London; the particularly vicious nature of the wartime German state; and the extent to which it enjoyed popular support. Japan also presents itself as a victim of wartime bombing.

Technology has affected the perception of bombing. The discussion of ethics is not only historical. In recent years, digital photography linked to easily accessible satellite communications has become more insistent. The need for accuracy and precision in the employment of air-delivered weapons is now linked inexorably with the ability to report its impact in real time. The impact of collateral damage cannot be hidden, which makes the hunt for ever-greater accuracy a political imperative, thus greatly increasing the cost of weapon systems and their delivery platforms and limiting the number of occasions when air power might be used. This is an aspect of the degree to which air power is frequently viewed as somehow unfair, cruel, and mechanistic. Air power itself may lend itself to populist hyperbole, as with the very loose journalistic use of terms such as "carpet bombing."

This discussion over morality interacted with the discussion over the advisability of bombing in COIN operations. The success of air power against Iraqi ground forces in 1991 and to a lesser extent in 2003 had been considered a template and a precursor for future operations, but reality proved otherwise. The advisability of bombing in COIN operations was questioned given the frequent difficulty of identifying targets separable from civilians and the problems posed by a hostile response to bombing in a context within which local support was sought. Thus, in Afghanistan, air strikes compromised such support and also had an adverse impact elsewhere, notably in neighboring Pakistan.[28]

Indeed, as part of the reaction against what was held to be inappropriate triumphalism, a reaction that the apparent intractability of interventions in Iraq and Afghanistan encouraged, considerable skepticism about air power was expressed in the late 2000s, including by prominent American and British military figures and commentators. A stress on "boots on the ground" increased skepticism and exacerbated criticism, although, in practice, the presence, firepower, support, intelligence, and command and control of such troops depended, both immediately and ultimately, heavily on air power. Situational understanding and network-enabled capabilities were especially reliant on air power.

As throughout the history of air power, these and related differences over its value and use, and concerning the nature of its integration with other services, played out differently in accordance with contrasting national strategies and institutional inheritances.[29] At the same time, the particular characteristics of air power took a role, as with the Israeli ability in 2007 to destroy by air attack the nuclear reactor being built in Syria, repeating the success against the more distant Iraqi reactor at Osirak in 1981. However, in 2007, it was cyber-capabilities that disrupted Syrian radar and also located the site of the plant.

Having begun the chapter with an emphasis on COIN and on the problems facing air power, it is instructive, at the close, to consider continued confidence in air power. In March 2006, the Singaporean air force announced its intention to develop into a new generation of capability, extending from being able to defend Singapore from the air, the "first generation," and controlling the skies, the "second generation," to shaping the surface battles on the ground and sea. A series of new commands were accordingly established in 2007–8 for each of the major missions: the Air Defense and Operations Command, the UAV Command, the Participation Command (for taking part in land and sea combat), the Air Combat Command, and the Air Power Generation Command. The Singaporeans used American F-15s, F-16s, Apache helicopters, and munitions and trained in exercises held in the United States. Singaporean training focused not on COIN operations, but on air-to-air combat, which reflected the troubling regional environment, notably rivalry with Indonesia and the threats in the South China Sea.

A more urgently troubling regional environment lay behind a transformation in European air concerns in 2014–15 as the Ukraine crisis escalated. This crisis had seen the use of air power, as Ukraine sought to support its beleaguered position in its eastern provinces, notably by transporting troops, while Russian-backed separatists, in turn, shot down aircraft. A Russian Buk missile was also used to shoot down an overflying Malaysian passenger aircraft that was presumably mistaken for a Ukrainian aircraft, although it is not clear whether separatists or forward-deployed Russian army personnel shot it down. The crisis became a broader fear about Russian intentions, especially against NATO members in the Baltic, one encouraged by the movement of advanced missile systems to Crimea, large exercises near the Polish border, and the increase in Russian air activity, including the shadowing of NATO warships in the Black Sea in 2015.

In response, there were attempts to answer the threat of Russian aggression, notably with the use of air policing in Operation Atlantic Resolve to support the Baltic republics, and also with exercises to show support for Poland. In February 2015, the United States deployed twelve A-10s to Germany, a sign of increased military commitment to Europe. Aircraft, yet again, represented a rapid way to deploy and demonstrate power and commitment.

12

INTO THE FUTURE

Before the present century has run its course, there is nothing fantastic in suggesting that complete armies will be whisked through pure speed a thousand miles above the Earth's surface, to speed at 10,000 miles an hour toward their enemy. —J. F. C. Fuller, 1944[1]

Consideration of the present leads automatically into the future, as procurement and training are for these ends. The key arguments of the present about policy and doctrine necessarily relate to the future. There is the tension of major conventional conflict versus COIN, that of expensive, big-ticket systems versus flexible, inexpensive ones, and that of a primary versus supportive mode of operation. The first argument is about skills and functions, the second about budgets and systems, and the third about who leads and who is led.

Precision and stealth apparently offer politicians an almost guaranteed source of lethal violence, limited by the intelligence on which to plan. However, questions include the utility of that violence, at what tempo, at what scale, and targeted against whom? Thanks to technological development and potential, there is increasing speculation about the likely trajectory of air power, in both the short and the long term. In particular, the relative role of unmanned aircraft, missiles (such as highly developed, long-range cruise missiles), and electromagnetic pulses attract attention, both in their own right and for what they mean for the future of manned flight. However, these do not exhaust the possible future repertoire of air power. There are a range of technologies, and a related range of platforms, on offer. Thus, with swarms of robotic "insects" (i.e., micro-flyers capable, thanks to miniaturization, of military tasks), already in operational employment, there is increasing interest in their possible uses.

Past ideas of future air capabilities and conflict are instructive because they highlight what could be hoped. Some ideas remain implausible. Thus, in 1930, Archibald Wavell, then a British army brigadier, later a field marshal, noted, "A fleet of flying tanks landing behind an enemy and then shedding their wings and attacking him in rear is an inviting dream but not likely of fulfillment for a long time, if ever." More significantly, Wavell doubted the availability of sufficient aircraft to fulfill large-scale supply needs.[2] That past possibilities were frequently not fulfilled does not mean, however, that others will not be brought to fruition, with concept leading to development, manufacture, procurement, and use, possibly in a rapid process. Of all the services, the air force usually has the clearest vision of how it wants to fight, in part because it is the service that most heavily depends on the promise of new technology.[3]

Alongside a focus on technology, it is also possible to concentrate on the likely social, political, and environmental contexts of air power. This approach entails an appreciation of the challenges facing states, as air power is, due to its requirements, a means of conflict particularly wielded by the state. Thus, the question can be posed, what does air power mean in the case of "wars among the people," to employ a term coined by General Rupert Smith, UN commander during the Bosnia crisis in 1995,[4] or, alternatively, in the case of more state-to-state conflict? The interacting impact of context, policies, procurement, and tasks provides a dynamic and unsettled background. Tasking often puts air power to the fore, as in the repeated possibility, in the 2000s and 2010s, of an Israeli strike against the Iranian nuclear program.

Air power offers a swiftness in deployability and delivery that has tactical, operational, and strategic benefits. Air power, moreover, provides utility across a wide range of military tasks, as well as many soft-power roles. In part, this capability is a question of utility through reach and reach through utility.

TECHNOLOGY

Much of the development in the future will stem from an extension in the current characteristics of aircraft, missiles, and related systems. These include changing possibilities in propulsion, fuel, materials, aerodynamics, and computing capability.

At the simplest level, current and future weaponry suggests a continuing overlap between air power and artillery, in terms of delivering force at a distance, which underlines the need for their integration. For example, from 2010, Israel's capability vis-à-vis Hamas forces in Gaza was affected by the deployment by Hamas of the Russian-made Kornet antitank missile, which is capable of piercing forty-seven-inch-thick armor at a range of over three miles. There are technologies at issue that are more classically air-power related, as well as others that offer different overlaps. In the first case, there is the possibility of higher-speed aircraft. These may be capable of "skipping" on the upper atmosphere of the Earth and of transporting troops anywhere in the world within two hours, as Fuller suggested. In the shorter term, it is more likely that the upper atmosphere will be used for the delivery of ordinance. Conceptually, the USAF seeks an aircraft that can deliver globally in two hours. Although not without major problems, notably in terms of ensuring accuracy, such power projection is, and will be, less problematic than that of moving troops at hitherto unprecedented speed. In the early 2010s, the Americans tested the Falcon, a hypersonic vehicle (above Mach 5 speed) propelled into space by a rocket and then moved on a preset trajectory to attack a target on earth. Moreover, the Lockheed SR-72, which could enter service in 2030 if it can retain its funding, is designed to provide a hypersonic high-level reconnaissance aircraft, which could be manned or remotely piloted. There is no equivalent for the movement of troops. Indeed, the characteristic of humans, in the shape of their tolerance to circumstances—for example, g-forces—would need to be reengineered to match even a portion of the possibilities for weapons and delivery systems. So also for the materials used. The possibility of space-to-earth weapons is also significant, with only nuclear space-to-earth weapons outlawed by treaty.[5]

A different form of overlap was provided by cyberwarfare, which became more prominent from the late 2000s. Air and space forces, at the technological leading edge, are highly reliant on computer-based systems, on data links, and on space-based communications. At its most blatant, computers and code can be damaged, if not destroyed, by the detonation of an exoatmospheric nuclear weapon that could produce an electromagnetic pulse over a wide area, typically the size of a third of the United States. However, in a more subtle, and thus deniable, way, enemy code could be inserted, or even activated from a dormant state, within an enemy's defenses with the host having little knowledge. Most nations are developing cyber and anticyber capabilities and organizations. Cyberwarfare also poses a major threat to the use of information by aircraft and UAVs, and thus to their operations. However, much of cyberwarfare is vulnerable to detection, deception, and disruption, which is also the case with electromagnetic pulses.

The spread of drones has emphasized the extent to which technological change can be rapid and nonlinear. The likelihood of rapid change in the capabilities of UAVs is high. Already certain high-altitude UAVs employ solar panels, thus greatly extending their endurance, although also increasing a dependency on weather and the climate. Enhancing the extent to which weapons were operated by remote control, but moving beyond this modus operandi, missiles and drones that carried out attacks without direct human control were deployed by a number of powers in the mid-2010s, including Britain, Israel, Norway, and the United States. Termed autonomous weapons, though in practice usually highly automated weapons, for example Israel's Iron Dome, they relied on artificial intelligence and sensors to select targets and initiate an attack.[6] As a challenge to major powers, drones may also empower the underdog.

As a different instance of an existing capability that provides possibilities for future change, stealth technology offers a challenge. It also underlines the extent of defense inflation, which has proved particularly serious for aircraft costs, and all costs: procurement, maintenance, and running costs, including munitions and training pilots.[7] Stealth technology led to much matching and leapfrogging competition in the 2000s and early 2010s, with espionage a key element. The Chinese Chengdu J-20 stealth aircraft allegedly drew heavily on details of the plans of the American F-35 supplied by hackers. In response to Chinese and Russian advances, Boeing produced designs for a next-generation stealth aircraft, and on January 29, 2015, Robert Work, the American deputy defense secretary, announced that the American government would earmark funding for a "next-generation X-plane" in the proposed 2016 defense budget, which would also see investment in missile defense, space-control capabilities, nuclear weaponry, and advanced sensors. Planned stealth fighters would provide high-speed strike weapons. Given that systems are costly and take time to develop, produce, and deploy, it is necessary to introduce platforms, weapons, and capabilities that will have a valuable longevity, not simply a value when they are introduced.

Alongside the emphasis on change, it is pertinent to note that aircraft remain, and are likely to remain, limited in their capacity to carry volume and weight, certainly when compared to container ships. The importance of rapid long-range deployment explains the significance of acquiring modern air transports, notably the Boeing C-17 Globemaster. The contrast between aircraft and shipping is even more striking in the case of transporting fuel, which is very much a bulk product. The contrast is also seen with the movement of people, including troops. Thus, there is a need for the prepositioning of heavy equipment as well as for the rapid deployment of troops.

ORGANIZATION AND DOCTRINE

The use of aircraft will be more significant than their capabilities, not least because these capabilities emerge through use. This point is true for the present and the near future, and will be true for further ahead. This is clear with the leading air power, the United States. At present, the tension between close air support and strategic air power remains particularly apparent in usage, whatever the attempt to resolve this tension in doctrine. This tension was to the fore in an incident that occurred on June 9, 2014, in the Gaza Valley in Zabul Province, Afghanistan. A unit of American and Afghan soldiers cleared the Taliban from part of a valley and then awaited the arrival of Chinook helicopters to take them back to a forward operating base. The men came under enemy fire, a B-1B arrived in response, and, from twelve thousand feet on a five-mile orbit, it dropped two five-hundred-pound bombs that, in the event, killed not the Taliban, but, instead, five Americans and one allied Afghan. This mistake reflected a series of operational, equipment, and training errors, not least flying beyond the range of the pilots' night-vision goggles, and the provision of inaccurate information by the USAF ground controller, as well as the difficulties in tactical radio communications with the B-1B in mountainous terrain.

In turn, the episode brought up broader issues, with the head of the Army Special Operations Command rejecting the US Central Command's official investigation, by a USAF general, which criticized the troops. This rejection, and the subsequent criticism of the investigation, highlighted the inadequacy of training in the air and on the ground and the unsuitability of the equipment in strategic bombers for the complex mission of close air support, as well as the questionable effort by the USAF to replace the only aircraft dedicated to such support, the A-10 Warthog. The effective A-10 flies lower than the B-1B, and its pilot is accustomed to close air support and to making appropriate use of night-vision goggles.[8] However, even an A-10 pilot can make mistakes and hit friendlies. Indeed, operational errors are inevitable, and no amount of technology is ever going to eliminate them.

Possibly, but with the cost of duplication, the army would be better off creating its own fixed-wing fleet, buying a new model A-10, or acquiring more drones for the role of ground support. This course would be on the pattern of the marines, who provide, with their integral air arm, the best instance of ground-air cooperation. Moreover, they very much focus on practicalities in the deployment of air power as part of an integrated pattern in which traditional themes are to the fore. Thus, in 2012, during Exercise Geiger Fury, the marines rapidly refurbished the Second World War–era bases and runways at Tinian Island in the Western Pacific in order to re-create a mission where marines have to establish an airfield able to refuel aircraft.[9] This task was very different from that of aerial refueling.

Highlighting a tension seen from the 1910s, strategic air operations are best left to experts, in the shape of a separate air force committed to deep strike, bombing, air-to-air combat, strategic nuclear capabilities, and space. Close air support, in contrast, is best directed by the supported, not the supporting, arm or service, in short by the army, navy, and marines, each with their own integral air support, which provides a way to obtain the necessary military-service culture. Air dominance and strategic bombing remains the USAF's priority, and netcentric warfare its thesis, which puts the USAF at variance with the army over the nature and purpose of war and how it should be prosecuted. The air force feels most comfortable when acting alone and according to a strategy of its own making. In Afghanistan in the 2000s and early 2010s, divisions between the American services were such that the marines refused to integrate air controllers and other assets with the air force, while it was difficult for army units to get marine air-power support.

So also with Britain, which, with France, provides the bulk of the European Union's military strike capability. The history of the RAF is a proud one. Their leadership think corporately and strategically, and they are technically proficient—all, to a degree, more than among the officers of the British army. The latter are tribal (regimental) by nature, are instinctively more comfortable with "bushfire" contingency operations than general war and its accompanying strategic requirements, and, in some cases, appear to consider technology as best left to tradesmen. This cultural contrast has influenced, and continues to influence, the RAF approach to close air support. Being born out of the army originally, the RAF, like any new and younger organization, was anxious to distance itself, and thus preferred to operate independently. The RAF felt itself very much the junior service and, therefore, was anxious to assert and prove itself.

Moreover, the generally egocentric nature of fighter pilots does not lend itself to acting in operational support of anyone. Like the USAF, the RAF wish to be working at the strategic level, where, they claim, the technical superiority of air power provides a greater return for the investment in equipment, training, and effort involved, and thus justifies the cost. Indeed, in retirement in 1943, Lord Trenchard, the former head of the RAF, wrote a pamphlet in which he claimed, "The Air will dictate strategy and therefore dominate all wars because of its over-all influence."[10] Conversely, as a result of institutional memory, corporate culture, and organizational interests, close air support tends, in some states and in much of the theory, to be the Cinderella, or poor relation, of air power. Air support works best where the army and navy have retained their own integral close air support (for Britain the Army Air Corps, including Apache helicopters, and the Fleet Air Arm, respectively), or after a long period of enforced joint operations, as in Afghanistan by the early 2010s. In the mid-2010s, the RAF modified its Typhoons to carry the Brimstone, which was designed solely to destroy ground targets, notably tanks and artillery.

Similar problems, of operation, organization, and style, affect the use of air power by other states. For example, in Afghanistan, the killing of civilians as a result of the dropping of two five-hundred-pound GBU-38 precision-guided JDAMs near Kunduz on September 4, 2009, reflected the extent to which German commanders chose risk-averse weapon systems and tactics to protect their forces from possible harm.[11]

TASKING

Tensions in the present within states over military tasking throw light on the future, and also suggest why states will have contrasting outcomes in terms of policy, organization, doctrine, procurement, and performance. Alongside disagreements, the concept of synergy indicates that, in any future conflict, success will hinge on the ability to achieve successful combinations of air, land, sea, cyber, and space forces, as with the army fixing the enemy before air power destroys them. This ability will require the development of new, better-integrated organizational structures, as well as careful training of commanders and units, and appropriate systems of command, control, communications, and information appraisal and analysis. The heavy American investment in military infrastructure in space in the 2000s and 2010s indicates the commitment to such a synergy. At the same time, serious problems of coordination were suggested by the mismatch between the arrival times for different parts of the program. Such problems of coordination affect joint operations more generally.

As another cause of issues, indeed problems, the political imperatives will continue to ensure major requirements for air power while also affecting its use as well as the judgment of success. Depending on the circumstances, there will be contrasting requirements and very different alliance combinations, access, basing, overflight rights, targeting guidelines, and political support with which to pursue the resulting goals. Thus, in 2011, Norway withdrew its planes from the air operations over Libya because it did not agree with the goal of regime change.[12] Air power is a method of political signaling, to friends and foes alike.

States will be greatly challenged by nonstate actors, and at a variety of scales, including, but not only, in failed and failing states, while states that have not failed will continue to wield much of the world's power and to control much of its resources. Whatever the nature of the distribution of international power in the future, it is likely that major states will continue to have to plan for symmetrical and asymmetrical conflict, and for high- and low-tech military operations. In turn, these categories are malleable, may require continual redefinition, and can overlap. Nevertheless, states will see their legitimacy and ends defined in part in terms of conventional military forces, and will seek to use them to secure their interests, both actively and in terms of maintaining a deterrent capability. Air power will provide a key element in this equation, and those countries that allow themselves to become weak in the air may become pawns in a future conflict against an enemy with a command of the air.

13

CONCLUSIONS

"**W**e were very young in those days" is the most weighty phrase near the beginning of *The Case of the Constant Suicides*, a novel by the major Anglo-American detective writer John Dickson Carr. Published in 1941, this novel begins in London on September 1, 1940, before the heavy German air attacks on the city had started: "An air-raid alert meant merely inconvenience, with perhaps one lone raider droning somewhere."[1] By 1941, as today, the experience of bombing was very different, although not as different as it was to be by the end of the war in 1945. Bombing by 1945 had become a key experience notably of urban life, both in Europe and in East Asia. Refracted through the media and the arts, the civilian experience has to be remembered as a backdrop to the discussions about effectiveness and practicality throughout this book, although it was far from the only backdrop.

Air power has played a key role in the military history of the last century, both independently and affecting land and sea conflict. Air power has been particularly important at the tactical and operational levels. It has also been seen as a strategic tool, even if bringing this element to fruition has proved very difficult; and difficult, moreover, for the range of states that have sought to pursue this means. The debates about what air power can provide have taken considerably different directions based on whether the army was the dominant service and the degree to which the air force was independent. These issues raise questions not only about how best to present the history of air power, but also concerning its past and continuing rationale and relevance.[2] Air power, especially if missiles are included, has always appealed to those who are looking for "the modern," the "latest and the greatest," and for a strategic "magic bullet." However, the accounts of contemporaries about effectiveness, and the hopes of the advocates of air power, have frequently proved misplaced, and often seriously so. This is the case both for the military outcomes of its use and for their political consequences.

Nevertheless, despite the problems confronted in adapting circumstances, learning lessons, coping with the pressures of commitments, and responding to fiscal exigencies,[3] air power has dramatically changed equations for firepower and mobility. More specifically, both in its own right and as part of combined air operations, air power has made maneuver warfare a more central part of conflict. As a result, air power has greatly increased the tempo of war as well as its potential deadliness.

As with armored warfare when it was introduced in the 1910s, the perception of the capability of air power and its reality were very different. This was also true for fears of what it might mean for warfare. There is generally a poor understanding of the reliability of aircraft systems. In practice, the more complex a system, the less reliable it is. And there is the issue of appropriate use. Thus, air power is not a panacea. However, in one particular respect, air power fulfilled the hopes of some early advocates. Thanks to the successful integration of reconnaissance information with artillery, aircraft helped overcome the relative stasis of First World War land operations. In doing so, aircraft helped restore mobility and, at least, a sense of results to ground operations, although this achievement was heavily qualified in terms of outcomes. In the 1918 Allied victory on the Western Front, more was due to the effective use of artillery incorporating the advantages of air-derived information than to new weapons, whether tanks or aircraft, operating in ground-support roles, let alone to long-range bombing. Nevertheless, air power indeed proved part of the equation in translating advantages into the ability to defeat opposing forces on the ground, as it also did in 1918 with the British success against the Turks in Palestine.

This factor remained important in the understanding, presentation, and use of air power. All of the combatants in the Second World War believed in the value of air dominance or supremacy and in its impact on operations on the ground, even if not all pursued the latter with the immediacy understood by the term "ground support." Indeed, the stress on the war-winning dimension of air power encouraged Britain and the United States, neither of which saw their army as war winning, to focus not on ground support but on gaining an air dominance that could be used for strategic bombing campaigns against their opponents' home countries, rather than, at least as primarily intended, to affect operations on the ground. However, the latter was also an objective, even if the relationship between strategic bombing and theater dominance was frequently somewhat unclear in practice.

These goals and priorities were not static. They were affected by resources, opportunities, doctrine, and the ability to respond. Thus, the American ability to demonstrate flexibility and rethink the situation, and to plan and produce accordingly, led to the development and use of a long-range escort fighter capability. Similarly, in large part in response to Japanese advances in China and Japanese advances in the Pacific, the Americans moved their focus for air attacks on Japan from China-based aircraft to those operating from Pacific bases, and this had significant strategic and operational consequences. Ground support proved more significant from the outset for militaries that were reliant on their armies for war winning, rather than on strategic bombing. This was the case in the Second World War for Germany, Japan, the Soviet Union, and China.

The demonstration of air power in the 1940s challenged the traditional geopolitical dichotomy of land and sea.[4] Contemporaries, such as Carl Schmidt in *Land and Sea* (1942), argued that this would revolutionize geopolitics. The range and tempo of geopolitical rivalry was certainly different. During the Cold War, contrasting national legacies, priorities, and opportunities very much affected the protagonists. The United States and Britain continued to place an emphasis on strategic bombing, one greatly enhanced by the availability of nuclear weapons. In contrast, although the Soviet Union had effective long-range bombers, as it had not done during the Second World War, the stress there was on ground support.

In China, the stress was also on ground support. There, the legacy of the Second World War, when air operations in China against Japan had been handled by the Americans, was compounded by the revolutionary character of Maoist military thought. In particular, Mao Zedong, in his emphasis on guerrilla warfare, took further the anti–technological/

weaponry emphasis of early communist ideas and their conviction of the value of the revolutionary mass. This emphasis remained central to Chinese communist military thought until the 1990s, even though, under Mao, there was a commitment to new weaponry, certainly in the forms of jet aircraft and of missiles with atomic warheads.

Mao's ideas did not bring victory over the American-led UN forces in the Korean War (1950–53), but an emphasis on will, mass, and the negating of the technological advantages of the other side all proved significant across the world in the anti-Western insurrectionary struggles of the late 1940s to the mid-1970s. In practice, success or failure for the insurrections proved more complex in its causes and contexts, both militarily and politically, as the Vietnam wars, among others, showed. Moreover, when applied, in part or whole, later, these ideas met with mixed success, as in the case of Saddam Hussein's plans in 2003 for resistance against American attack.

Nevertheless, the problems latent in employing air power in COIN, or counterinsurgency operations, were present from the outset.[5] Tactical and operational limitations, including maintenance, logistics, and the security of air bases, were matched by strategic counterparts, notably the difficulties of obtaining an end to insurrection, in short of translating battlefield advantages into outcomes. The latter problem highlighted a disadvantage not only of air power but also for operations of the regular military as a whole. This problem, more generally, affected asymmetrical warfare, a type of warfare that could be waged against regular militaries by conventional forces as well as irregulars. At the close of the period, this issue remained a key element in the equations of force.

However, the limitations, both of air power and of conventional military methods, did not equate with uselessness, even if a cost-benefit analysis of air power could be bleak, notably due to the rapidly rising costs of cutting-edge aircraft, munitions, and the support system of air power. Indeed, it would be mistaken to treat air power simply as a lesson in failure. The hopes of its advocates were frequently misplaced, notably in terms of outcomes or political consequences, but air power has become both the key means of power projection and the most deadly and rapid form of delivering force at a distance.

Moreover, in the period since the 1960s, a period when debate over the ethics of war and, specifically, bombing became more critical, air attack has, in fact, become more accurate and thus less deadly. The increased use of precision weaponry has combined with a much improved intelligence and targeting capability, notably for the leading air powers. Targeting policy, furthermore, is driven in part by a determination to limit collateral damage. As a result, civilian casualties and collateral damage have fallen. The contrast between Vietnam in the 1960s and Afghanistan in the 2000s is highly instructive, although critics of the use of air power in Iraq and Afghanistan made reference to the strategic bombing of the Second World War.[6] Napalm, which was used by the United States in large quantities in the Vietnam War (388,000 tons of napalm bombs, compared to 16,500 against Japan and smaller quantities against German troops), was no longer acceptable, and there was controversy over the use of napalm-like incendiaries in the 2000s in Iraq.[7] This is curious, as the notion that bullets and bombs are less unpleasant is flawed, while incendiaries have been a part of warfare since at least the deadly employment of Greek fire in antiquity.

Values vary: at the same time as the number of civilian casualties due to Western bombing has fallen, in Syria there has been the deliberate bombing of civilians. Moreover, bombing could be presented as an exemplary process. In February 2015, Egyptian state television showed footage of F-16s taking off to bomb Islamic fundamentalist sites in Libya, as a statement was read on the air that included, "We stress that revenge for the blood of Egyptians, and retribution from the killers and criminals, is a right we must dutifully enforce." Egyptian planes hit training facilities and munition sites close to the town of Derna. For Western powers, alongside the determination to keep civilian casualties at a minimum, the problems of identifying belligerents and differentiating them from civilians remain serious and have become more prominent. Discussion of the morality and legality of using drones to kill from a distance is a new aspect of the already established debate about the ethics of air power. It is instructive to contrast such criticism, directed most prominently at the United States and Israel, with the large-scale killing of civilians by other means, including ground attacks, terrorism, ethnic cleansing, and sanctions. This contrast underlines the extent to which bombing, throughout, has been responsible for a minority of civilians killed, possibly 5 percent, for example, in the Second World War. It is also necessary to underline the difficulties caused by the determination of opponents to locate their military facilities among the

civilian population, an illegal practice seen, for example, with North
Vietnam during the Vietnam War, and again with Hamas in Gaza in
2014 while in conflict with Israel.[8]

Whatever the public discussion and context, the viability of air power was generally considered by governments and military planners with
reference to issues of cost and effectiveness. This consideration was a
continual process as funds were contested and allocated and plans were
debated and drawn up. At the same time, it was a process affected by
broad assumptions as well as by the pressure of circumstances. In the
first, air power benefited in its early decades by being new and apparently all possible, both because it was new and in the sense that claims
made on its behalf could not be readily assessed and questioned. However, from the late 1950s, air power, in the shape of manned flight,
risked the fate of obsolescence at the hands of unmanned flight, first
from missiles and subsequently from drones. Indeed, in 1957, a British
defense review, *Defence: Outline of Future Policy*, proposed the ending
of manned aircraft in the face of the potential of missiles.

Such ideas vied with those of the continued value of such flight,
notably if considering nonnuclear warfare, although, in practice, missiles could deliver firepower in this sphere and became more effective.
Alongside doubt about the value of manned aircraft, there was a trajectory of success that invited attention and citation. In particular, there
was a clear link between the Israeli successes in 1967–82 and the Western confidence in air power in 1991–2003. Not only could air power
provide superiority over air opponents, as with Iraq in 1991 and 2003,
but it also offered clear advantages for the expeditionary warfare and
interventionist operations of the period, notably swift deployability,
asymmetric capability, integration with land forces, and targeted destructiveness.[9] The focus in the 1990s on success through air campaigns
was a logical extension of the earlier emphasis on strategic bombing. In
the United States in the 1990s, there was a military doctrinal debate
after the Gulf War with Iraq about what was termed the "halt phase."
The air force argued that it was capable of halting a major conventional
advance on its own before the onward movement phase. The army had
a different opinion, and a rich body of literature, derived from a considerable body of modeling and simulation, crystalized many of the arguments. However, much of the related rivalry centered around a general
conventional scenario that largely was put aside after the 9/11 attacks.

Separately, the conflicts in Afghanistan and Iraq served to demonstrate anew the value of air power alongside the difficulty of translating power projection and force delivery into a successful military and political outcome. Ideas of the obsolescence of manned aircraft were queried anew during the crises of 2011–15 from the East China Sea to Mali. Each crisis underlined the significance of manned aircraft. Repeatedly, indeed, arguments from operational experience have fueled the optimism that many had regarding air power.

As of the present, air power has confirmed, not challenged, the overall ranking of military strength, even if it has not enabled that strength to operate as effectively as had been proclaimed and as might have been anticipated. At the higher level, air power, like space power, has greatly changed global reach capabilities, but it has not changed the way the global system operates politically nor radically altered the concentration of military capabilities. Britain and the United States, the leaders in sea power, became (so far) the leading air powers (especially if naval air power is also part of the equation), albeit subject to short-term intense challenges as well as to more lasting questions about their successive effectiveness as the leading states and about the effectiveness of air power. These leading powers have been technological leaders and, like other states with cutting-edge technology, have tended to rely, at least in part, on air power as a function of their economic and technological advantages, whether or not the results have encouraged the process. Moreover, the arrival and, even more, diffusion of new technologies suggested that air power in the shape of unmanned aircraft has great potential. Air power therefore very much continues to be part of the military agenda.

At the same time, the question of functional effectiveness does not address the continuing difficulty in relating military means and political goals. While this relates to all services, this has been a long-standing problem in particular with air power.[10] The lack of the political dimension is apparent in, for example, the discussion of American planning in D. T. Putney's *Airpower Advantage: Planning the Gulf War Air Campaign, 1989–1991* (2004). Linked to this lack has come an inadequate response to the learning of lessons and the corresponding need for the adaptation of doctrine.[11]

The complex relationship between military means and political goals is both specific to particular moments and more general. For example, there is a major contrast between the use of these means, and of technological advance more generally, in order to pursue a major change in the international system and, in contrast, to resist such change. The principal states that saw air power as a strategic tool, Britain and the United States, presented their policy in the latter terms, for example, in opposing the advance of communism. Thus, air power, an offensive capability, was understood by them in essentially defensive terms, which was not how it struck those who experienced its impact.

This contrast was related to the more general problem of having the capability and the will to predict and understand the battle space, and its context and consequences, prior to attempts to shape them. This problem has proved a major issue in, and with, the use of air power. It is possible to offer a discussion of the capability and effectiveness of air power, as largely resting on being the product of an advanced industrial economy and part of an integrated fighting system, and with an operational doctrine that relies on cooperation between arms and seeks to implement realizable military and political goals. There is a tendency to see today's Western way of war as integrated (joint and combined), which is often contrasted with the Second World War, when all services simultaneously fought their own wars. These military and political goals, however, have often been propounded with a lack of appreciation of practicalities, and the notion (implied or explicit) of strategic air power has contributed greatly to this problem. It is very possible that the future will witness the same problem. In practice, strategic and tactical tasks are difficult to reconcile, which suggests a necessary division of labor.

Moreover, the contextual analysis of the social, political, and environmental factors that affect the acceptability, operations, and impact of air power has been insufficient. In contrast, during the Cold War, the American air force spent a great deal of money trying to develop its understanding of the impact that air power and nuclear weapons would have on societies at war. To investigate these questions, there was much analysis of how the Soviet Union was organized, how it worked, and generally on the effects of air power at the societal level. In addition, there were many studies of the physical, societal, and psychological effects that air power had on Germany and Japan during the Second World War. Without endorsing this work, some of which was problematic in its approach, the fact that it was done reflected a realization that these questions were important. Comparable recent work relating to air power is less common, and it is unclear, anyway, that this work affects the decision-making process, or does so sufficiently.

For a number of reasons, air power, while still potent, is in a state of crisis, notably in the West. It is becoming very difficult for the air forces of the United States and other NATO powers to justify their costs in the face of competing social and political agendas, although other states, notably China, India, and Russia, continue to invest in cutting-edge aircraft. Moreover, at present, the growing influence of other service branches that are better tailored to countering terrorists and insurgencies makes it difficult to maintain accounts focused on the role of strategic air power.

NOTES

1. INTRODUCTION

1. Published in *Geographical Journal* 23 (1904): 421–44.
2. Joseph C. Scott, "The Infernal Balloon: Union Aeronautics during the American Civil War," *Army History* 93 (2014): 6–27.
3. Peter Hugill, "Trading States, Territorial States, and Technology: Mackinder's Contribution to the Discourse of State and Politics," in *Global Geostrategy: Mackinder and the Defence of the West*, ed. Brian Blouet (London: Frank Cass, 2005), 118.
4. Jennifer Van Vleck, *Empire of the Air: Aviation and the American Ascendancy* (Cambridge, MA: Harvard University Press, 2013).
5. James Libby, *Alexander P. de Seversky and the Quest for Air Power* (Washington, DC: Potomac Books, 2013).
6. Austin Jersild, *The Sino-Soviet Alliance: An International History* (Chapel Hill: University of North Carolina Press, 2014).

2. THE START OF A NEW ARM

1. Quoted in Richard Whatmore, "Shelburne and Perpetual Peace: Small States, Commerce, and International Relations within the Bowood Circle," in *An Enlightenment Statesman in Whig Britain: Lord Shelburne in Context, 1737–1805*, ed. Nigel Aston and Clarissa Orr (Woodbridge: Boydell and Brewer, 2011), 262.
2. David Chandler, *The Art of Warfare on Land* (London: Hamlyn, 1974), 152.

3. Gunther Rothenberg, *The Art of Warfare in the Age of Napoleon* (Bloomington: Indiana University Press, 1978), 123–24.

4. Frank Winter, *The First Golden Age of Rocketry: Congreve and Hale Rockets of the Nineteenth Century* (Washington, DC: Smithsonian Institution Press, 1990).

5. John Nowers, *Steam Traction in the Royal Engineers* (Rochester, NY: North Kent Books, 1994), 14; Jeffrey Stamp, "Aero-Static Warfare: A Brief Survey of Ballooning in Mid-Nineteenth-Century Siege Warfare," *Journal of Military History* 79 (2015): 767–82.

6. Michael Paris, *Winged Warfare: The Literature and Theory of Aerial Warfare in Britain, 1859–1917* (Manchester: Manchester University Press, 1992).

7. Hamilton to Sir William Nicholson, January 2, 1909, LH, Hamilton papers 4/2/7.

8. NA, WO, 106/6/87.

9. Rodney Atwood, *The Life of Field Marshal Lord Roberts* (London: Bloomsbury Academic, 2014), 249.

10. Hugh Driver, *The Birth of Military Aviation: Britain, 1903–1914* (Woodbridge: Boydell and Brewer, 1997); Andrew Whitemarsh, "British Army Manoeuvres and the Development of Military Aviation, 1910–1913," *War in History* 14 (2007): 325–46.

11. Marie-Catherine Villatoux, "De l'inspection permanente de l'aéronautique à la direction de l'aéronautique. Histoire d'une institutionnalisation, 1910–1914," *Revue Historique des Armées* 203 (last quarter, 2003): 19–20; Patrick Facon, *L'Histoire de l'Armée de l'Air. Une jeunesse tumultueuse, 1880–1945* (Rennes: Larivières, 2004), 26; Jean-Baptiste Manchon, *L'Aéronautique militaire française outre-mer, 1911–1939* (Paris: PUPS, 2013), 37–38, 47, 50. This is a key work.

12. Ernst Peter, *Die k.u.k. Luftschiffer- und Fliegertruppe Österreich-Ungarns 1794–1919* (Stuttgart: Motorbuch, 1981).

13. William F. Trimble, *Hero of the Air: Glenn Curtiss and the Birth of Naval Aviation* (Annapolis, MD: Naval Institute Press, 2010).

14. Michael Paris, "The First Air Wars—North Africa and the Balkans, 1911–13," *Journal of Contemporary History* 26 (1991): 97–109; Charles Stephenson, *A Box of Sand: The Italo-Ottoman War, 1911–1912* (Ticehurst, Sussex: Tattered Flag Press, 2014), 106–8, 114, 137; Bruce Vandervort, *To the Fourth Shore: Italy's War for Libya, 1911–1912* (Rome: Stato Maggiore dell'Esercito Ufficio Storico, 2012).

15. Gregory Vitarbo, *Army of the Sky: Russian Military Aviation before the Great War, 1904–1914* (New York: Peter Lang, 2012).

16. Michael Molkentin, *Australia and the War in the Air* (Oxford: Oxford University Press, 2014).

17. Manchon, *Aéronautique militaire français*, 51–121, 98–99, 109–11.

18. Roy Irons, *Churchill and the Mad Mullah of Somaliland* (Barnsley: Pen and Sword, 2013), 167–70.

19. Randolph Churchill, *Winston S. Churchill*, vol. 2, *Young Statesman, 1901–1914* (London: Heinemann, 1967), 690–705.

20. Ibid., 691.

3. THE FIRST WORLD WAR

1. *Times*, March 20, 1917, 9.

2. Holger Herwig, *The Marne 1914: The Opening of World War I and the Battle That Changed the World* (New York: Random House, 2009), 223–24; BL, Add. 49714, fol. 28.

3. Matthew Seligman, "A View from Berlin: Colonel Frederick Trench and the Development of British Perceptions of German Aggressive Intent, 1906–1910," *Journal of Strategic Studies* 23 (2000): 131.

4. Alec Brew, *The History of Black Country Aviation* (Stroud, UK: Sutton, 1993).

5. Susan R. Grayzel, "'The Souls of Soldiers': Civilians under Fire in First World War France," *Journal of Modern History* 78 (2006): 588–622, esp. 597–600, 621.

6. Alan to Edith Thomson, November 3, 1915, cf. September 24, 1915, Thomson papers, privately owned.

7. BL, Add. 49703, fols. 184–89.

8. Georges Pagé, *L'Aviation française, 1914–1918* (Paris: Grancher, 2011), 88–93.

9. Michel Bénichou, *Un siècle d'aviation française* (Clichy: Éditions Larivière, 2000), 28–29.

10. John Morrow, *The Great War in the Air: Military Aviation from 1909 to 1921* (Washington, DC: Smithsonian Institution Press, 1993), 105.

11. Callwell to Birdwood, March 31, 1915, AWM, 3 DRL/3376, 11/4.

12. Alan to Edith Thomson, October 5, 7, 1915, Thomson papers, privately owned.

13. W. Weston to Earl Fortescue, July 24, 1915, DRO, 1262 M/FC 60.

14. LMA, CLC/533/MS 09400.

15. Christopher Duffy, *Through German Eyes: The British and the Somme 1916* (London: Weidenfeld and Nicolson, 2007).

16. LMA, CLC/533/MS 09400.

17. Dean Juniper, "Gothas over London," *RUSI Journal* 148, no. 4 (2003): 74–80.

18. Jonathan Bailey, *The First World War and the Birth of the Modern Style of Warfare*, Occasional Paper No. 22 (Camberley: Strategic and Combat Studies Institute, 1996).

19. August 31, 1918, DRO, 5277M/F3/30.

20. Gary Sheffield, *A Short History of the First World War* (London: Oneworld, 2014), 48.

21. Malcolm Cooper, *The Birth of Independent Air Power* (London: HarperCollins, 1986).

22. George K. Williams, *Biplanes and Bombsights: British Bombing in World War I* (Maxwell AFB, AL: Air University Press, 1999).

23. Child-Villiers to his mother, September 26, 1918, LMA, ACC/2839/D002.

24. Robert Feuilloy, Lucien Morareau, et al., *L'Aviation maritime française pendant la Grande Guerre* (Paris: Ardhan, 1999), 277–79.

25. Ibid., 210–19.

26. R. D. Layman, *Naval Aviation in the First World War: Its Impact and Influence* (Annapolis, MD: Naval Institute Press, 1996).

27. Dean Juniper, "'Some Were Chosen': A Study of Aeroplane Procurement in the First World War," *RUSI* 149, no. 6 (December 2004): 62–69.

28. Alan to Edith Thomson, November 11, 1918, Thomson papers, privately owned.

29. Manchon, *Aéronautique militaire française*, 149.

30. Monash to wife, July 18, 1916, AWM, 3 DRL/23/6, 1/1, pp. 201–2.

31. Brett Holman, "Dreaming War: Airmindedness and the Australian Mystery Aeroplane Scare of 1918," *History Australia* 10 (2013): 180–201.

32. Margaret McClure, *Fighting Spirit: 75 Years of the RNZAF* (Auckland: Random House NZ, 2012).

33. Margam Philpott, *Air and Sea Power in World War I: Combat Experience in the Royal Flying Corps and the Royal Navy* (London: I. B. Tauris, 2013); Samuel Hynes, *The Unsubstantial Air: American Fliers in the First World War* (New York: Farrar, Straus and Giroux, 2014).

4. THE 1920s

1. Andrew Barros, "Razing Babel and the Problems of Constructing Peace: France, Great Britain, and Air Power, 1916–28," *English Historical Review* 126 (2011): 75–115, esp. 75–77, 114.

2. Neville Parton, *The Evolution and Impact of Royal Air Force Doctrine, 1919–1939* (London: Continuum, 2011).

3. Richard Overy, *The Bombing War: Europe 1939–1945* (London: Penguin, 2013), 25–26.

4. John Ferris, "The Theory of a French 'Air Menace': Anglo-French Relations and the British Home Defence Air Force Programmes of 1921–25," *Journal of Strategic Studies* 10 (1987): 62–83.

5. V. Butt, A. Murphy, N. Myshov, and G. Swain, eds., *The Russian Civil War: Documents from the Soviet Archives* (Basingstoke: Palgrave Macmillan, 1996), 102.

6. George Noble Molesworth, *Afghanistan, 1919: An Account of Operations in the Third Afghan War* (New York: Asia Publishing House, 1962).

7. Note by the General Staff on British Military Liabilities, June 9, 1920, NA, CAB, 24/109, fols. 255, 259; Julian Lewis, *Racing Ace: The Fights and Flights of Samuel "Kink" Kinkead* (Barnsley, South Yorkshire: Pen and Sword, 2011), 104–8.

8. Andrew Roe, "'Pink's War'—Applying the Principles of Air Control to Waziristan, 9 March to 1 May 1925," *Air Power Review* 13, no. 3 (Autumn/Winter 2010): 97–118.

9. *Times*, June 6, 1923.

10. Damian P. O'Connor, "The Twenty Year Armistice: RUSI between the Wars," *RUSI Journal* 154, no. 1 (February 2009): 86–89.

11. Military Report on Mesopotamia (Iraq), Area 1 (Northern Jazirah), 1922, NA, WO, 33/2758, p. 39.

12. David Omissi, *Air Power and Colonial Control: The Royal Air Force, 1919–1939* (Manchester: Manchester University Press, 1990); Priya Satia, "The Defense of Inhumanity: Air Control in Iraq and the British Idea of Arabia," *American Historical Review* 11 (2006): 16–51.

13. Brian Burridge [Commander-in-Chief Strike], "Technical Development and Effects Based Operations," *RUSI Journal* 149, no. 5 (October 2004): 28–29.

14. Jean-Baptiste Manchon, *L'Aéronautique militaire française outre-mer, 1911–1939* (Paris: Presses de l'université Paris-Sorbonne, 2013); M. Thomas, "Markers of Modernity or Agents of Terror? Air Policing and French Colonial Revolt after World War I," in *Britain in Global Politics*, vol. 1, *From Gladstone to Churchill*, ed. Christopher Baxter, Michael Dockrill, and Keith Hamilton (Basingstoke: Palgrave Macmillan, 2013), 68–98.

15. E. van Loos, "Die Indische militaire luchtvaart 1914–1950. Metalen vogels on der de tropenzon," *Onze luchtmacht* 4 (2014): 12–18.

16. Bruce J. Calder, *The Impact of Intervention: The Dominican Republic during the US Occupation of 1916–1925* (Austin: University of Texas Press, 1984).

17. *Times*, July 28, 1927, March 21, 1928.

18. *Times*, January 10, 1927.

19. David Killingray, "A Swift Agent of Government: Air Power in British Colonial Africa, 1916–39," *Journal of African History* 25 (1984): 429–44; Jafna L. Cox, "A Splendid Training Ground: The Importance to the RAF of Iraq, 1913–32," *Journal of Imperial and Commonwealth History* 13 (1985): 157–84.

20. Robin Higham, *Britain's Imperial Air Routes, 1918–1939* (Hamden, CT: Shoe String Press, 1960); Robert L. McCormack, "Imperialism, Air Transport and Colonial Development: Kenya 1920–1946," *Journal of Imperial and Commonwealth History* 17 (1989): 374–95.

21. *Times*, March 9, 1926.

22. Mauer Mauer and Calvin F. Senning, "Billy Mitchell, the Air Service, and the Mingo County War," *West Virginia Historian* 30 (October 1968): 339–50.

23. Leslie McLoughlin, *Ibn Saud* (Basingstoke: Palgrave Macmillan, 1993), 81, 221. On Iran, see Stephanie Cronin, *The Army and the Creation of the Pahlavi State in Iran, 1910–26* (London: I. B. Tauris, 1997).

24. Leon B. Poullada, *Reform and Rebellion in Afghanistan, 1919–1929* (Ithaca, NY: Cornell University Press, 1973).

25. Lieutenant General Congreve, Commander Egyptian Expeditionary Force, "Appreciation of the Situation: Egypt and Palestine," May 4, 1920, NA, CAB, 24/107, fol. 258.

26. Chiefs of Staff, "The Situation in China," April 4, 1927, NA, CAB, 24/186, fol. 108.

27. Robert B. Workman, *Float Planes and Flying Boats: The U.S. Coast Guard and Early Naval Aviation* (Annapolis, MD: Naval Institute Press, 2012).

28. BL, Add. 49045, fols. 1–2.

29. William F. Trimble, *Admiral William A. Moffett: Architect of Naval Aviation* (Washington, DC: Smithsonian Institution Press, 1994).

30. *Times*, September 6, 1927.

31. Ian M. Philpott, *The Royal Air Force: An Encyclopedia of the Inter-War Years*, vol. 1, *The Trenchard Years, 1918 to 1929* (Barnsley, South Yorkshire: Pen and Sword, 2005), 194–208.

32. Clark Reynolds, *The Fast Carriers: The Forging of an Air Navy* (New York: McGraw-Hill, 1968); Geoffrey Till, "Adopting the Aircraft Carrier: The British, American, and Japanese Case Studies," in *Military Innovation in the Interwar Period*, ed. Williamson Murray and Alan Millett (Cambridge: Cambridge University Press, 1996), 191–226.

33. NA, KV, 2/871.

34. Thomas Hippler, *Bombing the People: Giulio Douhet and the Foundations of Air-Power Strategy, 1884–1939* (Cambridge: Cambridge University Press, 2013).

35. Thomas Wildenberg, *Billy Mitchell's War: The Army Air Corps and the Challenge to Seapower* (Annapolis, MD: Naval Institute Press, 2013).

36. Galen Perras and Katrina Kellner, "'A Perfectly Logical and Sensible Thing': Billy Mitchell Advocates a Canadian-American Aerial Alliance against Japan," *Journal of Military History* 72 (2008): 786.

37. Report on India, 1926, Rutgers University Library, Department of Manuscripts, Fuller papers, p. 4.

38. Colin Sinnott, *The RAF and Aircraft Design, 1923–1939: Air Staff Operational Requirements* (London: Frank Cass, 2001).

5. THE 1930s

1. Memorandum by G. H. Thompson, recently a British diplomat in Spain, circulated to Cabinet on October 14, 1937, NA, CAB, 24/271, fol. 303.

2. Richard Overy, "Air Power and the Origins of Deterrence Theory before 1939," *Journal of Strategic Studies* 15 (1992): 73–101.

3. Roger E. Bilstein, "Airplanes," in *A Companion to American Technology*, ed. Carroll Pursell (Oxford: Blackwell, 2005), 263.

4. The Bayerische Flugzeugwerke was renamed Messerschmidt AG in 1938 when Willy Messerschmidt acquired the company. The air frames were all marked "Bf" rather than "Me," but they are better known by the latter designation.

5. Bernd Jürgen Fischer, *Albania at War, 1939–1945* (London: Hurst, 1999), 24.

6. Dirk Starink, *De Jonge Jaren Van de Luchtmacht. Het luchtwapen in het Nederlandse leger 1913–1939* (Amsterdam: Boom, 2013), 377, 380–81.

7. Ministerial Committee, July 16, 1934, NA, CAB, 24/250, fol. 119.

8. Sebastian Ritchie, *Industry and Air Power: The Expansion of British Aircraft Production, 1935–1941* (London: Frank Cass, 1997); John Buckley, *Air Power in the Age of Total War* (London: UCL Press, 1999), 109–10.

9. Steven Weinberg, "What Price Glory?" *New York Review of Books*, November 6, 2003, 59.

10. Peter Fritzsche, *A Nation of Flyers: German Aviation and the Popular Imagination* (Cambridge, MA: Harvard University Press, 1992).

11. Richard Overy, "From 'Uralbomber' to 'Amerikabomber': The *Luftwaffe* and Strategic Bombing," *Journal of Strategic Studies* 1 (1978): 154–78.

12. Edward L. Homze, *Arming the Luftwaffe: The Reich Air Ministry and the German Aircraft Industry, 1919–39* (Lincoln: University of Nebraska Press, 1976); Klaus A. Maier, "Total War and Operational Air Warfare," in *Germany and the Second World War*, vol. 2, *Germany's Initial Conquests in Europe*, ed. Klaus A. Maier et al. (Oxford: Oxford University Press, 1991), 31–59; James Corum, *The Luftwaffe: Creating the Operational Air War, 1918–1940* (Lawrence: University of Kansas Press, 1997); James Corum and Richard R. Muller, *The Luftwaffe's Way of War: German Air Force Doctrine, 1911–1945* (Baltimore, MD: Nautical & Aviation Publishing, 1998).

13. James Corum, *Wolfram von Richthofen: Master of the German Air War* (Lawrence: University of Kansas Press, 2008).

14. Jason Warren to Jeremy Black, e-mails, March 5, 2015.

15. Joel Hayward, "The Luftwaffe's Agility: An Assessment of Relevant Concepts and Practices," in *Air Power: The Agile Air Force*, ed. Neville Parton (Shrivenham: Royal Air Force Centre for Air Power Studies, 2008), 40–49.

16. Diego Navarro Bonilla and Guillermo Vincente Caro, "Photographic Air Reconnaissance during the Spanish Civil War, 1936–1939: Doctrine and Operations," *War in History* 20 (2013): 345–80.

17. Lionel Evelyn Oswald Charlton, *War from the Air: Past, Present, Future* (London: Nelson, 1935).

18. Scot Robertson, *The Development of RAF Bombing Doctrine, 1919–1929* (Westport, CT: Praeger, 1995); Philip Meilinger, "Trenchard and 'Morale Bombing': The Evolution of Royal Air Force Doctrine before World War II," *Journal of Military History* 60 (1996): 243–70.

19. LH, MM, 10/6.

20. James Corum, "The Spanish Civil War: Lessons Learned and Not Learned by the Great Powers," *Journal of Military History* 62 (1998): 313–34.

21. Robert Young, "The Strategic Dream: French Air Doctrine in the Inter-War Period, 1919–1939," *Journal of Contemporary History* 9 (1974): 56–76; Lucien Robineau, "French Air Policy in the Interwar Period and the Conduct of the Air War against Germany from September 1939 to June 1940," in *The Conduct of the Air War in the Second World War*, ed. Horst Boog (Oxford: Oxford University Press, 1992), 85–107.

22. Scott W. Palmer, *Dictatorship of the Air: Aviation Culture and the Fate of Modern Russia* (Cambridge: Cambridge University Press, 2006).

23. Uri Bialer, *Shadow of the Bomber: The Fear of Air Attack and British Politics, 1932–1939* (London: Royal Historical Society, 1980), 132; G. G. Lee, "'I See Dead People': Air-Raid Phobia and Britain's Behavior in the Munich Crisis," *Security Studies* 13 (2003–4): 230–72.

24. Arnold D. Harvey, "The Bomber Offensive That Never Took Off: Italy's Regia Aeronautica in 1940," *RUSI Journal* 154, no. 6 (December 2009): 96–97.

25. George C. Peden, *British Rearmament and the Treasury: 1932–1939* (Edinburgh: Scottish Academic Press, 1979), 183.

26. David Edgerton, *England and the Aeroplane: An Essay on a Militant and Technological Nation* (Basingstoke: Palgrave Macmillan, 1991).

27. Peter Flint, *Dowding and Headquarters Fighter Command* (London: Airlife, 1996), 11–12.

28. Cyril Newall, "The Air Force Guards the Empire," *Empire Air Day Official Programme—Royal Air Force* (1939), 22.

29. Barbara Rearden Farnham, *Roosevelt and the Munich Crisis: A Study of Political Decision-Making* (Princeton, NJ: Princeton University Press, 1997).

30. Milne, "The Role of the Air Force in Relation to the Army," LH, Milne, Box 3; Tami Davis Biddle, *Rhetoric and Reality in Air Warfare: The Evolution of British and American Ideas about Strategic Bombing, 1914–1945* (Princeton, NJ, and Oxford: Princeton University Press, 2002).

31. Philip Meilinger, "Clipping the Bomber's Wings: The Geneva Disarmament Conference and the Royal Air Force, 1932–1934," *War in History* 6 (1999): 306–30; Waqar Zaidi, "'Aviation Will Either Destroy or Save Our Civilization': Proposal for the International Control of Aviation, 1920–45," *Journal of Contemporary History* 46 (2011): 150–78.

32. David Edgerton, *Britain's War Machine: Weapons, Resources and Experts in the Second World War* (London: Allen Lane, 2011), 37–39.

33. James Gleick, *The Information: A History, a Theory, a Flood* (London: Knopf Doubleday, 2011), 187, 237–39.

34. Frank H. Winter, *Prelude to the Space Age: The Rocket Societies, 1924–1940* (Washington, DC: Smithsonian Institution Press, 1983); Arkady Kosmodemyansky, *Konstantin Tsiolkovskiy* (Moscow: Nauka, 1985).

35. Frederic Krome, ed., *Fighting the Future War: An Anthology of Science Fiction War Stories, 1914–1945* (New York: Routledge, 2011), 176–83.

36. James Duffy, *Target: America: Hitler's Plan to Attack the United States* (Santa Barbara, CA: Greenwood Press, 2004).

37. Hugo Gernsback, "The Air-Police Patrol," *Everyday Science and Mechanics*, February 1936, cited on Smithsonian.com, January 6, 2012, http://www.smithsonianmag.com/history/mobsters-tremble-before-the-crime-fighting-red-flying-gondola-16277987 (accessed December 29, 2014).

38. Angelina L. Callahan, "Reinventing the Drone, Reinventing the Navy," *Naval War College Review* 67 (2014): 98–122; Patrick Coffey, *American Arsenal: A Century of Waging War* (New York: Oxford University Press, 2014).

39. Martin J. Bollinger, *Warriors and Wizards: The Development and Defeat of Radio-Controlled Glide Bombs of the Third Reich* (Annapolis, MD: Naval Institute Press, 2010).

40. David Zimmerman, *Britain's Shield: Radar and the Defeat of the Luftwaffe* (Stroud: Sutton, 2001).

41. Michael Budden, "Defending the Indefensible? The Air Defence of Malta," *War in History* 6 (1999): 453.

42. Wesley K. Wark, *The Ultimate Enemy: British Intelligence and Nazi Germany, 1933–1939* (Ithaca, NY: Cornell University Press, 1985); Gerald Lee, "'I See Dead People': Air-Raid Phobia and Britain's Behaviour in the Munich Crisis," *Security Studies* 13 (2003–4): 230–72, esp. 245, 251, 254.

43. Brett Holman, *The New War in the Air: Britain's Fear of the Bomber, 1908–1941* (Farnham: Ashgate, 2014).

44. LH, MM, 10/6; NA, CAD, 24/259.

45. Secretary of state for war to Cabinet colleagues, January 17, 1936, NA, CAB, 24/259.

46. Giorgio Rocha, *Les Guerres Italiennes en Libye et en Ethiopie, 1921–1939* (Paris: SHAA, 1995).

47. Annual Review, November 1933, NA, CAB, 24/244, fol. 138.

48. Geoffrey Till, *Air Power and the Royal Navy, 1914–1945: A Historical Survey* (London: Macdonald and James, 1979).

49. Thomas C. Hone, Norman Friedman, and Mark D. Mandeles, *American and British Aircraft Carrier Development, 1919–1941* (Annapolis, MD: Naval Institute Press, 1999); Thomas Wildenberg, *Destined for Glory: Dive Bombing, Midway, and the Evolution of Carrier Airpower* (Annapolis, MD: Naval Institute Press, 1998).

50. Geoffrey Till, "Maritime Airpower in the Interwar Period: The Information Dimension," *Journal of Strategic Studies* 27 (2004): 298–323.

51. Jon Sumida, "'The Best Laid Plans': The Development of British Battle-Fleet Tactics, 1919–1942," *International History Review* 14 (1992): 682–700.

52. Richard Overy, *The Air War 1939–1945* (London: Europa, 1980), 25.

53. Arnold Harvey, "The Royal Air Force and Close Support, 1918–1940," *War in History* 15 (2008): 482–84, and "How Ill-Equipped was the Fleet Air Arm in 1939?" *RUSI Journal* 155, no. 3 (June/July 2010): 67.

6. THE SECOND WORLD WAR

1. Statement issued on behalf of President Harry S. Truman of the United States after the first atomic bomb was dropped on Hiroshima. Harry Truman, *Year of Decisions, 1945* (London: Hodder and Stoughton, 1955), 352–53.

2. NA, PREM, 3/328/5, pp. 23–26.

3. Pound to Admiral Cunningham, May 20, 1940, BL, Add. 52560, fol. 120.

4. Robert Doughty, *The Breaking Point: Sedan and the Fall of Paris, 1940* (Hamden, CT: Archon, 1990).

5. Robert Doughty, "Winning and Losing: France on the Marne and on the Meuse," in *Arms and the Man: Military History Essays in Honor of Dennis Showalter*, ed. Michael S. Neiberg (Leiden: Brill, 2011), 183–84.

6. Brian Burridge, "Technical Development and Effects Based Operations," *RUSI Journal* 149, no. 5 (October 2004): 27.

7. Richard Overy, *The Battle of Britain* (London: Penguin, 2000), 116–17.

8. Gavin Bailey, "The Narrow Margin of Criticality: The Question of the Supply of 100-Octane Fuel in the Battle of Britain," *English Historical Review* 123 (2008): 351–78.

9. Anthony J. Cumming, *The Royal Navy and the Battle of Britain* (Annapolis, MD: Naval Institute Press, 2010).

10. Garry Campion, *The Good Fight: Battle of Britain Propaganda and the Few* (Basingstoke: Palgrave Macmillan, 2009).

11. War Cabinet, Chiefs of Staff Committee, Weekly Résumé, no. 56, Churchill Papers, Churchill College, Cambridge.

12. Helen Jones, *British Civilians in the Front Line: Air Raids, Productivity and Wartime Culture, 1939–1945* (Manchester: Manchester University Press, 2006); Susan R. Grayzel, *At Home and Under Fire: Air Raids and the Culture in Britain from the Great War to the Blitz* (Cambridge: Cambridge University Press, 2012).

13. Cunningham, British naval commander in the Mediterranean, to Pound, May 28, 1941, BL, Add. 52567, fols. 117–18.

14. Cunningham to Pound, May 28, 1941, BL, Add. 52567, fol. 118.

15. Blamey to Minister for Air, August 15, 1941, AWM, 3 DRL/6643, 1/2, cf. August 2, 1941.

16. Rolf-Dieter Müller, *Enemy in the East: Hitler's Secret Plans to Invade the Soviet Union* (London: I. B. Tauris, 2015), 232–33.

17. The YAKs did not enter service in ascending model number.

18. Andrew Brookes, *Air War over Russia* (Hersham, Surrey: Ian Allan, 2003).

19. Hedley Paul Willmott, *Pearl Harbor* (London: Orion, 2001); Alan Zimm, *Attack on Pearl Harbor: Strategy, Combat, Myths, Deceptions* (Havertown, PA: Casemate, 2011), and "A Strategy Has to Be Able to Work to Be Masterful," *Naval War College Review* 68 (2015): 128–35.

20. Geoffrey Layton to First Sea Lord, 1947, BL, Add. 74806.

21. Mark R. Peattie, *Sunburst: The Rise of Japanese Naval Air Power, 1900–1941* (Annapolis, MD: Naval Institute Press, 2001); Arnold Harvey, "Army Air Force and Navy Air Force: Japanese Aviation and the Opening

Phase of the War in the Far East," *War in History* 6 (1999): 174–204, esp. 177–80.

22. Thomas C. Hone, ed., *The Battle of Midway* (Annapolis, MD: Naval Institute Press, 2013); Carl Hodge, "The Key to Midway: Coral Sea and a Culture of Learning," *Naval War College Review* 68 (2015): 119–27.

23. Joel Hayward, *Stopped at Stalingrad: The Luftwaffe and Hitler's Defeat in the East, 1942–1943* (Lawrence: University Press of Kansas, 1998).

24. Blamey to Curtin, September 27, 1941, AWM, 3 DRL/6643, 1/2.

25. Jonathan Fennell, "Air Power and Morale in the North African Campaign of the Second World War," *Air Power Review* 15, no. 2 (Summer 2012): 1–15.

26. Strategic review for regional commanders, August 16, 1941, AWM, 3 DRL/6643, 1/27.

27. Benjamin Coombs, *British Tank Production and the War Economy, 1934–1945* (London: Bloomsbury Academic, 2013).

28. Robert Johnson, "The Army in India and Responses to Low-Intensity Conflict, 1936–1946," *Journal of the Society for Army Historical Research* 89 (2011): 174.

29. Von Hardesty and Ilya Grinberg, *Red Phoenix Rising: The Soviet Air Force in World War II* (Lawrence: University Press of Kansas, 2012).

30. Anthony Rogers, *Churchill's Folly: Leros and the Aegean—The Last Great British Defeat of World War Two* (London: Weidenfeld and Nicholson, 2003).

31. Report by General Thomas Blamey, commander-in-chief of the Australian army, July 1943, and report by General Stanley Savige, AWM, 3 DRL/6643, 3/10, 12.

32. Michael Dobbs, "Homeland Security Implications from the Battle of the Atlantic," *RUSI Journal* 148, no. 5 (October 2003): 38. For an important revisionist account, see Christopher Bell, "Air Power and the Battle of the Atlantic: Very Long Range Aircraft and the Delay in Closing the Atlantic 'Air Gap,'" *Journal of Military History* 79 (2015): 691–719.

33. Phillips Payson O'Brien, *How the War Was Won: Air-Sea Power and Allied Victory in World War II* (Cambridge: Cambridge University Press, 2015), 484.

34. Claudia Baldoli and Marco Fincardi, "Italian Society under Anglo-American Bombs: Propaganda, Experience, and Legend, 1940–1945," *Historical Journal* 52 (2009): 1022–25.

35. Ibid., 1026–28.

36. James Sterrett, *Soviet Air Force Theory, 1918–1945* (Abingdon: Routledge, 2009); Joel Hayward, "Air Power: The Quest to Remove Battle from

War," in *The Ashgate Research Companion to Modern Warfare*, ed. George Kassimeris and John Buckley (Farnham: Ashgate, 2010), 58.

37. Alexander to Brooke, January 26, 1944, LH, Alanbrooke papers, 6/2/19.

38. Milan Vego, "The Allied Landing at Anzio-Nettuno," *Naval War College Review* 67 (2014): 114–15, 129–30.

39. Richard Overy, *The Air War, 1939–1945* (London: Europa, 1980); Stephen McFarland and Wesley Newton, *To Command the Sky: The Battle for Air Superiority, 1942–4* (Washington, DC: Smithsonian Institution Press, 1991); Horst Boog, ed., *The Conduct of the Air War in the Second World War: An International Comparison* (Oxford: Berg, 1992); Eric Hammel, *The Road to Big Week: The Struggle for Daylight Air Supremacy over Western Europe: July 1942–February 1944* (Pacifica, CA: Pacifica, 2009).

40. Romedio Thun-Hohenstein, "Response to 'How Effective Were Tank-Busting Aircraft in the Second World War?,'" *RUSI Journal* 154, no. 1 (February 2009): 92–93.

41. Ian Gooderson, *Air Power at the Battlefront: Allied Close Air Support in Europe, 1943–1945* (London: Routledge, 1998); Michael Bechtold, "'The Development of an Unbeatable Combination': U.S. Close Air Support in Normandy," *Canadian Military History* 8 (1999): 7–20.

42. David I. Hall, "From Khaki and Light Blue to Purple: The Long and Troubled Development of Army/Air Co-operation in Britain, 1914–1945," *RUSI Journal* 147, no. 5 (October 2002): 82, and "The Birth of the Tactical Air Force: British Theory and Practice of Air Support in the West, 1939–1943" (DPhil dissertation, Oxford University, 1996), esp. 165, 177, 287.

43. Montgomery, "Some Notes on the Use of Air Power in Support of Land Operations and Direct Air Support," December 1944, LH, Alanbrooke papers, 6/2/35, pp. 1, 5, 9, 29; John Buckley, *Monty's Men: The British Army and the Liberation of Europe, 1944–5* (New Haven, CT: Yale University Press, 2013).

44. Antony Beevor, *Ardennes 1944: Hitler's Last Gamble* (London: Viking, 2015).

45. Richard Overy, "Identity, Politics and Technology in the RAF's History," *RUSI Journal* 153, no. 6 (December 2008): 77.

46. Ralf Blank, "The Battle of the Ruhr, 1943: Aerial Warfare against an Industrial Region," *Labour History Review* 77 (2012): 45.

47. Tracy Dungan, *V-2: A Combat History of the First Ballistic Missile* (Yardley, PA: Westholme, 2005).

48. Sebastian Ritchie, *Industry and Air Power: The Expansion of British Aircraft Production, 1935–1941* (London: Routledge, 1997).

49. David Stubbs, "A Blind Spot? The Royal Air Force (RAF) and Long-Range Fighters, 1936–1944," *Journal of Military History* 78 (2014): 673–702.

50. Stephen McFarland, "The Evolution of the American Strategic Fighter in Europe, 1942–44," *Journal of Strategic Studies* 10 (1987): 189–208.

51. Gian Gentile, "General Arnold and the Historians," *Journal of Military History* 64 (2000): 179.

52. Ronald Schaffer, *Wings of Judgment: American Bombing in World War II* (Oxford: Oxford University Press, 1985); Stephen Garrett, *Ethics and Airpower in World War Two* (New York: Palgrave Macmillan, 1993).

53. Neil Gregor, "A *Schicksalsgemeinschaft*? Allied Bombing, Civilian Morale, and Social Dissolution in Nuremberg, 1942–1945," *Historical Journal* 43 (2000): 1051–70.

54. Gian Gentile, "Advocacy or Assessment: The United States Strategic Bombing Survey of Germany and Japan," *Pacific Historical Review* 66 (1997): 53–79.

55. Alfred Mierzejewski, *The Collapse of the German War Economy, 1944–1945* (Chapel Hill: University of North Carolina Press, 1998).

56. For this approach see Jeremy Black, *Other Pasts, Different Presents, Alternative Futures* (Bloomington: Indiana University Press, 2015).

57. The best general account of the subject is Richard Overy, *The Bombers and the Bombed: Allied Air War over Europe, 1940–1945* (New York: Viking, 2014), and, for a longer text, notably on the war in Eastern Europe, see the English edition of this book (London: Penguin, 2014).

58. Philip Sabin, "Why the Allies Won the Air War, 1939–45," in *Rethinking History, Dictatorship and War*, ed. Claus-Christian W. Szejnmann (London: Continuum, 2009), 158.

59. Mike Pavelec, *The Jet Race and the Second World War* (Westport, CT: Naval Institute Press, 2007).

60. Keneth Werrell, *Blankets of Fire: U.S. Bombers over Japan during World War II* (Washington, DC: Smithsonian Institution Press, 1996); Herman Wolk, *Cataclysm: General Hap Arnold and the Defeat of Japan* (Denton: University of North Texas Press, 2010).

61. Russell Spurr, *A Glorious Way to Die: The Mission of the Battleship Yamato, April 1945* (New York: Newmarket, 1981).

62. Michael Neiberg, *Potsdam: The End of World War II and the Remaking of Europe* (New York: Basic Books, 2015), 239–46; David McCullough, *Truman* (New York: Simon and Schuster, 1992), 458.

63. Sado Asada, "The Shock of the Atomic Bomb and Japan's Decision to Surrender—A Reconsideration," *Pacific Historical Review* 67 (November 1995): 99–115.

64. Elizabeth C. Corwin, "The Dresden Bombing as Portrayed by German Accounts, East and West," *UCLA Historical Journal* 8 (1987): 74–84; Richard

Overy, "The Post-War Debate," in *Firestorm: The Bombing of Dresden, 1945*, ed. Paul Addison and Jeremy Crang (London: Pimlico, 2006), 123–42.

65. Penney Diary, April 14, 1943, LH, Penney 3/2.

66. John Plating, *The Hump: America's Strategy for Keeping China in World War II* (College Station: Texas A&M Press, 2011).

67. Taylor Downing, *Spies in the Sky: The Secret Battle for Aerial Intelligence during World War II* (London: Little, Brown, 2011).

68. Donald Hanle, *Near Miss: The Army Air Forces' Guided Bomb Program in World War II* (Lanham, MD: Scarecrow Press, 2007).

69. Judith Barger, *Beyond the Call of Duty: Army Flight Nursing in World War II* (Kent, OH: Kent State University Press, 2013).

70. David Edgerton, "Brains at War: Invention and Experts," in *The Oxford Illustrated History of World War II*, ed. Richard Overy (Oxford: Oxford University Press, 2015), 358–60.

71. Blamey to Minister for Army, September 1, 1941, AWM, 3 DRL/6643, 1/2.

72. Arnold Harvey, "The Bomber Offensive That Never Took Off: Italy's Regia Aeronautica in 1940," *RUSI Journal* 154, no. 6 (December 2009): 99–100.

73. Pound to Layton, February 9, 1943, BL, Add. 74796.

7. THE EARLY COLD WAR, 1946–62

1. Nicholas Sarantakes, "One Last Crusade: The US-British Alliance and the End of the War in the Pacific," *RUSI Journal* 149, no. 4 (August 2004): 63–64, 66.

2. Stephen MacFarland, *America's Pursuit of Precision Bombing, 1910–1945* (Washington, DC: Smithsonian Institution Press, 1995).

3. Steve Call, *Selling Air Power: Military Aviation and American Popular Culture after World War II* (College Station: Texas A&M University Press, 2009).

4. Russell D. Buhite and William Christopher Hamel, "War for Peace: The Question of an American Preventive War against the Soviet Union, 1945–1955," *Diplomatic History* (1990): 367–84.

5. Jeffrey A. Engel, "'We Are Not Concerned Who the Buyer Is': Engine Sales and Anglo-American Security at the Dawn of the Jet Age," *History and Technology* 17 (2000).

6. Huw Dylan, *Defence Intelligence and the Cold War: Britain's Joint Intelligence Bureau 1945–1964* (Oxford: Oxford University Press, 2014), 117.

7. Andrew Brookes, *Vulcan Units of the Cold War* (Oxford: Osprey, 2009).

8. Conrad Crane, "To Avert Impending Disaster: American Military Plans to Use Atomic Weapons during the Korean War," *Journal of Strategic Studies* 23 (2000): 2–88.

9. Christopher Preble, *John F. Kennedy and the Missile Gap* (DeKalb: Northern Illinois University Press, 2004).

10. Robert Earl McClendon, *Autonomy of the Air Arm* (Washington: Air University Press, 1996); Herman Wolk, *Towards Independence: The Emergence of the US Air Force, 1945–1947* (Washington, DC: Air Force History and Museums Program, 1996); William Borgiasz, *The Strategic Air Command: Evolution and Consolidation of Nuclear Forces 1945–55* (Westport, CT: Praeger, 1996); Carl Builder, *The Icarus Syndrome: The Role of Air Power Theory in the Evolution and Fate of the U.S. Air Force* (New Brunswick, NJ: Transaction Publishers, 1994); Bill Yenne, *SAC: A Primer in Modern Strategic Air Power* (Novato, CA: Presidio Press, 1985).

11. Stuart Ball, *The Bomber in British Strategy: Doctrine, Strategy and Britain's World Role 1945–60* (Boulder, CO: Westview, 1995).

12. Thomas Hughes, *Overlord: General Pete Quesada and the Triumph of Tactical Air Power in World War II* (New York: Free Press, 1995).

13. Paul Cornish, *British Military Planning for the Defence of Germany, 1945–50* (Basingstoke: Palgrave Macmillan, 1996).

14. Harold Tanner, *Where Chiang Kai-shek Lost China: The Liao-Shen Campaign, 1948* (Bloomington: Indiana University Press, 2015).

15. Quirijn van der Vegt, *Take-Off: De opbouw van de Nederlandse luchtstrijdkrachten 1945–1973* (Amsterdam: Uitgeverij Boom Nelissen, 2014), English summary, 459–66.

16. Tim Benbow, *British Uses of Aircraft Carrier and Amphibious Ships: 1945–2010* (London: Corbett Centre for Maritime Policy Studies, 2012), 14.

17. Xiaoming Zhang, *Red Wings over the Yalu: China, the Soviet Union, and the Air War in Korea* (College Station: Texas A&M Press, 2002).

18. Conrad Crane, *American Airpower Strategy in Korea, 1950–1953* (Lawrence: University Press of Kansas, 2000).

19. Christine Goulter, "The Greek Civil War: A National Army's Counterinsurgency Triumph," *Journal of Military History* 78 (2014): 1051.

20. They were called police actions because the Dutch considered the archipelago theirs: thus, in their eyes, it was an internal issue and not an international one.

21. O. G. Ward, *De Militaire Luchtvaart van Het KNIL in de Na-oorlogse Jaren 1945–1950* (Houten, The Netherlands: Van Holkema and Warendorf, 1988), English summary, 372–73.

22. Stephen Chappell, "Air Power in the Mau Mau Conflict," *RUSI Journal* 156, no. 1 (February/March 2011): 64–70.

23. Tommy H. Thomason, *US Naval Air Superiority: Development of Shipborne Jet Fighters, 1943–1962* (North Branch, MN: Specialty Press, 2007).

24. Employment of Joint Helicopter Unit on Op Musketeer, January 14, 1957, NA, WO, 288/76/JEHU/S.816/G.

25. Helicopters at Port Said, Air Ministry Secret Intelligence Summaries, 1957, NA, AIR, 40/2771, vol. 12, no. 5, p. 12.

26. Stuart Ball, "'Vested Interests and Vanished Dreams': Duncan Sandys, the Chiefs of Staff and the 1957 White Paper," in *Government and the Armed Forces in Britain, 1856–1990*, ed. P. Smith (London: Hambledon Press, 1996), 217–34, esp. 232–33.

27. Paul Nitze et al., *Securing the Seas: The Soviet Naval Challenge and Western Alliance Options* (Boulder, CO: Westview, 1979).

28. Michael S. Goodman, *Spying on the Nuclear Bear: Anglo-American Intelligence and the Soviet Bomb* (Stanford, CA: Stanford University Press, 2007).

29. Janet Abbate, *Inventing the Internet* (Cambridge, MA: MIT Press, 1999).

30. Bill Yenne, *B-52 Stratofortress: The Complete History of the World's Longest Serving and Best Known Bomber* (Minneapolis, MN: Zenith Press, 2012).

31. Len V. Scott, *Macmillan, Kennedy and the Cuban Missile Crisis: Political, Military and Intelligence Aspects* (Basingstoke: Palgrave Macmillan, 1999).

32. Sheldon M. Stern, *The Cuban Missile Crisis in American Memory: Myths versus Reality* (Stanford, CA: Stanford University Press, 2012).

8. THE COLD WAR: THE MIDDLE PERIOD, 1963–75

1. Bernard C. Nalty, *Air Power and the Fight for Khe Sanh* (Washington, DC: USAF, Office of Air Force History, 1986).

2. Earl Tilford, *Setup: What the Air Force Did in Vietnam and Why* (Maxwell AFB, AL: Air University Press, 1991).

3. Fuller to William Sloane, July 2, 1965, LH, Fuller IV/6/42/1.

4. Stephen W. Wilson, "Taking Clodfelter One Step Further: Mass Surprise, Concentration and the Failure of Operation Rolling Thunder," *Air Power History* 48 (2001): 40–47.

5. Merle Pribbenow, "The 'Ology War': Technology and Ideology in the Vietnamese Defense of Hanoi, 1967," *Journal of Military History* 67 (2003): 175–200.

6. Craig M. Cameron, "The U.S. Military's 'Two-Front War,' 1963–1988," in *The Sources of Military Change: Culture, Politics, Technology*, ed. Theo Farrell and Terry Terriff (Boulder, CO: Lynne Rienner, 2002), 120–22.

7. Shelby L. Stanton, *Anatomy of a Division: The 1st Cav. in Vietnam* (Novato, CA: Presidio Press, 1999).

8. Wayne Thompson, *To Hanoi and Back: The U.S. Air Force and North Vietnam, 1966–1973* (Washington, DC: Smithsonian Institution Press, 2000).

9. Timothy N. Castle, *One Day Too Long: Top Secret Site 85 and the Bombing of North Vietnam* (New York: Columbia University Press, 1999).

10. Stephen P. Randolph, *Powerful and Brutal Weapons: Nixon, Kissinger, and the Easter Offensive* (Cambridge, MA: Harvard University Press, 2007).

11. Melden E. Smith, "The Strategic Bombing Debate: The Second World War and Vietnam," *Journal of Contemporary History* 12 (1997): 175–91.

12. Robert D. Sander, *Invasion of Laos 1971: Lam Son 719* (Norman: University of Oklahoma Press, 2014); Richard Wood, *Call Sign Rustic: The Secret Air War over Cambodia, 1970–1973* (Washington, DC: Smithsonian Institution Press, 2002).

13. Eliezer Cohen, *Israel's Best Defense: The First Full Story of the Israeli Air Force* (New York: Orion, 1993).

14. Dima Adamsky, "'Zero-Hour for the Bears': Inquiring into the Soviet Decision to Intervene in the Egyptian-Israeli War of Attrition, 1969–70," *Cold War History* 6 (2006): 119–29.

15. David Tal, "A Tested Alliance: The American Airlift to Israel in the 1973 Yom Kippur War," *Israel Studies* 19, no. 3 (Fall 2014): 29–54.

16. David Witty, "A Regular Army in Counterinsurgency Operations: Egypt in North Yemen, 1962–1967," *Journal of Military History* 65 (2001): 401–40.

17. P. V. S. Jagan Mohan and Samier Chopra, *The India-Pakistan Air War of 1965* (New Delhi: Manohar, 2005).

18. P. V. S. Jagan Mohan and Samier Chopra, *Eagles over Bangladesh* (New Delhi: HarperCollins, 2013).

19. Michael I. Draper, *Shadows, Airlift and Air War in Biafra and Nigeria, 1967–70* (Aldershot: Hikoki Publications, 1999).

20. The UN also used air power during its intervention in Congo in 1960–61: Walter Dorn, *Air Power in UN Operations: Wings for Peace* (Farnham: Ashgate, 2014).

21. Uriel Dann, *Iraq under Qassem: A Political History, 1958–1963* (Jerusalem: Israel Universities Press, 1969), esp. 366–70.

22. John B. Nichols and Barrett Tillman, *On Yankee Station: The Naval Air War over Vietnam* (Annapolis, MD: Naval Institute Press, 1987).

23. Nicholas Sarantakes, "The Quiet War: Combat Operations along the Korean Demilitarized Zone, 1966–1969," *Journal of Military History* 64 (2000): 439–58.

24. Anthony Gorst, "CVA0–01," in *The Royal Navy, 1930–2000: Innovation and Defence*, ed. Richard Harding (Abingdon: Frank Cass, 2005), 172–92.

25. Steven R. Ward, *Immortal. A Military History of Iran and Its Armed Forces* (Washington, DC: Georgetown University Press, 2009), 197–98, 207–8; Kaveh Farrokh, *Iran at War, 1500–1988* (Oxford: Osprey, 2011), 307–8.

26. Isabella Ginor and Gideon Remez, "The Spymaster, the Communist and Foxbats over Dimona: The USSR's Motive for Instigating the Six Day War," *Israel Studies* 11 (2006): 116–17.

9. THE LATER COLD WAR, 1976–89

1. Hugh Beach, "The End of Nuclear Sharing? US Nuclear Weapons in Europe," *RUSI Journal* 154, no. 6 (December 2009): 48–49.

2. Frances Fitzgerald, *Way Out There in the Blue: Reagan, Star Wars, and the End of the Cold War* (New York: Simon and Schuster, 2000).

3. Jonathan Haslam, *Russia's Cold War* (New Haven, CT: Yale University Press, 2011), 353–54.

4. Benjamin Lambeth, *Moscow's Lessons from the 1982 Lebanon Air War* (Santa Monica, CA: RAND Corporation, 1984).

5. Richard Whittle, *The Dream Machine: The Untold History of the Notorious V-22 Osprey* (New York: Simon and Schuster, 2010).

6. Joseph T. Stanik, *El Dorado Canyon: Reagan's Undeclared War with Qaddafi* (Annapolis, MD: Naval Institute Press, 2003). For an account by a participant, see Robert Venkus, *Raid on Qaddafi* (New York: St. Martin's, 1992).

7. Ayesha Siddiqa-Agha, *Pakistan's Arms Procurement and Military Build-up, 1979–99* (Basingstoke: Palgrave Macmillan, 2003).

8. Greg Mills and Grahame Wilson, "Who Dares Loses? Assessing Rhodesia's Counter-Insurgency Experience," *RUSI Journal* 152, no. 6 (December 2007): 22–31; Paul Moorcraft and Peter McLaughlin, *The Rhodesian War: A Military History* (Barnsley: Pen and Sword Books, 2008).

9. Lon Nordeen, *Harrier II Validating V/Stol* (Annapolis, MA: Naval Institute Press, 2007).

10. Robert C. Owen, *Air Mobility: A Brief History of the Air Experience* (Washington, DC: Potomac Books, 2013).

10. AIR POWER AND THE REVOLUTION IN MILITARY AFFAIRS, 1990–2003

1. Edward Mann, *Thunder and Lightning: Desert Storm and the Airpower Debates* (Maxwell AFB, AL: Air University Press, 1995); John A. Olsen, *John Warden and the Renaissance of American Air Power* (Dulles, VA: Potomac Books, 2007).

2. John Warden III, *The Air Campaign: Planning for Combat* (Washington, DC: National Defense University Press, 1988), and "The Enemy as a System," *Airpower Journal* 9 (1995): 40–45; John Olsen, ed., *Airpower Reborn: The Strategic Concepts of John Warden and John Boyd* (Annapolis, MD: Naval Institute Press, 2015).

3. Christopher Bowie et al., *The New Calculus: Analyzing Airpower's Changing Role in Joint Theater Campaigns* (Santa Monica, CA: RAND Corporation, 1993).

4. Robert C. Rubel, "A Theory of Naval Airpower," *Naval War College Review* 67 (2014): 76.

5. Thomas A. Keaney, "The Linkage of Air and Ground Power in the Future of Conflict," *International Security* 22 (Fall 1997): 147–49.

6. Richard Hallion, *Storm over Iraq: Air Power and the Gulf War* (Washington, DC: Smithsonian Institution Press, 1992); John Olsen, *Strategic Air Power in Desert Storm* (London: Frank Cass, 2003); Sebastian Ritchie, "The Royal Air Force and the First Gulf War, 1990–91: A Case Study in the Identification and Implementation of Air Power Lessons," *Air Power Review* 17, no. 1 (Spring 2014).

7. Bertil van Geel, "The Netherlands Air Force in the Post Cold War Era," *Netherlands Militaire Spectator* 1 (2013).

8. Valur Ingimundarson, "Confronting Strategic Irrelevance. The End of a US-Icelandic 'Security Community'?," *RUSI Journal* 150, no. 6 (December 2005): 69–70.

9. Greg Mills and David Williams, "From Warfare to Welfare and Back: The SA National Defence Force Ten Years On, Part 2," *RUSI Journal* 149, no. 2 (April 2004): 28; no. 3 (June 2004): 48.

10. Eliot A. Cohen, "The Mystique of U.S. Air Power," *Foreign Affairs* 73, no. 1 (January–February 1994): 109–24.

11. Mark Moyar, "The Era of American Hegemony, 1989–2005," in *The Cambridge History of War*, vol. 4, *War and the Modern World*, ed. Roger Chickering, Dennis Showalter, and Hans Van de Ven (Cambridge: Cambridge University Press, 2012), 566–88.

12. Tim Ripley, *Conflict in the Balkans, 1991–2000* (Oxford: Osprey, 2001), 21–24.

13. John Keegan, "Please Mr Blair, Never Take Such a Risk Again," *Daily Telegraph*, June 6, 1999.

14. *Washington Post*, May 16, 1999.

15. Joel Hayward, "NATO's War in the Balkans," *New Zealand Army Journal* 21 (July 1999): 1–17; Benjamin Lambeth, *NATO's Air War for Kosovo* (Santa Monica, CA: RAND Corporation, 2001); Stephen Wrage, ed., *Immaculate Warfare: Participants Reflect on the Air Campaigns over Kosovo, Afghanistan, and Iraq* (Westport, CT: Praeger, 2003); Dag Henriksen, *NATO's Gamble: Combining Diplomacy and Airpower in the Kosovo Crisis, 1998–1999* (Annapolis, MD: Naval Institute Press, 2007); Daniel Lake, "The Limits of Coercive Airpower: NATO's 'Victory' in Kosovo Revisited," *International Security* 34 (2009): 83–112. On the time component, see Susan Allen, "Time Bombs: Estimating the Duration of Coercive Bombing Campaigns," *Journal of Conflict Resolution* 51 (2007): 112–33.

16. Benjamin Lambeth, "Russia's Air War in Chechnya," *Studies in Conflict and Terrorism* 19 (1996): 365–88.

17. Ved Prakash Malik, *Kargil: From Surprise to Victory* (London: HarperCollins, 2006).

18. Greg Mills, "The Boot Is Now on the Other Foot: Rwanda's Lessons from Both Sides of Insurgency," *RUSI Journal* 153, no. 3 (June 2008): 76.

19. Dennis Drew, "U.S. Air Power Theory and the Insurgent Challenge: A Short Journey to Confusion," *Journal of Military History* 62 (1998): 809–32, esp. 824, 829–30.

20. Stephen Biddle, *Afghanistan and the Future of Warfare: Implications for Army and Defense Policy* (Carlisle, PA: University Press of the Pacific, 2002), summarized in Biddle, "Afghanistan and the Future of Warfare," *Foreign Affairs* 82, no. 2 (March/April 2003): 31–46. For a different approach, see Stephen Wrage, ed., *Immaculate Warfare: Participants Reflect on the Air Campaigns over Kosovo, Afghanistan, and Iraq* (Westport, CT: Praeger, 2003).

21. Benjamin S. Lambeth, *The Unseen War: Allied Air Power and the Takedown of Saddam Hussein* (Annapolis, MD: Naval Institute Press, 2013).

22. John Warden III, *The Air Campaign: Planning for Combat* (Washington, DC: National Defense University Press, 1988).

23. Eliot Cohen, "The Mystique of U.S. Air Power," *Foreign Affairs* 73, no. 1 (January–February 1994): 109–24.

24. Carroll Pursell, introduction to *A Companion to American Technology* (Oxford: Blackwell, 2005), 1.

25. Keith Shimko, *The Iraq Wars and America's Military Revolution* (Cambridge: Cambridge University Press, 2010).

26. Eliot Cohen, ed., *Gulf War Air Power Survey*, 5 vols. (Washington, DC: US Government Printing Office, 1993).

27. For differing views, see Robert Pape, *Bombing to Win: Air Power and Coercion in War* (Ithaca, NY: Cornell University Press, 1996), and Barry Watts, "Ignoring Reality: Problems of Theory and Evidence in Security Studies," *Security Studies* 7, no. 2 (Winter 1997–98): 115–71.

28. Harlan K. Ullman and James P. Wade, *Shock and Awe: Achieving Rapid Dominance* (Washington, DC: National Defense University, 1996).

29. Jock Stirrup, Chief of the Air Staff, "Air Power: Old Challenges, New Opportunities," *RUSI Journal* 150, no. 3 (June 2005): 26–27.

30. Ullman and Wade, *Shock and Awe*.

31. Antoine J. Bousquet, *The Scientific Way of Warfare: Order and Chaos on the Battlefields of Modernity* (New York: Columbia University Press, 2009); Karl E. Haug and Ole J. Maaø, eds., *Conceptualising Modern War* (London: Hurst, 2011).

32. Ian Bellany, "Deaths among Iraqis Due to the War," *RUSI Journal* 150, no. 1 (February 2005): 13.

33. George Perkovich, *India's Nuclear Bomb* (Berkeley: University of California Press, 1999).

34. Colin Gray, *Airpower for Strategic Effect* (Maxwell AFB, AL: Air University Press, 2012), 200.

11. A COMPLEX REALITY, 2004–15

1. Joel Hayward, ed., *Air Power, Insurgency and the "War on Terror"* (Cranwell: Royal Air Force Centre for Air Power Studies, 2009); Mark Clodfelter, "Back from the Future: The Impact of Change on Airpower in the Decades Ahead," *Strategic Studies Quarterly* (Autumn 2009): 111.

2. Dag Henriksen, *Airpower in Afghanistan 2005–2010: The Air Commanders' Perspectives* (Maxwell AFB, AL: Air University Press, 2014); Alan Vick et al., *Enhancing Airpower's Contribution against Light Infantry Targets* (Santa Monica, CA: RAND Corporation, 1996).

3. Stephen Grey, *Ghost Plane: The Untold Story of the CIA's Secret Rendition Programme* (London: Hurst, 2006).

4. Stephen Dalton, "The Future of British Air and Space Power: A Personal Perspective," *Air Power Review* 12, no. 3 (Autumn 2009): 5.

5. Joel Hayward, "Air Power: The Quest to Remove Battle from War," in *The Ashgate Research Companion to Modern Warfare*, ed. George Kassimeris and John Buckley (Farnham: Ashgate, 2010), 71–72.

6. Amos Harel, *34 Days: Israel, Hezbollah, and the War in Lebanon* (New York: Palgrave Macmillan, 2008).

7. Tamir Libel and Emily Boulter, "Unmanned Aerial Vehicles in the Israeli Defence Forces: A Precursor to a Military Robotic Revolution?" *RUSI Journal* 160, no. 2 (April–May 2015): 71.

8. Geoffrey Till and Martin Robson, *UK Air-Sea Integration in Libya, 2011: A Successful Blueprint for the Future?* (London: Corbett Centre for Maritime Policy Studies, 2013).

9. Karl P. Mueller, Jeffrey Martini, and Thomas Hamilton, *Airpower Options for Syria: Assessing Objectives and Missions for Aerial Intervention* (Santa Monica, CA: RAND Corporation, 2013).

10. Steven Abbott, "Window on the World: Rebuilding Kabul International Airport in 2002," *RUSI Journal* 150, no. 3 (June 2005): 30–31.

11. Republic of Singapore Air Force, *Our Air Force Story* (Singapore: Air Force, 2013), 72–73.

12. Michael Ignatieff, *Virtual War* (London: Chatto and Windus, 2000), 161; Daniel Byman, "Taliban vs Predator: Are Targeted Killings inside Pakistan a Good Idea?" *Foreign Affairs* website, March 18, 2009, http://www.foreignaffairs.com/articles/64901/daniel-byman/taliban-vs-predator (accessed January 31, 2015); Lloyd C. Gardner, *Killing Machine: The American Presidency in the Age of Drone Warfare* (New York: New Press, 2013).

13. Peter Singer, *Wired for War* (New York: Penguin, 2009); Peter Lee, "Remoteness, Risk and Aircrew Ethos," *Air Power Review* 15, no. 1 (Spring 2012): 1–20; "Rights, Wrongs and Drones: Remote Warfare, Ethics and the Challenge of Just War Reasoning," *Air Power Review* 16, no. 3 (Autumn/Winter 2013): 30–49; and *Truth Wars: The Politics of Climate Change, Military Intervention and Financial Crisis* (Basingstoke: Palgrave Macmillan, 2015), 114–29; Royal Norwegian Air Force, *UAV: Just New Technology or a New Strategic Reality?* (Trondheim: Akademica Forlag, 2013).

14. Toshi Yoshihara and James R. Holmes, *Red Star over the Pacific: China's Rise and the Challenge to U.S. Maritime Strategy* (Annapolis, MD: Naval Institute Press, 2010); Felix K. Chang, "China's Naval Rise and the South China Sea: An Operational Assessment," *Orbis* 56 (Winter 2012): 23–24; Andrew Erickson, Abraham Denmark, and Gabriel Collins, "Beijing's 'Starter Carrier' and Future Steps," *Naval War College Review* 65 (2012): 26–27.

15. Robert Rubel, "The Future of Aircraft Carriers," *Naval War College Review* 64, no. 4 (Autumn 2011): 19–26.

16. http://defensetech.org/2015/03/24/software-glitch-causes-f-35-to-incorrectly-detect-targets-in-formation (accessed March 24, 2015).

17. David Barno, Nora Bensahel, and Travis Sharp, *Hard Choices: Responsible Defense in an Age of Austerity* (Washington, DC: Center for a New American Security, 2011).

18. Nicholas Spykman, "Frontiers, Security and International Organizations," *Geographical Review* 32 (1942): 438.

19. Hugh Beach, "The End of Nuclear Sharing? US Nuclear Weapons in Europe," *RUSI Journal* 154, no. 6 (December 2009): 49–50.

20. Alessio Patalano, *Post-war Japan as a Sea Power: Imperial Legacy, Wartime Experience and the Making of a Navy* (London: Bloomsbury, 2015), 162.

21. Michael Pilsbury, "China and Taiwan—The American Debate," *RUSI Journal* 154, no. 2 (April 2009): 84.

22. Stephen P. Cohen and Sunil Dasgupta, *Arming without Aiming: India's Military Modernization* (Washington, DC: Brookings Institution Press, 2010).

23. *Times*, December 27, 2008, 43.

24. For more positive accounts of British naval aviation, see Tim Benbow, ed., *British Naval Aviation: The First 100 years* (Farnham: Ashgate, 2011).

25. David Blagden, "Strategic Thinking for the Age of Austerity," *RUSI Journal* 154, no. 6 (December 2009): 62.

26. Anthony Grayling, *Among the Dead Cities: Is the Targeting of Civilians in War Ever Justified?* (London: Bloomsbury, 2006).

27. Jörg Friedrich, *Der Brand: Deutschland im bombenkrieg* (Munich: Propyläen Verlag, 2002); Bill Niven, ed., *Germans as Victims: Reading the Past in Contemporary Germany* (Basingstoke: Palgrave Macmillan, 2006); Bas von Benda-Beckmann, *A German Catastrophe? German Historians and the Allied Bombings, 1945–2010* (Amsterdam: Amsterdam University Press, 2010); Gilad Margalit, *Guilt, Suffering and Memory: Germany Remembers Its Dead of World War Two*, trans. Haim Watzman (Bloomington: Indiana University Press, 2010); Mary Nolan, "Germans as Victims during the Second World War: Air Wars, Memory Wars," *Central European History* 38 (2005): 7–40; Anne Fuchs, *After the Dresden Bombing: Pathways of Memory, 1945 to the Present* (Basingstoke: Palgrave Macmillan, 2012); Tony Joel, *The Dresden Firebombing: Memory and Politics of Commemorating Dresden* (London: I. B. Tauris, 2013).

28. Theo Farrell and Stuart Gordon, "COIN Machine: The British Military in Afghanistan," *RUSI Journal* 154, no. 3 (June 2009): 23.

29. Étienne De Durand and Bastien Irondelle, *Strategie Aérienne Comparée: France, États-Unis, Royaume-Uni* (Paris: Centre d'Études on Sciences Sociales de la Défense, 2006).

12. INTO THE FUTURE

1. J. F. C. Fuller, "The Future of War," *Newsweek*, December 25, 1944, predicting developments by 2000.

2. Archibald P. Wavell, "The Army and the Prophets," *RUSI Journal* 75, no. 500 (1930), reprinted, vol. 155, no. 6 (December 2010): 91.

3. Conrad Crane, "Transformation Plans and Barriers," in *Transforming Defense*, ed. Conrad Crane (Carlisle, PA: Defense Technical Information Center, 2001), 93, 97.

4. "Interview with General Sir Rupert Smith," conducted by Toni Pfanner, *International Review of the Red Cross* 88, no. 864 (December 2006): 719–27.

5. Erik Seedhouse, *The New Space Race: China vs. the United States* (Chichester, West Sussex: Praxis, 2010).

6. John Markoff, "New Weapons Pick Whom to Kill," *New York Times*, November 23, 2014, 1, 4.

7. Kevin Terrett, "Stalemate: How the Future of Air Power Might Look in the Shadow of the Emerging Fifth-Generation Air Threat," *Air Power Review* 15, no. 2 (Summer 2012): 17–32.

8. Rowan Scarborough, "Green Berets Cleared in Afghanistan Friendly Fire Deaths," *Washington Times*, December 28, 2014, http://www.washingtontimes.com/news/2014/dec/28/green-berets-cleared-in-afghanistan (accessed December 31, 2014).

9. Robert Bebber, "Countersurge: A Better Understanding of China's Rise and U.S. Policy Goals in East Asia," *Orbis* 59, no. 1 (Winter 2015): 57–58.

10. Hugh Trenchard, *The Effect of the Rise of Air Power on War* (privately produced, 1943), 14. Currently held in UK National Archives, AIR 20/5567.

11. Constantin Schüssler and Yee-Kuang Heng, "The Bundeswehr and the Kunduz Air Strike 4 September 2009: Germany's Post-heroic Moment?" *European Security* 22 (2013): 362.

12. Tormod Heier, "Is 'Out of Area' Also 'Out of Control'? Small States in Large Operations," *RUSI Journal* 160, no. 1 (February/March 2015): 58–66.

13. CONCLUSIONS

1. John Dickson Carr, *The Case of the Constant Suicides* (1941; repr. London: Penguin, 1953), 5.

2. Christian Anrig, *The Quest for Relevant Air Power* (Maxwell AFB, AL: Air University Press, 2011).

3. Sebastian Ritchie, "Air Power Lessons Learnt and Not Learnt: The Royal Air Force and the Gulf War, 1990–91," in *Rethinking History, Dictatorship and War*, ed. Claus-Christian W. Szejnamann (London: Continuum, 2009), 211–25.

4. Jennifer L. Van Vleck, "The 'Logic of the Air': Aviation and the Globalism of the 'American Century,'" *New Global Studies* 1 (2007): 23; Or Rosen-

boim, "Geopolitics and Empire: Visions of Regional World Order in the 1940s," *Modern Intellectual History* 12, no. 2 (2015): 353–81.

5. For a strong assault on the validation of American counterinsurgency doctrine, see Douglas Porch, *Counterinsurgency: Exposing the Myths of the New Way of War* (Cambridge: Cambridge University Press, 2013).

6. Tami Davis Biddle, "Shifting Dresden's Ashes," *Wilson Quarterly* 29 (2005): 60–80.

7. Robert M. Neer, *Napalm: An American Biography* (Cambridge, MA: Harvard University Press, 2013).

8. Matthew Evangelista and Henry Shue, eds., *The American War of Bombing: Changing Ethical and Legal Norms, from Flying Fortresses to Drones* (Ithaca, NY: Cornell University Press, 2014).

9. Philip Sabin, "The Future of UK Air Power," *RUSI Journal* 154, no. 5 (October 2009): 8.

10. Mark Clodfelter, *The Limits of Air Power: The American Bombing of North Vietnam*, 2nd ed. (Lincoln: University of Nebraska Press, 2006), xi, 220–23.

11. Raymond Leonard, "Learning from History: Linebacker II U.S. Air Force Doctrine," *Journal of Military History* 58 (1994): 267–303, esp. 269, 303.

SELECTED FURTHER READING

Addison, Paul, and Jeremy Crang, eds. *Firestorm: The Bombing of Dresden, 1945*. London: Pimlico, 2006.

Anrig, Christian. *The Quest for Relevant Air Power*. Maxwell AFB, AL: Air University Press, 2011.

Arkin, William. *Divining Victory: Airpower in the 2006 Israel-Hezbollah War*. Maxwell AFB, AL: Air University Press, 2007.

Armitage, Michael, and Richard Mason. *Air Power in the Nuclear Age, 1945–1982*. London: Macmillan, 1985.

Ball, Simon. *The Bomber in British Strategy: Doctrine, Strategy and Britain's World Role 1945–60*. Boulder, CO: Westview, 1995.

Bolkcom, Christopher, and Kenneth Katzman. *Military Aviation: Issues and Options for Combating Terrorism and Counterinsurgency*. Washington, DC: Congressional Research Service Report for Congress, 2005.

Boog, Horst, ed. *The Conduct of the Air War in the Second World War: An International Comparison*. Oxford: Berg, 1992.

Borgiasz, William. *The Strategic Air Command: Evolution and Consolidation of Nuclear Forces, 1945–55*. Westport, CT: Praeger, 1996.

Bowie, Christopher, et al. *The New Calculus: Analyzing Airpower's Changing Role in Joint Theater Campaigns*. Santa Monica, CA: RAND Corporation, 1993.

Boyd, Alexander. *The Soviet Air Force since 1918*. London: Macdonald and Jane's, 1977.

Boyle, Andrew. *Trenchard*. London: Collins, 1962.

Brookes, Andrew. *Air War over Russia*. Horsham: Ian Allen, 2003.

Buckley, John. *Air Power in the Age of Total War*. London: UCL Press, 1998.

Budiansky, Stephen. *Air Power: From Kitty Hawk to Gulf War II*. London: Penguin, 2004.

Builder, Carl. *The Icarus Syndrome: The Role of Air Power Theory in the Evolution and Fate of the U.S. Air Force*. New Brunswick, NJ: Transaction Publishers, 1994.

Caldwell, Donald, and Richard Muller. *The Luftwaffe over Germany: Defence of the Reich*. London: Greenhill, 2007.

Call, Steve. *Selling Air Power: Military Aviation and American Popular Culture after World War II*. College Station: Texas A&M Press, 2009.

Cohen, Eliezer. *Israel's Best Defense: The First Full Story of the Israeli Air Force*. New York: Orion, 1993.

Cooke, Ronald, and Roy Nesbit. *Target: Hitler's Oil; Allied Attacks on German Oil Supplies 1939–1945*. London: William Kimber, 1985.

Cooper, Malcolm. *The Birth of Independent Air Power*. London: HarperCollins, 1986.

Cooper, Tom, and Farzad Bishop. *Iran-Iraq War in the Air, 1980–1988*. Atglen, PA: Schiffer, 2000.

Corum, James. *Wolfram von Richtofen: Master of the German Air War*. Lawrence: University Press of Kansas, 2008.

Cox, Sebastian, and Peter Gray, eds. *Airpower in Small Wars: Fighting Insurgents and Terrorists*. Lawrence: University Press of Kansas, 2003.

Crane, Conrad. *American Airpower Strategy in Korea, 1950–1953*. Lawrence: University Press of Kansas, 2000.

Creveld, Martin van. *The Age of Airpower*. New York: PublicAffairs, 2011.

Dobinson, Colin. *Building Radar: Forging Britain's Early-Warning Chain, 1935–45*. London: Methuen, 2010.

Driver, Hugh. *The Birth of Military Aviation: Britain, 1903–14*. Woodbridge: Boydell and Brewer, 1997.

Dunning, Christopher. *Regia Aeronautica: The Italian Air Force 1923–1945*. Hersham, Surrey: Ian Allan, 2009.

Durand, Étienne de, and Bastien Irondelle. *Strategie Aérienne Comparée: France, États-Unis, Royaume-Uni*. Paris: Centre d'Études en Sciences Sociales de la Défense, 2006.

Evangelista, Matthew, and Henry Shue, eds. *The American Way of Bombing: Changing Ethical and Legal Norms, from Flying Fortresses to Drones*. Ithaca, NY: Cornell University Press, 2014.

Frankum, Ronald. *Like Rolling Thunder: The Air War in Vietnam, 1964–1975*. Lanham, MD: Rowman and Littlefield, 2007.

Fredette, Raymond. *The Sky on Fire: The First Battle of Britain, 1917–18, and the Birth of the Royal Air Force*. Washington, DC: Smithsonian Institution Press, 1991.

Fritzsche, Peter. *A Nation of Flyers: German Aviation and the Popular Imagination*. Cambridge, MA: Harvard University Press, 1992.

Gates, David. *Sky Wars: A History of Military Aerospace Power*. London: Reaktion, 2003.

Gentile, Gian. *How Effective Is Strategic Bombing? Lessons Learned from World War II to Kosovo*. New York: New York University Press, 2000.

Gorman, Gerald Scott. *Endgame in the Pacific: Complexity, Strategy, and the B-29*. Maxwell AFB, AL: Air University Press, 2000.

Grau, Lester, and Michael Gress, eds. *The Soviet-Afghan War: How a Superpower Fought and Lost*. Lawrence: University Press of Kansas, 2002.

Gray, Colin. *Airpower for Strategic Effect*. Maxwell AFB, AL: Air University Press, 2012.

Hallion, Richard, ed. *Air Power Confronts an Unstable World*. London: Brassey's, 1997.

———. *Storm over Iraq: Air Power and the Gulf War*. Washington, DC: Smithsonian Institution Press, 1992.

Hayward, Joel, ed. *Air Power, Insurgency and the "War on Terror."* Cranwell: Royal Air Force Centre for Air Power Studies, 2009.

Henriksen, Dag. *Airpower in Afghanistan 2005–2010: The Air Commanders' Perspectives*. Maxwell AFB, AL: Air University Press, 2014.

Higham, Robin, and Stephen Harris, eds. *Why Air Forces Fail: The Anatomy of Defeat*. Lexington: University Press of Kentucky, 2006.

Holloway, David. *Stalin and the Bomb: The Soviet Union and Atomic Energy, 1939–1956*. New Haven, CT: Yale University Press, 1994.

Hughes, Thomas A. *Overlord: General Peter Quesada and the Triumph of Tactical Air Power in World War II*. New York: Free Press, 1995.

Joel, Tony. *The Dresden Firebombing: Memory and Politics of Commemorating Dresden*. London: I. B. Tauris, 2013.

Johnson, David. *Fast Tanks and Heavy Bombers: Innovation in the U.S. Army, 1917–1945*. Ithaca, NY: Cornell University Press, 1998.

Jones, Neville. *The Beginnings of Strategic Air Power: A History of the British Bomber Force, 1923–1929*. London: Frank Cass, 1987.

Kennett, Lee. *The First Air War, 1914–1918*. New York: Free Press, 1991.

Kozak, Warren. *LeMay: The Life and Wars of General Curtis LeMay*. Washington, DC: Regency Publishing, 2009.

Lambeth, Benjamin S. *The Unseen War: Allied Air Power and the Takedown of Saddam Hussein*. Annapolis, MD: Naval Institute Press, 2013.

Libbey, James K. *Alexander P. de Seversky and the Quest for Air Power*. Washington, DC: Potomac Books, 2013.

MacFarland, Stephen L. *America's Pursuit of Precision Bombing, 1910–1945*. Washington, DC: Smithsonian Institute Press, 1995.

Mahnken, Thomas. *Technology and the American Way of War since 1945*. New York: Columbia University Press, 2008.

McClendon, Robert Earl. *Autonomy of the Air Arm*. Washington, DC: Air University Press, 1996.

Meilinger, Philip, ed. *The Paths to Heaven: The Evolution of Airpower Theory*. Maxwell AFB, AL: Air University Press, 1997.

Mets, David. *The Air Campaign: John Warden and the Classical Airpower Theorists*. Maxwell AFB, AL: Air University Press, 1999.

Morrow, John. *The Great War in the Air: Military Aviation from 1909 to 1921*. Washington, DC: Smithsonian Institution Press, 1993.

Murray, Williamson. *Air War, 1914–1945*. London: Weidenfeld and Nicholson, 1999.

Neer, Robert M. *Napalm: An American Biography*. Cambridge, MA: Harvard University Press, 2013.

Olsen, John, ed. *Airpower Reborn: The Strategic Concepts of John Warden and John Boyd*. Annapolis, MD: Naval Institute Press, 2015.

———, ed. *European Air Power: Challenges and Opportunities*. Dulles, VA: Potomac Books, 2014.

———, ed. *Global Air Power*. Dulles, VA: Potomac Books, 2011.

———, ed. *A History of Air Warfare*. Dulles, VA: Potomac Books, 2010.

———. *John Warden and the Renaissance of American Air Power*. Dulles, VA: Potomac Books, 2007.

———. *Strategic Air Power in Desert Storm*. London: Frank Cass, 2003.

Omissi, David. *Air Power and Colonial Control: The Royal Air Force 1919–1939*. Manchester: Manchester University Press, 1990.

Overy, Richard. *The Bombers and the Bombed: Allied Air War over Europe, 1940–1945*. New York: Viking, 2014.

———. *Goering: Hitler's Iron Knight*. 3rd ed. London: I. B. Tauris, 2012.

Page, Robert, *Bombing to Win: Air Power and Coercion in War*. Ithaca, NY: Cornell University Press, 1996.

Paris, Michael. *Winged Warfare: The Literature and Theory of Aerial Warfare in Britain, 1859–1917*. Manchester: Manchester University Press, 1992.

Parton, Neville, ed. *Air Power: The Agile Air Force*. Royal Air Force, 2007.

———. *The Evolution and Impact of Royal Air Force Doctrine, 1919–1939*. London: Continuum, 2013.

Probert, Henry. *Bomber Harris*. London: Greenhill, 2006.

Ritchie, Sebastian. *The RAF, Small Wars and Insurgencies in the Middle East, 1919–39*. Cranwell: Royal Air Force Centre for Air Power Studies, 2011.

Robinson, Douglas. *The Zeppelin in Combat: A History of the German Naval Airship Division*. London: G. T. Foulis, 1962.

Royal Norwegian Air Force. *UAV: Just New Technology or a New Strategic Reality?* Trondheim: Akademica Forlag, 2013.

Sherry, Michael. *The Rise of American Air Power: The Creation of Armageddon*. New Haven, CT: Yale University Press, 1987.

Shimko, Keith. *The Iraq Wars and America's Military Revolution*. Cambridge: Cambridge University Press, 2010.

Stephens, Alan. *The Royal Australian Air Force: A History*. Melbourne: Oxford University Press, 2006.

Sterrett, James. *Soviet Air Force Theory, 1918–1945*. Abingdon: Routledge, 2009.

Stillion, John, and Scott Perdue. *Air Combat Past, Present, and Future*. Santa Monica, CA: RAND Corporation, 2008.

Tooze, Adam. *Wages of Destruction: The Making and Breaking of the Nazi Economy*. London: Allen Lane, 2006.

Towle, Philip. *Pilots and Rebels: The Use of Aircraft in Unconventional Warfare, 1918–1988*. London: Brassey's, 1989.

Trimble, William. *Hero of the Air: Glenn Curtiss and the Birth of Naval Aviation*. Annapolis, MD: Naval Institute Press, 2010.

Van Vleck, Jennifer. *Empire of the Air: Aviation and the American Ascendancy*. Cambridge, MA: Harvard University Press, 2013.

Vick, Alan, et al. *Enhancing Airpower's Contribution against Light Infantry Targets*. Santa Monica, CA: RAND Corporation, 1996.

Warden, John. *The Air Campaign: Planning for Combat*. 2nd ed. San Jose, CA: toExcel, 2000.

Wells, Mark. *Courage and Air Warfare: The Allied Aircrew Experience in the Second World War*. London: Frank Cass, 1995.

Wildenberg, Thomas. *Billy Mitchell's War: The Army Air Corps and the Challenge to Seapower*. Annapolis, MD: Naval Institute Press, 2013.

Williams, George K. *Biplanes and Bombsights: British Bombing in World War I*. Maxwell AFB, AL: Air University Press, 1999.

Wolk, Herman S. *Towards Independence: The Emergence of the US Air Force, 1945–1947*. Washington, DC: Air Force History and Museums Program, 1996.

Yenne, Bill. *SAC: A Primer in Modern Strategic Air Power*. Novato, CA: Presidio, 1985.

Zhang, Xiaoming. *Red Wings over the Yalu: China, the Soviet Union and the Air War in Korea*. College Station: Texas A&M Press, 2002.

INDEX